Cultural Policy in the Polder

Cultural Policy in the Polder

25 years of the Dutch Cultural Policy Act

Edwin van Meerkerk
and
Quirijn Lennert van den Hoogen (eds.)

Routledge
Taylor & Francis Group

LONDON AND NEW YORK

First published in 2018 by Amsterdam University Press Ltd.

Published 2025 by Routledge
4 Park Square, Milton Park, Abingdon, Oxon OX14 4RN
605 Third Avenue, New York, NY 10158

Routledge is an imprint of the Taylor & Francis Group, an informa business

ISBN: 9789462986251 (pbk)
ISBN: 9781003693536 (ebk)
NUR   754 | 757

Cover illustration: Koopman & Bolink: *Boothuis*, Noordoostpolder. Fotograf 1e: Dirk de Zee.
Cover design: Coördesign, Leiden

DOI   10.5117/9789462986251

For Product Safety Concerns and Information please contact our EU representative:
GPSR@taylorandfrancis.com
Taylor & Francis Verlag GmbH, Kaufingerstraße 24, 80331 München, Germany

Table of Contents

Acknowledgements   9

An Introduction to Cultural Policy in the Polder   11
    Edwin van Meerkerk and Quirijn Lennert van den Hoogen

    A Well-Balanced Cultural Policy   37
    An Interview with Minister of Culture Ingrid van Engelshoven
    Marielle Hendriks

1. Legal Aspects of Cultural Policy   41
    Inge van der Vlies

2. An International Perspective on Dutch Cultural Policy   67
    Toine Minnaert

    'A Subsidy to Make a Significant Step Upwards'   85
    An Interview with Arjo Klingens
    André Nuchelmans

3. The Framing Game   89
    Towards Deprovincialising Dutch Cultural Policy
    Johan Kolsteeg¹

4. Values in Cultural Policymaking   107
    Political Values and Policy Advice
    Quirijn Lennert van den Hoogen and Florine Jonker

    An Exercise in Undogmatic Thinking   131
    An Interview with Gable Roelofsen
    Bjorn Schrijen

5. Towards a Cultural Policy of Trust   133
    The Dutch Approach from the Perspective of a Transnational Civil
    Domain
    Thijs Lijster, Hanka Otte and Pascal Gielen

6. Dutch Media Policy   151
    Towards the End of Reflective Diversity?
    Erik Hitters

    'A More Holistic Approach to Problems'   165
    An Interview with Hans Poll and Jacqueline Roelofs
    Jack van der Leden

7. Cultural Education Policy   169
    Its Justification and Organisation
    Teunis IJdens and Edwin van Meerkerk

8. Culture for Everyone   195
    The Value and Feasibility of Stimulating Cultural Participation
    Koen van Eijck

    'A Strong Field Needs Variation and Experimentation'   215
    An Interview with Saskia Bak
    Rogier Brom

9. The People's Palaces   219
    Public Libraries in the Information Society
    Frank Huysmans and Marjolein Oomes

10. Cultural Policy at a Crossroads?   243
    How the Matthew Effect, New Sociocultural Oppositions and
    Digitalisation Challenge Dutch National Cultural Policy
    Erik Schrijvers

    'Production is Preceded by Talent Development'   265
    An Interview with Sandra den Hamer
    Kimberly van Aart

Epilogue: A Systemic View of Dutch Cultural Policy in the Next
    25 Years   269
    Quirijn Lennert van den Hoogen and Edwin van Meerkerk'

Overview of Dutch Ministers of / Secretaries for Culture and their
    most important cultural policy documents   287

Appendix   291
    Facts and Figures on Culture and Cultural Policy in the Netherlands
    Kimberly van Aart, Rogier Brom, Bjorn Schrijen

Authors' Biographies   315

Index   319

List of Tables and Figures

Figure 4.1: Distribution of values in cultural policy documents   114
Figure 4.2: Distribution of values in advice by Council for Culture   114
Table 4.1.   Ranking of values in the interviews with committee
             members of the Council for Culture   117
Figure 4.3: Evaluation of the policy plans of theatre companies by
             the Council for Culture   120
Figure 4.4: Possible evaluation of the policy plans under 'embed-
             ded autonomy'   125
Table 8.1:   Trends in *passive* cultural participation in the Nether-
             lands, 2006-2014 (% of the population who attended at
             least once in the preceding 12 months)   204
Table 8.2:   Trends in *active* cultural participation in the Nether-
             lands, 2005-2015   205
Figure 9.1: Expansion of the Dutch public library system (in
             millions)   224
Table 9.1:   Income of Dutch public library organisations, 2005-
             2016 (in millions of Euros)   235
Figure 1:   Population density in the Netherlands in 2017   292
Figure 2:   Share of inhabitants with a non-Western foreign
             background in total population in 2017   293
Table 3:   Number of municipalities in the Netherlands, 1900-2016   294
Table 4:   Government expenditures on cultural services in
             1995-2016 (in million euros)   295
Table 5:   Number of institutions subsidised on a long-term basis
             by the Ministry of Education, Culture and Science
             (OCW) and national funds for culture in 2009-2020   296
Figure 6:   Overview of institutions in the Basic Infrastructure for
             Culture (BIS) in 2017   297

Figure 7:   Overview of institutions receiving long-term funding
            from national funds for culture in 2017   298
Figure 8:   Share of cultural sectors in BIS subsidies in 2017-2020
            (in million euros)   299
Figure 9:   Share of performing arts subsectors in performing arts
            BIS subsidies in 2017-2020 (in million euros)   299
Table 10:   Share of national budget for culture in total national
            budget in 1993-2015 (in %)   300
Table 11:   Expenditures on cultural services of general govern-
            ment levels in the Netherlands, in surrounding
            countries and in the European Union in 2016   300
Figure 12: Share of self-generated income in cultural sectors in
            the Netherlands in 2015 (in %)   301
Figure 13: Overview of museums in 2016   302
Figure 14: Overview of members of the Association for Theatre
            and Concert Hall Directors (VSCD) on 1 January 2018   303
Figure 15: Overview of members of the Association for Pop Music
            Venues and Festivals (VNPF) on 1 January 2018   304
Figure 16: Overview of built, non-archaeological national monu-
            ments on 31 December 2017   305
Table 17:   Labour market in the arts and cultural heritage sector
            in 2005-2016   306
Table 18:   Active and receptive cultural participation from April
            2016-April 2017   307
Figure 19: Market shares of public and commercial television
            channels in total television ratings in 2017   307
Figure 20: Donations to culture from households, bequests, funds,
            companies and charity lotteries in 1997-2015 (adjusted
            for inflation, based on the price level of 2015, in million
            euros)   308
Table 21:   Donations to culture via crowdfunding platform
            Voordekunst.nl in 2015-2017, adjusted for inflation,
            based on the price level of 2015   309
Figure 22: Share of cultural sectors in donations to culture via
            crowdfunding platform Voordekunst.nl in 2017 (in euros)   309
Table 23:   Volunteers in museums, libraries and performing arts
            venues in 2005-2016   310

Acknowledgements

In February 2016, in the middle of a class on cultural policy, it suddenly dawned on us that in two years' time, the Cultural Policy Act would celebrate its 25th anniversary. This book is the result of that brainwave. Cultural policy researchers from various academic institutes in the country have contributed chapters to this book. The book as a whole, however, is not intended as a historical overview. On the contrary, it is aimed at the future that our students will encounter. In this volume, we have implicitly asked ourselves: for what kind of cultural policy field are we training our students? What do they need to know to be able to participate in that field as academics, future programmers, directors, politicians, curators, researchers or public officials? What topics will shape the debate for the next 25 years?

This book is the first publication of the Dutch Network for Cultural Policy Researchers, which is hosted by the Boekman Foundation in Amsterdam. Twice a year, researchers of Dutch cultural policy from various academic and vocational education institutes in the country meet in the Boekman Foundation's library to discuss the issues they face when teaching and researching cultural policy. Internationalisation is one of the most prominent of these challenges. With a few exceptions, over the course of just a few years, all but one of the Dutch-language programmes offering courses on Dutch cultural policy were transformed into English-language programmes. This poses a challenge that goes far beyond the mere translation of course content: it implies that the empirical material that courses on cultural policy are based on can no longer be in Dutch. For example, the Dutch 'standard' handbook on cultural policy, Roel Pots' *Cultuur, Koningen en Democraten* (Culture, Kings and Democrats) can no longer be prescribed to students in an international classroom. And yet our students still have the ambition to enter the Dutch cultural policy system after finishing their studies. The growing body of international students, however, have no access to the politics that play out behind the cultural field they are a part of while studying in the Netherlands. This book is intended to solve this issue. In doing so, the book also introduces the Dutch cultural policy system to an international (academic) audience.

We are grateful to the many people who have contributed to the publication of this book, first and foremost our colleagues at various Dutch universities and research institutes who were willing to write chapters in this book on the topics we selected. Also, we would like to extend our gratitude to those colleagues who were not able to contribute but who provided helpful comments along the way. Their collective wisdom is reflected in the contents of this book. Second, we are grateful to the people at the Boekman Foundation who supported the book's publication logistically and who provided the appendix and the interviews with key figures in the Dutch cultural scene. Our thanks are also due to Thijs Hermsen of the Humanities Lab at the Faculty of Arts of Radboud University, who created the insightful maps for the appendix. A special word of acknowledgement goes to Marielle Hendriks for her relentless support and for securing funding for the book's publication as well as the conference where it was presented, and to André Nuchelmans for co-ordinating the efforts of the Boekman Foundation and acting as image editor. And finally, we would like to thank Robert Oosterhuis of the Ministry of Education, Culture and Science for his helpful suggestions and for being the linking pin between the study and practice of Dutch cultural policy.

Edwin van Meerkerk and Quirijn van den Hoogen, April 2018

An Introduction to Cultural Policy in the Polder

Edwin van Meerkerk and Quirijn Lennert van den Hoogen

1.   Dutch Cultural Policy Before the Cultural Policy Act

Historically, central public authority in the Netherlands has been considered problematic. The country's origin as a confederate republic without strong central leadership has had the effect that the government usually works in a decentralised manner, giving leeway to provinces and cities. The modern Dutch state still tends to work 'bottom up', as recent trends in social and welfare policies demonstrate. As a result, the Netherlands possesses relatively few national cultural institutions in comparison to other countries. In addition, the national media historically were organised according to the 'pillarised' society, i.e. they were linked to religious and political denominations rather than to the nation-state. Before the Second World War, there was hardly any national cultural policy to speak of, apart from the preservation of cultural heritage, including national monuments and museums, and direct subsidies to a limited number of cultural institutions, such as orchestras and theatre companies. There was no separate department or Minister of culture[1]: the arts were administered by the ministry of the interior. The visual arts were supported by stipends and one national prize, the Prix de Rome. The mainstay of governmental support for the cultural sector was taken up by cities, which provided facilities such as libraries, museums, art galleries, concert halls and theatre venues. Art producers such as theatre companies were largely left to their own devices.

A national, centralised cultural policy system gradually developed in the post-war years. In contrast to the centralised bureaucracy built by the Nazis, which sought to bring cultural expressions under political control, this new system, though similar in structure, aimed to support the aesthetic independence and quality of the cultural sector. The new system evolved as a result of pressure from the cultural sector, which feared quality would suffer if left to their own devices—as had been the case before the war—and from city authorities who felt ill-equipped to effectively support arts production in the country. Moreover, there was a general consensus on the need for a cultural, not just economic and architectural, reconstruction of the nation after the Nazi occupation (see the section on the support for the national system for more details). At the same time, the rise of modern cultural genres—especially cinema—and growing possibilities for mass dissemination through radio and television required stronger oversight over the cultural sector. Over time, a truly intricate web of institutions and subsidies evolved, which ultimately led to a discussion on the desirability of such extensive involvement by the national government in the cultural sector. While the cultural policy system developed into an all-encompassing bureaucratic system over the decades, it was only provided with a legal basis as late as 1993, when the Cultural Policy Act (*Wet op het Specifiek Cultuurbeleid*, CPA) came into effect.

Rather than regulating the cultural sector, the CPA merely defines the government's role towards the sector. It allows the government to fund the sector with specific grants in aid and direct subsidies to institutions. Moreover, the CPA allows for the establishment of funding agencies to provide project subsidies to artists. Furthermore, it stipulates that the government discusses the principles and main direction of cultural policy once every four years with parliament. This was a marked improvement, as it gave parliament a say in cultural policy over a longer period of time. Until 1993, political discussions of cultural policy pertained only to specific parts of the sector and were mostly based on incidents that had arisen within the sector. Moreover, the four-year planning cycle guaranteed a relatively secure basis for the management and planning of cultural institutions, which addressed a pressing need of the sector. Precisely because the CPA does not provide any guidelines regarding the *content* of cultural policy, the Dutch system is known internationally for its stability, transparency and democratic legitimisation (Laermans 2002: 189-191). Such praise exists despite the fact that on an organisational level, the system resembles the architect-state model of Hillman-Chartrand and McCaughey (1989), a model which they define as ill-suited to parliamentary democracies, as it gives politicians too much influence over the content of cultural production. In practice, however, the system relies heavily on expert advice when allocating subsidies. At the same time, this is also a point of criticism, as these experts—who remain outside the scope of democratic control—exert influence on the spending of public funds (Laermans 2002: 192) The national perspective on the system has become increasingly critical: ever since the publication of the third policy document (for 2001-2004), various agents in cultural policy and in the public discourse have argued for either amending or fundamentally redesigning the policy system.

While this volume's focus lies on the national debates that have taken place over the past 25 years and topical issues for Dutch cultural policy in the coming years, we also incorporate an international and comparative perspective on Dutch cultural policy. There are four main reasons for doing so. First and foremost, in the political debates on Dutch cultural policy, international comparisons often serve as arguments both for and against changing the system. Second, as part of a society that is characterised by its open economy, the Dutch cultural sector is continually influenced by international developments, both economically (government budget, art trade), politically (art and culture as part of diplomacy and international trade policy), and aesthetically (as part of a globalised art system). Third, in the context of the European Union and the process of globalisation, the question of how a relatively small nation such as the Netherlands can maintain a *national* policy system has become pressing. Finally, for an academic understanding of Dutch cultural policy, a comparative perspective is necessary to highlight its intricacies and peculiarities. This volume is therefore timely and provides a basis for the debate on cultural policy.

Cultural policy and politics are discursive activities that impact how we think about the role of art and culture in society and how cultural institutions organise themselves and provide a cultural offering to society. The distinction between policy and politics—i.e., between the plans and their execution on the one hand, and on the other hand the system from which these plans originate—will not be made systematically throughout this volume. Yet the authors all endorse the point of view that policy is as much about the organisational context (policy) as it is about the discourse (politics; see also Campbell 2002). As the policy system introduced by the CPA has been in effect for a quarter century, its particular logic shapes the debates and thinking on the societal position of the arts and culture as well. This introduction starts from a historical perspective of the discourse, thus laying the ground for the subsequent chapters in which topical issues and current developments are the focus. It discusses how the CPA came about, describes its key features, and tracks discussions on and changes to the act over the past 25 years. Moreover, we will introduce the key themes and issues for understanding the Dutch cultural policy system, which will form the threads that are woven throughout the book. These issues are taken up in the following chapters, presenting an academic perspective on the current debates and highlighting issues that are likely to be prominent in the coming decades, using the research output of the various departments of Dutch universities that focus on cultural policy research.

2.   The Origins of the Dutch Cultural Policy Act

As mentioned above, the Dutch cultural policy system came into being in the aftermath of the Second World War. During the Nazi occupation, a system of monitoring and censoring artists, writers and cultural institutions had been set up, which provided an institutional blueprint for the post-war period. Paradoxically, the call to maintain the infrastructure that had been built during the war came first and foremost from the artists who had been active in the resistance. For example, in the so-called 'Grey Book', clandestinely published in 1942, five leading figures in the Dutch theatre provided a blueprint for the organisation of Dutch theatre.[2] They envisioned a central authority at the national level that would coordinate the production and distribution of spoken theatre (Van Maanen 1997). After the war, the Artists' Federation took up the cause that the Grey Book had put on the agenda. This Amsterdam-based labour organisation-cum-lobby group that had sprung forth from the left-wing Artists' Resistance Movement put forward a radical, anti-capitalist agenda. The Federation was eyed suspiciously by many politicians as well as by the majority of artists outside of Amsterdam. Only through the efforts of its secretary, the politically talented Jan Kassies, did the group slowly gain influence on national cultural policy (Oosterbaan Martinius 1990, Pots 2010). Kassies' calls were taken up by several politicians from the confessional political parties, such as the Catholic poet and politician Bernhard Verhoeven. Thus when the Socialists and the Catholics joined forces in the first post-war coalition governments, the ground was laid for a more centrally organised cultural policy.

The first result of this collaboration between Socialists and Catholics was the establishment of a preliminary Arts Council in 1947. Half of the Council's members were artists, while the other half consisted of delegates from the 'art-loving public' and representatives of cultural institutions. The Council achieved permanent status in 1955, and in 1958 Kassies became general secretary to the Council. In this new role, Kassies managed to make the ideas of the Federation mainstream. The implementation of the plans, however, would turn out to be an arduous—and ultimately unsuccessful—task. To give but one example: when the first post-war Minister for Education, Sciences and Culture, Gerardus van der Leeuw (Social-Democrat), converted the Council's plans into concrete policy, he faced opposition from the Christian-Democrat parties and was forced to leave office. The Christian-Democrats, from both the Catholic and Protestant parties, were hesitant to give their consent to an all-too-strong central influence on what they regarded as the sphere of the church and the family. However, the seeds for a centralised cultural policy system had been sown. Despite a mantra of endorsing bottom-up initiatives from within the cultural sector, the government gained an increasingly strong hold on arts and culture from the late 1950s onwards. The extent to which 'the arts' had any influence on public policy was soon limited to the influence of an increasingly institutionalised cultural field that showed strong centrifugal tendencies (cf. Pots 2000: 284-286).

The 1950s saw an intensification of Dutch cultural policy as the economy slowly recovered from the post-war crisis and American youth culture spread over the continent. The growing popularity of cinema and rock 'n roll music made politicians anxious for the loss of 'high' culture, giving more political clout to those arguing in favour of a centralised cultural policy. The edification of the masses, already on the agenda of earlier Socialist politicians, became a central tenet of cultural policy. A decade later, artists and younger generations called for what they saw as a more societally relevant kind of art and for the protection of the individual rights of the artists. Rather than curtailing the influence of national cultural policy, the protests led to an increase in the areas covered by national cultural policy. Cultural policy goals became extended to include welfare goals, financial support for artists, and the further codification of the artistic freedom of institutions and individual artists. Moreover, a more democratic conception of the notion of culture gradually gained ground, which implied that popular music and film became subject to government attention as well. While before the war, policies regarding cinema had long remained confined to the domain of censorship (age control having been decreed in the 1926 Cinema Act), after the war the focus of cinema policy moved towards stimulating film production and supporting the upcoming Dutch film industry, resulting in the establishment of the Film Production Fund in 1956 and the Film Academy in 1958. The first national subsidy for pop music was allocated in 1977.[3] In spite of this increasing involvement, the national government remained reluctant to interfere with the arts directly and sought to restrict cultural policy to stimulating indirect conditions.

Government involvement in various areas of life expanded, particularly in health and welfare issues. During the 1960s and 1970s, the emphasis of cultural policy shifted towards welfare rather than education. The expansion of policy themes resulted in a growing set of rules and regulations. As a consequence, the bureaucracy pertaining to the cultural sector grew rapidly, and attempts to curb this growth or at least guarantee its transparency often only resulted in even more bureaucratic institutions (Zijderveld 1983). Whereas in the early post-war years, the interests of artists and the elevation of the public had been the central focus, now social relevance, welfare and leisure moved to the foreground of cultural policy. This was most clearly visible in the move of the department of culture from the Ministry of Education and Sciences to that of Culture, Recreation and Welfare.[4] A general Welfare Act was being prepared to provide the legal basis for the ministry. Meanwhile, the relationship between the secretary for culture and the arts sector became tense, as artists rebelled against both institutions in general and against canonical art in particular. The minister for culture in the years 1966-1971, Marga Klompé, must be credited for her role in maintaining the dialogue with protesting artists and for not allowing her political orientation (she was a member of the Catholic party) to interfere with the position of the department. At the end of her term, Klompé had prepared a policy brief on cultural policy in which she encouraged the further democratisation of cultural policy. The brief was published by her successor Piet Engels as the *Discussion Paper on Art Policy* (*Discussienota Kunstbeleid*) in 1972. In his version of the brief, Engels emphasised that cultural policy ought to be part of welfare policy rather than a domain of its own. The document vehemently argued against a centralised cultural policy (Pots 2000: 298-301).

By contrast, the cultural sector was still greatly in favour of drawing up a separate act to address its relationship to the government, fearing that the inclusion of culture and art in a general Welfare Act would obstruct the focus on artistic or cultural quality (Van IJsselmuiden 1993). Again, left-wing politicians took up this challenge. In 1976, Harry van Doorn of the Radical Pacifist Party sent his policy document *Art and Art Policy* (*Kunst en Kunstbeleid*) to parliament. The document reflected the contemporary ideals of the 1968 generation, but for many, these ideals were too radical. It was the first policy document describing cultural policy in a systematic way. In three subsequent policy briefs, Van Doorn outlined specific policies for theatre, classical music and museums. Taken together, these four documents represented the increasing rationalisation of Dutch cultural policy. However, *Art and Art Policy* was never approved by parliament due to the fall of the Den Uyl government in 1977.

Alongside the tendency to systematize cultural policy, another current can be distinguished in the relationship between government and the cultural sector. From the early 1950s, with the introduction of the so-called percentage rule, public policy provided financial support for individual (visual) artists. The percentage rule held that 1% of all investments in public infrastructure and government buildings should be spent on public art on site. In addition, in order to provide artists with a basic income, the government established the Visual Artists Scheme (*Beeldend Kunstenaars Regeling*, BKR) in 1956. The number of artists calling upon the scheme grew rapidly after 1965, growing from 365 in that year to 3,377 in 1982 (Pots 2000: 318). The BKR was not an official part of cultural policy, however, as it was executed (and paid for) by the Department of Social Affairs. The economic crisis of the early 1980s put a stop to the expansion of government involvement, particularly in welfare. From 1982 onwards, the national government strove to take a more efficient and managerial approach to cultural policy, and artistic excellence—rather than the social relevance of art and culture—was re-established as a policy goal. As a result of this new approach, the BKR was repealed in 1987.

In short, discussions in parliament on art and culture oscillated between on the one hand pleas for a restricted role of the government in this particularly sensitive area of society and, on the other hand, a more active involvement in the cultural field in order to stimulate citizens' creative development. Although the political parties did not manage to come to an agreement on an official policy, budgets continued to increase, and the number of artists and institutions receiving government support grew steadily. The latter tendency was also the result of successful protests by artists, mainly in the theatre and music scene, calling for artistic freedom. During the same period, the BKR enabled many sculptors and painters to make a living from their work regardless of public recognition. Partly as a result of this expansion, which to many seemed virtually unchecked, a growing consensus emerged that the ever-expanding government 'interventions' had to be regulated. The time was ripe for the CPA. In a report for the Scientific Council for Government Policy in 1983, Jan Kassies—the godfather of Dutch cultural policy—concluded that the programmes of political parties did not differ in a way that led to conflicting policy orientations with regard to culture (Kassies 1983: 11). A decade later, the same Council concluded that there was no causal link between the ideas of different parties pertaining to culture and their behaviour in political decision-making (Hoefnagel 1992: 103). As a result, *specific* cultural policy as addressed in the CPA is formulated under relative political agreement, as the essential values underlying cultural policy are shared by the dominant political fractions (ibid. 105).[5]

Given this political consensus, it is surprising that it took until 1992 for the Act to be passed, becoming effective in 1993. This long delay might be a testament to the sensitive nature of this particular area of government policy, as it does indeed pertain to very personal choices of individuals, but it can also be attributed to the legal intricacies of the policy instruments involved. A legal development provided the final incentive to codify Dutch cultural policy, not the development of the cultural sector. In 1983, the General Administrative Law Act (*Algemene Wet Bestuursrecht*, AWB or GALA) became effective, an act that applied to any interaction between the government and agents in society. Two general requirements of the GALA are of particular interest in the context of cultural policy. First, the act required that all subsidies be allocated (or denied) with a motivation of the decision. This motivation must refer to the legal basis for the decision, i.e., it requires a formal act. Second, all such decisions on the allocation or denial of subsidies should be open to appeal by any interested party. The primary function of the CPA, therefore, was to provide this legal framework. Thus its final design can be seen as the result of a rather pragmatic legislative process rather than being driven by ideologies (Van IJsselmuiden 1993).

The CPA, however, not only provided the legal basis for Dutch cultural policy, it also codified the roles of all parties involved in cultural policy formation. Professionals from the cultural sector, who had hitherto argued in favour of government intervention in order to ensure artistic and cultural quality, were now cast as advisors to the government on matters of the content of cultural policy. Private individuals, who had previously been an important force behind cultural initiatives, were relegated to the role of members of boards of cultural institutions. Interestingly, the national government was put in the driver's seat of the cultural policy system, a position that also follows from the fact that cultural institutions increasingly became reliant on government support for their survival. Gradually, subsidy levels had risen, in many cases even above 80% of the total income of institutions (Pots 2010). Moreover, local authorities, while still providing two-thirds of the national public budget for arts and culture, started copying the themes of the national policy documents, in many cases adopting the same four-year policy cycle, so they could align local policy with national decisions (Van den Hoogen 2010). The resulting primacy of the national government in the policy system was an unintended consequence of the legislative process (see also Van IJsselmuiden 1993). Paradoxically, while cultural institutions were increasingly bound to the government, both politically and financially, their legal position became more independent. For instance, the national museums were privatised in 1993, the same year that the CPA was introduced, and many national, local and provincial institutions followed suit.[6]

3.   The Substance of the Cultural Policy Act

Although the CPA has been amended several times, its core articles have remained unchanged over the past quarter century. Articles 1 to 3 define the responsibilities of the Minister for Culture and the Council for Culture

(*Raad voor Cultuur*). The main responsibility assigned to the Minister for Culture is to provide the conditions for the preservation, development and social and geographic distribution of cultural expressions of national significance. In this, the Minister should follow the principles of excellence and diversity (the latter referring to diversity in disciplines rather than audience, the Dutch wording of Article 2 is 'kwaliteit en verscheidenheid'). While this limits the responsibility of the national government—which was intentional—these limits are not carved in stone: determining what is of national significance (i.e., excellence) is left open for discussion. The discussion on cultural policy as defined in the CPA is institutionalised in the Council for Culture. In establishing the Council, the CPA continued the practice of consulting the advisory councils on cultural heritage, the arts, the media and libraries. In 1995, these four councils would merge into the Council for Culture.

The role of parliament in cultural policy is defined in Article 3. In it, the policy cycle is defined: at least every four years, the Minister for Culture is required to submit a policy plan to parliament. The policy plans should contain a report on the previous policy cycle and developments impacting policy execution (Article 3, sub 2) as well as give general guidelines for the coming years (Article 3, sub 3). In practice, parliament was not satisfied with discussing the general policy guidelines without information on the implications for subsidy allocations. As a result, the policy plan started to function as the starting point of cultural policy formulation, which allowed cultural institutions to apply for subsidy. Subsidies would be allocated in a subsidy plan, which was published in September of the year preceding the new subsidy period. Effectively, this means that the whole procedure, including advice by the Council for Culture, takes almost two years.

Articles 4 to 8 of the CPA define the conditions under which the Minister for Culture is allowed to allocate subsidies to cultural institutions and to issue grants in aid to local authorities or funds. This provision forms the basis for all subsequent procedures for subsidies to cultural institutions at the national level.[7] In keeping with the consensus model that characterises Dutch politics, these articles imply that the Minister will confer with local partners (provinces and municipalities). This is necessary, as cultural institutions frequently receive subsidies from the national *and* local levels, a situation that the CPA explicitly allows for. It should be noted that the CPA itself does not provide guidelines as to how responsibilities for the cultural sector should be distributed among national, regional and local authorities. In general, the Dutch national government subsidises the *production* of cultural values, and the municipalities provide funds and/or facilities for the *dissemination* of the arts (theatre and music venues, other art spaces, festivals, museums, amateur arts and cultural participation, cultural education, and local heritage). The larger cities, however, also frequently provide direct support for artistic production. The provincial authorities have a far less clear role in the system, focussing on regional cultural heritage (including dialects and regional languages), cultural planning, and facilities in rural areas. Furthermore, some provinces also provide funds for support functions in amateur arts (e.g., the training of amateur directors and conductors) and public libraries.[8] This distribution of responsibilities predates the CPA and is subject to constant negotiations, in some cases leading to significant local differences. The CPA merely provides the legal framework to distribute funds according to whatever agreements are reached between authorities. This again demonstrates a very system-oriented way of thinking about cultural policy, without codification of responsibilities regarding the matter. This is in sharp contrast to other policy areas such as welfare, social security and education, where local authorities execute national policies.

Article 8 provides the opportunity to develop criteria for the allocation of subsidies and entitlements through governmental decree. In practice, every four years a new decree is drawn up detailing the format for applications (i.e., what information should be included) and the criteria to be used by the Council for Culture and the national funds when evaluating subsidy applications. This allows for a transparent and flexible procedure. It also allows for the addition of criteria not explicitly formulated in the CPA. This is a peculiarity of the CPA: it shuns explicit directives for all parties involved. The only criteria mentioned in the Act are quality and diversity (in Article 2). However, criteria can be added, and in practice they are.[9] Only in specific domains do stricter regulations apply, and usually these are governed by particular acts such as the Heritage Act, the Media Act or the Library Act. The general cultural policy seems relatively under-regulated, providing an arena for 'poldering' in the best of Dutch traditions.

The introduction of the four-year policy cycle was one of the major points of debate when the original version of the act was discussed in parliament in 1992. Members of parliament raised questions as to whether a new government could be expected to present its vision on cultural policy relatively shortly after coming into office if subsidy allocations were already fixed for a number of years. Parliament was also concerned about its right to assess the budget, given that the policy plans practically defined the budget for a period of four years. Minister Hedy D'Ancona replied that the CPA does indeed clash with parliament's right to assess budgets, but she claimed that the stability that the four-year policy cycle provides was necessary for the cultural sector to be able to plan their activities for the longer term, something that was essential for the sector. Principles of good governance also imply that an incumbent administration cannot instantly change allocations made by previous governments. But these issues do not prevent a new Minister of Culture from drafting a new policy document, as long as these documents provide general guidelines for cultural policy and not specific requirements pertaining to specific institutions. In hindsight, Van IJsselmuiden comments, the relative stability provided to cultural institutions is probably the most successful part of the legislation (1993: 286).

Since 1993, several changes have been made to the CPA. Most of them regard technical issues, e.g., changes in the General Administrative Law Act that needed to be implemented in the CPA. The most substantial change to the CPA took place with the introduction of the Basic Infrastructure (*Basisinfrastructuur*, BIS) in 2009. This was the result of discussions regarding what should be the basis for cultural policy: should it focus on cultural institutions as such (as it had until then) or rather on the *function* that institutions perform in the cultural system? Parliament agreed to focus on the latter and approved a proposal for a system that would define types of institutions that are deemed necessary to realise the policy goals derived from the CPA. The list of BIS functions includes knowledge institutes, national museums, institutes for the performing arts, and festivals, and the BIS stipulates the distribution of these institutions over the country. The inclusion of cultural institutions in the BIS can no longer be regarded as recognition of their quality. Rather, these are institutions that guarantee the core of cultural provision in the Netherlands, i.e., the basic functions that should always be maintained. Before 2009, a negative evaluation of a theatre or dance company or orchestra in a city like Groningen or Arnhem could mean the end of support for such a facility in that particular city or region (as the subsidy would go to a positively evaluated institution elsewhere). Now the geographical location of such a facility is fixed, and the evaluation regards the question whether the application is substantial enough to fulfil the particular function. To give an example: the BIS includes the function of a Frisian theatre company to be located somewhere in the province of Friesland (in practice in its capital Leeuwarden). This reflects the position of Frisian, the nation's second official language. In theory, anyone willing to make Frisian-language theatre can apply for the position in the BIS.[10] In reality, the Frisian language area is so small that there are no professional alternatives to the current Frisian-language company, Tryater. However, the BIS does not include Tryater itself, it only includes its function in the system.

In 1995, the statute of the Council for Culture was added in the CPA. The Council for Culture also underwent a significant change over the past two-and-a-half decades. Before 1995, the Arts Council consisted of a large number of artists and representatives from cultural institutions, whereas the new Council for Culture consisted of a core council of nineteen members who are considered experts in one of the artistic disciplines or central fields of cultural policy, most of them presiding over one of fifteen committees for artistic and cultural disciplines, three 'special' committees for archives, monuments, and legal issues, and a potentially unlimited number of ad-hoc committees, usually no more than half a dozen. The resulting bureaucracy, and the fact that experts rather than artists or representatives of the public made the most important decisions, eventually led to a reorganisation of the Council for Culture. As of 2005, the Council consists of only seven members in addition to a president. The Council is supported by a general-secretary, now called director . Each member is selected for his or her expertise but is required to possess a broad overview of the entire cultural field. The new members only advise on general issues and can no longer be members (or presidents) of the committees. The number of permanent committees has been reduced to three. These permanent committees perform functions in the field of monuments and heritage, such as the selection of UNESCO herit-age sites. For topical issues, ad hoc committees are established. In addition, the Council for Culture works with policy advisors for particular domains (e.g., cultural education, performing arts or visual arts). These officials are supported by temporary committees of advisors for their sector consisting of experts in their field. All committees give their advice to the Council, which then decides upon the final advice given to the Minister of Culture and to parliament. These changes were incorporated in the CPA in 2014.

A final tendency in Dutch cultural policy, surfacing in the last few years, is the compartmentalisation of the field into separate policy acts. One might hypothesise that a fragmentation of cultural policy and eventual dissolution of the CPA is imminent, but such conclusions cannot yet be drawn. The overall tendency towards discipline-specific policy, however, is unmistakable. One example is the public library system which was included in the CPA (then Article 11) in 1993, indicating the national government had responsibility for a national system of libraries. This implied that public libraries operating independently of the national system lost their title as 'public' library. The recognition that the libraries operate in a national system was important, as it promoted and enabled the development of a common digital framework in which all public libraries are obliged to participate. In 2015, Article 11 was dropped from the CPA when the Public Library Act came into effect.[11]

The most important example of the tendency towards compartmentalisation, however, is the field of museums and heritage. In 2016, the Heritage Act was effectuated, combining previous legislation on heritage in order to systematise the 'definitions, procedures, and rules for preservation' in prior regulations (OCW 2014). The Heritage Act may be seen as the final stage in a process of emancipation of heritage policy over the past decades. An important stepping stone in this process was the introduction of the State Art Collection (*Collectie Nederland*), a delineated list of objects defining Dutch national identity. The debate on the State Art Collection was sparked by the acquisition of a Mondriaan painting, *Victory Boogie Woogie*, in 1998 by the state (financed by the Dutch National Bank on the occasion of the introduction of the euro). A year earlier, the concept of a national collection was institutionalised in the State Art Collection Institute (*Instituut Collectie Nederland*), a decision that in retrospect could hardly have been more timely. The idea of a collection of art representing Dutch identity struck a chord in Dutch society, resulting in the decision in 2006 to establish a formalised canon of national history and a museum for national history, although the plan for the museum was abolished in 2011. In 2017, the Dutch Open Air Museum in Arnhem opened an (indoor) permanent exhibition representing the canon of Dutch history in 50 'windows' representing people, events and places from the past and the present.

The exhibition in Arnhem was the final result of a long debate in politics and the press on the status of national history in education. Although the plans for a separate Museum of National History were aborted, a standard curriculum for history education was adopted in 2010. The discussion on heritage, history and national identity is part of a broader re-assessment of the value of heritage in society. With the introduction of the Heritage Act, heritage was separated from the rest of cultural policy. The Heritage Act is concerned with all heritage, from monumental buildings to intangible heritage. The State Art Collection mentioned above is also subject to the Act, as are 39 specifically listed museums. The Heritage Act regulates the management of museum collections and finances the museum's accommodation. For other ends and purposes, such as exhibitions and educational programmes, museums are still referred to the regulations resulting from the CPA. For the 39 national museums under the Heritage Act, this provides a high degree of stability. They are no longer subjected to four-year policy cycles and the whims of consecutive Ministers of Culture. Other museums were, and still are, largely dependent on municipal funding for their existence. Because of this development, heritage will not be discussed separately in this volume.

4.   Key Themes in 25 Years of Cultural Policy Debate

As indicated above, an important recurring issue in the Dutch debate on cultural policy concerns the balance of influence between the central government and local and regional authorities. Usually, authorities in the periphery, i.e. outside the Rim City (the megalopolis that covers the major cities in the western part of the country: Amsterdam, Utrecht, Rotterdam and The Hague) feel underprivileged, as most central cultural institutions in the Netherlands are located in Amsterdam—such as the Rijksmuseum, the 'filmmuseum' EYE and the National Opera—or in Rotterdam, such as the New Institute (*Het Nieuwe Instituut*, the national institute for Architecture and Design). However, Article 2 of the CPA explicitly sets as a goal the geographical spread of cultural facilities. 'Regional' representatives have regularly pointed out the uneven distribution of public funds, for example by calculating per capita subsidies per province (e.g. Van Deijck & Raijmakers 1994). However, such calculations have not made a significant impact on the distribution of funds. Whether as a result of the predominance of the Rim City in cultural policy or a wider tendency of the cities in the west to become more dominant, the cultural sector in the Netherlands has gravitated towards Amsterdam. Indeed, many of the institutions located there provide programmes over the whole country. Nonetheless, for local politicians the process of drawing up a cultural policy plan has evolved into lobbying for national support of regionally oriented institutions. And indeed, the success of local policies is measured in terms of national subsidies flowing to peripherally located institutions.

The Council for Culture has recently suggested a redesigning of the policy process so that the process starts with the policy plans of regional authorities rather than a national plan. Instead of the current centralised system with its corollary of regional distribution, the national government should 'support' local ambitions. The Council has also advised that a reevaluation take place of what functions should be part of the BIS with a greater focus on the functioning of cultural institutions in their local environment. Taking the local or regional rather than the national perspective as a point of departure might solve some of what the Council denotes as 'persistent issues' (Raad voor Cultuur 2015: 21) of cultural politics in the Netherlands which mainly relate to the ineffective interaction of the local and national levels. In a recent publication (Raad voor Cultuur 2017), the Council takes a step back in this debate by suggesting that the government first draw up new goals for the CPA, as the current formulation of Article 2 is very vague and does not guide concrete actions for all agents involved in the policy process. The Council reasons that if the national and local levels agree on the goals of cultural policy, their joint actions might become more effective. The current government seems to be taking up these suggestions (Van Engelshoven 2018).[12]

One of the issues stressed by the Council for Culture in their suggestion to focus on the local or regional level is cultural participation. This has been a persistent theme in cultural policy ever since 1993. Enhancing cultural participation was one of the goals behind the efforts to reconnect cultural policy and educational policy when the Directorate for Arts and Culture was moved from the Welfare Department to the Ministry of Education and Sciences in 1994. Two years later, Secretary for Culture Aad Nuis (of the Social-Liberal Democrats, D66) launched a new era in arts education policy with his *Culture and School* policy brief (Netelenbos & Nuis 1996). Ever since, the ministry has devised programmes to improve in-school cultural education (see chapter 7). National programmes were meant to entice teachers and school boards to take cultural education to the next level and to improve its quality. As described above, notions of cultural democracy started to become increasingly important in cultural policy from the 1960s onwards. Pop music and film became suitable subjects in cultural education programmes. Moreover, in 1999, Nuis' successor, Rick van der Ploeg (of the Labour Party) introduced a new policy instrument, an 'Action Plan' for cultural participation, which aimed to increase younger generations and ethnic minorities' access to the cultural system. As with the Culture and School programme, the Action Plan relied heavily on the cooperation of provincial and local governments, thus initiating a phase of inter-governmental cooperation. The basis for the Action Plan was a co-funding programme by local authorities and the ministry. This involved the ministry more directly in subsidising culture than had been intended in the CPA. Although the programme was extended for another four years, this level of involvement was deemed undesirable. In 2009, the Cultural Participation Fund (*Fonds Cultuurparticipatie*) was set up to continue the programme, bringing it in line with the requirements of the CPA.

Despite these initiatives on cultural participation, evidence of a substantial rise in participation has not occurred (see also chapter 8). It should be stressed that participation is a particularly difficult issue to address from the national level, as most facilities in the Netherlands are the remit of municipalities. Van Maanen (2008) indicates the split as a particularity of the Dutch performing arts system, a rarity in international comparison, which hinders effective communication between producers and programmers. The same problem occurs in the visual arts and in heritage, as museums and galleries are nearly all the responsibility of municipalities and provinces. This may be one of the key problems of the policy system: apart from some subsidy schemes directed at 'programming' institutions that are executed by the national funds, the system is oriented towards production, allowing artists to 'ignore' considerations of reach and public attention to a large extent.

The cultural system also turned out to be particularly resistant to government intervention with regard to the inclusion of ethnic minorities. As early as 1999, when Van der Ploeg had published his brief *Make Way for Cultural Diversity (Ruim baan voor culturele diversiteit)*, some politicians explicitly aimed to influence the cultural sector in this respect. However, the proposed policy instruments did not receive much political or public support. It was only as recently as 2010 that the Code of Cultural Diversity (*Code Culturele Diversiteit*) was launched by the cultural sector. The Council for Culture finally employed diversity as a subsidy criterion in 2017 (see chapter 4), when the government had already dropped the issue from the policy agenda. Moreover, as the ethnic diversity of city populations varies greatly in the Netherlands, the Council for Culture's stress on the local or regional position of cultural institutions might make the issue more easily addressable in cultural politics.

Related to the issue of cultural participation and ethnic diversity, cultural governance and entrepreneurialism have been constant concerns of Dutch cultural politics. Secretary for Culture Van der Ploeg introduced the notion of 'cultural entrepreneurship' in 1999 in an effort to attune cultural institutions more towards the needs of their audiences and to seize business opportunities in order to enhance their reach. A knowledge and training institution, Culture+Entrepreneurship (*Cultuur+Ondernemen*), was incorporated in the policy system based on British examples, and a norm for financial self-reliance was introduced. Also, art schools were required to address entrepreneurship in their curriculum. Ever since, cultural entrepreneurship has been present in almost all policy documents. The issue finally became the central tenet of cultural policy in 2011, when secretary Halbe Zijlstra issued his policy brief *More than Quality: A New Vision of Cultural Policy (Meer dan kwaliteit: een nieuwe visie voor cultuurbeleid)*. Here, the notion of entrepreneurship was used to redress the 'addiction' of the cultural sector to subsidies. The (short-lived) minority coalition government of Liberals and Christian-Democrats, supported in parliament by the right-wing populist Freedom Party, cut some 20% of the national budget for arts and cultural.

This austerity measure had an even greater impact on the fine arts and performance sector, as cultural heritage was spared.[13] The budget cuts were accompanied by a Gift and Inheritance Tax Act (*Geefwet*), which tried to promote private donations to the arts by introducing tax benefits for donors. Interestingly, the Act put the tax incentive on the side of the donor rather than the cultural institution. Even though the act was presented as a way to offset the accompanying austerity measures, no significant rise in the volume of donations has been recorded (meaning that only donors have benefited from the act).

It is important to note that for the first time, criteria regarding cultural entrepreneurship and cultural governance were made *equally important* to criteria regarding artistic quality or public reach. Although Zijlstra's successor, Jet Bussemaker, eased the focus on economic profits for cultural institutions to encompass what she calls 'societal value', entrepreneurial criteria still play a crucial role in evaluations by the Council for Culture and the national Performing Arts Funds, for instance (see chapter 4). The introduction of entrepreneurship and cultural governance in cultural politics can be regarded as a reflection of the growing focus on professionalisation in Dutch cultural policy. Increasingly, the government has taken an interest in how cultural institutions are managed, how (and what kind of) audiences are reached, and how subsidised institutions manage their risks. In 2003, a handbook for cultural governance was published, which was replaced by the Code of Cultural Governance in 2006. In 2013, the code was updated by experts from the field. Currently, the code provides guidelines for the rules of conduct of the boards and management of cultural institutions and their accountability towards subsidisers and the society at large. The code is enforced not only by the ministry and national funds; private cultural funds such as the Prince Bernhard Cultural Fund (*Prins Bernhard Cultuurfonds*) also expect recipients of subsidies to respect the code. The fact that the code has been developed by representatives from the sector itself, however, suggests that the issue also reflects the professionalisation of the sector itself.

One of the constant threads in the legitimisation of cultural policy has been the economic impact of arts and culture. This issue is particularly relevant for local governments, as the economic impact of the arts and heritage mostly accrue to local economies. The heritage in cities such as Amsterdam, Delft or Den Bosch attracts many tourists. Their spending mostly leads to local tax income, while salaries earned in the tourism industry also lead to tax income for the national government. Large-scale art facilities also attract tourists to cities. Since the 1980s, cities have focused on cultural facilities in their promotion campaigns, often focussing on particular facilities. For example, Arnhem has a focus on fashion; Eindhoven (home to the Philips company) specialises in light, technology and design; and Amsterdam has the heritage of the Dutch Golden Age and world-famous dance music. Frequently, economic arguments are the driving motives behind local government investments in large cultural facilities.

The 'classical' argument of economic impact has been losing its appeal as an argument in cultural policy. Originally, the notion of the creative class and the creative city (Florida 2002, 2004) was taken up wholesale in Dutch cultural politics, particularly at the local level (Van den Hoogen 2010). Around the turn of the millennium, national cultural policy also began to be influenced by these ideas. The core argument was that the variety of cultural facilities rather than their size is what determines (economic) impact. The cultural sector came to be considered an asset in the creative economy. In 2005, Secretary Medy Van der Laan took up this idea in a policy document she drew up together with her colleague at the Ministry of Economic Affairs. *Our Creative Capital* (*Ons Creatieve Vermogen*, Van der Laan & Van Gennip 2005) is the first policy brief to investigate the possibilities of connecting cultural and economic policies. Ever since, both ministries have regularly published policy briefs on the subject. Arts and culture have been considered part of the creative sector, one of the top priorities in the national economic Top Sector Policy.

Economic aspects of cultural policy also relate to the income of artists. Apart from the social policy regarding individual artists (BKR) mentioned above, several measures to improve the income of artists have been implemented and also withdrawn. After the end of the BKR, initiatives such as the Artists Income Provision Act (*Wet Inkomen Kunstenaars*, WIK) and its successor the Labour and Income Provision for Artists Act (*Wet Werk en Inkomen Kunstenaars*, WWIK) sought to provide provisions to the general unemployment regulations. These acts provided artists with a basic income, allowing them to build a career in the arts. The WWIK was repealed in 2012. Parliament felt that artists should not be regarded any differently than other professionals. Just like the BKR, this specific legislature was not part of cultural policy and fell under the remit of the Ministry for Social Affairs. With the repeal of the WWIK, efforts to support artists via social policy came to an end.

This, however, had not resolved the problems that artists faced. In 2016, the Social and Economic Council (*Sociaal-Economische Raad*, SER) and the Council for Culture published an alarming report on the income of

Dutch artists, concluding that artists could hardly make a living from their activities. 42% of all artists are self-employed. Many others are on unemployment benefits and have only short-term engagements or combine such engagements with a job on the side. Although this is in line with a growing flexibilisation of the labour market as a whole, the arts seem to be taking the brunt of the burden. Not without merit, Pascal Gielen (2013) has argued that cultural workers have been the model employees for the new post-Fordist economy. Minister of Culture Jet Bussemaker acknowledged the problem and took up criteria for 'good employership' in her regulations. This implies that the proper payment of cultural workers has become a matter of good governance on the part of cultural institutions. As Bussemaker was not able to supply additional funds to implement the measures, the issue has been left to the sector to solve. Bussemaker's reaction does present a deviation from earlier government involvement with the issue of artists' income. Moreover, the CPA does not address the issue at all. Nor does it address economic impact in general. However, cultural policy officials have increasingly busied themselves with these issues, blurring the lines between cultural policies—geared towards the quality and diversity of cultural expressions—and issues of income and economic impact.

A final recurrent theme in debates on Dutch cultural policy regards the international position of Dutch art. The theme is already present in the first policy document published under the CPA. As a former member of the European Parliament, Minister of Culture Hedy D'Ancona was acutely aware of the international perspective on Dutch art and culture. Representation of Dutch culture abroad is facilitated through Dutch cultural institutes. The Foundation for International Cultural Activities (SICA, now DutchCulture) was set up in 1999 to promote the international activities of Dutch cultural institutes and to organise cultural exchange initiatives. The organisation is funded by both the Ministry of Education, Culture and Science and the Ministry of Foreign Affairs. International cultural policy aspires to achieve two aims: to support Dutch artists and cultural institutions in their efforts to gain an international audience and to use art and culture to enhance international relations. The Ministry of Foreign Affairs also hosts the department for international cultural cooperation, a unit that facilitates the activities of cultural attachés employed at Dutch embassies and consulates. International cultural policy is coordinated by the department, reporting to both the Minister for Culture and the Minister of Foreign Affairs. Specific policy briefs on the topic are produced on a regular basis. As a result, the general cultural policy documents devote little attention to the matter.

International cultural policy is discussed in more detail in chapter 2 of this book.

5.   The Structure of This Book

As the following chapters focus on particular issues within the debates sketched above, the chapters do not describe the policy system itself, nor do they give an overview of the data underlying the system. To provide the background necessary to follow the discussion surrounding Dutch cultural policy, the basic structure of the cultural policy system has been described in an appendix. Furthermore, the appendix provides a shorthand dataset on the functioning of art and culture in the Netherlands. The data available at cultuurindex.nl is the basis for this overview. This is where the geographical distribution of the supply and use of art and culture is provided per sector. Topical data can also be acquired at www.cultuurindex.nl, a website devoted to statistics related to Dutch cultural policy. The appendix is authored by employees of the Boekman Foundation (*Boekmanstichting*), the institute that documents Dutch cultural policy and academic research conducted on the discipline. Interspersed throughout the book are six interviews with cultural leaders of the Dutch cultural sector, which provide the perspective from 'the floor', so to speak. The interviews, conducted by the Boekman Foundation, lay out the view of these leaders on the developments of the Dutch cultural sector in the coming decades.

The chapters in this volume are written by Dutch cultural policy researchers from various academic institutes in the country devoting departments to this area of study. The volume is organised in three parts. The first part focuses on the legal and organisational arrangements and the intended outcomes of Dutch cultural policy. Inge van der Vlies discusses the legal framework of Dutch cultural policy in chapter 1. The framework is rather peculiar from an international perspective, as the discussion above may also have indicated. In chapter 2, Toine Minnaert addresses the international perspective by discussing the extent to which 'the Dutch model' differs from other national models. He also explains the Dutch perspective on international cultural policy and cooperation. In chapter 3, Johan Kolsteeg examines cultural entrepreneurship and the conflicting responsibilities that its inclusion in cultural politics has entailed for management of cultural institutions. Chapter 4 focuses on the interplay between cultural politics and expert advice. Quirijn van den Hoogen and Florine Jonker explain how value orientations of the policy documents have changed and whether and how these have impacted the evaluation of subsidy applications by the Council for Culture. In chapter 5, Thijs Lijster, Hanka Otte and Pascal Gielen discuss how cultural policies relate to the public sphere and how notions of the arts as a public sphere are represented in Dutch cultural policies in practice.

The second part looks at typical issues that have come up during the last decades and will remain issues for the coming years. This part includes two chapters focusing on a particular sector of the cultural field: one on public media by Erik Hitters (chapter 6) and one on public libraries by Frank Huysmans and Marjolein Oomes (chapter 9). It is an important insight into Dutch cultural policy that these fields, as in the case of heritage policy, are no longer subject to the CPA. Each domain has, more or less recently, received its separate legal arrangement. Nonetheless, these fields are frequently discussed in cultural policy documents and are seen as an integral part of the country's cultural infrastructure. Hence, not including these in this volume would have been an omission. The chapters discuss the particular rules that apply to these domains and the main developments expected in the coming decades. Furthermore, Part II discusses one of the most prominent topics in Dutch cultural policy in recent decades: accessibility. Teunis IJdens and Edwin van Meerkerk shed light on how cultural education policies evolved in the Netherlands and discuss the key issues to be addressed in the coming years. Koen van Eijck addresses cultural participation in the Netherlands in chapter 8 and the type of research that is necessary to properly evaluate the success of cultural policy in this respect.

In Part III of the book, the threads connecting previous chapters are picked up. Chapter 10 takes a long-term perspective. Erik Schrijvers, one of the authors of *Reassessing Culture* (*Cultuur herwaarderen*) , a recent report on Dutch cultural policy by the Scientific Council for Government Policy (*Wetenschappelijke Raad voor het Regeringsbeleid*, WRR), addresses key tensions that he believes will determine the coming decades, focussing on the impact of digitalisation, the growing unease within Dutch society about its cultural roots, which introduces difficult questions as to how cultural policy can and should deal with those who feel 'culturally insecure'.

In the epilogue, we apply a systemic approach to Dutch cultural policy, discussing its bureaucratic tendencies and linking these up with the current debate on the redesign of the policy system. We hope this book contributes to the debate on the future of Dutch national cultural policy, or at least its future for the next 25 years.

Notes

1. Throughout this book two titles are used to indicate the person responsible
    for cultural policy in the Dutch government. 'Minister of Culture' is used to
    indicate those members of government with the rank of *minister*, 'Secretary
    for Culture' for *staatssecretaris*. There is no essential difference between
    their roles or legal position other than the minister's final responsibility for
    the budget (see the overview of Ministers of / Secretaries for Culture at the
    end of the book).

2. This booklet was written by five authors from the artist resistance move-
    ments but was also discussed in a wider committee of theatre practition-
    ers, amongst them well-known actors and directors (Van Maanen 1997:
    47). Therefore the booklet's contents can be regarded as a vision of Dutch
    spoken theatre shared by the profession.

3. The subsidy was allocated to the Pop Music Foundation Netherlands
    (*Stichting Popmuziek Nederland*). Its aim was to realise a pop music institute
    that would develop several artists, lobby pop music interests and act as
    impresario. However, the first subsidies did not allow for the realisation of
    this ambition (Nuchelmans 2002).

4. In 1982, the Ministry of CRM was reorganised into the Ministry of Welfare,
    Public Health and Culture (*Welzijn, Volksgezondheid en Cultuur*, WVC). In 1994,
    cultural policy 'returned' to the Ministry of Education and Sciences which
    henceforth has been renamed OCW (*Onderwijs, Cultuur en Wetenschap*).

5. However, slight differences still exist. Traditionally, the Christian-Democrats
    focus on amateur arts and the geographical distribution of cultural facili-
    ties, the Social-Democrats focus on the social reach of facilities, and the Lib-
    erals traditionally focus on artistic quality and the autonomy of the sector
    (and its consumers). Also, parties employ different phrasings on cultural
    policy: the Liberals tend to use more economical and legal reasoning than
    the other parties do, whereas Christian-Democrats stress the responsibility
    of communities, for instance (Hoefnagel 1992: 105).

6. The CPA is deeply affected by notions of New Public Management which
    have risen to prominence in Dutch public administration from the 1980s.
    See chapter 4 for more information on this topic.

7. The possibility to set up funds was only introduced by Minister D'Ancona in
    the final reading of the CPA in parliament. In doing so, she incorporated a
    general principle of the Lubbers government (1989-1994), which was to de-
    volve decision-making power from the central authority either to local au-
    thorities (geographical decentralisation) or to private foundations set up for
    specific purposes (functional decentralisation). National funds were set up
    for the performing arts, the visual arts and design and film, and for amateur
    arts. A literature fund was already effective. At first these funds allocated
    project subsidies and bursaries to artists, but in later years they were also
    allowed to provide two or four-year funding to cultural institutions.

8. The distribution of responsibilities regarding cultural education is different. While the content of education programmes is the responsibility of the schools, in line with the national education policy, the national government determines the end levels to be achieved by students. These include end levels for musical and cultural education. Although the nationally subsidised cultural institutions are evaluated by the Council for Culture based on how they develop educational programmes, the connection between the cultural and education sectors is facilitated mostly by local authorities who in many cases develop elaborate cultural education programmes and provide funds for instating liaison officers in schools. Moreover, local authorities subsidise institutions for cultural education outside schools.

9. It is worth mentioning that criteria regarding the management of cultural institutions or cultural entrepreneurship have become very important in the last decade. Since 2013, criteria of cultural entrepreneurship—in practice, financial criteria—have become as important as the evaluation of subsidy applications. Until 2013, they had always been criteria that were assessed *after* quality had been established, but now they are calculated prior to the quality assessment. See chapter 4 for a discussion of the implications of such changes over time.

10. The Frisian language is recognised as an official language by the Dutch state at the level of Chapter II of the European Charter for Minority Languages. All other Dutch regional languages are merely recognised at the level of Chapter III. In practice, this means they are dialects, while Frisian can be used in official government documents and in court.

11. See chapter 9 for a discussion of Dutch public libraries.

12. This current debate is not fully discussed in this book, as all chapters were written prior to the publication of Secretary Van Engelshoven's policy document *Cultuur in een Open Samenleving (Culture in an Open Society)*. We will revisit the current debate in the epilogue.

13. Although the cultural budget had been pruned by earlier governments in times of economic crisis, e.g. during the 1980s and the early 2000s, the cultural sector was always spared to some extent; in percentage terms, budget cuts were always relatively mild in relation to reductions of the total government budget. In 2011, austerity measures amounted to 10% of government spending while in the cultural sector they ran up to 20%. The media budget was reduced by similar percentages.

Bibliography

Campbell, John L. 2002. "Ideas, Politics, and Public Policy", *Annual Review of Sociology*, vol. 28: 21-38.

Gielen, Pascal. 2013. *Creativity and Other Fundamentalisms*. Amsterdam: Mondriaanfonds.

Florida, Richard. 2002. *The Rise of the Creative Class And How It's Transforming Work, Leisure, Community and Everyday Life*. New York: Perseus Book Group.

—. 2004. *Cities and the Creative Class*. Abingdon: Taylor & Francis.

Hillman-Chartrand, Harry, and Claire McCaughey. 1989. "The Arm's Length Principle: An International Perspective". In: Milton C. Cummings Jr. and J. Mark Davidson Shuster (eds.), *Who is to Pay for the Arts. The International Search for Models of Arts Support*, pp. 43-79. New York: American Council for the Arts.

Hoefnagel, Frans J.P.M. 1992. *Cultuurpolitiek: het mogen en het moeten* [Cultural Politics: Between What One Might and Should Do]. The Hague: Wetenschappelijke Raad voor het Regerings-beleid [Scientific Council for Government Policy].

Kassies, Jan. (1983) *Notities over een heroriëntatie van het kunstbeleid* [Notes on Reorienting Arts Policy]. The Hague: Wetenschappelijke Raad voor het Regeringsbeleid [Scientific Council for Government Policy].

Laermans, Rudi. (2002) *Het cultureel regiem. Cultuur en beleid in Vlaanderen* [The Cultural Regime. Culture and Policy in Flanders]. Tielt: Lannoo

Netelenbos, Tineke, and Aad Nuis. 1996. *Cultuur en School* [Culture and School]. The Hague: SDU.

Nuchelmans, André. 2002. *Dit gebonk dient tot het laatste toe te worden bestreden* [This Pounding Must Be Fought to the Very Last Moment]. Amsterdam: Boekmanstudies.

Pots, Roel. 2010. *Cultuur, Koningen en Democraten. Overheid en Cultuur in Nederland* [Culture, Kings and Democrats. Government and Culture in the Netherlands]. Amsterdam: Boom.

Oosterbaan Martinius, Warna. 1990. *Schoonheid, Welzijn, Kwaliteit; Kunstbeleid en verantwoording na 1945* [Beauty, Welfare, Quality; Art Policy and Legitimisation after 1945]. The Hague: SDU.

Raad voor Cultuur [Council for Culture]. 2015. *Agenda Cultuur 2017-2020 en verder* [Agenda for Culture 2017-2020 and Beyond]. The Hague: Raad voor Cultuur.

—. 2017. *Cultuur voor stad, land en regio, de rol van stedelijke regio's in het cultuurbestel* [Culture for City, Land and Region. The Role of Urban Regions in the Cultural System]. The Hague: Raad voor Cultuur [Council for Culture].

Sociaal-Economische Raad and Raad voor Cultuur. 2016. *Verkenning Arbeidsmarkt Cultuursector* [Enquiry Labour Market for the Cultural Sector]. The Hague: SER and Raad voor Cultuur [Social-Economic Council and Council for Culture]. Avaliable at https://www.ser.nl/~/media/files/internet/publicaties/overige/2010_2019/2016/verkenning-arbeidsmarkt-cultuursector/verkenning-arbeidsmarkt-cultuursector.ashx (downloaded 27 February 2018).

Van Deijck-Hofmeester, Carla, and Willem-Jan Raijmakers. 1994. *Er is meer tussen stad en staat; de provicie: partner in kunst- en cultuurbeleid* [Between City and State; The Province: Partner in Art and Culture Policies]. The Hague: IPO.

Van den Hoogen, Quirijn Lennert. 2010. *Performing Arts and the City; Municipal Cultural Policy in the Brave New World of Evidence-Based Policy*. PhD dissertation, Groningen University.

Van der Laan, Medy, and Carien van Gennip. 2005. *Ons Creatieve Vermogen* [Our Creative Capital]. The Hague: Ministerie van OCW en EZ [Ministry of Education, Culture and Science & Ministry of Economic Affairs]. Available at https://www.rijksoverheid.nl/documenten/rapporten/2009/08/26/ons-creatief-vermogen-brief-cultuur-en-economie (downloaded 27 February 2018).

Van Engelshoven, Ingrid. 2018. *Cultuur in een Open Samenleving* [Culture in an Open Society]. The Hague: Ministerie van OCW [Ministry of Education, Culture and Science].

Van IJsselmuiden, Peter. 1993. "Gevonden Waarheden. De ontstaansgeschiedenis van de Wet op het specifiek cultuurbeleid" [Found Truths. The Genesis of the Cultural Policy Act], *Boekmancahier* 5 (17): 280-292.

Van Maanen, Hans. 1997. *Het Nederlandse Toneelbestel van 1945 tot 1995* [The Dutch Theatre System between 1945 and 1995]. Amsterdam: Amsterdam University Press.

—. 2008. "A World of Independents in the Dutch Theatre System". In: Cas Smithuijsen and Ineke van Hamersveld (eds), *State on Stage. The Impact of Public Policies on the Performing Arts in Europe*, pp. 122-138. Amsterdam: Boekman Foundation.

Winsemius, Aletta. 1999. *De overheid in spagaat: theorie en praktijk van het Nederlandse kunstbeleid* [Government Doing the Splits: Theory and Practice of Dutch Art Policy]. Amsterdam: Thela Thesis.

Zijderveld, Anton C. 1983. "Transformatie van de verzorgingsstaat. De moeilijke balans van vrijheid, gelijkheid en solidariteit" [Transformation of the Welfare State. The Difficult Balance of Freedom, Equality and Solidarity]. In: Philip Abraham Idenburg (ed.), *De nadagen van de verzorgingsstaat. Kansen en perspectieven voor morgen* [The Latter Years of the Welfare State. Opportunities and Threats for Tomorrow]. Amsterdam: Meulenhoff.

A Well-Balanced Cultural Policy

An Interview with Minister of Culture Ingrid van Engelshoven

We meet several days after the presentation of *Culture in an Open Society*, which outlines Minister of Culture Ingrid van Engelshoven's vision of cultural policy. It is a publication that every Dutch minister for culture makes at the beginning of his or her administration. The cultural world is pleased with the arrival of this particular D66 (Social-Liberal Democratic Party) Minister. After years of austerity, the investment tap has once again been turned on. In addition, throughout the document she writes 'on behalf of the cabinet', indicating that her vision is shared by the rest of the government. Combined with her emphasis on the intrinsic value of art, few in the sector could be more delighted with her. The question then is: how does she view the role of culture in society? What does she think of the Cultural Policy Act? And how does she envision Dutch cultural policy to be 25 years from now?

'I don't want to make a statement about the effectiveness of the law after five months in office,' she says. 'What I find particularly important is that in the current Cultural Policy Act, the responsibility of the national government is well-anchored. Of course, there are constant discussions about what that means, also depending on the prevailing political spectrum and the *Zeitgeist* of the times.' One such discussion topic is the duration of Basic Infrastructure funding. The Council for Culture recently proposed stretching this from four to six years. 'I can quite imagine this from the cultural standpoint, but it would mean putting politics aside for six years,' she says, 'whereas I think politics should be able to keep pace with our rapidly changing society.' Additionally, the Minister does not want to make exceptions for iconic cultural institutions like the Rijksmuseum. After all, fixing the budget also comes at the expense of the system's flexibility. Perhaps the policy cycle should be even shorter, so that there is room for interim adjustments and so that young, up-and-coming makers have a chance within the system.

Nevertheless, Van Engelshoven is not in favour of substantially changing the system. The current law provides a sufficiently solid basis and an adequate degree of certainty. She therefore sees no need to create legal frameworks at the local level, despite the fact that municipalities are more likely than before to take the pruning shears to the cultural sector, due to their increased responsibilities for care and other priorities. Municipal autonomy is a great thing, however, and the Minister – previously an alderman in The Hague – believes that the idea of legislating to make local politics toe the desired culture-political line is an illusion. She thinks that when voters opt locally for a right-wing populist government (who tend to be less in favour of cultural subsidies), it is not up to the national government to lecture them. It is up to the municipalities to set priorities themselves. Care for the elderly, youth provision and safety are also important issues at the local level. The cultural sector must be careful not to believe that it is above everything, for this is exactly how it makes itself vulnerable to criticism. 'Be convinced of your own power within society, and enter into the public debate,' she advises. 'Dare to put yourself out there and say: "I know what I stand for and I can defend it."'

However, she does feel that coordination between the three levels of government can be improved. 'It is inconvenient for the sector to have to make separate subsidy applications for municipalities, provinces and the national government,' she remarks. 'That leads to a lot of uncertainty and administrative pressure. That is why we are going to try to connect them to each other. It would make me very happy if that succeeds. ' However, Van Engelshoven does not want to return to the interlocked subsidies that were abolished by the Cultural Policy Act. She advocates stronger regional cultural profiling and has the ambition to realise this in consultation with the provinces, municipalities and institutions.

How does she view European cooperation? A quarter-century from now, might Dutch cultural policy have degenerated into a 'local variant' of European cultural policy? The Minister does not think so, as she believes firmly that the Netherlands will always continue to pursue its own national cultural policy. However, cultural policy only exists thanks to the free movement across borders. 'We must keep the hatch open,' she says. 'That's important in every respect.'

Van Engelshoven is the first Minister in years to be allowed to increase the state budget for culture. She notes with satisfaction that even the political opposition has endorsed the additional 80 million euros for culture. 'People could have said, "What intrinsic value? Let's look at the economic returns." Or: "Couldn't we spend more money on teachers' salaries?"', she notes. According to her, this shows that, on both the left and the right end of the political spectrum, people understand the value of culture for society. For culture is not only about the abrasive, innovative arts but also about heritage and the cultural expressions that contribute to our identity – simply because everyone needs them. In cultural policy, the balance has sometimes come to lie too much with one or the other. 'Both sides of culture are important, more important than any systematic discussion,' she declares. She emphasises that a great task awaits culture, and she has urgent advice for the sector: do not write people off in advance. 'Not every cultural expression has to reach everybody, but we have to have something to offer for everyone,' she says. 'And that applies not only to the proverbial "Henk and Ingrid" but also to Mohammed and Fatima.'

Marielle Hendriks

1. Legal Aspects of Cultural Policy[1]

Inge van der Vlies

1.1 Introduction

Freedom of expression, including artistic expression, is a fundamental right. The regulation of the legal aspects of cultural policies must respect this right. The implications of the legal system for this freedom varies from one country to the next. In some countries, the legal system is strict: artists, like any other citizen, are expected to serve their country or the common interest, and the audience can only enjoy state-approved productions. Elsewhere, artistic freedom reigns supreme. Most countries, however, have a mix of these approaches: the legal system protects the freedom of the arts, but only as far as necessary in a democratic state under the rule of law.

Ai Weiwei is an example of the first type. As an artist, he is confronted with a government that limits his personal artistic activities in a way he refuses to accept. China defines what cultural activities are permissible and what are not. In countries where freedom of expression is the norm, artistic freedom is codified as a right. Many constitutions and international treaties cite the freedom of expression while limiting it as well. Laws put limits on cultural expressions everywhere. The prohibition of racism, for instance, is generally accepted as a fundamental and universal rule, thus restricting the freedom of expression for artists. The assessment of what limits are admissible is subject to change over time and from one place to the next.

The Dutch legal system regarding cultural policy is an example of a legal regime that is imbued with the wish to respect freedom of the arts, specifically limiting the power of politicians to influence the making of art. Cultural producers are granted full freedom of choice. This is especially challenging in the context of a positive cultural policy: a policy that strives to give equal chances to all. This positive right can be seen as a necessary condition to ensure freedom of expression. People are entitled to the means for creating and enjoying the arts. They need education and access to cultural productions. In other words, freedom is not only a negative right (an obligation for the government not to intervene) but can be valued as a positive one as well. A state must facilitate a flourishing cultural climate, even when no legal obligation is stated.

The complexity of combining the negative with the positive is a challenge for lawmakers: the law must grant freedom of cultural expression (state opts out) while simultaneously ensuring that culture can be developed and maintained (state opts in). To achieve the latter goal, governments must make choices in encouraging and protecting cultural productions and goods. How can it make these choices while refraining from interference in the cultural field?

In order to perform this task, the Netherlands has established a specific legal-cultural domain. The main components of this framework are: the concept of the rule of law, the constitutional freedom of expression, the Cultural Policy Act (CPA), cultural funds, the General Administrative Law Act (GALA), the rules of the EU, principles of good governance, and public-private partnerships. Various issues regarding art and law are regulated in international treaties, most of which have been ratified by the Netherlands. These have been implemented in Dutch cultural policy and will be examined in more detail below. These treaties and conventions do not constitute a third (global) legal order beyond the national and the European. It could be said that such a new global order is in the making, but it is not there (yet).

1.2   Rule of Law

The legal-cultural domain must be organised, like all other specific domains, under the rule of law. The meaning of the rule of law therefore bears further examination. Western democracies are regularly organised under the rule of law (Dicey 2013). The legal system enforces and protects the principles of a democratic state. A government based on democratic legislation ensures the equality of the people, as the government is bound to apply the law equally for all. The judiciary plays an important role in maintaining the rule of law and in guaranteeing equality. Independent judges may review an application by the government on a citizen's appeal. Legal courts thus provide checks and balances in the system and enforce the abiding of the rule of law by the government. The way a government applies the rules and develops cultural policy is thus guided by the spirit of fundamental rights, including the freedom of expression (Dawson 2017).

1.2.1   Government Based on the Law

Legal systems contain guarantees against the arbitrary use of power by the state. Without a legal basis, public authorities under the rule of law are not allowed to command or prohibit the actions of citizens. Therefore, legal acts have to contain exact descriptions of the power that authorities have in order for citizens to be able to know what authorities are and are not allowed to do. In some cases, it is impossible to do so. For instance, with regard to the maintenance of public order, authorities are endowed with far-reaching legal powers. An open air concert may bother people living in the neighbourhood. Local authorities have to find a balance between the freedom of expression and the wishes of residents to have a good night's sleep. The local authorities' reasoning to either protect the musicians and their audience or the residents in the neighbourhood must be convincing, but it cannot be laid down in detail in the law.

The fact that public authorities are not allowed to hinder cultural expressions or other actions of citizens without a legal basis dovetails with another demand pertaining to the concept of the rule of law: no obligation for citizens without a legal authorisation. The empowerment of administrative bodies to impose obligations on citizens or to steer them in a certain direction has to be done in a democratically established law.

As a consequence, subsidies and their conditions, which influence the actions of citizens via a system of granting money, must be based on a democratic law. These laws make the possibilities to apply for a subsidy public and accessible to all and prevent the arbitrary use of state power to subsidise certain groups of citizens.

1.2.2   The Legal Basis for Cultural Policy

There is no legal obligation for the state to subsidise the arts. Legal rules only guide the spending of money if public administration makes the political decision to subsidise. In the Netherlands, two legal acts regulate the power of state authorities to rule on cultural policies and create options for cultural development for all (Van der Vlies 2017). These acts are the General Administrative Law Act (*Algemene Wet Bestuursrecht*, GALA) and the Cultural Policy Act (*Wet op het Specifiek Cultuurbeleid*, CPA). They provide the legal basis for the government to act in the cultural field under the rule of law, thereby preventing arbitrariness in government policy.

The CPA concerns the administration of cultural policy at the national level and does not address municipalities or provinces, which set their own local rules to fulfil the demands of the rule of law. The other act, the GALA, codifies administrative law. It regards general rules and individual orders. Principles of good governance are defined and translated into practical rules. The GALA applies to local and regional authorities as well (see section 5).

1.2.3   Access to the Courts

Furthermore, in the concept of the rule of law, access to a judge is essential. Courts need to guard the correct application of rules. The public administration must, like any private party, follow up the case law. An applicant who has been denied a subsidy can therefore launch an appeal, according to the GALA. An administrative law court decides such cases.

1.2.4   Guarantees

The concept of the rule of law in the cultural domain is guaranteed by the freedom of expression and other fundamental rights, the CPA and detailing rules, local rules, the GALA and citizens' access to the courts.

1.3   Freedom of Artistic Expression

Freedom of expression is a fundamental right, essential in a state operating under the rule of law (Saunders 2017). This right allows people the freedom to express themselves in the way they choose without governmental interference. In most states—as in the Netherlands—the constitution ensures freedom of expression, within democratic limits.

The details of this right differ from country to country with respect to the limitations it places on freedom of expression. These limits are drawn along the lines of national customs. Even within Europe, ideas about what is allowed and must be tolerated and what can or shall be forbidden differ. This element—that the ambit of the freedom varies with the national customs—is expressed in the European Convention on Human Rights and shown in the case law of the European Court. Regardless of these differences, governments subscribing to the European Convention are obliged to enable people to enjoy freedom of expression (Berlin 1969, Blokland 1995, Nussbaum 1997).

1.3.1   Freedom of Artistic Expression as a Fundamental Right

Freedom of artistic expression is developed in case law with regard to freedom of expression as such.[2] Article 10 of the European Convention on Human Rights defines the right and its limitations:
1.   Everyone has the right to freedom of expression. This right shall include freedom to hold opinions and to receive and impart information

    and ideas without interference of public authority and regardless of
    frontiers [...].
2.   The exercise of these freedoms, since it carries with it duties and respon-
    sibilities, may be subject to such formalities, conditions, restrictions or
    penalties as are prescribed by law and are necessary in a democratic
    society.

The European Court of Human Rights gave an interpretation of this Article
(05-24-1988 Müller vs Swiss), stating the position of the artistic freedom as
follows:

> Admittedly, Art. 10 does not specify that freedom of artistic expression, in
> issue here, comes within its ambit; but neither, on the other hand, does it
> distinguish between the various forms of artistic expression. [...] it includes
> freedom of artistic expression [...] which affords the opportunity to take
> part in the public exchange of cultural, political and social information
> and ideas of all kinds.

At the European level, freedom of artistic expression is both recognised
and limited. In the case mentioned above, Swiss public authorities had
forbidden a gallery to display a certain painting on the grounds that the
picture offended public morals. The prohibition was acceptable in the eyes
of the court, as it was in accordance with national views. The authorities
concerned were empowered by national rules to act as they did. Freedom
of artistic expression is not absolute but will be respected in accordance
with cultural standards of the public, which are codified by law.

    Article 7 of the Dutch constitution contains a similar approach of rights
and limitations (Strengers & Van der Vlies 2017). A well-known limitation
is the prohibition of encouraging violence against people (Kearns 2013).
Another one is the protection of the public order, something necessary in
a democracy.

    A recent article states what this right is about in a more direct way.
Article 13 of the European Union Charter of Fundamental Rights states: 'The
arts and scientific research shall be free of constraint. Academic freedom
shall be respected.' It differs from the phrasing in Article 7 of the Dutch
Constitution and Article 10 of the European Convention for Human Rights.
In Article 13 of the European Union Charter, the freedom of the arts is
mentioned specifically, while traditional phrasing does not mention freedom
of artistic expression, implying that it is part of the freedom of expression
as such. Whether this explicit recognition in an International Convention

will change the implication of the freedom of artistic expression will be revealed in the future case law of the courts.

1.3.2   Social Aspects of Freedom of Expression

What does freedom of expression entail if someone cannot write, does not have money to buy paint or to take lessons on a musical instrument (Vlemminx 2002)? For people to be able to exercise their rights, they should be enabled to master the necessary tools such as writing and reading and have access to cultural productions and goods. Since 1983, Article 22 of the Dutch Constitution mentions the cultural development of the people as a permanent obligation of public administration. Cultural policy is imbued with the notion that conditions must be created to make cultural development achievable for the public. Many international treaties include a similar intention. Fundamental to the creation of tools for public cultural development is education. In many states, general education is free but does not always include artistic or cultural education.

Article 22 of the Dutch Constitution obliges public authorities to provide the conditions for a cultural atmosphere in which cultural activities are accessible to all. The Article does not establish a legal obligation to finance the arts. Rather, it states an overriding principle. It creates a legal basis, making it possible for the administration to fund cultural endeavours. Since the beginning of the twenty-first century, public finances for the arts have been cut significantly. Protest against these cuts could not fall back on a legal basis, and thus did not cause a change in the policy.

Subsequent governments maintained the new chosen policy. In the twenty-first century, politicians are rather reluctant regarding the arts, and no restoration of the twentieth-century policy is to be foreseen. Financial support for the arts has to be found primarily in private sources (Van der Vlies 2012). This change of policy, which was an unwelcome change to many, showed very clearly that legal protection is limited. The law guides the way in which support to the arts is organised and guides the ending of subsidising. It does not demand that support is given or continued. Procedures do give guarantees to a decent downsizing (see below), but no more.

National government has placed itself in a difficult position by legally obliging itself to support the arts while simultaneously binding itself to severe juridical limits in exerting influence on artistic expressions. Creating art is the privilege of artists, promoting the arts is the privilege of producers, and choosing to enjoy the arts is the privilege of the audience. After all, any support of the arts is related to the freedom of expression. The administration is not allowed to use its power to privilege artists from a political point of view. To achieve these contradictory goals, procedural measures have been taken in the Netherlands, separating the decision-making process from any opportunity of influence by the administration.

The Chinese walls that have been erected here between politics and cultural decision-makers differ between countries. In Germany, the federal and especially the state governments have more influence (Kessels 2004). In other countries, politicians are allowed to intervene by erecting cultural heritage sites (the *Grands Travaux* of the French presidents, such as the Bibliothèque Nationale or the Musée du Quay Branly, are prime examples). To ensure that cultural institutions and productions are valued on their artistic merits, independent experts play an important role in the Netherlands. Their advice is decisive, with a few exceptions. The process is made transparent in order to protect both the cultural institutions and the government. The GALA contains several procedural provisions to ensure that the process is executed as objectively as possible (see below).

Freedom of expression has two sides in a welfare state that is democratically organised under the rule of law. Artists have free choices and so do the audience. Furthermore, the state is under an obligation to enable the people to enjoy this right as much as possible.

1.4   The Cultural Policy Act

Cultural policymaking is derived from the legal obligation to stimulate and to provide. The contents of cultural policy varies from one Culture Minister to the next. For example, in the past, priority has been given to the regions, diversity, restoration, cultural entrepreneurship, accessibility, buildings and education. All these political choices are perfectly possible within the CPA.

Since the Second World War, support of the arts has been standing policy in the Netherlands. The gradual rise of cultural policymaking resulted in a rather scattered system of predominantly unwritten conventions. In the last decades of the twentieth century, new artists and institutions started to protest against the arbitrariness of the system and held the Minister of Culture accountable, calling for new guidelines on behalf of younger artists and newcomers. The Minister agreed and started to open up the system to newcomers by introducing new policy rules. Further, the gradual increase in budget for cultural policy also necessitated an adjustment of the system. A third reason was a series of political scandals involving the arts. In 1971, for instance, the State Secretary of Foreign Affairs withdrew a subsidy from a theatre company (Proloog) because it criticised him (Reinders & Van der Vlies 1972). The court reviewed the withdrawal and found it in violation of the company's freedom of expression. As a result, the wish for a new system with clear procedures that was less dependent on the whims of politicians became more urgent.

The new system is laid down in the Cultural Policy Act (CPA) of 1993. It defines the framework of cultural policy at the national level by describing the following aspects:

- cultural goals that can be served,
- empowerment of administrative bodies to grant subsidies,
- planning of cultural policy,
- mandates to develop further cultural policy rulings.

The Cultural Policy Act outlines procedures for establishing cultural policy. This Act strikes a balance between various contradictory demands. The arts seek creativity and flexibility, and the government seeks to plan. Cultural institutions want to be assured of a long-lasting subsidy relationship, while governments want to have the power to cut subsidies whenever they deem fit. Politicians seek to leave their own mark on the cultural sector and often seek to change the policy of their predecessors, while the legal system seeks continuity and equal treatment of cultural institutions. These three tensions have been the cause of frequent amendments to the CPA and the rules that are derived from it. The fact that the CPA could nevertheless survive for more than 25 years can be attributed to the flexibily of the system, which managed to stay identifiable notwithstanding the amendments made. It works because independent cultural experts play a part in individual cases, while politics are in charge of determining the total amount of money involved. Within this framework, the various Secretaries for Culture have been able to change the rules within the legal limitations set by the act without changing the system as such (see section 5).

The call for providing the cultural policy system with a legal basis had a juridical source as well. The General Administrative Law Act (GALA) required a legal basis of all subsidy decisions by the public administration. The GALA was developed in phases, drawn up and enforced chapter by chapter. The first three chapters contain important rules on decision-making by public authorities (1992). Chapter 4 contains rules for subsidies and demands a legal basis for subsidies (1994). The CPA and the GALA prescribe how to take decisions regarding the spending of the cultural budget, which is provided by another Act—the State Budget (*rijksbegroting*), which is adopted yearly. The core rules of the CPA establish the power of three important actors: the Minister of Culture, the Council for Culture and the Culture Funds.

1.4.1   Minister of Culture

Cultural policy in the Netherlands is set up with three public administrative tiers: the state, the provinces and the local communities. The legal system set up by the national government (the CPA) has to a certain extent been copied by other public bodies. At their respective levels, provincial and local authorities have set up general rules on cultural policy. Many municipalities make a cultural policy plan every four years. Each authority takes care of cultural policy within its own ambit. In this chapter, the focus is on the legal system at the national level—with some exceptions. The Minister of Culture is the ultimate authority that makes the CPA work. The task of the Minister is described in article 2:

> The Minister must create the conditions to maintain, develop, and socially and geographically or otherwise spread cultural expressions. He shall be guided by considerations of quality and diversity.

The Minister has to ensure that the cultural infrastructure is sound and accessible to all. The cultural infrastructure regards all pillars of cultural society such as artists, cultural producers, theatres, concert halls, education, institutions and audiences.

The CPA offers various instruments for a Minister to establish her policy:
- publication of the main issues of ministerial policy at least once every four years (Article 3);
- ministerial rulings that state which subsidies will be afforded for the coming four years;
- the granting of subsidies in compliance with these ministerial rulings;
- the establishment of cultural public funds.

Besides the CPA, other Acts create options to subsidise artistic activities in different contexts, such as within the health care system. These are not discussed here.[3] By communicating the main issues, for example a greater focus on cultural entrepreneurship, the art world is informed about what to expect. These communications will be translated into detailed secretarial rules. The detailed ministerial rules tell most cultural institutions whether they are likely to receive a subsidy. The most famous cultural institutions like the Royal Concertgebouw Orchestra or the Nederlands Dans Theater will almost always find they fulfil the requirements to receive subsidies. Once admitted into the system, institutions are guaranteed financial stability for four years. While from some perspectives, that period of time seems reasonable, it can prove difficult for arts organisations to successfully plan cultural activities within this time frame, especially for institutions working with world-renowned artists. Nevertheless, the four years' term is one of the pillars of the system.

1.4.2   The Council for Culture

Before a Minister of Culture can decide on a subsidy, he/she has to consult the Council for Culture. The Council for Culture advises the government and parliament on legislation or policy regarding culture and on individual requests for subsidies (Van der Vlies & Van den Berg 2017).

The CPA further requires that members of the Council for Culture be independent cultural experts. Their advice on individual cases is binding for the Minister, so long as the advice is carefully drafted. After the Minister has accepted the Council's advice, he/she is held responsible for declaring that the advice was set up carefully. The GALA (General Administrative Law Act) demands that a justification be given if the Minister decides to derogate from the advice of the Council for Culture (Art. 50 GALA). The justification may refer to exceptional circumstances such as apparent mistakes in advice given by the Council for Culture. Sometimes, however, the Minister's decision can be contrary to the advice and yet still justifiable without an elaborate explanation. For example, the Minister may identify funds for applications that had a positive artistic review of the Council for Culture but were denied a subsidy due to a limited state budget, as happened in 2016 when Minister Bussemaker subsidised institutions that had applied in vain for grants from the Performing Arts Fund. In such cases, no legal objections will arise against the Minister for her actions, and the content of the advice will be respected.

The advisory system with the Council for Culture was created in order to minimise political influence. The focus on the inter-subjective quality of the applications is safeguarded by the intervention of the Council for Culture. A final safeguard in the CPA for cultural institutions is an article that arranges a procedure for appeal for institutions whose applications have been denied (see section 5).

1.4.3   Public Cultural Funds

The available budget for cultural productions within the framework of the CPA is divided between the Minister of Culture and public culture funds. These culture funds are established by the Minister, who is empowered to do so by the CPA. The funds are a part of the cultural policy of the Minister. The Council for Culture advises on the tasks they are set up with. The Minister is responsible to parliament for his/her cultural policy.

The public culture funds are legally given the power to issue legislative rules and to grant subsidies. The Netherlands Film Fund, for example, subsidises the making of films. Culture funds are required to submit draft rules containing subsidy criteria to the Minister. Only after approval has been given can a culture fund publish its rules. This procedure allows the Minister to maintain coherence in the execution of cultural policy beyond the domain in which she can directly intervene. Culture funds have their own boards and establish their own committees, with independent cultural experts advising on individual applications. Since the culture funds are public authorities, due to the responsibilities bestowed upon them through the CPA, public law is applicable to their actions. They must concur with the GALA (see section 5).

Since 2013, six public culture funds have been operational: for stage arts, literature, film and media, visual arts and exhibitions, creative industries, and participation. The Participation Fund was set up to address a hot political issue: the cultural participation of all people. In the past, more culture funds existed, as specific art forms were each covered by their own fund. While this gave the impression of transparency, it in fact caused a lot of red tape for applicants. They had to solve a complex puzzle in choosing the appropriate culture fund. Is a book about paintings to be defined as a book, and should the author apply to the Literature Fund, or does it serve the interest or development of painters and should the author call upon the Visual Arts Fund? Every fund defined its own working field, leaving it to the applicants to find the right match. This was extremely complicated in the case of multi-media arts and interdisciplinary projects.

Procedures for filing requests with the culture funds are similar to those with the ministry: the funds draw up the rules for applications by cultural institutions and artists. The ruling on applications is based on expert advice. The most important difference between the ministerial procedure and that of the culture funds is the status of the receiving institutions. The Minister of Culture finances the most important cultural institutions through the Basic Infrastructure. Eligible institutions, with the artistic quality and (international) reputation required, obviously have a high chance of receiving the subsidy requested. Moreover, the Minister allows institutions more diversity in their budgets. The amount of money they get is higher, and they only need to file one application regarding all their activities for the next four years. In contrast, culture funds offer a wider variety of subsidies with specific goals, such as internationalisation, community activities, or education. This forces the smaller cultural institutions to apply for a variety of subsidies with the concerned funds for each activity, apart from obtaining income from other sources. Combined with their lower status and reputation, this creates a wide gap between institutions that receive their funding directly from the ministry and those that receive subsidies from culture funds.

1.4.4   Legal Evaluation

The CPA offers a stable framework to deal with the variety of tensions caused by the legal-political-cultural triangle. This framework allows the demands of the rule of law to be fulfilled on a very basic level: subsidies are based on parliamentary legislation, and a court may review the subsidy resolutions. Although the powers of the public authorities that give the subsidies are well arranged for (they have a legal basis, they have to comply with legal principles), they retain much discretion. However, the authority of the Council for Culture, focusing on the inter-subjective quality of the applications, serves to moderate possible political misbehaviour. Principles of good governance—codified in the GALA—also provide legal guidance (see section 5). The discretionary power of politicians is diminished but has not disappeared. Cultural institutions and artists can never be certain about what the political future may bring. The granting of a subsidy brings them certainty for a short period of time or enables a project, but thereafter they have to wait and see, knowing that new politicians will bring new policies. The CPA created a system that ensures a certain degree of transparency in the decision-making process, supported by the rules in the GALA (see section 5).

1.5   The General Administrative Law Act

The GALA constitutes the backbone of the rule of law in the cultural domain: dealings of the public administration (with a cultural implication) must be done in a legally correct way. The Act does not command the government to act, however. If the government does not take cultural decisions at all, it is still acting in a legally correct way. The GALA contains a chapter on rules with regard to subsidies. For the cultural field, this chapter is of great importance (see below). The GALA addresses all administrative bodies, whether state bodies, municipality bodies or public funds.

The General Administrative Law Act (GALA) lists the basic legal standards for all activities of the public administration (the parliamentary legislator not included) (Borman & De Poorter 2017). It defines 'administrative authority', classifies and defines its actions, and regulates those actions. If we say: 'the public administration grants a subsidy to the Toneelgroep Amsterdam', within the GALA it would say: 'the competent administrative authority decides to issue a decree on the application of the Toneelgroep Amsterdam (applicant) and to award the application in compliance with the applicable rules and the principles of good governance'. This is an illustration of the way that subsidies given to a certain person or institution are categorised as decrees of the administration[4] and that these decisions must follow the general rules of the GALA (Chapters 1, 2, 3 GALA). Chapter 4 of the Act describes special rules for subsidies.

The GALA translates the principle of legal certainty through the demand that decrees are written and sent in a timely manner to the applicant, the demand that facts are presented correctly, the demand that legal provisions are referred to, and the demand that sufficient reasoning be used. These provisions aim to transfer the principle of legal certainty into practical technical rules. In all chapters of the GALA, principles of good governance are partly codified as rules. Principles have to be translated into rules to make them applicable without creating problems of interpretation. The codification of the principle of legal certainty makes it clear that permanent continuity of a legal situation is not included. A complete prohibition of any changes in the rules in order to ensure legal certainty would, of course, be ridiculous. In cases where subsidy rights are changing, the principle of legal certainty is translated into operational rules regarding the timeframe and the costs of transition to a new situation. A subsidy resolution can be reviewed in court if an appeal is launched against it (chapters 6, 7, 8 GALA, see § 5.3 below).

1.5.1 Principles of Good Governance

Principles of good governance are general legal principles with regard to public administration (Schlossels & Zijlstra 2017). They can be codified in rules or be identified in case law. They regard the process of the making of a decree by a public authority: due diligence, the weighing of interests, proportionality, clear reasoning, legal equality and legal certainty. The principles also regard the position of the consultant of the administration and of the issuing authority: expertise, competence, integrity, independence and the prohibition of arbitrariness.

Principles of good governance contribute to the establishment of lawfulness in public administration. From the early twentieth century on, they have been developed by the courts into instruments to review the actions of administrative authorities. Later on, some were codified in various laws. The GALA constitutes an important step in making the principles practical. People can call upon these rules when dealing with the public administration.

The principle of legal equality is a fundamental legal principle. It is codified in many international conventions as well as in many national constitutions. The Dutch Constitution starts with a codification of the principle in Article 1 (Loenen 2009): all people are equal before the law. As a principle of good governance, the principle obliges public administration to apply laws and policy rulings equally to all. All similar institutions shall have equal opportunities. The crux of the matter is to find an approach that creates the non-equality that sometimes is also necessary. In one case, the question was: are all institutions established on a religious fundament, with a goal to improve society equal, or are all institutions established on an ethical fundament with a goal to improve society equal? The principle of equality, due to its broad, pre-existing codification, is not codified in the GALA.

The principle of due diligence is important because of its procedural character. It requires that all facts be researched before decrees are issued, that all concerned interests be weighed and that all prescribed procedures be followed. This principle is codified in Article 3:4 GALA. In practice, this principle plays an important role with regard to refusals of applications and the ending of subsidy relationships.

Due diligence played an important role in the case of Djazzex.[5] This company submitted an appeal against the refusal of its funding application. It put forward that the judgment of artistic quality, which was negative, was not based on fact. The public administration could not show any file with decent reviews of performances of the company, but it was also unable to show its sources for judgement. The negative subsidy decision was therefore in violation of the principle of due diligence. It was nullified by the court.

Due diligence is a condition for good reasoning. Many aspects of the principle of good reasoning are stated in various provisions of the GALA.

A decision should be based on well-researched facts (Art.3:46). Any decree holding the decision on the request of a subsidy must refer to the concerned legal provisions (Art.3:47). Moreover, the reasoning must be understandable.

The principle of good governance regarding reasoning obliges the public administration to show arguments in support of its decisions. The researched and mentioned facts and the reasoning must be convincing. The route from the facts to the outcome of the reasoning is sometimes difficult. For public administrators, it is challenging to explain why some applications are reviewed as high quality and other applications are not. How can one explain the standards of 'good quality'? People who disagree with the view on the quality will argue that the reviewers merely have different taste and therefore misjudged the quality of the application. The contested decision must contain sufficient grounds to make it acceptable to the courts that the application did not meet the required standards, in other words the public authorities must make it clear that it is not a matter of taste. Well-known formulas used to this end are: 'not sufficiently distinctive from other applications', 'has been done before', 'no proof that the proposed capable artists will indeed cooperate'. The most important legitimation in this perspective is the use of a procedure guaranteeing objectivity (going back to the principle of due diligence). A well-constructed procedure offers warrants for the objectivity of the reasoning.

The demands with regard to artistic quality of the production do not constitute the only quality standards that are required in the rules. Other quality grounds to review the application are, for example, cultural entre- preneurship, regional distribution, general dissemination, appreciation in the media and audience reach. These criteria give less cause for disputes, as they can be described more clearly. A ruling may state that subsidies must be awarded to two theatre groups in every region. A denial of an application is sufficiently reasoned if it is based on an advice that two other applications are of a similar artistic quality but are rated higher in other aspects.

Applicants have to accept their loss if the decision of the authority is in accordance with the rules of GALA, CPA and other cultural policy regula- tions. The courts have accepted that in the end, the view of different parties or independent experts with regard to the quality of an artistic production can differ without violating a rule or a principle of good governance.

The principle of legal certainty embodies many aspects (see also section 5.1). These various aspects are translated into detailed provisions of the GALA. Institutions and people may not be confronted with sudden changes

in what they could reasonably expect (Art. 4:51 GALA), Instead, they must
be forewarned. This provision has an important impact on the way in
which subsidies can be terminated. The relationship created as a result of
a subsidy is formally only temporary: it lasts as long as is stated in the decree.
Sometimes, however, the relationship between the administrative authority
that granted the subsidy and a cultural institution lasts for many years. As
a result, the cultural institution may very well become heavily dependent
on the subsidy. It is quite understandable in such circumstances for the
cultural institution to count on a positive response to its subsequent subsidy
applications, because it continues to perform the same activities for which
it received subsidies earlier. This expectation, however, has no legal ground
(subsidies are given for a certain period of time without a legal promise for
the next period of time, and the administration is free to change its policy).
The GALA indicates that while some expectations may be understandable,
that they do not implicate a *right* on a prolongation of the subsidy relationship. However, the fact that it concerns a long-lasting relationship cannot
be neglected. In the fictitious case described above, a public authority
that decides to withhold subsidy on the next application must inform the
applying institution in a timely manner, that is, before the current subsidy
ends, in order to enable the institution to prepare for the loss of funding.
In some cases, the institution is even entitled to additional financing for
coping with the costly effects of the subsidy cut, for example the costs of
firing personnel. The institution must deal with the legal ramifications of
these actions. If the result is that an institution must downsize or even close,
it involves dealing with the early termination of labour contracts, rental
space contracts and other special costs. The administration must therefore
consider these aspects when making the decision not to continue granting
a subsidy. Sometimes it must compensate for these costs.

The principle of integrity pertains to other elements in the process, for
example the choice of experts to advise the administration. In choosing the
experts, it must be clear that they are recognised as such in their field and
that they have no conflicts of interest. If they have an interest in a pending
case or if they are on a board of the cultural institution submitting an
application, they must recuse themselves from reviewing that application or
any others that are in competition with the concerned cultural institution
(Van den Berg et al. 2017: 232-239). The bottom line is they must avoid the
appearance of impropriety.

   The GALA provides specific rules for the consulting relationship of
administrative authorities with advisory bodies, such as the Council for

Culture (chapter 2). The administration is held accountable for the final decision, which is only made after the advisory councils have given their advice. Therefore, before a decree can be issued, the authorities must verify that the councils have complied with the rules regarding their assignment, that the facts were properly researched, and that the advice is thorough and given in accordance with the GALA rules (Van den Berg et al 2017: 239-243).

1.5.2   Legal Remedies

Applicants that are confronted with a subsidy denial can submit an appeal with the competent authority and eventually they can appeal to an administrative law court (Van den Berg et al. 2017: 263-267). Thereafter, they can file a claim with the highest administrative law court in the Netherlands: the Raad van State. The procedures for these actions are also outlined in the GALA (chapters 6-8).

Applicants can write an objection to the issuing authority within six weeks after receiving an unwelcome decision, in which they explain why it was wrong to reject their application or a part of it. Their protest can be directed against the amount of money or against the conditions, for example too stringent obligations such as playing at too many different locations. The protest has to be substantiated.

The administrative authority must then reconsider its decision fully on the basis of the reasoning in the objection. A hearing must be organised to gather all information. The public authority itself can hear the applicant, but it can also set up a special procedure. If it opts for the latter, various procedures are available. It can outsource the hearing to a person, establish a committee of civil servants with an external chairperson, or appoint a committee of independent experts. This committee will organise a hearing in which the applicants and one or more representatives of the public administration will be heard. The committee will base its advice on the inquired facts, policy considerations, and the law. The administrative authority must follow up the advice or explain why it does not do so (art. 3:50 GALA).

The appeals procedure is set up in favour of applicants who feel disadvantaged by the administrative authorities. The procedure contains safeguards to avoid new disadvantages for the applicant. The reconsidered decision of the administration must be based on the notice of objection and not seek to reconsider parts of the decision that are not questioned in the notice. The administration is not allowed to decide on appeal in a way that is disadvantageous to the applicant (the so-called rule of *no reformatio in peius*).

Applicants that are not satisfied with the decision on appeal can submit a notice of appeal with an administrative law court (art. 8:1 GALA). The appeal must include all supporting documents and information, together with substantiated objections. If the appellant has appointed a legal representative or agent to speak for him/her, the appeal must also identify the representative or agent. The procedure can be conducted without a legal representative, however. The procedure before the administrative law courts is supposed to be understandable for all. In practice, though, many legal obstacles may occur. The power of the courts to review is limited to legal grounds: a breach of law or a violation of the principles of good governance or the fundamental principles of a fair trial. The courts cannot take a new decision, apart from exceptional cases, but they can oblige the administrative authority to reconsider and issue a new decree. If the applicant does not agree with the verdict of the administrative law court, a higher appeal to the Raad van State, the highest administrative law court, is possible. The conditions under which this procedure can be followed are similar to the ones to appeal in the administrative law courts (chapter 8 GALA).

1.5.3   Legal Evaluation

Subsidy allocations are administrative law decisions, which are regulated in the GALA. The relationship between the authorities and cultural institutions benefits from the principles of good governance and the regulations in the GALA. Protection in law is well accounted for. A disadvantage of the legal approach may be the formalisation of the relationships between the cultural institutions and the administration, since anything can be of substance in a procedure before administrative law courts. This is a frequent complaint both from the cultural institutions and from the administrative authorities.[6] The problem is shared by all relationships regulated by administrative law: health care, environmental planning, the protection of nature, or traffic. The benefits of legally well-established relationships are still considered to be greater than the disadvantages.

1.6   Influence of the European Union

The European Union created a new legal system with a general influence on all legal dealings of the Member States.[7] The legal order of the EU has effects in the field of cultural policy just like in any other policy domain. The implications for the cultural domain are rather restricted at the moment, however. One of the legal issues at stake is the question of which party initiates cultural policymaking: a Member State or the EU? For the moment, the Member States are primarily responsible for their respective cultural policies (Art.6c, Treaty on the Functioning of the European Union, TFEU). The Member States of the European Union are allowed to continue their cultural policies within the general rules of the EU, especially with regard to the open market. Subsidising an entrepreneur implicates infringement with the articles regarding the open market, but not all cultural institutions operate on the open market as entrepreneur. Nonetheless, some cultural tasks are mandated to the administration of the European Union. These will be described first.

1.6.1   European Tasks

Article 167 of the TFEU provides details on EU action in the field of culture: 'The Union shall contribute to the flowering of the cultures of the Member-States, while respecting their national and regional diversity and at the same time bringing the common cultural heritage to the fore' (Art 167.1). The EU must safeguard cultural heritage of European significance, foster non-commercial cultural exchanges and artistic and literary creation, including in the audio-visual sector. The European Union can take action to improve the knowledge and dissemination of the culture and history of the European peoples. Cooperation between Member States must be encouraged and supported. When taking action under other provisions of the Treaty, the Union should balance the various interests at stake, of which cultural input is one.

1.6.2   Economic Rules

Article 36 of the TFEU requires open competition, but the rule of reason demands that some helpful regulations are allowed, for example to assert diversity.[8] Article 107.3d of the TFEU limits the scope of national cultural policy. State support for firms is forbidden, but the prohibition is not absolute. The European Court of Justice gave a more detailed description of the notion of an undertaking in the case of Höfner and Elser v Macrotron:[9] 'in the context of competition law, [...] the concept of an undertaking encompasses every entity engaged in an economic activity, regardless of the legal status of the entity and the way in which it is financed'. In some circumstances, financial aid to cultural enterprises is allowed. Article 107.3d states that financial aid is allowed to promote culture al and heritage conservation where such aid does not affect trading conditions and competition in the Union to an extent that is contrary to the common market.

Traditionally, cultural institutions such as museums were not commercial enterprises. They did not compete in a commercial entertainment market, though their services could be qualified as commercial activities. These activities were allowed by the European Court given the circumstances.[10] Many museums in the Netherlands are independent institutions, and they do not strive for profit maximisation. They conserve and often present state-owned collections. Their task is to preserve the collection for the next generations and to make the collections accessible to the public.[11]

Cultural activities are often of a non-economic nature and are thus organised in a non-commercial manner due to their special goal. Subsidies support cultural activities with (almost) free access for all. A ticket covering only a small part of the costs does not constitute a commercial business. Financial support given to museums has not been qualified as state aid up until now. If the national policy changes and museums or other cultural institutions start to act more like competitors of each other and of other enterprises in the entertainment industry, this qualification may change. In some more complicated cases, it already has in fact.[12] The subsidy given to a museum cooperating with commercial parties was qualified by the European Committee as state aid and had to be withdrawn. Museums and other cultural institutions must choose: they can only ask for a subsidy if they are not involved with a commercial partner that could benefit from the subsidy and thus get state aid in violation of the principles of the free market. Cultural institutions can cooperate with commercial institutions if that does not touch upon their subsidised activities. The case law is not very clear and still has to develop, as the circumstances are changing.

1.6.3   EU and Cultural Decrees

Dutch administrative authorities must ensure that cultural decrees are in compliance with EU rules. The more cultural institutions are operating on the open market, the higher the risk that subsidies for these institutions will be seen as contrary to the principles of the open market. Museums that are legally part of public bodies are not qualified as independent institutions. They do not compete commercially. Since 1993, however, the national museums in the Netherlands are no longer part of the public administration and have become independent legal entities. As such, they can be competitors on the European open market and thus have to comply with the rules of the EU.

1.7   Partnerships in Funding

1.7.1   Public-Public Partnerships

For a variety of reasons, administrative levels may choose to cooperate in facilitating cultural institutions. In most cases, cultural activities are linked to a municipal territory. The organising of a festival in a public space requires a high level of cooperation with the local authorities, even if the subsidy is completely provided by the national administration. There are no general legal rules to organise this type of cooperation (Van der Vlies 2012, Bergman 2012). Every cooperation is organised according its own rules.

Every legal domain has a specific division of legal obligations for the administrative authorities involved. Administrative law is organised in a top-down manner, with sections for every part of the organisation of the state. The concept of the rule of law demands a legal basis for every relationship: the national authorities can only command local authorities if they can refer to a legal provision. If a local administration has to perform a task under the direction of the state, a legal basis must be provided. The state can expand or limit its responsibilities in the cultural field at will, but it cannot command municipalities to set up a budget for the arts. General legal rules facilitating horizontal cooperation are not provided. This lack of legal options is dealt with in practice by semi-legal solutions. Sometimes administrative authorities coordinate their actions by setting up semi-legal procedures, for example by making gentlemen's agreements. These agreements are not binding in a legal sense but do have some binding effects, mostly at a moral level. These semi-legal inventions can make the communication between the various levels of the administration on cultural activities quite complex, because their status in law is not clear. The CPA and the GALA offer no solution here.

Various public bodies may cooperate to achieve a shared cultural goal. For example, the Holland Festival is supported by the Minister of Culture and by the city of Amsterdam. This world-renowned festival originated shortly after the Second World War, when the Dutch government took initiatives to stimulate Dutch culture as part of rebuilding society. Excellent international artists and groups came to the Netherlands to inspire local cultural activities. This aspect of the Holland Festival represents its national significance. As it is performed for a large part in Amsterdam, this also makes it of local significance. The Minister of Culture and the city of Amsterdam ensure that their respective input is well coordinated. They inform each other on their intentions, laying these down in a memo of understanding. They reach consensus on how to deal with the application of the Holland Festival. This memo of understanding cannot be qualified as a civil law contract but rather as a gentlemen's agreement. This means that its binding character comes only with a complicated legal reasoning or is absent. Furthermore, the agreement is addressed to the parties involved, but it has effects on the subsidy relationship of each of these parties with the Holland Festival. The Holland Festival, not being a party to the gentlemen's agreement, will nonetheless find its application for a subsidy answered along the lines of this agreement. Besides, the Holland Festival has to apply twice, since administrative bodies are formally not allowed to transfer the money to each other and allow just one of them to handle the paper work. Hopefully, the law regarding this issue will change.

1.7.2   Public-Private Partnerships

Private funds play a moderate role in the funding of the arts, but still their contribution is very important. A well-known private fund is the Prince Bernhard Cultural Fund (Prins Bernhard Cultuurfonds). It seeks cooperation with other private and public funds. The cooperation with other private funds can be conducted without legal problems. The cooperation with public funds or administrative bodies causes similar legal problems as the cooperation between public funds. The two funds may agree that one of them handles the procedures, with the other fund merely providing part of the money. This makes their cooperation public. The status of these combined forces is again vague: the public party cannot conclude agreements, as it is not allowed by law to do anything other than granting subsidies in a top-down relationship. For other legal actions, such as giving money to another fund, no legal basis is provided.

The rule of law requires a legal basis for handing over the money to private funds, yet there is none. Public funds can only do what the law allows them to do. In the law, public-private partnerships are not mentioned. Nevertheless, parties find a variety of informal ways to circumvent legal obstacles and work together. From a formal point of view, these procedures are not legally valid, which could cause troubles for the cooperation. It would be very helpful if the law regarding this issue would provide ways for a legal public-private cooperation. It is remarkable that in a country where 'poldering' is so important, the legal vehicles to do so are absent. For private-private partnerships, no legal limitations occur: they can cooperate as they choose.

1.7.3   Legal Evaluation

Partnerships in the world of cultural funding make the spending of money more effective and avoid contradictory conditions from several funds. Cooperation involving a public fund is difficult from a legal perspective. Administrative law, regulating the actions of administrative bodies, is meant for top-down relationships and leaves no room for horizontal contracts. Agreements, ruled by civil law, are legally not permitted for the public financing of the arts. In practice, informal roads have been found to make cooperation effective, but these are vulnerable as they are not fully legal. Parties nonetheless seek to 'polder' anyway.

1.8   Conclusion

The legal system for the cultural domain is focused on the rules for subsidies. These rules are in part specific to the cultural domain (the CPA) and in part to general administrative law rules for subsidies (the GALA). The legal system for the cultural domain is imbued with the wish to restrict the influence of the political administration on financial support of the arts. This wish is consistent with the freedom of expression: government is not allowed to interfere with the freedom to make art or to enjoy it. Respecting the freedom of the arts and supporting it as well for both the makers and the audience is a challenge. The refined system that has been set up to achieve these goals in the Netherlands has both advantages and disadvantages. It stimulates and protects the arts, but at the same time it is characterised by excessive red tape. Bureaucracy is a companion of administration under the rule of law, and this is an area that is hard to tackle. Successive governments have made known their intention to diminish the bureaucratic burden for decades, but none have yet been successful, either in the Netherlands or anywhere else.

The EU legal system has added to the difficulties due to the legally prioritised position of the open market. Cultural institutions partly work on the open market as entrepreneurs, and they partly work towards cultural goals. The latter can be supported by public means. In many cases, working for the market and working to provide culture are mixed. Such a mix is in fact promoted by many governments, including the Dutch Ministry for

Education, Culture and Science. The mix of activities, however, has not been accompanied by new systems of financing. Strict rules of administrative law hinder the development of coordinated financial support for the arts by various parties.

Notes

1. The author thanks Lauren Mescon and Martha Hawley for their comments on the use of the English language.
2. See also: Article 19 of the International Covenant on Civil and Political Rights.
3. E.g. The Cultural Heritage Act, Act on Municipalities.
4. In Dutch: beschikkingen (een beslissing van het openbaar bestuur in een individueel geval, gericht op rechtsgevolg). Due to the differences in the systems of civil law (the Netherlands) and common law, exact translations are not possible. In this context, 'order' refers to a legal decision of a public authority in an individual case.
5. Djazzex, http://deeplink.rechtspraak.nl/uitspraak?id=ECLI:NL:RBSGR:1998 :AA3432
6. See, amongst others, Nota Verschil Maken, 2005, K II 2004/05, 28 989, nr. 22.
7. See: European Committee, 'Commission Notice on the notion of State aid as referred to in Article 107(1) of the Treaty on the Functioning of the European Union. C/2016/2946; Houdijk (2009); HvJEG 7 mei 1997, C-321-324/94, ECLI:EUC:1997:229 (Pistre e.a.).
8. HvJ EG 13 december 2007, C-250/06, ECLI:EU:C:2007:783 (*UPC Belgium*).
9. HvJ EG 23 april 1991, C-41/90, ECLI:EU:C:1991:161 (*Höfner en Elser*).
10. HvJ EG 30 april 1974, 155/73, ECLI:EU:C:1974:40 (*Sacchi*).
11. This is now ruled in the Cultural Heritage Act.
12. EC 2016, p. 8-9; Rb. Den Haag (vzr.) 3 april 2017, ECLI:NL:RBDHA:2017:9251, with regard to Filmmuseum Eye.

Bibliography

Van den Berg, Irma, Gwenoëlle Trapman and Inge van der Vlies. 2017. "Hoofdstuk 5 Subsidie en andere financiering".[Chapter 5 Subsidy and other forms of Finance] In: Inge van der Vlies (ed.), *Kunst, recht en beleid* [Art, Law, and Policy], pp. 191-268. The Hague: Boom.

Bergman, Annemarie. 2012. "Samenwerken gaat goed, maar is het legaal?" [Collaboration Works, but is it Legal?], *Nederlands Juristenblad* [Dutch Journal for Jurists] 40 (16): 2824-2828.

Berlin, Isaiah. 2013. "Two concepts of Liberty". In :Henry Hardy (ed.) *Liberty*, pp. 166-218. Oxford: Oxford University Press.

Blokland, Hans. 1995. *Wegen naar vrijheid*.[Roads to Liberty] Amsterdam: Boom.

Borman, T., and J.C.A. de Poorter. 2017. *Tekst en Commentaar Algemene wet bestuursrecht* [Text and Annotations to the General Administrative Law Act], Deventer: Wolters Kluwer.

Dawson, Mark. 2017. *The Governance of EU Fundamental Rights*, Cambridge: Cambridge University Press.

Dicey, A.V. 2013. *The Law of the Constitution*, Oxford: Oxford University Press.

Houdijk, Joost A.C. 2009. *Publieke belangen in het mededingingsrecht: een onderzoek in vijf domeinen* [Public Interest in Competitive Law: a Research in Five Domains]. Deventer: Kluwer.

Kearns, Paul. 2013. *Freedom of Artistic Expression, Essays on Culture and Legal Censure*. Oxford and Portland: Hart Publishers.

Loenen, Titia. 2009. *Gelijkheid als juridisch beginsel. Een conceptuele analyse van de norm van gelijke behandeling en non-discriminatie.*[Equality as a Legal Principle. A Concenptual Analysis of the Norm of Equal Treatment and Non-Discrimination] The Hague: Boom.

Nussbaum, Martha C. 1997. *Cultivating Humanity, A Classical Defense of Reform in Liberal Education*, London: Harvard University Press.

Reinders, Alexander, and Inge van der Vlies. 1972. "Luns wikt en beschikt. Het verlenen en intrekken van subsidies" [Luns Weighs and Ponders. On the Granting and Discontinuing of Subsidies], *Ars Aequi* 21: 117-124.

Saunders, Kevin W. 2017. *Free Expression and Democracy, A Comparative Analysis*. Cambridge: Cambridge University Press.

Schlossels, R.J.N., and S.E. Zijlstra. 2017. *Bestuursrecht in de sociale rechtsstaat 1 en 2* [Administrative Law in the Social Constitutional State]. Deventer: Kluwer.

Kessels, Joyce. 2004. "Vrijheid van kunst en cultuursubsidies in Duitsland en Nederland. Een juridische beschouwing over de verenigbaarheid van de onthoudingsplicht en de zorgplicht van de overheid" [Freedom of Art and Art Subsidies in Germany and the Netherlands. A Judicial Consideration on the Government's Compatibility of the Responsibility to Abstain and the Responsibility to Maintain]. In: Cas Smithuijsen and Inge van der Vlies (eds.), *Gepaste afstand. De 'cultuurnotaprocedure' tussen de kunst, het recht en het openbaar bestuur* [Proper Distance. The 'Cultural Policy Brief Procedure' Between Art, Law, and Public Administration]. Amsterdam: Elsevier/Boekman Foundation.

Strengers, Carlijn, and Inge van der Vlies. 2017. "Hoofdstuk 3 Vrijheid van Expressie" [Chapter 3 Freedom of Expression]. In: Inge van der Vlies (ed.), *Kunst, recht en beleid* [Art, Law, and Policy], pp. 75-121. The Hague: Boom.

Van der Vlies, Inge (ed.). 2017. *Kunst, recht en beleid* [Art, Law, and Policy], 3rd edition. The Hague: Boom.

— (ed.). 2012. *Kunst, recht en geld* [Art, Law, and Money]. The Hague: Boom.

—. 2012. "Nieuwe financieringsvormen voor de kunsten" [New Forms of Funding the Arts], *Nederlands Juristenblad* [Dutch Journal for Jurists] 40 (16): 2822-2824.

Vlemminx, Frans. 2002. *Een nieuw profiel van de grondrechten: een analyse van de prestatieplichten ingevolge klassieke en sociale grondrechten* [A New Profile of Fundamental Rights: an Analysis of Performance Duties Resulting from Classical and Social Fundamental Rights]. The Hague: Boom.

2. An International Perspective on Dutch Cultural Policy

Toine Minnaert

Cultural policy, like any other domain, does not operate in a vacuum. The international context of cultural policy is relevant from two perspectives. First, a comparison between policy systems and policy practice can shed light on the typical characteristics of national cultural policy. And second, the tension between national and international perspectives on culture plays a part *within* national cultural policy. This chapter explores both perspectives. It starts out by exploring the ways in which it may be viable to compare policy systems. It will do so first with regard to the systemic aspect of cultural policy by answering the question of how the Dutch system differs from other national cultural policies. Second, it will explore the role of national culture in Dutch cultural policy so as to determine the *Dutchness* of Dutch cultural policy. With regard to the latter, this chapter focuses on the role that national culture plays in Dutch international cultural policy, i.e. that part of cultural policy that concerns itself with international cultural cooperation and exchange as well as cultural diplomacy.

2.1 National Culture and National Cultural Policy

National culture has been a key feature of industrialisation and an engine of modernity. The formation of a national culture at the beginning of nation-states 'helped to create standards of universal literacy, generalized a single vernacular language as the dominant medium of communication throughout the nation, created a homogeneous culture and maintained national cultural institutions, such as a national education system' (Hall 1992: 612). The construction of a unifying national culture thus played a crucial role in the stability of the nation-state as regime throughout the world. But as a result of globalisation, the role of culture as a national identity layer has become less self-evident. As Zygmunt Bauman points out, three waves of migration led to a gradual degradation of the stability caused by the close connection between culture and nation-states (2011: 34). The first migration wave, which mainly occurred in the nineteenth century, consisted of two elements: an increase in emigration to the new continents and colonisation.

The second wave occurred in the opposite direction: immigration (or re-migration) from the former colonies. Bauman: 'They [the immigrants, TM] settled in cities where they were to be fitted into the only worldview and strategic model available to date, the model of assimilation, created in the early phase of nation-building as a way of dealing with ethnic minorities, linguistic or cultural' (ibid. 34-35).

Bauman uses the term 'diaspora' for the third wave of migration, which shook up the previously seemingly unbreakable bond between identity and nationality, the individual and his residence, the physical neighbourhood and cultural identity (ibid. 36). In this third wave, all countries became both immigration and emigration countries, resulting in culturally di-verse populations all over the world. This trend is clearly visible in the Netherlands. Currently, roughly 22% of the Dutch population is labelled as a migrant, 66% of whom are non-Western.[1] Amsterdam is home to 177 different nationalities, making it one of the most culturally diverse cities in the world.[2] As a result, where culture could once be seen as an expression of a shared identity within national borders and a way to characterise differences between the Netherlands and abroad, it has also—and in some cases predominantly—become a way to express differences between people within the country's borders.

Besides the changed relation between nation and culture, there is another trend that justifies an international perspective on Dutch cultural policy. Over the years, there has been a significant increase in transnational and international cultural exchange, with Dutch artists travelling all over the world to participate in the global art world (cf. Bevers 2015). In 2016, nearly 4,000 Dutch artists and organisations undertook 14,925 activities abroad, almost three times as much as in 2008.[3]. According to the Council for Culture, for many Dutch cultural organisations, artists and makers, the city has become their home base and the world their playing field (Raad voor Cultuur 2015). In its most recent framework for international cultural policy, the government stated that borders between inland and abroad are fading, and that for a substantial number of artists, designers and cultural institutions, the work field has become global (Bussemaker & Koenders 2016).

In this chapter, I will discuss the Dutch national cultural policy system from an international perspective in two ways. First, I take a closer look at comparative analytic approaches to national cultural policies. I will argue that these comparative studies can help when trying to point out the specifi-cities of a particular cultural policy, or when considering alternative policies. However, they offer limited opportunities to extract the specific national nature of a cultural policy, because indicators used in the comparison and models designed to point out more general trends both lead to quite generic descriptions of cultural policies. In order to make the national nature of the system more explicit, I propose to add the level of politics, an arena in which cultural policies are more explicitly connected to their national context. In order to do this, the second part of this chapter is devoted to a specific policy area where the changed relationship between culture and the nation comes to the fore: international cultural policy (ICB is the Dutch acronym). It is interesting to note that ICB forms a specific part of Dutch cultural policy with a specific departmental unit and specific policy documents co-ordinated jointly by the Ministries of Foreign Affairs and of Culture. I will argue that ICB has shifted between cultural nationalism and cosmopolitanism in its approach to the changed relation between culture and nation, and that changing political power relations are at the base of these changes rather than new insights or altering opinions. These shifts are emblematic for Dutch cultural policy in general, but the limited space of a book chapter does not allow for an exploration of this argumentation for the full scope of Dutch cultural policy.[4]

2.2   Comparing Cultural Policies

There is a rich history of comparative research on cultural policy, which in recent decades has shown some interesting developments both with regard to the scope of the research and in its political orientation (Wiesand 2002). A recurring critique in the academic literature on this type of research (e.g., Belfiore 2004, Gray 2009, Kawashima 2009, Wiesand 2002, Wyszormiski 1998, Wyszormiski et al. 2003), however, is the lack of consistency in methodology and a primary focus on data collection rather than in-depth analyses. In her article on the methodological challenges of cross-national research, Eleonore Belfiore (2004) distinguishes two types of comparative analysis. The first type can roughly be described as the development of databases with a standardised set of indicators in order to make comparisons possible. The second type attempts to find archetypical models to describe and analyse cultural policy. Both types can serve as possible inputs for determining the specific national nature of cultural policy.

A good example of a database suitable for a quantitative comparison of cultural policies is the Compendium of Cultural Policies and Trends in Europe.[5] This online compendium is the result of a partnership between the Council of Europe Cultural Committee and Secretariat and the independent not-for-profit European Institute for Comparative Cultural Research

(ERICArts).[6] It contains a series of reports on a wide scope of countries (European and beyond), using local researchers for the composition of its reports. In the case of the Netherlands, the most recent Dutch report (2016) was prepared and updated by Jack van der Leden, librarian and editor at the Boekman Foundation, in cooperation with the Ministry of Education, Culture and Science. This Dutch solution is a mix of the two most common variants: an independent researcher (commonly affiliated with a university) and a civil servant working at the ministry responsible for cultural policy.[7] Since the reports are based on both official and unofficial information, this Dutch combination of both an independent researcher and the involvement of the relevant ministry seems like an ideal mix.

When browsing through the individual country reports, it becomes clear that they serve as a valuable access point for research into a nation's cultural policy. The fact that all reports are written in English helps in bridging the language barrier and allows access to content that otherwise would have been incomprehensible. Most information provided in the reports is factual in nature, but some of it is more interpretative. In the Dutch report, for example, some general trends are identified that are characteristic of the Dutch policy system: the relationship between the state and other levels of government (including the inter-administrative relations), the role of advisory committees, the role of funding bodies in the arts, and the law-based regulations for planning cultural policy.[8] These are indeed characteristic of the Dutch system, but due to the factual nature of the database, any nuance seems to be missing. The role of the different actors involved is presented as self-evident, but for example there were severe frictions between the Council for Culture and the Secretary for Education, Culture and Science Halbe Zijlstra during the debates in 2011 on cuts to the culture budget.

Due to the setup of the database, it is also possible to run comparative analyses based on the different mandatory sections. Each report, for example, has chapters on the main legal provisions in the cultural field, on the financing of culture, and on the main public institutions in the cultural infrastructure. The standardised table of contents makes it possible to look at any of the document's chief sections and determine any overarching trends. When performing such an analysis, it becomes evident that the cultural policies of the participating countries have much in common. It might prove helpful for cultural policymakers to observe and analyse how other countries are dealing with contemporaneous challenges, e.g. digitalisation, cultural diversity, decreasing national funds and the different responsibilities between government levels. At the same time, it is hard to point out the specific national nature of cultural policies, at least based on the information accessible through the database. It is also difficult to determine whether a particular approach is only applicable locally or whether it has the potential to be used abroad.

In addition to the separate country reports, the compendium contains a wide range of comparative analyses, subdivided into three sections: 'culture and democracy themes', 'monitoring and comparisons' and 'statistics'. For example, there are overviews of special income tax measures for freelance artists, measures to support book markets in Europe and policies and programmes to support intercultural dialogue. These topics might actually be more nation-specific, and browsing through the different reports brings up some very interesting alternatives. But the information provided is too limited to really comprehend the specificities of the measures. In addition, these analyses focus predominantly on the relationship between the national government and the cultural field and leave out the political context. Of course, this makes sense, since the databases are focused on cultural policy as text. But this also makes it very much dependent on the availability of resources.

The nature of the analyses is quite varied, proving the previous point about the lack of a clear methodology. Some of the comparative analyses are rather meagre. For example, the comparative analysis of the actors in the intercultural dialogue is nothing more than a simple table with an overview of the main institutes involved. The added value of such a list is hard to grasp. Lastly, the lack of detailed information on cultural policy at the lower levels of government neglects their crucial role in the nation's cultural infrastructure. For example, in 2012 the Netherlands the municipalities spent €1,960 million on the arts, whereas the state spent €1,004 million.[9] The database is limited to a breakdown of the three levels of government. Also it is mentioned that as of 2015, Statistics Netherlands (CBS) no longer collects these statistics on three levels. This again shows how dependent the database is on external resources.

A more general concern regarding the current state of this particular dataset is that in quite a few cases, the information is out of date. In the comparative analysis of the organisation and trends of international cultural cooperation, for example, the Dutch information is both outdated and inaccurate. It mentions the Service Centre for International Cultural Activities (SICA), the Netherlands Culture Fund, the Insititut Néerlandais in Paris, and the Flemish-Dutch House in Brussels as bodies and agencies charged with promoting international cultural relations. SICA has merged with two other organisations (TransArtists and Mediadesk Nederland) to form

DutchCulture, the Institut Néerlandais has closed, and the role of the embassies and consulates is missing. Maintaining a database is time-consuming, and the lack of a clear use of the database makes it vulnerable to decay. But a regular update is necessary for the database to remain relevant as a resource for research. As of April 2018, the Compendium has found a new home at the Boekman Foundation in the Netherlands, and there are plans to redesign the country profiles-grid and subsequently the website.[10] These changes can possibly tackle some of the issues raised above.

An alternative, more interpretative type of comparative policy analysis is labelled by Belfiore as 'cultural policy models'. The most influential studies in which cultural policy models were introduced appeared in the mid-1980s. She specifically mentions the collection by Cumming and Katz (1987) titled *The Patron State: Government and the Arts in Europe, North America and Japan*. In its time it was ground-breaking, but one of main critiques of this collection is its lack of methodological consistency. As Belfiore describes, '[n]o common framework has been adopted and shared by the many authors whose papers are brought together in the volume. No particular disciplinary perspective nor methodological approach has been consistently endorsed by all the authors.' (2004: 12). This resulted in a report in which ten different countries were analysed, each of which led to a different model.

A more consistent and systematic approach was offered by Harry Hillman and Claire McCaughey (1989), whose work distinguishes four different types of public support for the arts: the facilitator model, the patron model, the architect model and the engineer model. The models differ in their emphasis on either the support for the creative process or the specific artistic outcome. In their own words:

> The Facilitator State funds the arts through tax expenditures made according to the tastes of individual, corporate and foundation donors. The Patron State funds the arts through arm's length arts councils, which promote standards of professional artistic excellence. The Architect State funds the arts' social welfare policy through ministries or departments of culture and promotes community standards. The Engineer State owns all the means of artistic production and uses them for purposes of political education.

The models are by no means exclusive: most countries have, to varying degrees, adopted all four types of public support. The Dutch model, for example, with its large role for public funds and a basic infrastructure that is maintained by the Ministry of Education, Culture and Science, can be described as a mix of the architect and the patron models. The engineer model was present in heritage policies before the privatisation of the national museums. On the whole, the Engineer model seems ill-suited to parliamentary democracies and to ideas of New Public Management focusing on the outsourcing of cultural provision. At the local level, however, the engineer model can still be found, as in many cases facilities for the dissemination of culture, such as libraries, concert halls and theatres, are owned and run by local authorities.[11]

What is the purpose of these models other than to help identify the main characteristics of specific cultural policies and to note that the Dutch system has similarities with other countries? The models can help in pointing out some of the nuances of a particular system. As described before, two of the main characteristics of the Dutch system are the use of public funds and the role of advisory councils. In itself, these are elements that are also present in the cultural policy of other countries. In the Dutch case, the choice of an advisory council without any budgetary power might seem to make the council vulnerable. Its choices and advice can be ignored by the Minister or Secretary. In practice, this is rarely the case for individual institutions (see Introduction). Moreover, provisions of *good governance* (chapter 1) require that deviations from expert advice be motivated. Decisions that derogate from expert advice are particularly vulnerable when appealed in a court of law. Such provisions might be very different in other countries that use similar or rather different types of policy instruments. For example, in the UK, the Arts Council seems to have a much stronger position, simply because it has the authority to also allocate the funds. However, the Dutch four-year policy cycle provides a particular advantage over the British system, which allocates budgets on a *yearly* basis. In other words, the advantage of those models is not so much their possibility to precisely classify cultural policies but rather in the more delineated framework provided that allows for a comparison between systems. Yet, fully comparative analyses need to take into account the written and unwritten 'rules of conduct' within the system.

In short, both approaches appear to have their advantages and disadvantages. In the case of the databases, the strict and consistent use of standardised indicators makes it possible to carry out comparisons on a relatively large scale and also allows for longitudinal research to look for changes over time. A disadvantage is that in most cases it only leads to observations but does not generate new insights and lacks nuance and critical reflection. A qualitative approach traditionally generates insight into the specificities of cultural policy, because it actually tries to transcend the individual cultural policies themselves. A disadvantage, however, is that part of this process and its findings remain speculative, and that most models are never exclusive enough that a country's cultural policy fits precisely within one of the categories, nor do the organisational arrangements shed full light on the power dynamics between cultural policy agents.

A more general recurring problem when looking at both the quantitative comparisons and the cross-national analysis based on archetypical models is that they focus almost exclusively on cultural policy texts as their source of information and forgo examinations of the political context in which policy is formulated and implemented. As Belfiore states,

> [A] methodological approach is needed that allows and requires a more in-depth study of the cultural, social and political history and the cultural debates within the countries being compared, as well as an understanding of their legal and administrative systems as a precondition for discussing cultural policy mechanisms cross-nationally. (2004: 15)

An alternative approach is therefore necessary and might be developed using the four different types of cultural policy research articulated by David Bell and Kate Oakley: cultural policy as discourse, as text, as process and as practice (Bell & Oakley 2014). Textual analyses of cultural policies give an interesting insight into the types of terminology used to describe policy goals and the legitimisation of government funding, to give just two significant examples. The focus on process and practice moves the analysis towards the actual usage of policy texts, emphasising that they form the input for processes and are just one of the elements in actual practice. The focus on discourse moves the analysis even further away from the original policy text, placing it in a wider conversation on particular topics such as diversity and identity. Particularly in the latter type of research, there is the possibility of placing cultural policy in a broader societal context.

In the second part of this chapter, I will apply such a contextualised approach to Dutch international cultural policy. This policy domain is the shared responsibility of the Ministry of Foreign Affairs and the Ministry of Education, Culture and Science, which at times has resulted in conflicting interests and tensions between the actors involved (Minnaert 2009, 2016). It is the policy field in which the relation between culture and nation has been at the forefront. But before I delve into the policy discourse, I briefly elaborate on the theoretical discourse on national identity and the specific position of culture. I also briefly touch on a few key moments in the Dutch debate on national identity. Both are helpful in placing the policy debate in the broader discourse on national and cultural identity.

2.3 Nation, State, and Identity

In the *Oxford English Dictionary*, a nation is defined as 'a large body of people united by common descent, history, culture, or language, inhabiting a particular state or territory'.[12] According to Benedict Anderson (2006), these nations can be considered imagined communities, a concept that emphasises that the members of a nation form a community with a shared identity, even though they are never able to meet with all the other members of that community. The nation thus refers to the group of inhabitants, whereas the nation-state refers to a sovereign state of which most of the citizens or subjects are united by the factors listed above. With the establishment of nation-states, nations became organised political communities under one government, with territorial borders.

In her work on the discursive construction of national identity, Ruth Wodak (1999) defines identity as 'the relationship between two or more related entities in a manner that asserts the sameness or equality' (11). Following this definition, national identity is about what its members share. But this inclusiveness also breeds exclusiveness: differences between individuals—as well as nations—can also be expressed in terms of identity. To complicate matters even more, Wodak states that the identity of an individual is layered, that '[i]ndividuals as well as collective groups such as nations are in many respects hybrids of identity, and thus the idea of a homogeneous "pure" identity on the individual or collective level is a deceptive fiction and illusion' (16). In line with this thought, the idea of a Dutch identity as a pure identity that is shared by all Dutch citizens is simply an illusion.

The newspaper article 'The Multicultural Drama' ('Het multiculturele drama') by Paul Scheffer (2000) is considered an important turning point in the Dutch debate on national identity. Scheffer stated that the negative consequences of the increased cultural differences had been neglected for too long under the guise of a multicultural society, and he encouraged the government to take action by, for example, developing programmes to enable immigrants to gain knowledge of the Dutch language and culture. In the years that followed the publication of this article, the tensions that Scheffer described became visible after the 2001 terrorist attacks in the US and the murders of Pim Fortuyn in 2002 and Theo van Gogh in 2004. Gradually, the tone of the debate became more intense.

Although the government was reluctant to implement drastic changes, some initiatives were taken. Particularly noteworthy is the drawing up of the canon of Dutch history, commissioned by the Ministry of Education, Culture, and Science. In 2006, the Van Oostrom Committee presented the canon, which consisted of 50 so-called 'windows' that could be used to teach and discuss Dutch history. It was based on the assumption that a shared history is an important element of a nation's identity, and that knowledge about that history could contribute to the idea of a shared identity. On the website of the canon, it states that 'The windows of the canon of the Netherlands serve as a starting point to illustrate the periods',[13] emphasising that the committee did not envision a rigid list of the most important people and events. Some windows are connected to people, for example the famous children's book author Annie M.G. Schmidt and the philosopher Spinoza. Other windows highlight particular events, for example the discovery of natural gas in Slochteren and the flooding of parts of the Netherlands in 1953. The canon was implemented in schools, and in 2010 it became one of the core competences of both primary and secondary education. Representative of the debate on Dutch identity was that part of the critique focused on the national orientation of the canon, discussing Dutch history primarily as a national development. Also, some of the windows provoked opposing emotions and showed that the interpretation of history is never uncontested. For example, while the East Indies Company (VOC) was considered by some as a symbol of the glorious Dutch Golden Age, others connected it to the county's colonial past and its involvement in the slave trade.

In 2007, the Scientific Council for Government Policy (WRR) tried to foster a more nuanced political debate on national identity with its report *Identification with the Netherlands (Identificatie met Nederland)*. The Council identified six different views of national identity: territorial, modernist, cultural, ethnic, stately and symbolic. A shared culture can be one of the shared identities, and as mentioned at the beginning of this chapter, governments actively used culture to create a shared national identity.[14] The WRR tried to emphasise that the cultural view was not the only possibility. These different views on what constitutes the shared identity are quite useful when trying to differentiate the positions in the debate on national identity: from something relatively uncontested such as a national border—at least in the case of the Netherlands—to something highly contested such as an ethnicity.

Since then, the debate on national identity has been intense at times. In recent years, political parties increasingly seem to be pandering to voters by making strong statements and adopting far-reaching initiatives in relation to national identity. For example, plans for teaching the Dutch national anthem in high school and a mandatory visit by students to the Rijksmuseum and the House of Parliament have been included in the coalition agreement of the Rutte III government. In the debate on the tradition of Sinterklaas and the figure of Black Pete, political parties explicitly choose sides with either the proponents of change or the preservation of tradition. This last example also reveals another development, namely that the debate on national traditions has also become more global. In 2015, the tradition of celebrating Sinterklaas was admitted by the Dutch Centre for Intangible Cultural Heritage to their heritage list. Two years earlier, a similar attempt to put the tradition on the UNESCO list of intangible heritage failed.

2.4   A Brief History of International Cultural Policy

In this section, I will briefly introduce the most important policy principles during four important periods with regard to cultural policy and interpret the political perspective. There are different ways to label these four periods. Based on the policy processes that took place in these periods, they can be described as the phase of exploration (1970-1986), the phase of transition (1987-2006), the phase of togetherness (1997-2006), and the phase of divergence (2007-2012) (Minnaert 2009, 2016). More recently, the phase of divergence has gradually changed into a phase of complementarity (2013-). Another way to label these periods is to base them on the dominant ideology pertaining to national identity and culture: cultural nationalism (1970-1986), multiculturalism (1987-2006), cultural relativism (1997-2006), and instrumentalism (2007-2012) (Minnaert 2016). Since 2012, the focus of instrumentalism has changed from an economical focus to a more broadly oriented use of culture as an instrument in modern diplomacy.

In the first period, the focus was on the role of culture in international relations. Culture was seen as unique to a nation—much in line with the observations made at the beginning of this chapter—and through cultural exchange, other countries could gain knowledge about the Netherlands and vice versa. In that sense, there was clearly an instrumental use of culture for foreign policy aims; the use of the term 'Holland Promotion' in a policy paper in 1986 was perhaps the most clear indication that culture was used to promote a unified Dutch image abroad.

In 1987, a WRR report entitled *Culture without Borders (Cultuur zonder grenzen)* initiated a change of course that marked the beginning of a new phase. The WRR stated that the changing relation between culture and nation should be addressed in cultural policy, and consequently that the ministry responsible for culture should take the lead in this policy field. After a small period of resistance, the issue was indeed addressed in national policy, and international and national cultural policy gradually became more intertwined. This also led to a change in ideology. This shift towards multiculturalism in the second period was best exemplified by the change of course by Minister of Culture Hedy D'Ancona. She stated that, while there was a need for the increased cultural diversity within the nation-state to be addressed in cultural policy, national culture was also an important good that required protection. In her opinion, the internationalisation of culture also meant that the discourse on artistic quality was no longer strictly a national one. The risk, however, was that the international discourse would become the leading one; she considered it the task of the Council for Culture to find a balance between the two.

The third period was characterised by an increasing form of cultural relativism, in which the idea of a uniting culture was relinquished in favour of a more cosmopolitan approach. One of the characteristics of this period is a strong interweaving of national and international cultural policy, making it hard to separate the two. Throughout this period the Minister of Culture worked closely with his/her counterpart at the Ministry of Foreign Affairs, and a joint budget was helpful in developing a shared agenda with enough room for own initiatives. The Secretary for Culture Aad Nuis was quite explicit in his opposition to the idea of a shared identity and particularly the idea that all citizens needed to adjust to a model of Dutch national cultural identity. He considered the ability to adjust and to host different cultures to be at the core of Dutch cultural identity. He felt that the international context was a *fait accompli* and that the Netherlands should become a safe haven (*vrijhaven*) where a global community can be formed. Rick van der Ploeg, Nuis' successor, took this idea of cultural relativism even further. For him, the arts and heritage were not so much the binding factor of society but the 'catalyst of unarmed confrontations between many different cultural views and values'. He was more explicit in placing international policy in line with national policy. The next Secretary for Culture, Medy van der Laan,[15] was most explicit in her cultural relativism, literally stating that our national traditions are the result of centuries of intercultural dynamics 'because we travel, because we receive immigrants, because we translate books and watch television'.

The fourth period brought a return to a more instrumental use of culture and a move back to a more nationalist approach. Minister of Culture Ronald Plasterk focused more on excellence, which in effect translated into more exclusive access to funding for international ambitions. Together with Minister of Foreign Affairs Frans Timmermans, he announced a shift in the policy direction, focussing more on strategic choices and less on a more varied approach. Under the subsequent Secretary for Culture Halbe

Zijlstra, the economic and instrumental use of culture became much more explicit, exemplified in the use of the term economic diplomacy as one of the government's main policy goals. The dominance of the economic agenda in cultural policy was most evident in the central role that the list of nine top sectors (one of which was the creative sector) of the Ministry of Economic Affairs, Agriculture and Innovation played in the distribution of funds, including those for ICB.

Most recently, Minister of Culture Jet Bussemaker together with Minister of Foreign Affairs Bert Koenders described the predominantly economic course as undesirable. They argued that, apart from the more intrinsic value of international exchange and sustainable cooperation between cultural organisations globally, culture could also contribute to a safe, righteous and future-proof world and be effectively used in modern diplomacy. This change in tone of voice was a first step in a less economically oriented cultural policy, although the instrumental use of culture still seemed to be the predominant view.

2.5   Policy Meets Politics: An Ideological Pendulum

Political parties have used the policy domain of ICB to express their views on national culture. The main difference in these views seems to centre around the sustainability of a cultural view on national identity (Minnaert 2016: 230-231). The Christian-Democratic Party, the Liberal Party and the smaller confessional parties share a cultural view on national identity. This results in the primacy of foreign policy and the instrumental use of culture for economic and diplomatic relations. The increased internationalisation and cultural diversity we are experiencing are predominantly seen as a threat to national sovereignty. In contrast, the Social-Democratic Party (PvdA), the Social-Liberal Party (D66) and GroenLinks (the Green-Left party) are less inclined to adhere to a cultural view on national identity. The Dutch population is—or has become—part of a larger, global community. In their view, the role of territorial borders has become less important in the face of cultural connectedness, and the use of a uniting national culture has become increasingly untenable. These two views are not necessarily exclusive, and at times there was a possibility to pursue both. But particularly when budgets had to be cut, the political balance of power determined the main policy course.

The national government's actual policy towards culture has moved back and forth under the influence of liberal and social democratic pressures, none of which are unidirectional. This has resulted in a policy that tries to find a balance between liberalism's emphasis on the market and social democracy's priority on equality and multiculturalism (Minnaert 2014). A possible explanation for this is the interministerial nature of the policy domain and the ideological divide between the parties that hold responsibility for the two main areas: culture and foreign policy. Cultural policy has largely been the domain of the Social-Democratic Party (PvdA) and the Social-Liberals (D66), whereas foreign policy has largely been the domain of the Christian-Democrats (CDA) and the Liberal Party (VVD). This has made this policy field subject to an ideological pendulum that has been characterised by debates on both the primacy of the policy (either foreign affairs or cultural policy) and its inward or outward orientation towards nation and culture (Minnaert 2014).

In addition, there is a change in the tone of the political debate, despite the call for more nuance made by the WRR in 2007. A possible explanation is that the populist parties have been very explicit in their aversion to possible influences of other cultures on Dutch society, forcing the more traditional parties to move out of their comfort zone and also become much more explicit in their contributions to the debate. Particularly the parties in favour of cultural nationalism seem to have become more radical in their comments. For example, in 2017 the Liberal Party's Halbe Zijlstra complained that RTL had 'murdered the Sinterklaas tradition'[16] by replacing Black Pete with a Pete with some black smears on the face, and the Christian-Democrat Sybrand Buma declared that diversity was never an end in itself and that 'we cannot allow our tradition and culture to be diluted'.[17]

Another observation is that the populist parties have not been using the debates on cultural policy to express their view on national identity. Most of these parties were born during the first decade of the twenty-first century, around the time that the debate on national identity became more intense. Their political ideology was quite often nationalistic in nature. For example, one of the primary goals of the political party known as Trots op Nederland (*Proud of the Netherlands*), founded in 2006 by Rita Verdonk, was to safeguard Dutch culture. And the Freedom Party has made no secret of its worries about the threat that Islam poses for Dutch culture. But because they predominantly chose policies on immigration and integration as the main battlegrounds for the political debate on national identity, the other political parties had to follow. Of course, these parties could have chosen to continue the debate on identity within the context of cultural policy. But because at that time ICB was cosmopolitan in nature and national cultural policy was predominantly focused on the Basic Infrastructure, the starting points for such a debate were not present.

The developments outlined here illustrate a more fundamental problem with the interaction between the policy process and the political discussion of it that might be characteristic of the Dutch system. Because the terms of office of the responsible cabinet member are out of sync with the four-year cycle used for culture policy, the possibility of cultural policy becoming explicitly political in nature seems limited. Almost all the time, the political party that delivers the Culture Minister is a member of the opposition in the following cabinet period. Thus, although the CPA could in itself serve as an inducement to reflect on the changing role of culture in society, it is caught in a deadlock, and its role in setting the tone in the debate on the role of culture in society is in fact less far-reaching than anticipated. This limits the opportunity for political parties to strongly position themselves through cultural policy.

2.6   Concluding Remarks

This chapter has taken two approaches to the international perspective on Dutch cultural policy. First, it was argued that two types of comparative analyses are possible. Neither type of analysis points to what is particularly Dutch or national about the policy. Analyses taking the politics of cultural policy into account yield more insight. Therefore, the second part of the chapter was devoted to the question of how the notion of 'national' has evolved in Dutch international cultural policy. In response to the growing cultural diversity of Dutch society and increasing globalisation of cultural practice, the idea of a national culture as a shared identity was nearly abandoned in cultural policy at the end of the twentieth century in favour of a cosmopolitan approach to international cultural relations. This meant that the growing societal debate on national identity at the beginning of the twenty-first century was scarcely reflected in cultural policy. Initiatives such as the establishment of a canon of Dutch history and the attempts to found a museum on national history, together with the emergence of populist parties with a strong nationalist agenda, were out of sync with the strong tendency at the core of the policy texts to put national identity into perspective and the focus on foreign appreciation for Dutch art.

While the debate on national identity boiled down to a debate about dealing with different cultural backgrounds, cultural policy took a turn inwards, focusing on a national basic infrastructure. In the slipstream of that change in direction, the possible influence of the political arena on decisions made in the policy context was limited even further by placing budgets and decisions under the responsibility of culture funds. The barrage of criticism that the Council for Culture had to endure during that time exemplifies this shift in power relations.

Although the CPA does offer the possibility to reflect on the changing role of culture, the fact that it is encapsulated in a policy process means that its relevance in the political debate is in fact less far-reaching than expected or desired. To make a bold statement, perhaps this celebration of 25 years of CPA is also the moment to start the quest for its successor: a system that promotes political discussions on the role of culture in a globalising world rather than muffling such a crucial debate.

Notes

1.   Source: https://opendata.cbs.nl/statline/#/CBS/nl/dataset/37325/ table?ts=1521544067276, last visited 20-03-2018.
2.   Source: http://worldpopulationreview.com/world-cities/amsterdam-popu-lation/, last visited 20-03-2018.
3.   Source: https://dutchculture.nl/nl/buitengaats last visited 20-03-2018.
4.   For pragmatic reasons, I limit this chapter to the national perspective. It is, however, relevant to point out that larger cities like Amsterdam and Rotterdam have their own international cultural policy and operate quite independently from the national level. Also, much cultural cooperation is taking place near the borders, with cities like Maastricht and Arnhem working closely with neighbouring cities across the border. In its recent report, the Council for Culture also noted the increasing importance of the local and regional government level in cultural policy (Council for Culture 2017).
5.   http://www.culturalpolicies.net/web/index.php.
6.   http://www.ericarts.org/web/projects.php?aid=60&cid=600&lid=en, last visited 28-03-2018.
7.   Based on info at http://www.culturalpolicies.net/web/national-experts.php, last visited 17-03-2018.
8.   http://www.culturalpolicies.net/ → Country profile the Netherlands, p. 5, last visited 20-03-2018.
9.   http://www.culturalpolicies.net/web/netherlands.php?aid=622, last visited 28-03-2018.
10.   http://www.culturalpolicies.net/web/index.php, last visited 6-6-2018.
11.   The engineer model is emblematic of the German theatre system, in which Stadttheater are run by city authorities. As the original analysis of Hillman-Chartrand and McCaughey pertained to national policies, they were oblivious to such nuances, incorrectly assuming the model is particularly relevant

in the former Eastern block. See Edelman et al. 2017 for a more nuanced discussion of the models.

12. https://en.oxforddictionaries.com/definition/nation, last visited 28-03-2018.
13. Source: http://entoen.nu, last visited 20-03-2018.
14. As described in the Introduction, culture has played a limited role in the history of the Netherlands. As Roel Pots (2000) elaborately describes, during the Batavian Republic, Lodewijk Napoleon took some steps towards the creation of national institutes. Under King William I, this national cultural infrastructure was expanded slightly, but what is emblematic of Dutch history is the limited role of the central government, with initiatives by lower government levels and private individuals having been highly relevant for the development of the cultural field.
15. In between Van der Ploeg and Van der Laan, Cees van Leeuwen of the LPF briefly held the office of Secretary for Culture, but he did not launch any formal policy plans regarding international cultural policy.
16. https://nos.nl/artikel/2139439-vvd-er-zijlstra-vindt-afschaffen-zwarte-piet-domme-zet.html, last visited 28-03-2018.
17. https://www.volkskrant.nl/politiek/sybrand-buma-in-hj-schoo-lezing-onze-traditie-en-cultuur-mogen-we-niet-laten-verwateren~a4514939/, last visited 28-03-2018.

Bibliography

Anderson, Benedict. 2006. *Imagined communities*, 2nd print. New York: Verso.

Bauman, Zygmunt. 2011. *Culture in a liquid modern world*. Cambridge: Polity Press.

Bell, David, and Kate Oakley. 2014. *Cultural policy*. Londen: Routledge.

Bevers, Ton, Bernard Colenbrander, Johan Heilbron and Nico Wilterdink (eds.). 2015. *Nederlandse kunst in de wereld* [Dutch Art in the World]. Tielt: Lannoo.

Bussemaker, Jet, and Bert Koenders. 2016. *Beleidskader internationaal cultuurbeleid 2017-2020*. [Policy Framework for International Cultural Policy 2017-2020]. The Hague: Ministerie OCW [Ministry for Education, Culture and Science].

Edelman, Joshua, Louise Ejgod Hansen and Quirijn Lennert van den Hoogen. 2017. *The Problem of Theatrical Autonomy. Analysing Theatre as a Social Practice*. Amsterdam: Amsterdam University Press.

Gray, Clive. 1995. "Comparing Cultural Policy: A Reformulation", *The European Journal of Cultural Policy* 2(2): 213-222. (Published online 24 Feb 2009: https://doi.org/10.1080/10286639609358015).

Hall, Stuart. 1992. "The Question of Cultural Identity". In: Tony McGrew, Stuart Hall and David Held (eds.), *Modernity and Its Futures*, pp. 600-632. Cambridge: Polity Press.

Hillman-Chartrand Harry and Claire McCaughey. 1989. "The Arm's Length Principle and the Arts: an International Perspective—Past, Present and Future". In: Milton .C. Cummings Jr & J. Mark Davidson Schuster (eds). *Who's to Pay? for the Arts: The International Search for Models of Support*. New York: American Council for the Arts. (published online at http://www.compilerpress.ca/Cultural%20Economics/Works/Arm%201%201989.htm#The%20Facilitator, last visited 16-03-2018).

Kawashima, Naboko. 1995. "Comparing Cultural Policy: Towards the Development of Comparative Study", *The European Journal of Cultural Policy*. 1(2): 289-307 (Published online: 24 Feb 2009: https://doi.org/10.1080/10286639609358015).

Minnaert, Toine. 2009. "Drang naar samenhang: het internationaal cultuurbeleid van Nederland" (Urge for Coherence: Dutch International Cultural Policy], *Boekman* 21 (80): 6-13.

—. 2013. "Internationaal cultuurbeleid als ideologisch strijdperk" [International Cultural Policy as Ideological Battle Ground], *Boekman* 25 (95): 79-85.

—. 2014. "Footprint or Fingerprint: International Cultural Policy as Identity Policy", *International Journal of Cultural Policy* 20(1): 99-113.

—. 2016. *Verbinden en verbeelden* [Connecting and Imagining]. PhD dissertation, Utrecht University.

Scheffer, Paul. 2000. "Het multiculturele drama" [The Multicultural Drama], *NRC Handelsblad*, 29 January.

Pots, Roel. 2000. *Cultuur, Koningen en Democraten. Overheid & Cultuur in Nederland* [Culture, Kings and Democrats. Government and Culture in the Netherlands]. Nijmegen: Sun Uitgeverij.

Raad voor Cultuur. 2015. Agenda Cultuur 2017-2020 en verder [*Agenda for Culture 2017-2020 and beyond*]. The Hague: Raad voor Cultuur [Council for Culture].

—. 2017. *Cultuur voor stad, land en regio* [Culture for City, Country and Region]. The Hague: Raad voor Cultuur [Council for Culture].

Wiesand, Andreas. 2002. "Comparative Cultural Policy Research in Europe: A Change of Paradigm", *Canadian Journal of Communication* 27: 369-378 (Published online at http://www.culturalpolicies.net/web/comparisons-research.php, last visited 17-03-2018).

Wodak, Ruth. 1999. *The Discursive Construction of National Identity*. Edinburgh: Edinburgh University Press.

WRR [Scientific Council for Government Policy]. 2007. *Identificatie met Nederland* [Identification with the Netherlands]. Amsterdam: Amsterdam University Press.

WRR [Scientific Council for Government Policy]. 1987. *Cultuur zonder grenzen* [Culture without Borders]. The Hague: WRR.

Wyszomirski, Margaret J. 1998. "Comparing Cultural Policies in the United States and Japan", *Journal of Arts Management, Law, and Society* 27(4): 265-281. (Published online: http://doi.org/10.1080/10632929809597271, last visited 17-03-2018).

Wyszomirski Margaret J., Christopher Burgess, and Catherine Peila. 2003. *International Cultural Relations: A Multi-Country Comparison*. Columbus: Ohio State University.

'A Subsidy to Make a Significant Step Upwards'

An Interview with Arjo Klingens

De Staat © H.P. van Velthoven

In 2016, De Staat, a rock band from Nijmegen, was granted a subsidy of €236,200 per annum for the period of 2017-2020 by the Fund for Performing Arts (*Fonds Podiumkunsten*). It was one of 84 subsidies granted by the fund, but it was the only one that provoked rather fierce reactions. On social media, comments were largely negative. The criticism also came from other pop musicians and people related to the sector. These reactions are striking, as the plans that were laid out in the application barely differed from other applications like the Dutch Chamber Choir (*Nederlands Kamerkoor*) or The Hague Percussion (*Slagwerk Den Haag*) (Van Woersem 2016). Arjo Klingens, manager of De Staat, believes that subsidising popular music should be common sense. 'Why would you subsidise a chamber orchestra and not a rock band? In the classical music scene, it is totally acceptable to apply for a subsidy to make a complete production.'

The Cultural Policy Act lays down the responsibilities of the different government levels. For the popular music sector, municipalities are responsible for the infrastructure, i.e., the venues. The national government used to supply money for the Stage Plan (*Podiumplan*), an ingenious system that allowed venues to programme upcoming bands for a reasonable fee. At first, the National Pop Institute bore responsibility for the Plan, but after it merged with other organisations to form the Dutch Music Centre (*Muziekcentrum Nederland*), the Stage Plan became the responsibility of the Fund for Performing Arts.

These policies certainly contributed to the unique network of venues of various sizes in the Netherlands, according to Klingens. This network makes it possible for musicians to perform at various stages of their career, from amateur to professional. Klingens does harbour doubts about this system, however. 'One of the effects is the urge of municipalities to build the biggest venue. As a consequence, there is a proliferation of venues of a similar size, with all the consequences that that entails. After the building of the venue is finished, there is barely any money left for a team to run the venue professionally. Sometimes it is sad to send your artists to a venue that is hardly professional.'

Klingens finds it incomprehensible that the infrastructure only includes the venues. 'It would be very useful to also include the artists in it. Bands create bastions of people with the network they gather around them. Think of sound technicians, graphic designers, record labels, roadies, bookers and so on. In other art sectors, it is quite common to apply for a subsidy for a project including additional expenses so that you can also pay an acceptable fee for the other people involved.' She believes there is an important role for the government with regard to the income of artists such as pop musicians and the network surrounding them.

The four-year subsidy to De Staat not only creates a relaxed attitude within the band—they don't have to worry about how to finance each idea they have—it also allows the band to offer a reasonable fee to others involved, and this supports the certainty that they can do the things they want to do while stimulating their creativity. 'The atmosphere between the different band members is relaxed, there is no financial stress anymore.' The band does not intend to remain dependent on subsidies. 'We are going to use this subsidy to make a significant step upwards, so we can be more independent afterwards. We may apply for smaller project subsidies at one time or another, but the fact that we have been granted this subsidy has a surplus value to get to the next level.' Klingens believes it is her task as a manager to write the subsidy applications. 'That is not something for musicians at all, let them be creative instead of questioning whether it is useful to put their valuable time in it while not knowing if it will yield anything in the end.'

As a member of the Pop Coalition, a pressure group for the popular music sector that includes all branches of the Dutch popular music field, Klingens is also closely involved in lobbying the national government. 'The most important issue we are involved in right now is the Fair Practice Code. Pop musicians should get a reasonable fee for their work. The 100 to 150 euros that a band gets as a supporting act nowadays leaves almost nothing for the band after subtracting all costs involved. By giving them a reasonable fee, you also make it possible for them to invest in themselves.' Being a professional pop musician is, in her opinion, highly underestimated. 'That is true for all artists, but especially for pop musicians.' A Dutch band like Golden Earring (which was successful in the 1970s and 1980s) had a reasonable income from record sales, which enabled them to tide over periods that they did not perform in order to work on a new album, she states. 'Nowadays that isn't possible anymore. As record sales have collapsed, bands depend on performing for their income. That makes the life of a pop musician not only physically but also mentally heavy.' In the past, pop musicians could appeal to the Artists' Income Provision Act (*Wet Inkomensvoorziening Kunstenaars*, WIK) and subsequently the Labour and Income Provision for Artists Act (*Wet werk en inkomen kunstenaars*, WWIK) to tide over periods of lower income or no income at all, for instance in order to write new songs. With the repeal of the WWIK in 2012, life as a pop artist has become even more uncertain.

With regard to the future, Klingens has much faith in the recently established Pop Music Investment Fund (*Investeringsfonds Pop*), initiated by the Foundation for the Exploitation of Neighbouring Rights (*Stichting ter Exploitatie van Naburige Rechten*, SENA). This regulation was developed specifically for the pop sector, which is used to entrepreneurial thinking. 'As far as this is concerned, other fields of art can learn a lot from the pop sector.'

André Nuchelmans

Bibliography

Van Woersem, Lisa (2016) "Wie slaat de brug tussen de popsector en subsidieverstrekkers?" [Who's gonna bridge the gap between the pop sector and subsidisers?], Boekman 28(109): 34-37.

3. The Framing Game

Towards Deprovincialising Dutch Cultural Policy

Johan Kolsteeg[1]

This chapter discusses the use of the term cultural entrepreneurship in strategic documents produced by Dutch government and cultural institutions. I specifically focus on recent history (2012-2016), starting off with a historical sketch from the early 1980s onwards. In this sketch, I identify a dichotomy of values that can still be observed in recent sources: a narrow, economic interpretation of the term versus a broad, cultural interpretation. The government frames entrepreneurship as having to do with creating societal connections. In strategic plans, cultural institutions show considerable awareness of societal issues but do not label these concerns as belonging to entrepreneurship. Instead, the term is predominantly reserved for financial strategic deliberations. I do not introduce an a priori definition of cultural entrepreneurship but look at the construction of meaning in written documents. Finally, I extrapolate a possible conundrum of cultural entrepreneurship in the Netherlands based on the suggestion that attempts to connect culture to transnational societal agendas may be hindered by a provincialising effect of Dutch cultural policy.

3.1 Some Background

Since Christian-Democrat Elco Brinkman became Minister of Culture in 1982, Dutch cultural policy has become more aware of the business side and the market mechanisms of culture (Kuypers 1999: 12). State museums were privatised, and budget financing was introduced (Van Puffelen 2000: 155). From this point onwards, institutions had to make do with a fixed yearly subvention instead of one based on a deficit. This approach provided organisations with some freedom and 'led to a situation in which potential profits can be kept, while possible loss had to be compensated, for instance by generating more extra income, or requesting more government support' (Ministerie van WVC 1993: 209 and Elshout 2015: 170, also Boogaarts 1989: 93). In her 1989 report for the Scientific Council for Government Policy, Inez Boogaarts also observed a fundamental remark made by the cultural sector (and one that would return several times in the years to come), which is that increased financial risks for 'culture entrepreneurs' cannot be taken if institutions are not allowed to create a starting capital or strategic financial reserves.

Pim van Klink has observed that, generally, arts institutions considered it to be an improvement that the new system allowed them to plan four years ahead (2005: 160). Yet the grants were awarded with strings attached: audience reach is crucial. Cultural institutions were encouraged to take the public's perspective, leading to the fear that a marketing-oriented mentality was taking over cultural institutions from top to bottom (Pots 2010: 232-234). The trend continued in the period that Hedy d'Ancona was Minister of Culture, as also doubts in the sector continued to grow. Especially the demand that performing arts organisations should manage to obtain fifteen percent of their budget through self-generated income (D'Ancona, 1992) met with considerable resistance. As a protest, the advocacy organisation Arts'92 (*Kunsten'92*) was established. Later, it turned out that obtaining this percentage of self-generated income was not a problem for institutions (Pots 2010: 360).

Early government measures to give cultural institutions more financial responsibility are part of a general post-1960s/1970s deregulation tendency in government policy. In the policy documents *Culture as Confrontation* (*Cultuur als confrontatie*) and *Cultural Entrepreneurship* (*Cultureel Onderne-merschap*) written under the responsibility of Secretary for Culture Rick van der Ploeg (1999a and 1999b), this was explicitly connected to innovative aspects of what was then termed entrepreneurial behaviour:

> Without reducing the importance of a more business-like approach, the term [entrepreneurship] for me mainly means innovation. [...]. The innovation is not a goal in itself, it is a means to connect to different audi- ences, different disciplines or subcultures. This requires [...] an *outgoing* attitude and effective use of communication channels.[2] (Van der Ploeg 1999a: 17, emphasis in the original).

Also, subsidies should be seen as a safety net to cover financial risks and not as the start of everything. In his policy brief *Cultural Entrepreneurship*, Van der Ploeg (1999b) argues that the government should position itself as a good commissioner (*opdrachtgever*) and thus set an example for companies and private sponsors to connect with cultural organisations.

Cultural entrepreneurship, understood as a new and different outreach to the audience, became a key concept in popularising arts and heritage.

Following policies in health and education, the term 'market value' became more prominent in the cultural policy discourse (Van der Ploeg 1999a: 35-40). In all, the term 'entrepreneurship' related organisational practice in culture to a combination of not only the traditional artistic but also business and societal deliberations, and the required open and risk-accepting attitude, 'being attentive to exploit opportunities and possibilities' (Van Dulken 2005: 60, also Fransen et al. 2009: 12).

The sector fiercely debated the associations of the term entrepreneurship with the economy, the market, and commercial thinking—traditionally taboos in the cultural sector (Van der Ploeg 1999a: 35-40). The term was used to refer to both financial independence and the responsibility to broaden audience reach, but it remained unclear how these two could be related other than by foregoing artistic quality in order to boost ticket sales. This was experienced as problematic since artistic excellence remained the dominant criterion for the evaluation of subsidised cultural organisations. In 2008, this fear still existed when Secretary for Culture Ronald Plasterk agreed with the sector that entrepreneurship and artistic quality needed to be evaluated in connection with each other, since 'repertoire choices leading to more audience will be evaluated negatively if this evaluation is exclusively focussed on artistic quality' (Plasterk 2008: 7, also Kolsteeg 2014).

In its 2008 report, the advisory Profit for Culture-Committee (*Commissie Cultuurprofijt*) noted that increasing societal support for the arts requires improving art's engagement with society. The committee introduced the notion that the capacity to self-generate income is an indication of an organisation's societal support. The committee also advised the government to be more strict regarding organisations' self-generated income: 'Institutions that do not realise this goal have something to account for.' (Sanders et al. 2008: 9). In its defence, the committee felt that institutions should be allowed entrepreneurial freedom (as did Boogaarts twenty years earlier, see above) in order to create financial reserves out of extra income obtained on top of the standard. Most importantly, the committee reinforced Van der Ploeg's logic that entrepreneurship is required to strengthen the connection between cultural institutions and society.

The interpretation of the term 'entrepreneurship' developed further in the first government led by the Liberal Party under Mark Rutte (starting in 2010), when the Liberal Party Secretary for Culture Halbe Zijlstra reduced the state cultural budget substantially. Also the VAT on performing arts tickets went back up from six to nineteen percent (Zijlstra 2011: 50, Elshout 2015: 817-819). Zijlstra's interpretation of entrepreneurship reflects the idea that art and culture should operate on the basis of the same market mechanisms as any other product. This is illustrated by Zijlstra's claim that reducing government support leads to a stronger and more flexible cultural sector: 'cultural institutions should become less dependent on government money and thus more flexible and powerful. That's why the government economises on culture.' (Zijlstra 2011: 2).

Thus, generating self-generated income began as a moral obligation for cultural institutions and evolved into a measure of societal support and a condition for admission to the national subsidy system. The claim that the government is doing the sector a favour by getting out of its way, more reminiscent of an Ayn Rand novel than traditional values in Dutch cultural policy, echoes the classic capitalist emancipatory argument of the 'political freedom as the collateral of economic freedom' (Boltanski & Chiapello 2018: 13).

In 2015, the Social-Democratic Minister of Education, Culture and Science Jet Bussemaker added important nuances to this position and again brought the focus back to societal support for culture, using the argumentation that art 'supports our identity. Also because artists often contribute to a better, more beautiful, cleaner, and more liveable world.' (Bussemaker 2015: 15). As we shall see below, Bussemaker did hold on to the connection established by Van der Ploeg in 1999 of societal support and entrepreneurial behaviour in culture.

Conclusion

The government's relation with cultural institutions since the early 1980s has been characterised by the need for deregulation (which started before the Cultural Policy Act was introduced), followed by the suggestion of a relation between the financial emancipation of cultural institutions and an increased societal awareness of the arts, which subsequently turned into financial emancipation as an indicator of that societal connection and further into a perversion of that logic to justify the government's reduction of support for the arts. All throughout this history, the term 'entrepreneurship' was used to indicate the need to realise both financial emancipation and a societal connection.

Despite pressures from the culture sector, the national government largely refrained from accommodating the required entrepreneurial imperative, for instance by supporting risk-taking or allowing for the creation of financial reserves. As a result, the sector remained suspicious that the rhetoric would lead to nothing but a decrease of government subsidies. The sector's worst suspicions were realised in 2012.

3.2   Discourse on Cultural Entrepreneurship in Academia

In the early 1980s, arts management and arts marketing became topics in academic and educational discourses (Van Puffelen 2000: 79). Seminars were organised with the aim of opening up insights into management research for the arts sector. An early example of this is the seminar organised in October 1981 in the town of Tiel by the Interfaculty of Business Management at the Technical University in Delft entitled The Day of the Arts Entrepreneur (ibid.: 89). This seminar led to the first publication in this field: *Arts Companies and Business Administration* (*Kunstbedrijven en Bedrijfskunde*, Brevoord & Janmaat 1981).

Brevoord and Janmaat suggest that the state budget system increased the pressure on the cultural manager, since operational planning became more complicated and in fact more political. After all, cultural managers needed to manage the 'increasing complexity of policy processes, the falling short of income and increase of costs, more competition, need for audience targeting, more complex internal organisational processes' (ibid.: 51).

Even though Giep Hagoort later reminisces that in these early days, 'with new government policies on the rationalisation and reduction of the subsidized sector, and budget regulations emphasising the institutes' own responsibility, the period was pregnant of an 'urgent need to develop new management approaches' (Hagoort 2007: 12), some attendants at this seminar were suspicious that the association of the arts with the world of commerce and management was nothing more than a harbinger of cuts in government subsidies. Nevertheless the seminar was followed up in 1983 by a management course for experienced arts managers in the Dutch Theatre Institute. This course was a success and generated quite some spin-off (Van Klink 2005: 33) in several arts management curricula around the country.

Among the pioneers in the field are Giep Hagoort and Joost Smiers, who in 1983 started the Centre for Arts Management at the HKU Utrecht School of the Arts. Their position was that arts management is different from regular management practice because artists do not primarily react to market needs but rather to moral and societal issues. Arts managers need to respect 'the struggle with which art originates' (Van Puffelen 2000: 84-85). At the same time, Brevoord (1981) observed that the changes in government financing, the need for a modern business operation and a new up-to-date type of arts manager could no longer be ignored.

The field of interest developed rapidly. In 1990, the first *Handbook of Art Management* (eds. Hagoort & Smiers) appeared, and in 1992 Hagoort published a standard book on the topic, which has been translated into several languages. Hagoort made cultural entrepreneurship—i.e., awareness of the changing environment, risk awareness, innovation and audience outreach—instrumental to the moral obligation of upholding cultural values (Hagoort 2007), although balancing these agendas was, in Hagoort's own words, a 'Houdini act before anything else' (20).

How can this early phase of academic thinking about cultural entrepreneurship be interpreted? Writers in the Delft school such as Brevoord and others took the managerial perspective and investigated financial and marketing management obligations in arts institutions, while Hagoort looks at entrepreneurial strategy as a rational decision model inspired by cultural awareness and the personal characteristics and attitude of the arts-managerial professional. An arts manager connects two different worlds. Here, I once again see a dichotomy between rational managerial thinking and cultural/strategic thinking. Both schools are still present in the Dutch educational field of cultural entrepreneurship.

To overcome this economic-cultural dichotomy in order to understand the cultural entrepreneur, it is useful to consider the point made by economist Arjo Klamer (2011) that the cultural entrepreneur must be understood from a narrative perspective. Klamer's argument starts from the observed complexity of cultural entrepreneurial practice instead of its measurable outcomes, and it is embraced more heartily in the culture-sociological field than in the traditionally rather implacable cultural-economic field. Klamer looks at paradoxes that are not easily conceptualised in a strict economic framework, particularly the moral task of the entrepreneur to take responsibility for the cultural infrastructure. If entrepreneurial activity is 'a matter of coordination and organization' (150), following Schumpeter, then the most important 'cultural-economic' skills for an entrepreneur are being persuasive and not risk-averse, recognising how cultural entrepreneurship must 'work' differently in diverse regional and cultural contexts, for instance where levels of risk acceptance are culturally determined. Klamer's perspective of entrepreneurship as a (conversational) practice includes the realisation that the adoption of managerial and economic language may involve the risk that economic values overshadow cultural ones (155). But if cultural entrepreneurs 'generate support, organize communities, build partnerships [...] to extend the conversation for their art', then acquiring the right finances for this is merely 'one of the attributes of a good cultural entrepreneur' (ibid.).

Further research on cultural entrepreneurship as a narrative shows that the adoption of managerial and economic language in cultural practice is accompanied by a relabelling of these terms. Terms like growth, strategy, business model and professionalisation are re-labelled as belonging more to the development of creative identity than to economic rationalism (Kolsteeg 2017). Quite some balancing of cultural and economic interests is reflected in language by adding cultural values to economic terms.

Conclusion
The dichotomy between organisational/managerial and societal/cultural perspectives is visible in the academic discourse and seems to reflect the dichotomy in government discourse between entrepreneurship as financial austerity and societal connection. This dichotomy returns in present-day discussions about government definitions and sectoral practices of entrepreneurship.

3.3 Effects of Ambiguity on Cultural Entrepreneurial Practice

The aim of the rest of this chapter is to explore the working of this dichotomy in the policy discourse and the strategic management of cultural organisations. I approach this question by analysing government policy texts and organisational strategic texts written by cultural organisations for the basic infrastructure period 2017-2020. Representing the government position are the following documents:
- *Programme of Cultural Entrepreneurship* (*Programma Cultureel Onderne-merschap*, Zijlstra 2012). This document introduces the government programme designed to support entrepreneurship in culture in the period 2013-2016. It is accompanied by an internet survey in which representatives of the cultural sector were asked to explicate their ideas about cultural entrepreneurship. When the cultural policy for 2017-2020 started to be developed, the document was still regarded as the 'benchmark' of the government's ideas about cultural entrepreneurship.
- The discussion paper *Space for Culture* (*Ruimte voor Cultuur*, Bussemaker 2015). This document is included because it explains the position of government support for culture in 2017-2020, including its position regarding cultural entrepreneurship.

Further, I include the strategic plans of twelve randomly selected cultural organisations applying for a (prolongation of their) subsidy in the Basic Infrastructure for the 2017-2020 planning period. Even though the strategic plans discussed here are public documents, the findings are presented without reference to source documents, as information from these documents is anonymised for this publication.

In the analysis I will look at the topics discussed in relation to entrepreneurship, and elements that are not labelled as entrepreneurial but can be understood as entrepreneurial.

Limitations
The analysis is restricted to written sources. It does not include interviews in which respondents would have had the opportunity to elaborate their understanding of entrepreneurship and entrepreneurial action. While the downside of this choice is that it prevents us from investigating in more depth the motivations and ideologies behind formulations and actions—in other words to observe cultural entrepreneurship as an embodied practice—the approach is nevertheless chosen for the comparability of the written data. Strategic texts (in addition to being 'culturally-politically correct') have in common that they are the result of a long process of negotiation, in roughly similar dynamics (for most organisations), between business and artistic actors in the organisation. Another limitation is our suspicion that in the type of documents studied here, a certain degree of equivocality with regard to the term entrepreneurship may well be deliberately ingrained as a discursive manoeuvring space. It is not the aim of this chapter to evaluate the government programme Cultural Entrepreneurship itself. This has been done by Van der Horst et al. (2017). Finally, it should be said that the data allow some insight into the relationship between the government and institutions but ignore the 'go-between' in the whole process, the Council for Culture, which uses a definition of cultural entrepreneurship of its own (Raad voor Cultuur 2016: 13). It must be assumed that the Council's point also influenced the writers of the strategy documents.

Data
The *Programme of Cultural Entrepreneurship* (Zijlstra 2012) was presented to parliament on 31 May 2012. The document lacks an unequivocal definition of the term entrepreneurship. The meaning of the term must be deducted from the list of goals of the programme. These are:
–   Creating awareness of the need for expansion of the financing mix.
–   Creating awareness of the possibilities for donating to culture.
–   Participation in industry networks to develop entrepreneurial skills.
–   Improving leadership skills in the cultural sector.

The programme 'supports the cultural sector in strengthening its ties to potential financers and finding alternative sources for income' (ibid. 3). It is clear that in this document, the prevailing government position is that of entrepreneurship as a means to increase self-generated income. In preparing the Programme of Cultural Entrepreneurship, apart from consultations with financial and other experts, the government conducted an internet survey within the field to investigate what competencies and themes the sector considered important in developing entrepreneurship among small cultural organisations and individual artists. The results of this survey were incorporated into the Programme. Among the twenty-six respondents of this survey are three artists, ten commercial consultants and service providers, six unions or advocacy organisations, two educators and four cultural organisations.[3] This by all standards minimal set of respondents cannot be considered representative of the Dutch cultural sector as a whole, but given the importance it is given in the Programme, I elaborate on the survey here.

The following issues were signalled by the respondents of the consultation as vital for the development of an entrepreneurial practice in culture:[4]

- Several remarks stress the need for developing long-term strategies for organisations in which artistic and business aspects (exploration and exploitation) are combined, making artistry and entrepreneurship 'normal' and not to be experienced as opposites.
- Several remarks stress the importance of building on existing entre-preneurial grassroots practices in audience reach and participation, for instance, bypassing 'conservative managers of larger institutions'.
- Other remarks refer to the importance of building sustainable coopera-tion with sponsors and societal actors, creating a sustainable vision in which artistic profile is a vital element.
- Some remarks emphasise the importance of supporting the development of a professional level of operational management and employership in the sector.

The *Programme of Cultural Entrepreneurship* (Zijlstra 2012) provides a list of take-aways from the survey that were used, where possible, to inform the document. None of these take-aways reflect the survey's remarks on entrepreneurship as an integrative artistic/financial strategy.

In the policy brief *More than Quality* (*Meer dan Kwaliteit*, Zijlstra 2011), just preceding the Programme, entrepreneurship is introduced as a condi-tion for access to government funding. It is defined broadly as pertaining to 'positioning and profiling, context awareness and balanced finances' (Zijlstra 2011: 11). The elaboration of these themes in the document, however, is entirely devoted to the final, financial point. The *Programme of Cultural Entrepreneurship* itself again elaborates the concept by including necessary changes in the context, particularly in stimulating a culture of giving (*geef-cultuur*) in the private sector, in addition to training cultural managers in acquiring funds and donations and improving their leadership skills.

Tracking the use of the term entrepreneurship in the second government document in this analysis, *Space for Culture*, is quite a search. It starts with the three basic policy goals: (artistic) quality; space for innovation and profiling; and cooperation (Bussemaker 2015: 3). These policy goals should facilitate cultural institutions in dealing with 'changes in the experience and production of culture' (ibid.), more specifically changes in financing and audience taste, and the re-valuation of the autonomy of culture.

An indication of relevant societal changes is derived from *Agenda Cultuur* of the Council for Culture (Raad voor Cultuur 2015: 7) as well as documents published by the Scientific Council for Government Policy (WRR, Schrijvers et al. 2015) and the Social and Cultural Planning Office (SCP, Bovens et al. 2014). They include changes in financing, taste and audience behaviour (ibid.: 3, 9); demographic changes (ibid.: 41); and the position of cities and regions (ibid.).

Space for Culture specifies the second policy goal—space for innovation and profile—as artistic innovation; finding new and diverse audiences; entrepreneurship; and connecting to society (Bussemaker 2015: 9). From these specifications follows a set of criteria for awarding a subsidy for 2017-2020. These criteria are quality; education and participation; and societal value (ibid.: 20). The criterion of societal value is specified into entrepreneurship, expressing that this will allow cultural organisations to strengthen their ties with society and contribute to societal issues. The exact formulation is that 'through entrepreneurship, I [the minister] strengthen the broad-based support (*draagvlak*) for cultural institutions' (ibid.: 14). In its grandiosity, the statement rivals the causal reasoning in 2012 that a retreat of the government necessarily leads to a stronger sector.

Both governmental programmes understand societal support to include: connection to other societal sectors, self-generated income, geographical spread, and a good business management and governance structure, including marketing and audience development. These aspects are taken together as the 'broad definition of the concept of entrepreneurship in the Programme of Cultural Entrepreneurship' (ibid.: 21). Yet in the *Programme of Cultural Entrepreneurship*, the term 'broad' refers to broadening the financial strategy. The meaning of 'broad' in Space for Culture refers to societal impact. The document seems to be an attempt to work with this broader societal definition of cultural entrepreneurship while not abandoning the financial definition established earlier.

A closer reading of Space for Culture leads to the following observations:

- Entrepreneurship is required to enlarge societal support in a fast-changing society.
- Entrepreneurship starts with innovation and (artistic) profile. Societal support can only partly be measured by self-generated income. These nuances seem to be derived from the 2008 advice of the Profit for Culture-Committee mentioned above and seem to correct the parochial operationalisations of that advice delivered by the previous Secretary for Culture.
- Entrepreneurship is needed to react to societal changes.
- How exactly entrepreneurship can be instrumental in reacting to a fast-changing society is unspecified.
- In opposition to the view of the Profit for Culture-Committee that entrepreneurial risk should be supported by a safety net, *Space for Culture* sees the managing of risks of finding 'hybrid financing options' (ibid.: 16) as a responsibility for the organisations' governance.

The document creates a further divide between the two (by now familiar) understandings of cultural entrepreneurship. It is understood as a vehicle for relating to societal change. It all begins with artistic profile. Risk-taking, in an artistic sense, is arguably the strong point of cultural organisations. Yet the sector's plea for a financial safety net for entrepreneurial risks was not adopted by the government. *Space for Culture* disconnects artistic strategy (the applicants' artistic profile for 2017-2020) from a possible financial entrepreneurial strategy and hinders the understanding of entrepreneurship as a joint artistic/economic strategy.

Organisations
Space for Culture lists a number of challenges the sector should refer to: financing, taste and audience behaviour, demographic changes, and the position of cities and regions. These challenges are reflected in strategic documents written by cultural organisations applying for support in the basic infrastructure BIS in general terms. Prominently discussed in the strategic documents are changes in cultural consumption. Several organisations mention that the ever-changing 'cultural luggage' of audiences requires innovative educational activities. One organisation embraces these differences, another merely mentions the need to adapt but does not elaborate further, and yet another pleads for more research on how to deal with these changes.

Societal Issues

Organisations in our sample show ample concern with societal issues. Several organisations mention migration as a pressing societal issue. One organisation mentions in very general terms that globalisation, individualisation, new international relations, political crises, urbanisation and ageing have affected European Enlightenment thinking, then continues to relate this to phenomena such as new forms of art distribution, the loss of audience through the changing consumption of art and competition from other forms of leisure activities. One organisation describes its artistic strategy as creating a bridge between societal issues and the 'direct life-world of our visitors', inadvertently suggesting that these changes are not part of the life world of their audience yet. One other organisation mentions the 'demographic changes' in a SWOT analysis as one of the opportunities, while one other states that the ageing of the population will automatically have a positive effect on audience reach. In the documents in this sample, urbanisation is not mentioned as a relevant issue.

One organisation in this sample elaborates on the need to look at themes such as migration, privacy protection, the role of the state, themes in which the arts should take the lead in reflection and interpretation. One organisation's diagnosis is that after the budget cuts it changed into a 'participative organisation', involving all organisational members in diverse innovation trajectories.

The associations with the term 'societal support' (*draagvlak*) are diverse. Whereas the Ministry of Education, Culture and Science relates it to societal impact, diversity and entrepreneurship, several organisations connect activities to building support by better explaining the motivations and background of their projects and to attempts to enlarge societal support for art in general. Organisations present innovative strategies for connecting to society and audiences, which in *Space for Culture* is a policy goals leading to entrepreneurship.

Finances

Many organisations in the sample mention financial strategies such as the increasing willingness among young people to donate to culture, realising a better exploitation of catering, taking on national and international commercial productions (in response to the economic crisis), setting up a separate commercial enterprise, improving budget control, or simply exhausting existing financial reserves. Expanding and balancing the financial mix is often seen in relation to building up long-term relationships with financers, sponsors and donors, although two institutions remark that the 'market' for private and corporate money appears to be shrinking and that therefore the competition is growing. This line of strategy shows a clear intention to follow the suggestions on sponsoring and donations in the Programme of Cultural Entrepreneurship.

Entrepreneurship
In the strategic documents we have examined in this sample, concerns about realising innovative relations to societal issues are generally not labelled as entrepreneurial. Instead, entrepreneurship is mentioned in relation to developing more effective production routines and improving one's financial position by seeking long-term relationships with sponsors and donors. Entrepreneurship as a combination of business and artistic strategies, as hinted upon in the 2012 internet survey responses, is found where organisations explicitly connect entrepreneurship to artistic identity, increased societal value, effective business models and professional management. This is reflected in definitions of entrepreneurship provided by some organisations. Here are three definitions:

– Entrepreneurship is artistic profile, societal value, finance mix and professional business administration (this formulation is also found, almost word-for-word, in the responses to the internet survey four years earlier, Zijlstra 2012).
– Enlarging income, enhancing quality, having a better profile and larger audience reach.
– An attitude, a way of working and programming aimed at achieving maximum artistic, societal and financial output.

3.4   Discussion and Extrapolation

The variety of strategies used to make sense of the term cultural entrepreneurship can be understood as framings (Cornelissen & Werner 2014). These framings may be widely dispersed over a political spectrum. The government's framing in 2012 of the capitalist topos of financial independence leading to freedom lacks any sensitivity to the evolution of Dutch cultural policy over the past half century. Then, entrepreneurship was framed in 2015 as a way to realise societal value but simultaneously honouring the importance of financial austerity, yet without making clear how these two aspects—artistic/societal innovation and economic austerity—could possibly relate to each other. Among organisations applying for government subsidies in the Basic Infrastructure in 2015, the financial framing of cultural entrepreneurship is dominant. Creating societal value is not an activity generally labelled as entrepreneurial practice, confirming a dichotomy between the economic and artistic aspects of the term, despite the suggestion voiced by the sector to overcome the artistic and economic dichotomy in thinking about entrepreneurship.

This suggestion was introduced in 1999 by Van der Ploeg, re-triggered by the Profit for Culture-Committee in 2008, and supported four years later in the meta-analysis provided by Rebel Group on entrepreneurship in the strategic plans of cultural institutions applying for the Basic Infrastructure 2013-2016 (the period preceding the one I discuss here). This meta-analysis, written for the ministry, signals a separation of artistic and entrepreneurial strategies. It warns that entrepreneurship remains a 'paper value' when financial ambitions lack artistic substantiation (In 't Veld et al. 2012).

The dynamics discussed in this chapter reveal an underlying discussion on what it means to establish a relation between the arts and society. In the 1980s, this discussion centred around the word cultural management, in the 1990s around the term cultural entrepreneurship, and now it is centred around cultural leadership and cultural diplomacy. They reflect a good forty years of moral discomfort in defining the relation between art and society, while at the same time accommodating a political debate on the level of government subsidies for the arts. I contend that these dynamics effectively limit the amplitude of the discussion on the societal value of art. As we have seen, the societal issues mentioned in Space for Culture are derived from sources external to the Ministry of Education, Culture and Science. They can hardly be said to reflect present societal and political challenges, which are arguably not national but global in nature and include such issues as (cultural) identity, (performative) democracy, (real) participation, solidarity, migration, populism, (cultural) glocalisation and (true) integration. These global problems also tend to be manifest at the national level. They are unmistakably addressed in Dutch cultural production but hardly reflected in government cultural policy. In fact, the dynamics discussed in this chapter are a framing game inside the cultural-political discussion zone of relating-to-society-as-long-as-it-doesn't-cost-too-much. National policy does not encourage organisations to relate to pressing global issues but forces cultural policy in a loop of provinciality. The use of the term entrepreneurship is but a manifestation of this loop.

This framing game cannot be addressed without the construction of new types of frames of cultural entrepreneurship. Extrapolating on the findings and deliberations discussed in this chapter, I suggest the investigation of a new framing of entrepreneurial action. This new frame would be constituted by an understanding of how exactly cultural organisations realise societal connections, based on the point elaborated by Thibodeaux and Rühling (2015) that cultural organisations connect to their environment on the basis of an emotional/moral necessity instead of a transactional/economic one. This would provide the term entrepreneurship with a 'practice-based' interpretive frame. A bottom-up understanding of entrepreneurial action would be built on a plethora of managerial and leadership practices connecting arts to fundamental societal issues. It would allow us to consider societal actions beyond the provincial reach of Dutch cultural policy, relating to a more daring agenda constituted at the European level, for instance.

The European cultural agenda is not without its flaws, nor is it free from ideological pitfalls. It is coloured by its own dichotomy, that of economic globalism and a cultural identity ideology. But it does offer cultural entrepreneurs a possibility to connect to a transnational cultural/societal discourse. Organisations such as the European Cultural Foundation and Trans Europe Halles and initiatives like the Forum on European Culture continually discuss the societal role of culture. A closer connection to such transnational cultural idealism may inspire a government to investigate a deeper connection between societal and cultural agendas than the Dutch cultural policy now has to offer. The globalist/idealist agenda may paradoxically be a better way out of the framing battle than the present dynamics between the national government and cultural institutions. It would mean an upgrade from cultural entrepreneurship to the next frame, that of cultural leadership.

Notes

1.   I am very grateful to Dr. Dos Elshout for his contribution to this chapter.
2.   p. 17 "Het benutten van kansen vraagt van kunstenaars en instellingen een open, actieve, publieksgerichte en ondernemende houding: cultureel ondernemerschap. Zonder af te doen aan het belang van verzakelijking, heb ik met dit begrip vooral innovatie op het oog. De ondernemer is, in de betekenis die de econoom Schumpeter eraan gaf, iemand die iets nieuws wil maken of iets op een nieuwe manier wil doen, routines doorbreekt, ogenschijnlijk onbegaanbare wegen bewandelt. De vernieuwing is geen doel op zichzelf, maar een middel om verbindingen te leggen met andere publieksgroepen, met andere disciplines of andere subculturen. Dat vereist een bepaalde mentaliteit: een duidelijke oriëntatie op succes met een toegankelijke en wervende opstelling voor jongeren en ouderen, met een multiculturele aantrekkingskracht, een inhoudelijk veelzijdig aanbod, een

outgoing-houding tegenover de buitenwereld en een effectief en actief gebruik van alle in aanmerking komende kanalen van communicatie en publiciteit. In dat opzicht kan er veel worden geleerd van de niet-gesubsidieerde cultuursector."

3.   It must be noted here that the author of this chapter was among the respondents.

4.   I do not elaborate on input in the survey on developing a patronage for culture and its fiscal advantages, or the cultural leadership programme LINC.

Bibliography

Boltanski, Luc, and Eve Chiappelo. 2018[1999]. *The New Spirit of Capitalism. New Updated Edition.* London/New York: Verso. Originally published as: *Le nouvel esprit du capitalisme.* Paris: Gallimard.

Boogaarts, Inez. 1989. *Kunst en cultuur in Amsterdam: een inventarisatie van de financiële ontwikkelingen* [Art and Culture in Amsterdam: An inventory of financial developments]. The Hague: Wetenschappelijke Raad voor het Regeringsbeleid [Scientific Council for Government Policy].

Bovens, Mark, Paul Dekker and Will Tiemeijer (eds.). 2014. *Gescheiden werelden. Een verkenning van sociaal-culturele tegenstellingen in Nederland.* [Seperate Worlds. An Enquiry of Social and Cultural Tensions in the Netherlands]. The Hague: SCP and WRR. Available from: https://www.wrr.nl/publicaties/publicaties/2014/10/30/gescheiden-werelden-een-verkenning-van-sociaal-culturele-tegenstellingen-in-nederland (accessed 3 April 2018).

Brevoord, Cornelis (ed.) 1981. *Kunstbedrijven en bedrijfskunde.* [Arts Companies and Business Administration]. Leiden: SMO.

— (ed.). 1983. *Ondernemers en overheid: spanningen en knelpunten.* [Entrepreneurs and Government: Tensions and Bottlenecks]. Delft: Delftse Universitaire Pers.

Brevoord, Cornelis and Bert Janmaat. 1981. "Op weg naar een opleiding". In: Cornelis Brevoord (ed.), *Kunstbedrijven en bedrijfskunde* [Arts Companies and Business Administration] , pp 50-61. Leiden: SMO.

Bussemaker, Jet. 2015. *Ruimte voor cultuur. Uitgangspunten cultuurbeleid 2017-2020.* [Space for Culture: Principles for Cultural Policy 2017-2020]. The Hague: Ministerie OCW [Ministery of Education, Culture and Science].

Cornelissen, Joep P., and Mirjam D. Werner. 2014. "Putting Framing in Perspective: A Review of Framing and Frame Analysis across the Management and Organizational Literature", *The Academy of Management Annals*, (8)1: 181-235. DOI: 10.1080/19416520.2014.875669.

Commissie Cultuurprofijt. [Committee Culture-Profit]. 2008. *Meer draagvlak voor cultuur.* [More Support for Culture]. The Hague: Commissie Cultuurprofijt. Available from: http://binoq.nl/lib/Documenten/cultureel%20ondernemerschap/Meer%20draagvlak%20voor%20cultuur.pdf (accessed 4 April 2018).

D'Ancona, Hedy. 1992. *Investeren in Cultuur, Nota cultuurbeleid 1993-1996* [Investing in Culture Cultural Policy Plan for 1993-1996]. Rijswijk: Ministerie van WVC [Ministry of Welfare, Health and Culture].

De Wolf, P. 1981. "Op zoek naar het nieuwe...!". In: Cornelis Brevoord (ed.), *Kunstbedrijven en bedrijfskunde* [Arts Companies and Management] , pp. 22-29. Leiden: SMO.

Elshout, Dos. 2013. "Museumbeleid in Nederland". In: Quirijn van den Hoogen, Tjeerd Schiphof, Robert Oosterhuis, Wesna Snijder and Berend-Jan Langenbert (eds.), *Cultuurbeleid: Digitaal handboek voor de kunst- en cultuursector* [Cultural Policy: Digital Handbook for the Arts and Cultural Sector] (n.p.). Amsterdam: Reed Business.

—. 2015. *De moderne museumwereld in Nederland. Sociale dynamiek in beleid, erfgoed, markt, wetenschap en media.* [The Modern Museum World in the Netherlands. Social Dynamics in Policy, Heritage, Market, Science and Media]. PhD.diss. University of Amsterdam.

Franssen, Boris, Peter Scholten and Marc Altink. 2009. *Handboek Cultureel Ondernemen.* [Handbook Cultural Entrepreneuring]. Assen: Van Gorcum.

Hagoort, Giep. 1992. *Cultureel ondernemerschap. Een inleiding in kunstmanagement* [Cultural Entrepreneurship. An Introduction to Art Management]. Culemborg: Phaedon.

—. 1998. *Strategische dialoog in de kunstensector* [Strategic Dialogue in the Arts Sector]. Delft: Eburon.

—. 2007. *Cultural Entrepreneurship. On the Freedom to Create Art and the Freedom of Enterprise.* Inaugural lecture Utrecht University.

Hagoort, Giep and Joost Smiers. 1990. *Handboek Management Kunst en Cultuur.* Alphen aan de Rijn: Kluwer.

In 't Veld, Jeroen, Enno Gerdes and Boris Gooskens. 2012. *Meta-analyse ondernemerschap* [Meta-analysis Entrepreneurship]. Rotterdam: Rebel Group.

Klamer, Arjo. 2011. "Cultural entrepreneurship", *The Review of Austrian Economics*, 24(2): 141-156.

Kolsteeg, Johan. 2014. *Shifting Gear.* Delft: Eburon.

—. 2016. "Trust, a partnership's must". In: Giep Hagoort (ed.), *Cooperate. The Creative Normal*, pp. 108-119. Delft: Eburon.

—. 2017. "Transfer of economic concepts to cultural strategy – and back?". In: Wendelin Küpers, Stephan Sonnenburg, and Martin Zierold (eds.), *ReThinking Management. The Impact of Cultural Turns*, pp. 115-130. Wiesbaden: Springer.

Kuypers, Paul. 1999. *In de schaduw van de kunst. Een kritische beschouwing van de Nederlandse Cultuurpolitiek.* [In the Shadow of the Arts. A Critical Reflection on Dutch Cultural Policy]. Amsterdam: Prometheus.

Kunsten92. https://www.kunsten92.nl/over/geschiedenis/, retreived 30 March 2017.

Ministerie WVC. 1993. *Cultuurbeleid in Nederland.* [Cultural Policy in the Netherlands]. Rijswijk: Ministerie van WVC [Ministry of Welfare, Health and Culture].

Plasterk, Ronald. 2008. *Brief minister Plasterk aan de Tweede Kamer over Rapport Commissie Cultuurprofijt Meer Draagvlak voor Cultuur.* [Policy Brief Secretary Plasterk to the House of Representatives on the Report of the Committee Culture-Profit: More Support for Culture] .The Hague: Ministerie OCW [Ministery of Education, Culture and Science].

Pots, Roel. 2010. *Cultuur, koningen en democraten* [Culture, Kings and Democrats]. Amsterdam: Boom.

Raad voor Cultuur [Council for Culture]. 2015. *Agenda Cultuur. 2017-2020 en verder.* [Agenda Cultural Policy 2017-2020 and Beyond]. The Hague: Raad voor Cultuur [Council for Culture].

— 2016. *Beoordelingskader Basis Infrastructuur 2017-2020.* [Assessment Framework Basic Infrastructure 2017-2020]. The Hague: Raad voor Cultuur [Council for Culture].

Schrijvers, Erik, Anne-Greet Keizer, and Godfried Engbersen (eds.). 2015. *Cultuur herwaarderen* [Reassessing Culture]. The Hague: WRR [Scientific Council for Government Policy]. Available from: https://www.wrr.nl/publicaties/verkenningen/2015/03/05/cultuur-herwaarderen (accessed 3 April 2018).

Thibodeau, Bruce D. and Charles-Clemens Rüling. 2015. "Nonprofit Organizations, Community, and Shared Urgency: Lessons from the Arts and Culture Sector", *The Journal of Arts Management, Law, and Society*, 45(3): 156-177.

Van der Broek, Andries, Frank Huysmans and Jos de Haan. 2005. *Cultuurminnaars en cultuur-mijders*. [Culture Afficionados and Avoiders]. Rijswijk: Sociaal en Cultureel Planbureau.

Van der Horst, Annelies, Justin de Kleuver and Alwien Bogaard. 2017. *Ondernemerschap in Cultuur* [Entrepreneurship in Culture]. Amsterdam: DSP-Groep.

Van der Ploeg, Rick. 1999a. *Cultuur als Confrontatie. Uitgangspunten voor het cultuurbeleid 2001-2004*. [Culture as Confrontation. Principles for Cultural Policy 2001-2004]. The Hague: Ministerie OCW [Ministry of Education, Culture and Science].

—. 1999b. *Cultureel Ondernemerschap*. [Cultural Entrepreneurship]. The Hague: Ministerie OCW [Ministery of Education, Culture and Science].

Van Dulken, Hans. 2005. "Cultureel ondernemerschap, verkenning van een concept" [Cultural Entrepreneurship, Enquiry into a Concept]. In: Giep Hagoort and Janine Prins (eds.). *Dwarsdoorsnede 2005* [Cross-section 2015], pp. 57-66. Utrecht: HKU.

Van Eykelenburg, Carel. 2009. *Advies aan de minister van OCW. Eigen inkomstennormen voor de cultuur producerende instellingen in de basisinfrastructuur*. [Advice to the Minister of Education, Culture and Science. Self-generated Income Benchmarks for the Producing Cultural Institutions in the Basic Infrastructure]. The Hague: Ministerie van OCW. Available from: https://www.rijksoverheid.nl/documenten/kamerstukken/2009/06/16/bijlage-b-advies-eigen-inkomstennorm-voor-de-cultuurproducerende-instellingen-in-de-basisinfrastructuur (accessed 5 April 2018).

Van Klink, Pim. 2005. *Kunsteconomie in nieuw perspectief*. [Cultural Economy in New Perspective]. PhD. Diss. Groningen University. Groningen: K's Concern.

Van Puffelen, Frank. 2000. *Culturele economie in de lage landen* [Cultural Economics in the Low Countries]. Amsterdam: Boekman Foundation.

Zijlstra, Halbe. 2011. *Meer dan Kwaliteit. Een nieuwe visie op cultuurbeleid*. [More than Quality: A New Vision of Cultural Policy].The Hague: Ministerie OCW [Ministery of Education, Culture and Science].

—. 2012. *Programma ondernemerschap in de culturele sector*. [Programme Entrepreneurship in the Cultural Sector]. The Hague: Ministerie OCW [Ministery of Education, Culture and Science].

4. Values in Cultural Policymaking

Political Values and Policy Advice

Quirijn Lennert van den Hoogen and Florine Jonker[1]

4.1   Introduction

In his seminal historical analysis of Dutch cultural policy, Roel Pots (2010) concludes that the Cultural Policy Act (CPA) codifies the roles of the central actors in the policy system: the government, professionals from the cultural sector and private initiatives. The Act puts the government in the driver's seat of the policy system, initiating debates on cultural policy every four years. Professionals were cast as advisors to the government; at the national level, this became the role of the Council for Culture (*Raad voor Cultuur*). Private initiatives, which were very prominent in Dutch cultural policy before the Second World War, were reduced to the role of boards of cultural institutions. Although these boards tend to have a major influence, their impact is limited because of the advent of professional managers of cultural institutions and strict regulations of their responsibilities as a result of cultural governance.[2] This chapter takes a sociological perspective on the question of how the political system influences the cultural system, by looking at the underlying value orientations of cultural policies and expert advice. To put it more cynically, it investigates to what extent political values inform actual subsidy allocations.

As indicated in the introduction to this volume, the CPA has focused Dutch cultural policy on quality and diversity as the central objectives, quite overtly keeping its distance from any directives affecting the content of art and the cultural offering. The Act regulates the role of professionals as advisors on matters of quality in particular. This implies that politicians themselves do not meddle in subsidy allocation decisions, that is, they do not decide on allocations to individual institutions. Rather, they follow the advice of the Council for Culture.[3] However, this does not mean that politics takes a 'neutral' stance towards the cultural sector. Two developments since 1993 have profoundly affected Dutch cultural policy. The first is the advent of New Public Management (NPM). In and of itself, the CPA is a clear example of NPM, a business-like approach to public administration that has favoured increasingly more detailed requirements to gain funding. This trend is visible in other parts of Europe as well, such as the UK (Belfiore 2004) and Scandinavia (Lindqvist 2007, 2008), and outside Europe, for example, in Chile (De Cea 2008). This leads us to expect that business-like values have become more important over time, outweighing cultural or aesthetic considerations.

The second trend is specific to the Netherlands: each four-year policy plan tends to have a distinct focus, such as cultural democracy, social inclusion, or the economic impact of the cultural sector. As the criteria to be used by the Council for Culture are determined by governmental decree (*ministeriële regeling*), subsidy allocations may in the end be affected by non-artistic considerations, or, following Pierre Bourdieu (1993), 'heteronomous values'. As a result, we might expect the values driving subsidy allocations to differ for each four-year policy cycle, although another hypothesis is also possible: previous analyses of Dutch cultural policy have indicated that while political parties may apply their particular ideological perspective to cultural policies, in the practice of cultural policymaking, ideological differences are barely relevant (Hoefnagel 1992, Winsemius 1999). Given the advent of right-wing populist parties such as the Freedom Party and the Forum for Democracy, which vehemently oppose the right of the government to interfere in cultural matters, in particular concerning the arts, it remains to be seen whether this is still the case.

4.2   Value Regimes and Theatre Policy

This chapter takes the value regimes of Boltanski and Thévenot to be central to the theoretical framework. These value regimes provide a methodological framework to study questions concerning the autonomy of the arts (Edelman et al. 2017). By analysing the values present in the consecutive cultural policy documents and in advice provided by the national Council for Culture, the chapter provides a timeline of changes in the values behind policy and actual subsidy allocations in the Netherlands, analysing theatre policy in particular. Theatre provides an interesting example, as it is prominent in cultural policy debates, particularly because it is susceptible to the major criticism of cultural policy in the Netherlands: that there is a gap between the supply of and demand for art and culture and, as a consequence, the sector is 'overreliant' on subsidies.

Boltanski and Thévenot (2006) argue that people evaluate others and possible courses of action based on sets of relatively durable values. Such a set of values is referred to as a 'value regime'. These regimes are potentially present in all social situations. However, usually only a few of the regimes are relevant in any particular situation. Conflicts can arise when agents in the same social situation refer to different value regimes. According to Boltanski and Thévenot, such value conflicts are the drivers of social change. Below, we will briefly explain the various value regimes.

- Values that can be associated with artistic autonomy such as quality—both the quality of the work and of the nature of the experience it affords—belong to what Boltanski and Thévenot call the 'inspired regime'. They use the art world to explain this regime, as it focuses on ambiguity—that which cannot be expressed in words—and on emotions and revelation.
- The 'domestic regime' relates to history and ancestry. Heritage and the use of old aesthetic languages in the arts represent domestic values.
- The 'industrial regime' is a professional regime in which experts are important protagonists, as the regime values knowledge highly. The regime foregrounds efficiency and effectiveness, as its dominant orientation demands that things work and that they do their job in an efficient manner.
- The 'civic regime' is not bound to individuals but to the collective: its central principle is the general interest.
- The 'market regime' revolves around competition. It values those who try to make the best deal. Money, profit and the possession of luxury goods can be used to measure success.
- The 'fame regime' is about public recognition. It revolves around press attention, public meetings (press conferences, product demonstrations) and public relations.
- A seventh regime, the 'project city', was introduced by Boltanski and Chiapello (2005) in their critique of capitalist economies. This regime combines features of the inspirational (creativity), the market (competition) and industrial (efficiency) regimes. It is a project-based regime, focusing on the ability of agents to move from one project to the next.

The inspired and domestic regimes present obvious examples of autonomous values in cultural systems, as does the notion of artistic expertise, which belongs to the industrial regime. Cultural policies in and of themselves should be regarded as a compromise between civic and inspired values: reflecting the ideal of *Bildung*, in which the arts are seen as an opportunity for members of society to grow personally and as a member of that society, providing a line of Enlightenment reasoning that forms the core of the legitimisation of most cultural policies in Western societies (Belfiore & Bennett 2008, Edelman et al. 2017). However, cultural policies can be, and frequently are, also legitimised by an appeal to more heteronomous values. The use of heritage and the arts to attract visitors to cities or countries, the success of the creative economy, and cultural diplomacy can be seen as manifestations of the market, industrial and fame regimes. Using the arts as a means to prevent social exclusion reflects civic reasoning behind cultural policies. Finally, as NPM introduces ever-growing demands for the objectification and quantification of the outcomes of cultural policies (Gray 2007, Van den Hoogen 2010), it can be regarded as a trend that once again promotes industrial values.

The impact of politics on the cultural system can be empirically researched by tracing the development of values in cultural policies. Boltanski and Thévenot indicate that discourse analysis can be done qualitatively by means of the interpretation of texts, and quantitatively by classifying certain words used in a text under one (or two or more in the case of compromise words) of the regimes and thus counting the number of references to each regime in that text. They indicate that both nouns and verbs should be classified, as they represent the objects and the acts that are deemed important. In our research, we have included adjectives as well, as these are used to express evaluations. Boltanski and Thévenot provide lists of nouns and verbs that can be assigned to each regime. These lists have been amended, as the word lists need to be specific to the situation under study—in our case, a cultural policy context. The lists were fed into a specifically designed computer programme that counted the frequency of the words in each document. The programme also provided a list of non-assigned words which were then manually assigned by the two researchers. Proper assignment in some cases needed to be inferred from the context.[4]

A specific note must be made concerning the project city regime. As this regime consists of a compromise between three other value regimes, it may be difficult to assign words specifically to this regime. Therefore, the regime is usually neglected in quantitative analyses (see, e.g., Van Winkel et al. 2012). We have chosen to include the regime, allocating a specific meaning to it: the regime is used when the connection of cultural institutions to their environment is indicated. Thus, words such as 'connecting' and 'cooperation' may be counted as falling within this regime. The reason for its inclusion concerns the introduction of the Basic Infrastructure (BIS) in 2009.[5] As the BIS consists of geographically fixed positions for cultural institutions, we wanted to know whether the way they connect to their regional environment has become more important in subsidy allocations.

The regimes were also used as a basis for interviews with current and former members of the theatre committee from the Council for Culture.

Interviews were held during the summer of 2016, when the Council for Culture was drawing up its advice for the policy cycle of 2017-2020. The interviews included a 'card game' of 14 values, two for each value regime (see Table 1). Committee members were asked to rank the values according to how they perceived the Council for Culture evaluates the policy plans of theatre companies. Subsequently, they were asked to indicate relationships or oppositions between values and to name the values missing in the card game. Finally, they were asked whether they could indicate changes in the prominence of these values over time. The outcomes of the interviews are used to contextualise the trends found in the analysis of the policy documents. One downside of the method chosen is the difference in the extensiveness of the research undertaken by each side: on the political side, only a document analysis is available, while for the advisors, interviews were also held. This implies that political issues that were prominent in the policy debates but were never added to the four-year policy documents—for example, the emphasis on vernacular culture and the debate concerning the never-realised National History Museum around 2006—are ignored in the analysis. This should be borne in mind when interpreting the data.

4.3   Corpus for Document Analysis

The four-year policy cycle produces rich written material for research. Each four-year cycle starts with a discussion paper (*uitgangspuntennotitie*) published by the ministry. These documents contain the vision of the new or incumbent Secretary or Minister of Culture. With the exception of the first period (1993-1997),[6] the discussion papers are used in the analysis rather than the actual cultural policy plans approved by parliament, as these do not always contain the political views. Using the description of Dutch cultural policy by Pots, we can assume the following:

- 1993-1996: Minister of Culture Hedy D'Ancona emphasised the importance of 'audience reach' and 'market forces'. She cared less about artistic innovation for innovation's sake, and was heavily criticised by the cultural field for wanting to bring the judgment of the arts to a 'viewing rate-level' (Pots 2010: 330). We expect the civic and market regimes to be important in this document.
- 1997-2000: Secretary for Culture Aad Nuis believed that a strong cultural self-awareness could prove to be a valuable support to the Dutch people in a multicultural society. In his view, a cultural policy could and should contribute to greater cohesion and solidarity by celebrating the typical

Dutch openness to other cultures (ibid.: 333-334). Nuis also focused on cultural dissemination, education and the regional functioning of institutes (ibid.). We expect the civic (education) and domestic regimes to be important.

- 2001-2004: Secretary for Culture Rick van der Ploeg seemed to combine some of the values of his predecessors. Van der Ploeg continued to support the thriving of a multicultural society. He considered youth and immigrant audiences a priority, urging the cultural field to actively seek them out. With this line of thought, he emphasised the power of market mechanisms and cultural entrepreneurship (ibid.: 337). We expect the civic and market regimes to be important.

- 2005-2008: Secretary for Culture Medy van der Laan explicitly focused on the procedural side of cultural policy. She strove to reduce rules and bureaucracy (ibid.: 340). Furthermore, she believed that the autonomy of the arts needed to be protected and that the functions of the arts for society should be fully exploited. One of these functions required special attention: cultural awareness, fostered by focussing on cultural heritage, should contribute to the shaping of a multicultural society (ibid.). We expect industrial values (relating to procedures), and the inspired and domestic regimes to be important.

- 2009-2012: Minister of Culture Ronald Plasterk's main priority was creating ample opportunity for excellence to thrive. He believed that by focusing subsidy allocations on high quality, more money should be spent on fewer projects (ibid.: 343-344). His policy document also introduced the BIS. Thus, we would expect that the inspired regime will be important as well as the industrial regime, as it points to procedural matters.

- 2013-2016: Secretary for Culture Halbe Zijlstra wrote his policy document as a member of a minority government supported by the right-wing populist Freedom Party (PVV). Zijlstra argued that the cultural sector had become too dependent on support from the government, urging the sector to be more attuned to its audiences and to look for private investment. Unsurprisingly, the cultural policy of 2013-2016 included some major budget cuts (Zijlstra 2010). We expect the inspired regime to be less relevant and the market and industrial regimes to be very important.

- 2013-2016: Unlike her predecessor, Minister of Culture Jet Bussemaker emphasised that quality should not be measured solely by numbers. She focused on both artistic quality and the quality of activities with a strong social orientation. The main focus of her policy was on the combination of professional business management and the broadening of audiences and geographical dispersion of cultural practices (Bussemaker 2015). We expect a better balance between the inspired regime on the one hand and the industrial and market regimes on the other.

For each policy cycle, the Council for Culture produces a document on subsidy allocations. As indicated, only the allocations to theatre institutions are considered in this research. Between 1992 and 2009, the advice documents comprise the subsidy allocations of all theatre institutions at the national level. As the full list of subsidy decisions was very comprehensive (comprising between 111 and 219 individual decisions per cycle), samples of the individual subsidy allocations were taken. With the advent of the BIS, the role of the Council for Culture was restricted to allocating resources to BIS institutions and to the National Performing Arts Fund. Their allocations were included in the analyses.

4.4   Values in Policy Documents and Policy Advice by the Council for Culture

Figures 1 and 2 present the outcome of the quantitative discourse analysis.

The high scores for the industrial regime, both in the policy documents and the advice by the Council for Culture, might seem surprising. However, this can be easily explained. First, policy in itself is an industrial phenomenon; it concerns the measures being taken to achieve certain ends. Public policy also requires procedures, which are explained in the documents, particularly in the introductions to the advice documents where the Council's procedures are explained. Second, the theatre sector uses vocabulary which is industrial in nature such as 'production', 'institution' or 'producing'. Third, the exact nature of the industrial regime is easy to put into words, most notably when compared to the ephemeral nature of the inspired regime. This applies particularly to the advice documents. A sentence such as 'The expertise of the artistic management is solid' leads to a score of 1 for inspirational policy ('artistic') and 3 for the industrial regime ('expertise', 'management' and 'solid'), while in fact the message is about artistic quality. Moreover, industrial adjectives are frequently used in negative evaluations, with words such as 'not realistic', 'too ambitious' or 'insufficient'.[7]

Although there are differences between the relative importance of the value regimes over the course of 25 years, the overall distribution does not

Figure 4.1:   Distribution of values in cultural policy documents

CULTURAL POLICY DOCUMENTS

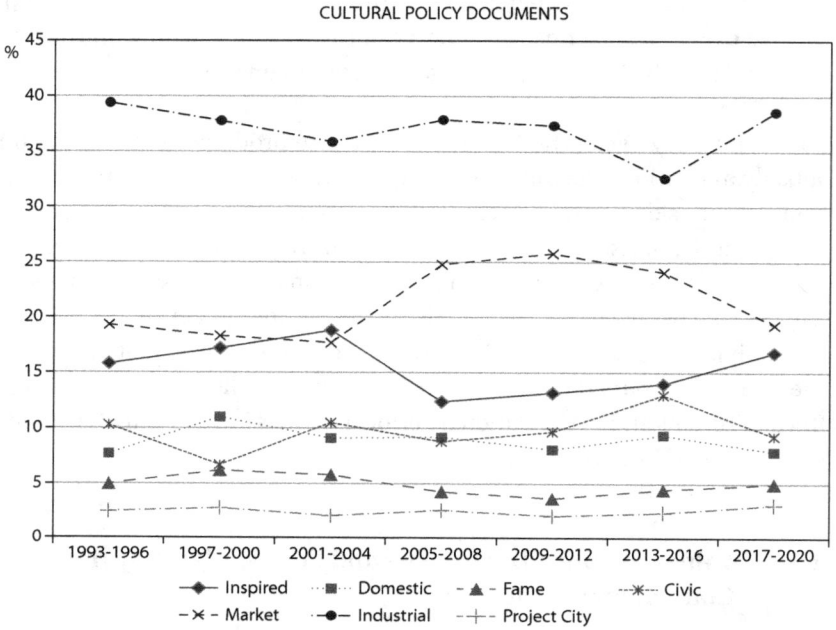

Figure 4.2:   Distribution of values in advice by Council for Culture

COUNCIL FOR CULTURE DOCUMENTS

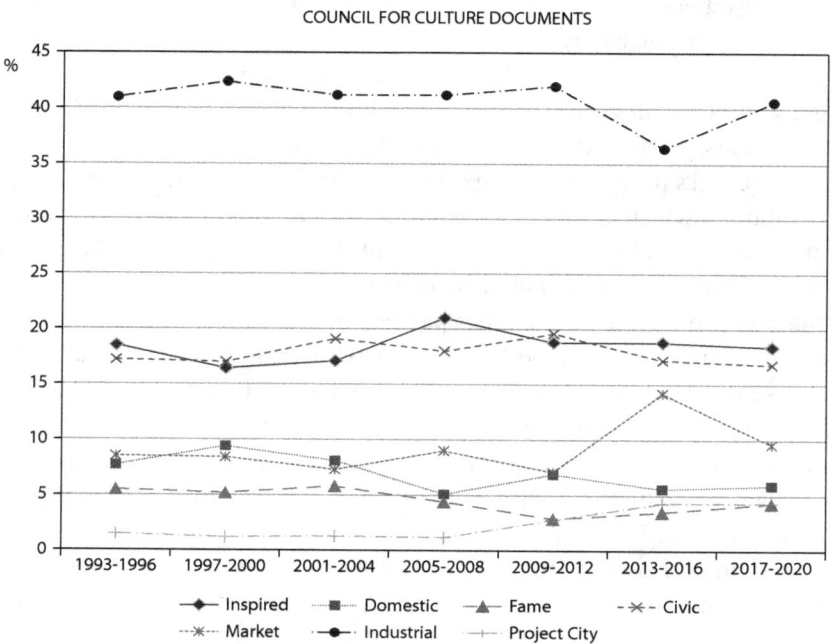

seem to change greatly. The industrial regime ranks highest for all periods and for both the policy documents and the policy advice.[8] The civic and inspired regimes are ranked second and third, again both in the policy documents and the advice. This reflects our hypothesis that cultural policy in itself is a compromise between these two regimes. All other regimes are of secondary importance and are never found in the top three, although market values come close—as predicted—in the period 2013-2016 (under Secretary Zijlstra).[9] None of the other predictions on the content of policy documents are supported by the figures. This suggests that cultural policy has been conducted under relative agreement on the values behind the policy over the last 25 years: inspired, civic and industrial values form the core of cultural policy. It can be concluded that the CPA system seems to limit the degree of deviation from the central values of Dutch cultural policy permitted to political agents. Even a major change to the system such as the introduction of the BIS did not change the underlying value orientation.

In the graph for the policy documents, we can see that after a relatively stable distribution during the first three policy periods, the scores for the civic and inspired values begin to change. By the 2005 document (published in 2003), the civic regime clearly outweighs the inspired one. This change concurs with the advent of right-wing populism in Dutch politics, first with Pim Fortuyn, a Rotterdam-based politician who founded his party in 2002, and later with the Freedom Party (PVV) of Geert Wilders (after 2005). Both politicians strongly opposed the role of the state in artistic matters. Fortuyn famously exclaimed during the Rotterdam election campaign that 'Artists are beggars [for subsidies], and we hate beggars'. Wilders supported the minority Rutte cabinet (2010-2012), which was responsible for pruning the national cultural budget by 20%, a move that was legitimised by the policy aim of redirecting the cultural sector towards the market. Market values clearly peak for the period 2013-2016, both in the policy document and the advice. This growing volatility of values in the policy documents indicates that the general agreement on cultural policy, as argued by Hoefnagel (1992) and Winsemius (1999), has waned.

When compared to the policy documents, the graph for the Council for Culture documents demonstrates that the value orientation behind individual subsidy allocations is far more constant. The advice by the Council appears to be insulated from the variations in political discourse. However, the insulation is not perfect. First, the peak in market values in the 2013-2016 document indicates that the Council had taken market values into account. The advice for the period 2017-2021 demonstrates that Minister Bussemaker's attempts to broaden the notion of market value to what she called 'societal value' were successful: market values recede in the advice, although they do not return to the low position they held in earlier advice. Second, these quantitative analyses do not represent a crucial change in politics: as of 2013, the criteria of artistic entrepreneurship and artistic criteria as such are equally important in Dutch cultural policy. Until 2013, artistic criteria were always paramount, and criteria such as entrepreneurship were secondary. From 2013, these entrepreneurial criteria were assessed by management consulting firms and operated as 'knock-out' criteria for the BIS. This will be explained in more detail below.

4.5   Ranking of Values in Evaluations of Policy Plans by the Council for Culture

Table 1 represents the quantitative outcomes of the card game. The scores of the card game were generated by giving 14 points to the value ranked highest by each respondent and 13 for the second, and so on, then adding the scores attributed to each value. For values scored equally by a respondent, average points were awarded.[10] The total scores for the values were then given a final rank from highest score to lowest.

The civic regime and inspired regime values are the most important, which corresponds to the outcomes of the analysis of the written policy advice. Some respondents related Artistic Development to Preservation of Traditions, values that are on opposition sides of the spectrum. In such cases, the latter also ranked higher. The fact that the civic regime outweighs the inspirational can be explained by the BIS. While the respondents acknowledged that Artistic Development and Autonomy of the arts were important, they feel fully focusing on these values is not suitable: given the position of the companies in the BIS, which represents the mainstay of the theatrical offering to Dutch audiences spread over the country, these companies also have the responsibility of developing audiences and introducing them to new artistic languages. Furthermore, these companies have a responsibility to the entire theatre system:

> what I do think is important for a first-line arts institution is that they are aware that they are in the vanguard. So they must also look around and be aware that they should be inspiring institutions that [are] not in the first line. (R3)[11]

Table 4.1.   Ranking of values in the interviews with committee members of the Council for Culture

Regime	Values operationalised in the card game	Score in card game	Final rank
Inspired regime (I)	Autonomy	104.5	4
	Artistic Development	129.0	2
Domestic regime (D)	Preservation of Traditions	66.5	9
	Local Identity	100.0	5
Fame regime (F)	Media Attention	68.5	8
	Image	44.0	13
Civic regime (C)	General Interest	127.5	3
	Accessibility (of art and culture)	136.5	1
Market regime (M)	Economic Surplus	47.5	12
	Competitive	43.5	14
Industrial regime (U)	Efficiency	60.0	10
	Expertise	97.5	6
Project City regime (PC)	Networking	85.5	7
	Flexibility	53.5	11

In other words, these companies cannot do whatever they want; they have a responsibility to represent the theatre sector to the Dutch audience, and they are seen as the signpost of the quality of Dutch theatre in general. As a result, the basic tension that theatre companies must deal with is between civic and inspirational values. As the BIS represents diversity, which is one of the two main goals of the CPA, it is logical that civic values outweigh inspirational values. Diversity also includes regional distribution, which is a clear policy objective. As a result, sometimes quality 'loses out' in subsidy allocation decisions:

> R1: On the one hand, you look at a company and assess it on its regional impact. At the same time, the Minister has instructed us to spread funds over the regions and attach certain amounts to this. And that means that you do not have the freedom to distribute across the country in a different way...
> I: So what you are actually saying is ... at a certain point the system forces you to give more weight to all kinds of things other than quality.
> R1: Exactly.[12]

For experimental companies (which are funded by the Performing Arts Fund as of 2009), the situation is different. Here inspirational values, most notably Artistic Development, can outweigh civic values.

Despite a high ranking, Autonomy turned out to be a difficult value for the interviewees to define. This value is associated with the notion of *l'art pour l'art*, which some respondents consider to be an outdated concept.[13] When the term is reduced to its etymological meaning (to set a rule or standard for yourself), it is easier to recognise the value: companies need to make autonomous choices, although within the confines of the rationality of the BIS.

> Autonomy makes me think of an autonomous artist and the opportunity to create what he or she has to create. The general idea is that there is also funding for that; that it does not have to satisfy the laws of the market but that the creator's artistic programme is leading.... But that autonomy actually stands in relation to all those other things, including the accessibility of the art itself: a BIS company should attract a certain number of visitors.[14] (R9)

Local Identity (domestic value), Expertise (industrial value) and Networking (project city value) are of secondary importance. These values are related to each other. As the BIS consists of geographically 'fixed' locations for theatre companies, the manner in which a company connects to its local environment becomes relevant (see also below). It is important to note that Expertise is also interpreted somewhat domestically: it is considered self-evident that theatre makers have the expertise to relate to different performing traditions. Market and fame values are of little importance in evaluating the policy plans of companies, as is the industrial value of Efficiency. Nevertheless, market values and efficiency were assessed, as financial and marketing aspects are evaluated by independent management consultants and their evaluations indeed determine discussions in the committee. Policy plans that have a mediocre score on these values are not immediately rejected, but this does land a company in trouble. Flexibility has a particular position in the evaluation. Some committee members immediately threw the value on the pile marked 'unimportant', while others linked flexibility to the artistic profile of the company, considering that they should be sufficiently flexible to absorb new ideas and developments.

In general, the order of values indicated by the interviewees corresponds to the outcomes of the document analysis of the written policy advice. Civic and inspirational values—that is, the general interest and cultural/artistic values—dominate in individual subsidy allocation decisions for theatre. Market values and Efficiency represent a focus on entrepreneurship, a notion that has become prominent in politics. However, this conclusion should be nuanced based on further content from the interviews, which is discussed below.

4.6 Relationships Between Values in the Assessment by the Council for Culture

Figure 3 offers a graphic representation of how the interviewees described the manner in which the Council for Culture evaluates the policy plans of theatre companies. This representation incorporates the values that members of the committee found missing in the card game and disregards values that were barely relevant. Therefore, the figure complements the data in Table 1.

Theatre companies are primarily evaluated on artistic quality. This is expressed by the position a company chooses between four central values: Autonomy, Artistic Development (which is immediately linked to the Preservation of Traditions, a value that does not score high in the card game, hence its smaller font size in the figure), the General Interest and Accessibility of Art. These are the civic and inspirational values in the card game that represent the central compromise behind cultural policy. A company should address the tensions between these values. Artistic Development and Accessibility may not automatically go hand in hand; for example, when considering the cultural competence of the audience. In the words of one of the respondents:

> We [theatre artists] have to reconcile enormous contradictions in ourselves. So developing your art and respecting tradition should be equally important in a career or in a company, as should autonomy. All sorts of things that are at odds with each other have to be linked through our artistic work.[15] (R11)

Committee members evaluate whether the choices of a company are internally logical and whether they fit within the total scope of subsidy applications in the BIS. In other words, the entire field of theatre should be attractive, and various positions should be 'covered' by different companies.[16] This is a pivotal moment in the evaluation. Apart from Accessibility, the four most important values are difficult to measure in quantitative terms. The evaluation is therefore qualitative in nature and heavily dependent on the expertise of the committee members. The balance a company or artistic director strikes between these key values represents the 'profile' of the company. The evaluation will assess whether a company avails itself sufficiently of Expertise in realising their profile and, to a lesser extent, whether they also use Flexibility in a way that allows them to realise their profile under changing circumstances. This implies that when the profile is not clearly described in the policy plan, or when it is illogical, the Council for Culture has difficulty assessing the other aspects of the plan, which are indicated as part of the secondary evaluation in Figure 3.[17]

Figure 4.3:   Evaluation of the policy plans of theatre companies by the Council for Culture

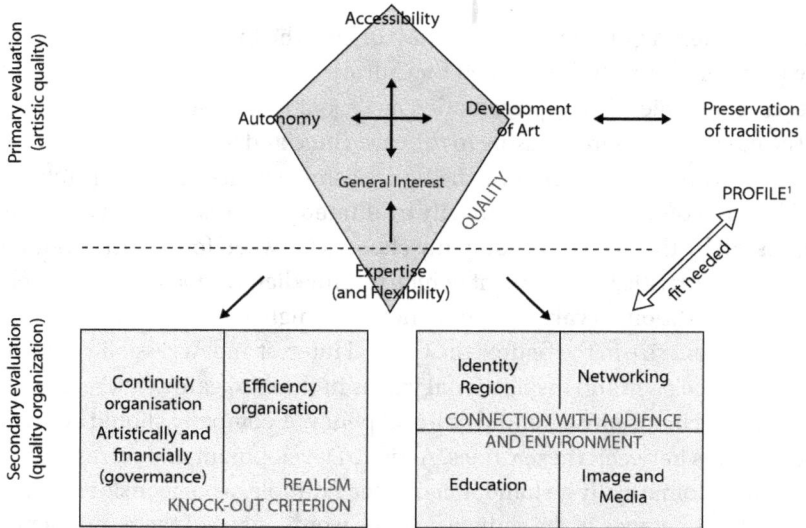

¹ company chooses its profile (autonomously) which forms the basis for the evaluation.

Secondary evaluation consists of two elements. The first aspects to be evaluated are the company's strategies for forging connections with the environment and the audience it seeks to serve. This entails the capacity to effectively market performances and the company as a whole to theatre venues and audiences. It also entails the capacity to develop effective cultural education programmes. Furthermore, this concerns questions as to how performances connect to the Identity of the region where the company is based. This is a domestic value that is the most important within this cluster of values, considered more important than, for example, market values. This implies that productions somehow relate to regional history or topics and, in particular for the larger cities in the west of the country, it is expected that the company's programme somehow reflects the ethnic diversity of these cities. This is a quite recent trend in the evaluations of the Council for Culture that is supported by all interviewees. It must be emphasised, however, that companies can relate to the identity of their region in various ways. In short, the manner in which the company connects to stakeholders in its region is an important factor that comes to the fore in questions concerning how the company presents itself to its environment (Image and Media), how it sets up Education and develops Networks with stakeholders inside and outside its region, and how the programme's content reflects the

Regional Identity. These issues relate to the market, fame and civic value regimes. In the quantitative discourse analysis, the issue of connection to the region has been related to the project city regime, which indeed gains importance during the second half of the 25 years analysed, although its rise is limited. However, this trend might continue (see below).

The second aspect of secondary evaluation concerns the 'internal' organisation of the company. Here, two issues are important: the continuity of the company (both in a financial and an artistic sense) and its Efficiency. Continuity relates to the question of whether a company has a rigorous financial plan and the ability to deal with financial risks. However, it also concerns artistic risks; for example, what will happen if an artistic leader leaves the company, or when the artistic leadership comes under internal or external scrutiny? These issues are subsumed under the notion of *cultural governance*. Furthermore, the Council for Culture wants public funds to be allocated efficiently. These issues all relate to the industrial value regime. Moreover, the realism of policy plans is evaluated: are the expectations (e.g. regarding audience numbers) realistic? Here, a development over time can be witnessed; while in former times, evaluations mainly regarded the Expertise of artistic personnel, currently committee members also want to know who will develop the educational programmes or who will be responsible for marketing and what their qualifications are.

> [You see] that everyone is really concentrating on this and on becoming more professional and ... that the choices your personnel make are very important. Nobody is concentrating on generating publicity. You need a marketing person! ... That is a development ... What is more, we [the respondent means the members of the committee] recently said to each other that it would be good if we not only heard who the artistic leaders and directors were, but also who will be the education staff, marketing staff and staff facilitating public participation, because that's what we know a lot about. If we see a certain name on the list, we can make an assessment: wow, that's someone really good! If he/she is behind this plan, we can be confident of its success. That is a new aspect, I think.[18] (R4)

As a result, respondents have started interpreting Expertise (industrial value) more broadly, also encompassing marketing and educational expertise. They see this as a form of professionalisation of the theatre sector, which might have been instigated by cultural policies, particularly in times of budget austerity; however, they also see this as a trend inherent to the sector, as artists are gradually taking the issues of audience development and audience reach on board as part of their responsibilities.[19] The same applies to civic values such as the representation of ethnic diversity in Dutch theatre. Respondents noted that, while in earlier decades this was very much a politically induced issue, for example, in the policy plan of Van der Ploeg (2000-2004), now the issue has become a 'natural' concern for theatre companies, although not for all. Committee members even feel that when the issue was politically emphasised, they were relatively unsuccessful, but now that the political pressure is off, the theatre sector seems to be adapting, albeit slowly, to the demographic changes in Dutch society.

It is important to note that, as already indicated above, since 2013 the financial criteria have become 'knock-out' criteria that are evaluated *before* the assessment of artistic quality. The Council for Culture has engaged two management consulting firms to calculate the financial rigorousness of institutions and to evaluate their marketing efforts. While their evaluations are not final, they are discussed in the committee meetings, so they focus attention on finances, marketing and cultural governance. In the evaluation round of 2016, one of the theatre company's plans (Theater Utrecht) was formally rejected on the basis of financial criteria, while the assessment of the company's profile was positive. In this case, the discretionary authority of the Minister of Culture was applied to ultimately allocate a subsidy to the company. Moreover, and more important for the current argument, it should be mentioned that the interviewees indicated that secondary evaluation has gained considerable importance over time, at the expense of the issues discussed under primary evaluation. As a result, the interviews corroborate the hypothesis that NPM favours non-artistic criteria—that is, the market, industrial and fame regimes—which have become more important at the expense of the inspirational-civic compromise that forms the central legitimisation of cultural politics.

4.7   The Relationship Between the Dutch Political and Cultural Systems

The analysis above demonstrates that while the impact of the political system on the cultural system—in this case, theatre—is substantial at the level of the system as a whole, determining budget levels and the geographical positions that are available, it is only moderate when individual subsidy allocations are concerned. The advisory role of the Council for Culture seems to provide a buffer: civic and inspirational values dominate subsidy allocations over time regardless of the issues raised in policy documents.

The cultural policy document graph demonstrates a similar distribution of value regimes, albeit more dynamic than for the Council for Culture. The policy priorities have not truly impacted the value orientation of the policy documents, except for the prominence of market values in the 2013-2016 period. This is testament to one of the successes of the CPA mentioned in the Introduction: formally codifying the state's relation to the cultural sector has provided stability for cultural institutions.

This does not, however, indicate that nothing has changed over the past 25 years. The issue of cultural diversity indicates that political desirables do have an impact, although the impact may not be immediate or successful. In addition, we should not think of such impact as a one-way street: in many cases, politics takes up issues that are already prominent in the cultural sector itself. This occurred in the 1960s and 1970s, as well as since 1993. The obvious rise of economic and market indicators and quantitative elements in the evaluations of policy plans should be linked to the rise of NPM. However, the emphasis on marketing and entrepreneurship cannot be regarded as only due to political impact, it should also be interpreted as a sign of the professionalisation of the cultural sector. Younger generations of artists tend to see marketing and management as 'part of their job' rather than as something alien to the artistic profession. Rather than an 'absolute' interpretation of artistic autonomy, they describe an 'embedded' form of autonomy, in which they see it as part of their obligation to think about artistic choices and how to reach and develop an audience for whom these choices are relevant. As a result, expertise is increasingly interpreted more broadly, not only as artistic expertise but also as management and marketing expertise. Politics, however, made these issues very prominent by establishing financial benchmarks, or 'knock-out' criteria, as thresholds, indicating that a cultural institution is first evaluated on this basis before 'entering' the system. These issues come at the expense of intrinsic criteria such as quality and the development of artistic languages.

4.8   Ramifications for the Future

The data presented in this chapter do not immediately indicate developments for the future of Dutch cultural policy. However, three possible routes may be inferred.

First, the quantitative analysis points in particular towards the stability provided by the CPA system, so it is logical to assume that cultural policy in the future will be based on similar value patterns, first and foremost balancing inspired and civic logics. The impact of political rhetoric may be expected to be limited, although it is difficult to assess whether the constant trend towards quantification and market-based logics, driven by both NPM and the professionalisation of the cultural sector itself, will continue to increase in significance or whether it has reached its zenith (see also the chapter on cultural entrepreneurship).

This brings us to the second possible route. Recent publications such as *The Value of Culture* (*De waarde van cultuur*) Gielen et al. 2014) and *Reassessing Culture* (*Cultuur herwaarderen*) Schrijvers et al. 2015)—the former a study commissioned by the Flemish government, the latter a report by the Scientific Council for Government Policy (WRR)—emphasise the importance of evaluating what heritage, culture and art mean for society in terms of *heritage, culture and art*. Although empirical evidence on intrinsic efficacy is limited because it is difficult to measure, the authors advise that a greater focus on intrinsic qualities is required—that is, a greater focus on the inspired value regime (and the domestic value regime in the case of heritage). Indeed, this appeal has been taken up by Minister Bussemaker and the Council for Culture.

The third route would imply more drastic change. Recent publications by the Council for Culture (2015 and 2017) recommend that the local or regional levels be taken as the point of departure for Dutch cultural policy rather than a national policy agenda. This would further embed cultural institutions subsidised by the national government in their local settings. Currently, this argument seems to be taking root in the sector. This would lead to an even more embedded interpretation of artistic autonomy than has already been alluded to in the qualitative research. The question of how a cultural institution connects to its local environment and attunes its offerings to that environment will then become paramount in cultural politics. This trend is already visible in the data presented in this chapter; although of relatively minor importance, the project-city value regime seems to be gaining weight, particularly in the advice documents. This trend could continue, probably not to the extent that project-city values will rise to the level of the centrally located inspired and civic compromise visible in Figures 1, 2 and 3. Thus, this might amount to a small change in Figure 3, where the arrow between the 'kite' representing artistic quality and the box representing the connection of cultural institutions to their environment will become more important. However, it might also indicate a greater change whereby artistic quality will, in the future, be determined on the basis of how cultural institutions manage to attune their position on the inspired and civic regimes to their local surroundings. That would imply elevating the entire box to the level of primary evaluation, as demonstrated in Figure 4.

Figure 4.4: Possible evaluation of the policy plans under 'embedded autonomy'

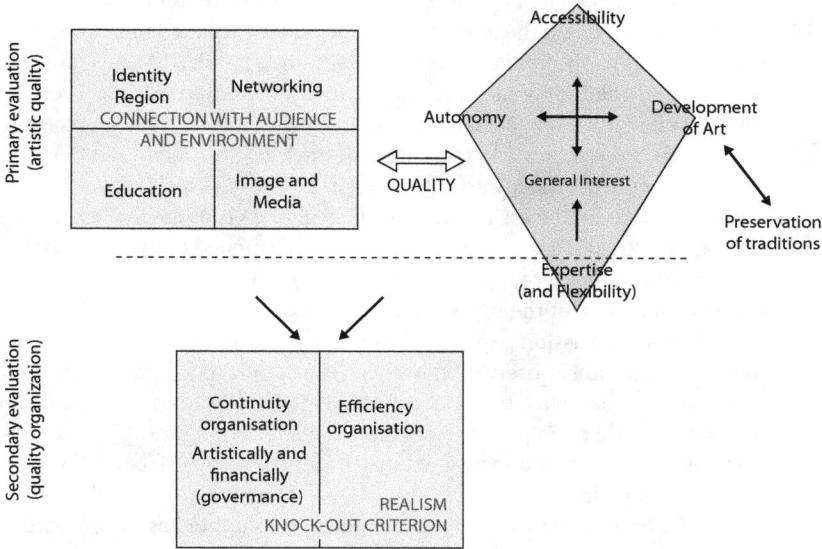

Such an expansion of the notion of embedded autonomy will enmesh the cultural sector more firmly into society. Independent advice then remains crucial in policy development and implementation, as only cultural and artistic experts can assess the intrinsic qualities of art and culture and how they are made relevant on the local and national levels. However, in a time of 'fact-free politics' and 'alternative facts', the legitimacy of expert advice seems to be seriously challenged. This poses difficult questions regarding the roles of politicians, professionals and art audiences which, according to Pots, were codified in the Dutch parliamentary system by the CPA. However, if shifts occur, new regulations may be necessary for the next 25 years of cultural policy in the Netherlands.

Notes

1.   The authors wish to acknowledge the invaluable contribution of Laura Cornelisse and Romy Akkerman, who assisted in gathering the empirical data for this chapter.

2.   Their primary role seems to be the appointment of artistic personnel. After these appointments, their role is limited.

3.   Exceptions are extremely rare, such as e.g. in 1995, when the Secretary for
     Culture Aad Nuis denied a subsidy to an amateur theatre production by
     Theater Toetssteen on the grounds that the play represented members of
     the royal family 'who could not defend themselves publicly'. More common
     are generic deviations, which include the implementation of budget restric-
     tions that had not been taken into account by the Council for Culture, e.g.
     in 2012. See chapter 1 for an explanation of the legal position of the Council
     for Culture vis-à-vis the Minister/Secretary.
4.   Some words cannot be assigned to a value regime as they are too generic,
     e.g. the verb 'to be'. In these cases, the word was assigned to the category
     'other' in the computer programme. This category was not counted.
5.   For an explanation of the BIS, see the appendix.
6.   There was no discussion paper document for this period.
7.   In fact, participatory observation revealed that, while in meetings the com-
     mittee may speak in inspirational terms, the text of the advice is amended
     by lawyers to use more precise terms, as the advice is open to appeal in
     court by theatre institutions. Again, this favours the industrial over the
     inspirational regime.
8.   We should note that the word 'raad' (council) was counted as a civic word,
     making up a relatively large proportion of the civic words in the advice
     documents (7% to 17%). We deemed this correct, as the Council represents
     the government in the cultural field rather than representing the cultural
     field in public administration. Contrary to what artists wanted, the Council
     has never served as an artists' parliament. If the word is omitted from the
     calculations, the inspired regime becomes more important than the civic in
     the advice documents. By including it, they are of equal importance.
9.   It is interesting to note that Rick van der Ploeg's policy document does not
     present a deviation from the general pattern. He is the only Secretary to
     have been criticised by parliament for disregarding quality as a central cri-
     terion and focusing on cultural outreach and entrepreneurialism (see Van
     den Hoogen 2010, chapter 2). His document, however, has the highest score
     for the inspired value regime, which is most associated with artistic quality.
10. For example: when a respondent ranks Autonomy and General Interest as
     the two top values but of equal importance, each of the values was awarded
     13.5 points.
11. 'Wat ik wel van belang vind bij een instelling in de basisinfrastructuur, is
     dat ze zich bewust zijn dat ze een voorhoedepositie innemen. En dat ze
     dus ook om zich heen kijken en dus ook andere instellingen die niet in de
     basisinfrastructuur, dat zij daar het boegbeeld voor zijn.'
12. 'R1: Aan de ene kant kijk je naar een gezelschap en beoordeel je het op z'n
     regionale functie. Tegelijkertijd hebben wij de opdracht vanuit de minister
     om te verdelen over regio's. En daar bepaalde bedragen aan te verbinden.
     En dat betekent dat je zelf niet de vrijheid hebt om dat anders over het land
     te verdelen. (...)

I: Dus eigenlijk zeg je ... het systeem dwingt je op een gegeven moment al-
lerlei dingen boven kwaliteit te laten gaan.

R1: Exact.'

13. The traditional interpretation of *l'art pour l'art* is also problematic and is
based on an error in the translation of the original document (see Lijster
2012 and Belfiore & Bennett 2008).

14. 'Bij autonomie denk ik aan de autonome kunstenaar en de mogelijkheid om
te kunnen maken wat diegene moet maken. Het algemene idee is natuurlijk
toch wel dat daar subsidie voor is. Dat het niet aan de wetten van de markt
hoeft te voldoen, maar dat het artistieke programma van de maker leidend
is (...). Maar die autonomie die staat toch wel in relatie tot al die andere
zaken, dus ook toegankelijkheid van de kunst: van een BIS-gezelschap
verwacht je wel een bepaald aantal bezoekers.'

15. 'Wij [theatermakers] moeten hele grote tegenstrijdigheden in onszelf
verenigen. Dus ontwikkeling van de kunst en het behouden van traditie
moeten in een carrière of in een gezelschap even belangrijk zijn, evenals de
autonomie. Allemaal dingen die op gespannen voet zijn ga je met elkaar in
verband brengen door middel van ons artistieke werk.' (R11)

16. At this point, the evaluation resembles Bourdieu's field logic, although it is
slanted towards the autonomous part of the field, as the Council for Culture
is not involved in the private production of theatre in the Netherlands.
Nevertheless, in the interviews, it became apparent that the committee
members do take the types of theatre produced by private companies in
the Netherlands into account in their evaluations, claiming that subsidised
theatre should be different (e.g. spend more money on set design).

17. On the one hand, the difference between primary and secondary values
stems from the order of importance as indicated in the card game. On
the other hand, the difference corresponds to that between primary and
secondary performance evaluation as defined in the *Balanced Scorecard* for
cultural institutions (Boorsma & Chiaravalotti 2010) and with the model for
the evaluation of municipal cultural policy as developed by Van den Hoogen (2010, 2012). Both models, however, regard retrospective performance
evaluation of cultural institutions, while the evaluation of the Council for
Culture has a prospective nature. It seems logical to apply the same distinction between primary and secondary values.

18. '[Je ziet] dat iedereen daar heel erg mee bezig is en daarin aan het profes-
sionaliseren is en (...) dat de keuzes van je personeel echt van belang zijn.
Er zit niet iemand een beetje publiciteit te maken. Je hebt een marketeer
nodig! (...) Daar zit een ontwikkeling (..) Sterker nog, wij [respondent doelt
op de leden van de commissie] zeiden onlangs tegen elkaar dat het goed
zou zijn als we niet alleen te horen krijgen wie de artistiek leiders en de
regisseurs zijn, maar ook wie de educatie-, marketing- en participatieme-
dewerkers zijn, omdat we daar namelijk best wel kennis van hebben. Als
daar een bepaalde naam staat kunnen we een inschatting maken van: hé,

dat is een hele goede! Als die het gaat doen, dan hebben we daar vertrouwen in. Dat is wel nieuw denk ik.' (R4)

19.   Hinrichs (2015) noted a similar development for the more experimental theatre institutions applying for subsidies from the Performing Art Fund.

Bibliography

Belfiore, Eleonore. 2004. "Auditing Culture; The Subsidised Cultural Sector in the New Public Management", *International Journal of Cultural Policy* 10(2): 183-202.

Belfiore, Eleonore, and Oliver Bennett. 2008. *The Social Impact of the Arts, An Intellectual History.* London: Palgrave Macmillan.

Boltanski, Luc, and Laurent Thévenot. 2006 [1991]. *On Justification, Economies of Worth.* Princeton University Press. Translated by Catherine Porter from *De la justification, Les économies de la grandeur.* Paris: Gallimard.

Boltanski, Luc, and Eve Chiapello. 2005 [1999]. *The New Spirit of Capitalism.* London/New York: Verso. Translated by Gregory Elliot from *Le nouvel esprit du capitalisme.* Paris: Gallimard.

Boorsma, Miranda and Francesco Chiaravalloti. 2010. "Arts Marketing Performance: An Artistic-Mission-Led Approach to Evaluation", *Journal of Arts Management, Law and Society*, 40(4): 297-317.

Bourdieu, Pierre. 1993 [1983]. "The Field of Cultural Production, or: The Economic World Reversed". Reprinted in Randal Johnson (ed.), *The Field of Cultural Production* pp. 29-73. Originally published in *Poetics*, 12/4-5: 311-56, translated by Richard Nice. Columbia: Columbia University Press.

Bussemaker, Jet. 2015. *Ruimte voor cultuur: uitgangspunten cultuurbeleid 2017-2020.* [Space for Culture: Principles for Cultural Policy 2017-2020]. The Hague: Ministerie van OCW [Ministry of Education, Culture and Science].

Council for Culture. 2015. *Agenda Cultuurbeleid 2017 en verder.* [Cultural Policy Agenda for 2017 and beyond]. The Hague: Raad voor Cultuur [Council for Culture].

—. 2017. *Cultuur voor stad, land en regio* [Culture for City, Nation and Region]. The Hague: Raad voor Cultuur [Council for Culture].

De Cea, Maite. 2008. "Expert Knowledge Mediation in the Relationship between Cultural Stakeholders, Politics and the State". Paper presented at the fifth International Conference on Cultural Policy Research, 20-24 August 2008, Istanbul.

Edelman, Josh, Louise Ejgod Hansen and Quirijn Lennert van den Hoogen. 2017. *The Problem of Theatrical Autonomy. Analysing Theatre as a Social Practice.* Amsterdam: Amsterdam University Press.

Gielen, Pascal, Quirijn van den Hoogen, Thijs Lijster, Sophie Elkhuizen and Hanka Otte. 2014. *De Waarde van Cultuur* [The Value of Culture]. Brussels: Socius.

Gray, Clive. 2007. "Commodification and Instrumentality in Cultural Policy", *International Journal of Cultural Policy* 13(2): 203-215.

Hinrichs, Bibi. 2015. *Cultureel Ondernemerschap. Een onderzoek naar cultureel ondernemerschap als subsidiecriterium bij een Nederlands publiek gefinancierd cultuurfonds* [Cultural Enrepreneurship. An Investigation of Cultural Entrepreneurship as a Criterion for Subsidy by a Public Art Fund]. MA thesis, Groningen University.

Hoefnagel, Frans J.P.M. 1992. *Cultuurpolitiek: het mogen en het moeten* [Cultural Politics: Between What One Might and Should Do]. The Hague: WRR [Scientific Council for Government Policy].

Lijster, Thijs E. 2012. *Critique of Art: Walter Benjamin and Theodor W. Adorno on Art and Art Criticism.* PhD dissertation, Groningen University.

Lindqvist, Katja. 2007. "Public Governance of Arts Organisations in Sweden: Strategic Implications", *International Journal of Cultural Policy* 13(1): 303-317.

—. 2008. "Managerialisation in the Name of Democracy: Governance Structures and Management Control in the Field of Public Art Organisations in Europe". Paper presented at the fifth International Conference on Cultural Policy Research, 20-24 August 2008, Istanbul.

Pots, Roel. 2010. *Cultuur, Koningen en Democraten. Overheid & Cultuur in Nederland* [Culture, Kings and Democrats. Government and Culture in the Netherlands]. Amsterdam: Boom.

Schrijvers, Erik, Anne-Greet Keizer and Godfried Engbertsen (eds.). 2015. *Cultuur Herwaarderen* [Reassessing Culture]. The Hague: WRR [Scientific Council for Government Policy].

Van den Hoogen, Quirijn Lennert. 2010. *Performing Arts and the City. Municipal Cultural Policy in the Age of Evidence-Based Policy.* PhD dissertation, Groningen University.

— 2012. *Effectief Cutuurbeleid: Leren van Evalueren* [Effective Cultural Policy. Learning from Assessment]. Amsterdam/The Hague: Boekman Foundation/VNG.

Winkel, Camiel van, Pascal Gielen and Koos Zwaan. 2012. *De hybride kunstenaar: de organisatie van de artistieke praktijk in het postindustriële tijdperk* [The Hybrid Artist: The Organisation of Artistic Practice in the Postindustrial Era]. Den Bosch/Breda: AKV/St Joost (Avans Hogeschool).

Winsemius, Aletta. 1999. *De overheid in spagaat: theorie en praktijk van het Nederlandse kunstbeleid* [Government Doing the Splits: Theory and Practice of Dutch Art Policy]. Amsterdam: Thela Thesis.

Zijlstra, Halbe. 2010. *Meer dan Kwaliteit. Uitgangspunten voor cultuurbeleid.* [More than Quality. Principles for Cultural Policy]. The Hague: Ministerie van OCW [Ministry of Education, Culture and Science].

An Exercise in Undogmatic Thinking

An Interview with Gable Roelofsen

From an old factory in Maastricht, Gable Roelofsen (1982) brings into practice what he thinks cultural policy needs: undogmatic thinking. Roelofsen is an actor, singer, writer, director, producer and currently chairman of the Council for Culture's advisory committee on the future of opera and music theatre. He leads Het Geluid, a music theatre collective that produces performances that shift between different genres, using both traditional and modern methods, and addressing local questions as well as global problems. Striking examples of their work are the virtual-reality opera *Weltatem* (2016), the pool performance about 'otherness' entitled *Contested Waters* (2015) and the artistic food truck *Cultuur Frituur* (2011).

While Het Geluid creates art in unorthodox ways, it does so in a cultural sector in which all too often traditional, dogmatic lines of thinking prevail, Roelofsen says. One example of this is the assumptions about the artistic quality of genres, as a result of which non-commercial musicals, for instance, are unlikely to receive much subsidy. Another example is the stereotypes associated with artistic innovation: much of people's view on innovation is coloured by a 'counterculture' form of romanticism that values Bob Dylan-like *enfants terribles*. This makes them potentially blind to innovative practices that do not fit this rhetoric.

Roelofsen also sees another dogma in the relation between the megalopolis (linking Amsterdam, Rotterdam, The Hague, and Utrecht) and other regions in the Netherlands. While money, institutions and resources seem to be distributed rather fairly across the country, Amsterdam is still perceived to be the place to go for arts and culture. Yet in reality, a lot of artistic content originates from the provinces, and Amsterdam is just one of many reference points. Take the case of the home base of Het Geluid: while there are few places in the Netherlands further removed from Amsterdam than Maastricht, the latter city is central in the axes between Amsterdam, Brussels and the German Ruhr area.

For Roelofsen, the biggest challenge in cultural policy for the coming decades is overcoming these types of old-fashioned ideologies. While this will not be achieved from one day to the next, several practical steps can and must be taken.

First, artistic resilience would benefit from a 'huge variety' of smaller grants, each serving different purposes. In an ideal situation, it would also become more common to get funding for artistic and innovative projects that may not at first glance have a clear use, target audience or profitability. Roelofsen gives the example of Dick Raaijmakers, whose early experiments with electronic music ultimately led to the emergence of this now extremely popular genre.

According to Roelofsen, it is not only grants that could benefit from more diversity but also the committees that review grant applications. At the moment, these committees (and the cultural sector in general) are a poor reflection of the Dutch population. An unintended result of this is that 'other' voices are underrepresented in the debate about subsidy and artistic quality. Quota and inclusiveness policies could be used to form more inclusive committees, provided that these committees remain completely free in the choices they make.

These choices, however, should reflect a broad definition of quality. The status of the applicant, the quality of the application or the expected audience should not be the only criteria for the assessment of applications; motivation, energy, resilience, cooperation and artistic research ought to also be taken into account. As these criteria are not easy to measure, this presupposes an atmosphere of trust and generosity in both the cultural sector and within the public debate.

Finally, the local context should be taken into account in the reviewing of grant applications. What are the most pressing problems in a region? What kind of contribution can the artist offer in that particular area? Asking these questions, however, means that the traditional dichotomy between 'artistic' and 'social' or 'educational' art must be transcended. Roelofsen gives the example of *Common Carnaval* (2016), a project in which Het Geluid participated. While ostensibly a societal project in which refugees were actively welcomed in the festivities of Maastricht carnival, Roelofsen sees this as one of his most artistic projects to date.

According to Roelofsen, future cultural policy should become an exercise in undogmatic thinking. This is a challenge for policymakers, but artists bear a responsibility as well. One favourable aspect of Dutch cultural policy, Roelofsen states, is that the cultural sector is actively involved in policymaking. The lines of communication between policymakers and artists are short, and everyone can be reached easily. He calls on artists to use this proximity, to let policymakers hear your voice.

Yet policymakers are not the only ones able to solve an artist's problem. Roelofsen hopes that in the future, artists will increasingly side with universities and other institutions or companies outside the art sector. For the Maastricht-based theatre makers—who are not subsidised by production houses—this has been a necessity from the start. It has been one of the factors that helped them withstand the disruptive storm that has raged through the cultural sector this decade: Het Geluid recently celebrated its tenth birthday.

Bjorn Schrijen

5.   Towards a Cultural Policy of Trust

The Dutch Approach from the Perspective of a
Transnational Civil Domain

Thijs Lijster, Hanka Otte and Pascal Gielen

5.1.   Introduction

Throughout modernity, institutions and cultural organisations such as museums, theatres, opera houses, theatre companies, orchestras and so on have played a crucial role in the constitutive process of civil society and of a democratic public sphere. The conceptual framing of this civil domain, from Hegel up until Habermas (1989), has focussed mainly on the national level: the 'civil' as the middle ground between the private individual and the political body of the nation-state. Dutch cultural policy also focuses on this level, supporting a so-called national Basic Infrastructure that provides high-quality offerings of culture, to be displayed on podia that are mainly locally supported but do comply to this national standard. The same applies to subsidised organisations and cultural projects allocated by the six national cultural funds established and supported by the Dutch Ministry of Education, Culture and Science.

This framing is up for discussion, for several reasons. On the one hand, the social, political and cultural issues facing civil society today go increasingly beyond the scope of the nation-state (Walzer 1995, Koopmans & Statham 2010, Fraser et al. 2014). Globalisation forces us to re-evaluate the notion of civil society, as well as civic values and virtues, and raises questions about the possibility of a transnational public sphere, which would be crucial for democratic deliberation. On the other hand, all over the globe we witness the emergence of grassroots cultural and civil organisations that do not fit the traditional profile of national institutions. These organisations lack the hierarchical order and rigid organisational structure of traditional institutions, and no longer or not primarily refer to the (national) artistic canon (Castells 2015).

In January 2017, Jet Bussemaker, Minister of Education, Culture and Science, requested a study from the Council for Culture (*Raad voor Cultuur*) for a new framework for cultural policy after 2021. With this request, she was responding to a long-standing wish of the cultural field and to earlier signals coming from the Council for Culture itself but also from Kunsten

'92 (the interest group for the cultural sector) and the G-9 (the nine largest municipalities) to shift the focus of cultural policy from the national to the local and regional level. In the advice, entitled *Agenda Culture. 2017-2020 and Beyond* (*Agenda Cultuur. 2017-2020 en verder*, 2015), the Council for Culture had already pointed out that the cultural field is increasingly characterised by small independent organisations and temporary projects and associations. These small-scale organisations have the benefit of being both embedded in a local (often urban) setting and therefore equipped to sense the needs and concerns of specific communities, while at the same time being flexible enough to enter into networked relations with communities in other cities both within and outside of the Netherlands. There is, however, a huge tension between on the one hand a cultural policy that traditionally focuses on large, established institutes or organisations that follow the same hierarchical logic/structure, and on the other hand the needs of these small-scale initiatives. The Council warned that these smaller organisations have difficulties finding their way in a subsidy system that has become more and more specific in its demands (with regard to quality, public outreach, output, dissemination, cost legitimisation and so on), and which for that reason tends to clash with the informal and casual character as well as with the 'horizontalist' and sometimes international scope of these kinds of organisations. Therefore, the Council recommended a reevaluation of the national focus of Dutch cultural policy and its funding systems.

Although we share the concerns of the Council for Culture and would welcome a shift in attention from the national towards the local/municipal level, we think this in itself would be insufficient to cater to the needs of either the contemporary cultural field or to those of contemporary society in general. As we will argue, the Dutch cultural policy system has traditionally suffered from two blind spots: 1) on the reception side, it considers art and culture first and foremost as something to *enjoy* on an individual level rather than something of inherent civil or political value, and 2) on the production side, it has focused primarily on established institutions rather than on small-scale organisations emerging from specific concerns in society. After having further discussed these blind spots in the first section, we will reframe the civil role of cultural organisations in the second section, through a discussion of what we call the 'civil sequence': the process through which individual emotion can transform into collective action. Art and culture can, as we will argue, play a crucial role in this process. Finally, on the basis of a comparison of the Dutch cultural policy system with the approach of the European Cultural Foundation, we will come up with some recommendations for an alternative framework for a new 'Dutch approach'.

5.2   Blind Spots

One might investigate the aforementioned blind spots from a historical and systematic perspective. Ten Thije (2017) gives an elaborate and clear historical reconstruction of debates concerning the Dutch cultural policy system, a debate that is usually considered as one that pits the liberal and the social-democratic views on cultural policy against each other, two sides embodied by the statesmen Johan Rudolph Thorbecke (1798-1872) and Emanuel Boekman (1889-1940), respectively. As a liberal, Thorbecke opposed any involvement of the state with the arts, apart from the occasional support of already existing private initiatives. By contrast, Boekman argued that the government had a responsibility to support the arts as well as people's *interest* in art. In his view, enjoyment of the arts had for too long been a privilege of the elite, and he considered it the government's task to bring as many people as possible in contact with art and culture.

However, although this implied more involvement of the state, Boekman still considered the arts themselves to be a private matter, namely as a means for individual emancipation or enlightenment and human flourishing. In other words, and as Ten Thije observes, although the perspectives of Thorbecke and Boekman are clearly contrasted, they are in a different way fully aligned: both consider art and culture primarily as something to *enjoy* or as a basic anthropological need of the private individual:

> Where the views of these two men align is that both feel that the involvement of the government should be done discretely and that the active involvement of the government introduces the risk of drawing art into the political sphere... The idea, in other words, that art in some sense is inherently public in the sense that art participates in the most public activity of all—politics—is not entertained by either Thorbecke or Boekman (Ten Thije 2017: 78).[1]

Thorbecke and Boekman cast a long shadow over debates concerning cultural policy, and one might even argue that the condescending characterisation of the arts as (either leftist or elitist) 'hobbies', voiced by the advocates of the recent budget cuts, is derived precisely from this individualist perspective on the arts as a means for personal flourishing. Now that the belief in *Bildung* has deteriorated in recent decades, this flourishing is now increasingly defined in terms of economic prospering—which is, of course, still a matter of the private sector. This, then, is the first 'blind spot': the dominant idea—shared by left and right-wing governments alike—that cultural policy caters to the individual aesthetic experience rather than to a fundamentally public or civil domain.

The second blind spot of the Dutch cultural policy tradition has been its top-down approach and, consequentially, its relative inability to recognise, stimulate and support the kinds of small-scale grassroots organisations that, according to the Council, are characteristic of the contemporary cultural landscape. The focus on long-term, well-established and nationally oriented institutions and the bureaucratisation of subsidising and funding procedures has undoubtedly had its benefits in creating continuity for high-quality cultural organisations, but this also makes it quite difficult for newcomers or organisations that favour a different approach to enter or survive in this playing field. This proves to be particularly problematic once an increasing part of the population no longer recognises itself in the existing cultural provision and as a consequence has the feeling that the cultural sector is run by a self-involved and self-sustaining 'elite'. This means that, even if the Dutch cultural policy system were to consider art and culture as a potential public arena, it will have difficulties localising or articulating specific exist-ing civil concerns due to its top-down approach and the relative inflexibility and rigidity of the subsidising systems. Although cultural policymakers and socially engaged artists may in fact share many concerns and ambitions with regard to the role of the arts in society, in practice their approaches and discourses more often clash than intersect (cf. Kolsteeg 2017).

We doubt whether the mere shift in focus from the national to the re-gional/local level will really compensate for these blind spots. In fact, 60% of the total budget for culture is already in the hands of the municipalities, which means that they already have a big say in how this budget is spent. Nevertheless, at this municipal level the established institutions also seem to have priority (i.e., the second blind spot just mentioned). In his research comparing seven municipalities, Van Herpen (2017) notes that 75% of the cultural budget goes to 'brick' institutions, such as libraries, city theatres and museums. Pop music venues, or venues programming multiple and cross-disciplinary arts, receive far less subsidy per inhabitant (for instance: an average of €26 for a city theatre against €3.66 for a more 'hybrid' venue). A likely explanation for this difference is the fact that these hybrid venues also have a more hybrid financial basis, earning a substantial part of their income from catering, for instance. Still, it is telling that the Dutch national and the local/municipal cultural policy systems share a preference for established institutions, which implies that they also share the blind spot for grassroots initiatives. An additional reason for the shared blind spot is that, at least up until now, the municipalities may have been responsible for the buildings and stages, but the national government determined the programming by supporting the big (national) theatre and opera companies and the like. In other words, this approach leaves very little space for change. Apparently, the national/local distinction and the top-down/bottom-up distinction are not one and the same, and a shift in the former may be of no consequence at all for the latter.

With regard to the first mentioned blind spot, it is equally unlikely that a mere shift in responsibilities from the national to the local level will have immediate drastic consequences. The primary goal, as formulated on the website of the Ministry of Education, Culture and Science, remains to ensure that 'as many people as possible in the Netherlands have access to culture of high quality'[2] and, as Bussemaker emphasises in the tradition of Boekman, that 'everyone in the Netherlands should be able to *enjoy* culture' (Bussemaker 2015: 21, our emphasis). In other words: the focus of Dutch cultural policy still is on the arts and culture as a leisure activity or else as a means of economic stimulation (to bring tourism or as a Dutch 'export product'). At the municipal level, this is no different. In policy plans, the big municipalities emphasise the economic importance that the arts and culture have for their city.[3] They voice the wish that high-quality cultural venues, festivals and events will attract tourists both from inside and outside the Netherlands, thus having a positive effect on local business. Even though the empirical evidence for such an economic effect is quite scarce (cf. Gielen et al. 2015), and even though Richard Florida has noticed the downsides of the gentrification processes for the urban environment and the middle class (Florida 2017), the choir of municipal cultural policymakers singing the praises of the cultural and creative industries remains as loud as it ever was.

At the same time, and in recent years, there has been a new emphasis in Dutch cultural policy on stimulating the 'participation society', as the second Rutte cabinet has called it. The idea of the 'participation society' expects a more proactive role of citizens and a more responsible attitude with regard to their community and surroundings as the government retreats (which is why the concept was, according to its critics, merely an excuse for austerity measures driven by neoliberal ideology). This active citizenship can also be regarded as a shift from an emphasis on 'formal' citizenship to one on 'moral' citizenship (Van Houdt & Schinkel 2009: 50-51). Whereas formal citizenship concerns the legal status of a citizen, moral citizenship is about the extra-juridical, moral (and perhaps we should add: cultural) interpretation of what a good citizen is or should be and should do.

In cultural policy, this translates into subsidies for cultural participation and community art projects, which were supposed to integrate individuals into existing communities, create new communities, or bridge the gap between communities (cf. Otte 2015) as well as open subsidising programmes such as The Art of Impact.[4] Although to a certain extent this shift in Dutch cultural policy indeed meant a step beyond the Thorbecke/Boekman deadlock, involving a more social and/or civil understanding of the arts and culture, it still implied a rather functionalistic approach. It either considered the arts as a form of social glue and a plaster on the wounds of the community—wounds that, apart from developments such as population decline and digitisation, were also often inflicted by neoliberal policy itself (cf. Gielen 2011)—or it considered the arts, opportunistically, as some kind of creative problem solver or 'motor for innovation', as in The Art of Impact.

So what would an alternative framework for the role of the arts and culture in civil society look like, and what would the consequences be for cultural policy? How can we see through or beyond the blind spots? To answer those questions, we need to step back and take a theoretical detour.

5.3   The Civil Sequence

In 2015-2016, two of the authors of this chapter conducted a pilot research study, commissioned by the European Cultural Foundation, on a new civil role for contemporary cultural organisations in Europe.[5] The kinds of organisations the ECF was interested in are involved in projects or creative services that address global challenges or tackle community issues (or a combination of both). These organisations move into new creative working areas where they explore 'glocally' relevant themes that often lead them to actions far beyond the immediate arts and culture sector (De Cauter et al. 2010, De Bruyne & Gielen 2011, Gielen 2015). Moreover, as already outlined in the report by the Dutch Council for Culture mentioned earlier, these organisations lack the strict hierarchical organisational structure that characterises most traditional arts institutions. Long-term strategic plans seem to be increasingly replaced by a shared creation of general organisational value frameworks. These provide an overall strategic orientation point for the organisation while ideally creating room for individual initiatives and experimentation. Many new cultural initiatives today remain rather small and informal. They build temporary alliances with other like-minded initiatives in order to pursue shared strategic goals or to share knowledge, resources and ideas for tackling similar cultural questions and artistic working fields. The cultural field is increasingly characterised by rhizome-like network structures that traditional cultural organisations are not (or not fully) equipped to handle. In many cases these networks emerge and continue to operate outside of the traditional infrastructure.

The theoretical framework of this research study, which we called the 'civil sequence', is most relevant for our current concerns. We will also shortly refer to two case studies, for they demonstrate the important function that culture can play in the organisation and efficacy of the civil domain, or in the so-called 'participation society'.

The 'civil sequence' starts from the premise, derived from the work of Spanish sociologist Manuel Castells (2015), that all civil action is born from emotion. The urge to change something in society emerges from emotions of an often negative nature: outrage, anger, fear or frustration. You may feel dissatisfied by the lack of playgrounds in your city, feel threatened by youngsters in the neighbourhood, or you might be experiencing stress and anxiety from your workload or from the lack of future prospects in your job. Obviously, not every emotion will lead to civil action. People dissatisfied about their city can also move; employees experiencing stress can go to a therapist or coach. Emotions can be channeled in many ways. One can choose to opt for a rather private and individual solution to one's problem, but that has nothing to do with civil action. In order to 'enter' civil society, we need specifically to address a collective and generate public support. The initial emotion must be recognised as a shared emotion—a shared fear, frustration or irritation. Civil action is only possible if we 'de-privatise' our personal discomfort.

Such a step towards civil space requires an important skill: *rationalisation*. Rationalisation, which in the first place means self-rationalisation, is required to articulate an initial intuition or basic emotion. It is the cognitive competence of analysing one's own feelings and perhaps pointing out possible causes. Self-rationalisation therefore precedes communication, although the causes of certain emotions may be further clarified in dialogue with others. And finally, after the stages of rationalisation, communication and de-privatisation, the skill of *organising* is required in order to set the civil action in motion and, if necessary, keep it going in the long run. For instance, one must organise oneself in order to write an opinion piece but also encourage others to do the same. Protesting in the streets or rolling up our sleeves to clean the neighbourhood requires at least a modicum of organisation.

What is important here is that these processes of self-rationalisation and self-organisation can diminish the emotions that initiated them in the first place. For instance, having to find one's way in a maze of legal rules, being obliged to study political procedures, or having to follow the long and winding road through bureaucratic institutions in order to arrive at the right form of organisation can make one lose the energy to go on. Both processes therefore require us to literally rationalise the initial emotion, to distance ourselves from it and in a sense 'bureaucratise' it (all forms of organisation presuppose setting up a minimum number of rules and procedures and sticking to them).

In itself, such processes are not dramatic or even necessary to initiate civil action. However, it does mean that we all too easily forget about the basic emotions that formed the initial 'drive' or the energy of the civil undertaking. It is the engine that powers all civil organisation or any initiative with a civil mission. This also means that civil action derives its basic energy from very direct, daily and mostly local human experience. The chances of a civil initiative succeeding and enduring therefore depend on finding the right balance between rationalising and organising on the one hand and keeping up the energy that is obtained from the initial basic emotion on the other hand. This balance is all the more urgent the more organisations 'scale up' their activities, for instance from a local to a regional level or from the national to the transnational level. Each step up the ladder demands more rationalisation and organisation, which thereby risks depleting the initial drive and emotion as well as losing track of the local problems that started it all.

From the above we may conclude that cultural organisations that adopt a civil role are situated at the end of a sequence of distinctive operations. Analytically, this succession of processes—which we call the *civil sequence*—looks like this: (1) emotion, (2) rationalisation, (3) communication, (4) de-privatisation (or going public), and finally (5) organisation. Here we have to emphasise that this sequence is not a one-way street, and this is something we actually found out during our empirical research. An organisation can be arranged more or less 'rationally' or be re-ignited with a certain emotion. Moreover, as we will discuss further below, the relevance of a *cultural* organisation can precisely be to spread the emotion throughout a community, thereby returning again to the start of the sequence.

But first let us look at the model analytically one last time. We can see that the civil sequence can only be fulfilled through *three transitions*. The first one takes place at the emotional level. An initially negative feeling (of discomfort, injustice, etc.) must be converted into a sense of positive energy, of simple enthusiasm to 'get cracking' or at least of not resigning oneself to the situation. Castells gives the example of fear that must be 'positively' converted into hope and outrage (2015: 247-248). By 'positively', we mean that only hope can lead to action. No matter how negative the results of bursts of outrage may sometimes be, they always indicate an accumulation of energy. A second necessary transition is to be found at the level of communication, as it is only through communication that a transformation can take place from the individual to the collective level, and it is only through communication that we can test or correct our emotions or find out whether they are shared in the first place. It might be the case that someone's feelings of fear and insecurity in the neighbourhood are unjustified or have a different source than the one they were expecting. Organisations that adopt a civil role often originate in such shared sentiments. So, without collectivisation, there is no civil action and no organisation.

The civil sequence requires yet another transition, from the private to the public sphere. As indicated earlier, feelings and issues can be shared and therefore collectivised in both the private and the public sphere. The employee consulting a therapist is not engaged in civil action. It is only when the initial emotion is articulated in social terms that it acquires civil value. Stress is then not only about the irritated nerves of the individual employee or about the annoying personality of a boss but also about high work pressure, increasingly precarious working conditions such as flexible and mobile project labour, or the decrease in long-term employment contracts and job security. In other words, in the transition from the private to the public sphere, a personal issue (being a stress-sensitive person) is not only translated into a collective problem (a stressful environment, stressful working conditions); the cause of the problem or feeling of discomfort is also located in broader social phenomena. This is why the transformation from the private to the public sphere implies the *politicisation* of the initial feeling.

What, in general, is the role of *culture* in all this? For our field research into the civil role of cultural organisations, we investigated two grassroots cultural organisations: Les Têtes de l'Art in Marseille and Culture 2 Commons in Zagreb. Although this is not the place to discuss these cases at length, what is relevant for our present concern are the two specific ways in which the civil sequence worked in practice. We call them 'the art of mirroring' and 'transversal action'. When we asked these organisations how they kept the 'fire burning'—that is, how they kept alive the initial emotion that started their activities—the people of Les Têtes de l'Art emphasised that for them the simple act of making art together with others or 'doing things' plays the most important part. The drive is not so much communicated in words, and energy rarely comes from a well-articulated view. Rather, they emerge from the activities that are organised and the artistic interventions that are staged. Just like the transference of emotions can take place subconsciously and non-verbally through mirror neurons, the drive and energy are primarily communicated through the actions themselves. This is what we have chosen to call 'mirroring': seeing others act makes us act too. Actions generate actions and energy generates energy. Herein lies the power of culture-specific artistic interventions. They generate a 'mimetic effect', which spurs others into action. Artistic interventions and performances in public space often indirectly—and in a particularly positive manner—point out the social issues within a group, neighbourhood or town. Cultural civil actions not only bring to light what is not visible, they also reveal how the surroundings, a space or a neighbourhood may be experienced differently.

In this respect, artistic activities differ from other civil actions such as protests, opinion pieces or petitions. Whereas such civil actions are generally limited to social criticism, the artistic civil action has an additional element: an alternative experience. For a brief moment, the artists provide an often quite modest but possibly different world, which in most cases generates positive energy. Les Têtes de l'Art illustrated this quite literally with their initiatives named Place à l'Art, a sort of 'fair' where people in the neighbourhood could engage in all sorts of creative and artistic activities together, producing a very positive social dynamic in places where drug dealers and other petty criminals had previously created an unsafe social environment. The outrage over an unsafe environment is immediately 'compensated' for with a positive alternative.

The other 'mode' in which we encountered the civil sequence was 'transversal action'. What we mean by this is how action can spread out from one social domain to the other, connecting different stakeholders, interest groups and the like. In other words, civil action is disseminated across society geographically, for example via the rhizome network of organisations, actions or initiatives within the cultural scene but also at the social level, where we see an extension of the artistic and cultural sector into trade unions and ecological pressure groups, for example. The cultural scene thus joins, or in some cases even commences, a broader social movement that transversally connects to many different segments of the population and spheres in life. One example of this is *Pravo na Grad* (Right to the City), which was established as a collaboration between civil society organisations working in the field of culture and youth and was later formalised as an NGO.[6] This social broadening is crucial in increasing the power and charging the energy of civil actions. In this respect, too, the well-known civil activities of traditional representational politics—in which such organisations as trade unions played a central part—are forsaken in favour of actions that no longer rely on quantitative representation alone but look for the convincing quality of a singular dissonant voice.

5.4   Alternative Approaches

What does the civil sequence and its two modes of existence teach us with regard to cultural policy in general and the Dutch system in particular?

First of all, we need to observe that cultural policy usually enters the stage only at the very end of the sequence, once the initial emotion has already been rationalised, communicated and organised—that is, only when one has already 'organised' oneself and made up one's mind about what to do and how to initiate action will one encounter policy, for instance to obtain permits for a manifestation, to arrange an exhibition space, or to get sufficient funding. So, it is in the nature of policy itself (and part of the model of the civil sequence) that policy appears at the end of the chain, but once it becomes part of the game it can either 'boost' or frustrate the sequence. It can either give you the feeling of finally getting things done, making actions possible, or being recognised; or it can slow things down, temper your enthusiasm, or force you to unwillingly change your plans due to legal objections. Cultural policy can play a crucial role in all three transitions that we mentioned above: from negative to positive emotion, from individual to collective communication, and from private to public sphere. And in each transition, it can go either way: it can either stimulate or frustrate, it can either give voice or silence, it can either isolate or connect.

Now it is not difficult to see that there is a huge tension between, on the one hand, the two blind spots of the Dutch cultural policy system mentioned in the first section (the focus on the individual aesthetic enjoyment, and the emphasis on top-down policy) and, on the other hand, the two modes of existence of the civil sequence mentioned in the second section (the art of mirroring and transversal action). First, if one considers the primary objective of cultural policy to cater to the individual aesthetic experience, as the Dutch system traditionally seemed to do, one is likely to miss out on the kinds of civil responsibilities that these new organisations have taken upon themselves and the civil roles they ascribe to themselves. Moreover, by focusing on aesthetic enjoyment as the desired end goal of cultural products, one misses out on the connection that aesthetic pleasure can have with all kinds of other (civil) emotions. The 'art of mirroring', after all, presumed both the very 'communality' of emotions (arousing, recognising, sharing, spreading, 'infecting') and the conversion of emotions (for instance from fear and anxiety to enthusiasm and hope).

Second, it is equally clear that 'transversal action' is not likely to be stimulated as long as the Dutch cultural policy system suffers from the second mentioned blind spot, the top-down approach, the uneven focus on long-term, well-established, nationally oriented institutions and the bureaucratisation of the subsidising and funding procedures. All of these characteristics frustrate the civil sequence rather than foster and stimulate it. After all, in a top-down approach one already has a clear view of what one wants to establish or accomplish, and therefore there is little room for improvisation and unexpected connections with other fields and, hence, unexpected outcomes within the civil domain. The same goes for the established organisations themselves, who already have a fixed 'identity' and artistic vision. If they have had to broaden their scope, pressured by policymakers who want them to attract more and different audiences, this often seems very forced. Orchestras working together with rappers and DJs hardly lead to interesting crossovers, neither artistically nor with regard to their respective publics. Also, the 'bracketing' or compartmentalisation inherent to bureaucratic subsidising systems is likely to cause difficulties for cultural organisations wishing to work together with trade unions, NGOs or other social platforms. It is results, after all, that are expected in the artistic domain, while civil action 'in the streets' immediately brings along other rules that are more difficult to judge on the basis of aesthetic criteria alone.

Could the Dutch cultural landscape benefit from an alternative approach to better cater to the needs of these new kinds of cultural organisations and the civil role they see in store for themselves? Perhaps here a comparison between the Dutch cultural policy system and the strategy of the European Cultural Foundation may be useful. Of course, the ECF and the Dutch Ministry for Education, Culture and Science have quite different goals and are of a very different scale, but what we are interested in here is the framework within and method through which they approach these new kinds of cultural organisations we have been talking about, and to what extent they manage to do so. The ECF's objective—'to nurture a socially engaged and culturally rooted civil society across Europe' (ECF 2017)—is clearly distinct from the Dutch ministry's emphasis on quality and enjoyment. The ECF propagates the transformative force of culture, aiming 'to shift the tide from exclusion to inclusion' in Europe. Obviously, the ECF's focus is more international and pan-European, and that makes a comparison with Dutch national cultural policy difficult. In that regard, a comparison between the ECF's approach with Dutch *international* cultural policy (ICB), as formulated in the *Policy Framework 2017-2020* (*Beleidskader 2017-2020*, Bussemaker & Koenders 2016), may be more appropriate.[7]

As mentioned in the Policy Framework itself, the focus of ICB in recent years has been almost exclusively economic: promoting Dutch culture as a successful export product. By now, however, the ministry has realised that this approach has been too narrow and that it does insufficient justice to the other (intrinsic and social) values of art and culture. Apart from stimulating the visibility and success of Dutch culture abroad, ICB now also wants to 'effectively implement culture' in diplomacy and use culture as a way of making the world more 'safe, just and sustainable'. As a result of the involvement of three different ministries and their agendas, this shift in focus from the purely economic towards the social and political is certainly promising. However, though it may be too soon to tell, both the tone of the document and the expected approach (in terms of subsidising systems) is still very top-down. For instance: it is the ministry that is setting out the strategy of focusing on seven specific countries around Europe, most notably countries east and south of the Mediterranean Sea. Funding bodies and embassies receive the money to distribute among the organisations that fit *their* criteria and goals.

While part of the ICB is directed at the improvement of international relations between other countries and the Netherlands, the ECF is primarily directed at a pan-European, transnational civil domain. In practical terms, this means the ECF supports local cultural organisations, both financially and in terms of network and knowledge exchange. For instance, in the 'Connected Action for the Commons' programme, six so-called 'hubs' are supported and brought into contact with one another (including the two cases mentioned above, Les Tetes de l'Art and Culture 2 Commons).[8] This creates a bottom-up structure in which the ECF tries to listen as much as possible to what the already existing local cultural initiatives want and need. Or to formulate it in terms of our theoretical model: the ECF hooks into a 'civil sequence' that already exists rather than trying to construct one from scratch. One might say that it tries to provide the 'grease' to smoothen the varied transitions that characterise the civil sequence. An appropriate funding structure would also be organised in a bottom-up manner, and at the moment of writing the ECF is in the process of developing just such a structure, a process that is itself also organised in a bottom-up way. Recently, the ECF organised a meeting with 30 activists who developed prototypes or organisational models, which were in turn further developed in working groups consisting of artists, researchers and representatives of cultural funds into what the ECF calls 'participative funding models'. These models, which are characterised by a structure of open membership, are inspired largely by Cultura Nova, a funding system for independent culture in Zagreb. Cultura Nova is financed by the national government, but the cultural sector itself decides—by way of an annual assembly composed of all the members of the cultural field—on how the money is allocated. From this year on, members of the ECF, rather than a top-down chosen committee of experts, will also allocate the grants of four new funds.

Finally, besides a more bottom-up approach of cultural policy itself, it is important to provide for conditions that make the cultural public spaces more public. The cultural sector is becoming more and more distanced from society as a result of two trends. Currently, the sector offers a (top-down subsidised) artistic programme that might call for reflection and debate but only attracts a small group of higher educated, mostly white upper-to-middle-class people, a group that is no longer representative of the increasingly diversifying population in most cities. And with the government asking/stimulating cultural organisations such as theatres to compile a market-oriented programme from the market (i.e. national and international, commercial best-selling products), this probably attracts a broader but at the same time more passive audience.[9] It does not help to build big new buildings in the city without investing in other domains that are necessary for the arts to support and stimulate an urban fabric. It is no coincidence that grassroots activities are often initiated and performed in alternative, seemingly more accessible public places than the official cultural institutes. They might flourish better in places where they have room to develop and discuss their products and where they can directly hold up that mirror to the people who are concerned and involved with what is going on in their city.

5.5   Conclusion: The Policy Paradox

One might call this the 'policy paradox': in order to scale up, one must first scale down. That is, in order to face contemporary cultural, ecological and economic problems that are increasingly transnational in nature, one must start from the level where these kinds of issues are immediately experienced: the local level of specific regions and neighbourhoods. Once they find each other across borders, local grassroots initiatives can form transnational networks, which are often more powerful and sustainable than 'forced' and artificially created cooperations of larger institutions. This paradox relates to what Benjamin Barber has argued in his famous book *If Mayors Ruled the World* (2013): that the greatest challenges of the twenty-first century—global warming, poverty, safety and cultural clashes—are better dealt with at the municipal than at the national level. Cities not only now house more than half of the population of our planet, they are also the 'incubator of the cultural, social, and political innovations which shape our planet' (ibid.). Local leaders (e.g., mayors) traditionally have a more pragmatic and non-partisan way of dealing with these issues and opportunities and moreover are often more trusted by their citizens as well as by their colleagues in other cities abroad than national politicians.

Could an alternative approach to Dutch cultural policy and a new subsidy system that gives urban regions more influence on how to spend money on culture, as recently proposed by the Dutch Council for Culture, indeed lead to more space for small-scale and grassroots cultural organisations to intertwine cultural practices with civil actions on a transnational level? Following Barber, we might indeed expect local authorities to be able to recognise these kinds of initiatives more easily and stimulate them more effectively because of their greater sense of what's happening in the region, and also because of their relatively lower thresholds and greater approachability. However, as we argued in this chapter, this is not only—and perhaps even not primarily—a matter of the national/local (municipal) distinction, i.e., a matter of where the responsibilities over the budget lie, although this certainly plays an important part. As we have argued, cultural policies of local authorities can be (and in the Dutch case often are) organised in the same top-down manner, and this means that they have the same blind spots. It is only once the cultural policy system has developed more of an eye for the kinds of grassroots local initiatives that we have been describing and once the funding methods themselves are organised in a bottom-up fashion that a shift in responsibility from the national to the local level will have any effect.

The 'trust' that Barber speaks of, moreover, should go both ways: there must be not only trust on the part of citizens in their (local) leaders but also trust on the part of policymakers in those organisations they are supporting. How a cultural policy for such new organisations would exactly look like is something to be discovered. However, we do know, as the examples we mentioned in this article show, that such a policy will be a bottom-up policy. Things will no longer be done by the hierarchic rules and principles that both social democracy and liberalism designed for us. Such a policy is by its very nature bottom-up, meaning that artists and other cultural actors make their own rules and can design their own logistical and financial structures. Cultural governance would then be no more than 'inductive', which means that it can only reject or confirm the legality of the regulations that cultural actors have already developed for themselves. Politicians and administrators just need to make room for self-development, self-organisation and self-regulation. Such an inductive policy requires, in the first place, a fundamental shift from the actual top-down governance and its management of distrust to a cultural politics of openness and trust. This is perhaps the biggest challenge of such an alternative approach, especially in the Dutch context where every penny must be accounted for and legitimised according to fixed sets of criteria and expected 'output' or 'deliverables'. A bottom-up approach, after all, presumes that a policymaker relinquishes control and gives governance to the organisations themselves. This is the challenge that we face if we are to realise a cultural dynamic on which the civil realm of a real participation society can be built.

Notes

1. We should note that politics is understood here in a very broad sense: as creating and giving form to the world. Ten Thije draws on Jacques Rancière's understanding of aesthetics and politics as the distribution or redistribution of the sensible.

2. Retrieved on 27 October 2017 from: https://www.rijksoverheid.nl/onderwerpen/kunst-en-cultuur/kunst-en-cultuurbeleid.

3. Even if these policy plans sometimes pay lip service to the 'intrinsic' value of the arts, this value is still formulated in terms of individual enjoyment (cf. the first blind spot mentioned). Moreover, in practice, cultural organisations are in fact primarily held accountable on the basis of these economic effects (cf. Van den Hoogen 2012).

4. See: http://theartofimpact.nl/#s1.

5. The report itself is unpublished but was later turned into the chapter 'The Civil Potency of a Singular Experience' for the book *The Art of Civil Action* (eds. Gielen & Dietachmair, 2017). See Gielen & Lijster 2017.

6. An example closer to home is 'Hart boven Hard', a civil initiative against the Flemish and Belgian government that was started in 2014 by artists but was soon joined by representatives of the cultural sector, trade unions, academics and NGOs. See also http://www.hartbovenhard.be

7. https://www.rijksoverheid.nl/documenten/beleidsnota-s/2016/05/04/beleidskader-internationaal-cultuurbeleid-2017-2020.

8. http://www.culturalfoundation.eu/connected-action/.

9. It is even debatable how broad the audiences of the more commercial theatres are. In the Dutch city of Groningen, only 8.4% of the mature population attends one or more of the performances supplied by all professional theatres in the city per year (Van Maanen et al. 2015: 296).

Bibliography

Barber, Benjamin R. 2013. *If Mayors Ruled the World. Dysfunctional Nations, Rising Cities.* New Haven: Yale University Press.

Bussemaker, Jet. 2015. *Ruimte voor cultuur. Uitgangspunten voor cultuurbeleid 2017-2020* [Space for Culture: Principles for Cultural Policy 2017-2020]. The Hague: Ministerie van OCW [Ministry of Education, Culture and Science].

Bussemaker, Jet, and Bert Koenders. 2016. *Beleidskader internationaal cultuurbeleid 2017-2020* [Policy Framework for International Cultural Policy 2017-2020]. The Hague: Ministerie OCW [Ministry for Education, Culture and Science].

Castells, Manuel. 2015. *Networks of Outrage and Hope. Social Movements in the Internet Age,* Second edition, enlarged and updated. Cambridge: Polity Press.

De Bruyne, Paul, and Pascal Gielen (eds.). 2011. *Community Art. The Politics of Trespassing.* Amsterdam: Valiz.

De Cauter, Lieven, Ruben de Roo and Karel Vanhaesebrouck (eds.). 2010. *Art and Activism in the Age of Globalization.* Rotterdam: NAi Publishers.

European Cultural Foundation, 2017. *Our Mission.* Retrieved on 15 September 2017 from http://www.culturalfoundation.eu/about-us.

Florida, Richard. 2017. *The New Urban Crisis. How Our Cities are Increasing Inequality, Deepening Segregation, and Failing the Middle Class – and What We Can Do about It.* New York: Basic Books.

Fraser, Nancy. 2014. "Transnationalizing the Public Sphere. On the Legitimacy and Efficacy of Public Opinion in a Post-Westphalian World". In: Kate Nash (ed.), *Transnationalizing the Public Sphere,* pp. 8-42. Cambridge and Malden: Polity Press.

Gielen, Pascal. 2011. "Mapping Community Art". In: Paul De Bruyne and Pascal Gielen (eds.), *Community Art. The Politics of Trespassing,* pp. 15-33. Amsterdam: Valiz.

—. 2015. "A Caravan of Freedom: Mobile Autonomy beyond 'Auto-Mobility'". In: Nico Dockx and Pascal Gielen (eds.), *Mobile Autonomy. Exercises in Artistic Self-Organisation,* pp. 63-83. Amsterdam: Valiz.

Gielen, Pascal, Sophie Elkhuizen, Quirijn van den Hoogen, Thijs Lijster and Hanka Otte. 2015. *Culture. The Substructure for a European Common. A Research Report.* Brussels: Flanders Arts Institute.

Gielen, Pascal, and Thijs Lijster. 2017. "The Civil Potency of a Singular Experience. On the Role of Cultural Organisations in Transnational Civil Undertakings". In: Philipp Dietachmair and Pascal Gielen (eds.), *The Art of Civil Action. Political Space and Cultural Dissent,* pp. 39-63. Amsterdam: Valiz.

Habermas, Jürgen. 1989[1962]. *The Structural Transformation of the Public Sphere. An Inquiry into a Category of Bourgeois Society.* Translated by Thomas Burger from: *Strukturwandel der Öffentlichkeit. Untersuchungen zu einer Kategorie der bürgerlichen Gesellschaft.* Cambridge, MA: MIT Press.

Kolsteeg, Johan. 2017. "Understanding Global/Local Cultural Leadership: Issues and Methods". Paper presented at the 25th ENCATC Congress on Cultural Management and Policy, Brussels, Belgium.

Koopmans, Ruud, and Paul Statham (eds.). 2010. *The Making of a European Public Sphere. Media Discourse and Political Contention.* Cambridge: Cambridge University Press.

Otte, Hanka. 2015. *Binden of overbruggen? Over de relatie tussen kunst, cultuurbeleid en sociale cohesie* [Binding or Bridging? On the Relation Between Art, Cultural Policy and Social Cohesion]. PhD dissertation, Groningen University.

Raad voor Cultuur [Council for Culture]. 2015. *Agenda Cultuur. 2017-2020 en verder* [Agenda Culture: 2017-2020 and Beyond]. The Hague: Raad voor Cultuur.

Ten Thije, Steven. 2017. "The Blind Spot. Art and Politics in the Netherlands". In: Jeroen Boomgaard and Rogier Brom (eds.), *Being Public. How Art Creates the Public*, pp. 69-88. Amsterdam: Valiz.

Van den Hoogen, Quirijn Lennert. 2012. "Cultuurbeleid in de Brave New World van evidence-based policies. Probleemgebied evaluatie van cultuurbeleid [Cultural Policy in the Brave New World of Evidence-Based Policies. Problem Area Evaluation of Cultural Policy]". In: Quirijn van den Hoogen, Berend-Jan Langenberg, Robbert Oosterhuis, Tjeerd Schiphof and Wenda Snijder (eds.), *Handboek Cultuurbeleid* [Handbook of Cultural Policy], pp. III.1-4-1 t/m 32. Doetinchem: Reed Business Media.

Van Herpen, Stan. 2017. "Gemeentelijk cultuurgeld: traditionele instellingen blijven grootverbruikers". Retrieved 7 September 2017 from https://www.cultuurmarketing.nl/verdeling-gemeentelijk-cultuurgeld/#.WbEGOa2iGu4.

Van Houdt, Friso and Willem Schinkel. 2009. "Aspecten van burgerschap. Een historische analyse van de transformaties van het burgerschapsconcept in Nederland" [Aspects of Citizenship. A Historic Analysis of the Transformations of the Concept of Citizenship], *Beleid & maatschappij* 36, 50-58.

Van Maanen, Hans, Maja Sorli, Hedi-Lis Toome, Malieke Wilders, Josh Edelman, Attila Szabó, and Magdolna Balkányi. 2015. "Spectators, Who are They? A Demographic Analysis of Theatre Audiences in Four European Cities", *Amfiteater, Journal of Performing Arts Theory* 3, 1-2: 280-299.

Walzer, Michael. (ed.). 1995. *Toward a Global Civil Society*. Providence and Oxford: Berghahn Books.

6. Dutch Media Policy

Towards the End of Reflective Diversity?

Erik Hitters

6.1 The Third Channel

On 4 April 1988, the Dutch public broadcasting service launched its third television network. This third public channel marks a turning point in the history of public broadcasting in the Netherlands, while at the same time serving as a strategic move to counter the effects of increasing commercialisation. Furthermore, the third channel was the embodiment of the cultural and even artistic policy goals of the media policy (Pots 2000: 409). In the preceding years, the Scientific Council for Government Policy (WRR 1982: 10) had proposed that one of the objectives of Dutch policy on the media should be the protection of the country's cultural achievements and their dissemination through the increasing possibilities of radio and television. From this moment, government policy was to be determined by a media policy based on democracy, pluralism and freedom of expression, together with a cultural policy focused on the preservation and promotion of cultural values. A third television channel could cater to these cultural, artistic expressions that were not sufficiently covered on the two existing channels, which were programmed by independent, non-profit broadcasting associations.

The third public television channel was programmed with a mix of news and information, sports, education and culture. Over the years, the cultural aspirations of the network were toned down as the public broadcaster was attempting to compete with the advent of commercial broadcasting in the 1990s. The cultural objectives of media policy continued to be the subject of debate from the 1990s onward but remained resilient in the drastically changing media landscape in the Netherlands.

This chapter will assess recent media policies and the changes therein by applying insights from policy regime theory, against the background of societal and technological changes. It will explore both this political process, the coalitions that have been forged, and the implicit value system that underlies it.

We consider policy decisions as the outcome of a process characterised by the formulation of different views and interests, expressed by actors or stakeholders that adhere to a certain logic and that engage in debate (Van den Bulck 2012). We will discuss the development of media policy in the Netherlands in relation to the changing nature of cultural policies, the wider public service media debate and debates about the legitimacy of public media policy in general. Our focus will primarily be on two subsectors of media policy: broadcasting and digital media, as these are the spheres in which substantive cultural objectives are most clearly visible. Furthermore, broadcasting (and notably public television) has always been the main focus of media policy, characterised by a relatively high degree of state intervention in the system of public service broadcasting (Bakker & Vasterman n.d.). We will therefore not discuss the press and print media policies.

6.2   The Media Act and the Rationales for a Media Policy

Traditionally, in many Western European countries, the government's cultural and media policies have been organisationally linked. The two policy areas often fall under the same ministry. The same applies to the Netherlands. Since the mid-1980s, both policy areas come under the same Directorate General of Culture and Media of the Ministry of Education, Culture and Science. However, since 2010 the political responsibilities have been divided between the Secretary and the Minister of Education, Culture and Science.

Media policy in the Netherlands is secured in a separate Media Act and thus not subject to the Cultural Policy Act of 1993, as discussed in the other chapters of this book. Interestingly, the Media Act has always been very closely linked to cultural policies, even though they are legally separate policy fields. Media policy, it is safe to argue, has traditionally had very strong cultural objectives. In the consecutive Media Acts of 1987, 2008 and 2016, the legislature has deliberately chosen to integrate media policy into the government's broader cultural policy objectives. In essence, media policy aims to safeguard the independence and reliability of public media, to guarantee plurality and diversity of content and to maintain access and affordability for all citizens. In order to achieve this, the state intervenes at the organisational or intermediary level. Public and commercial media organisations operate in one market for audiences, advertisers and rights and distribution infrastructure. These institutional providers of content are the subject of broadcasting policy, as they are the direct beneficiaries in terms of admission to the broadcasting infrastructure, and also because they are the recipients of funding and other facilities as well as shelters of their programmatic autonomy. In its intentions—and to a limited extent also in its formal, legal effect—classic broadcasting policy is traditionally only partly and indirectly focused on representing the interests and preferences of citizens and consumers. The actual decision-making, nevertheless, is largely a matter of coalitions between specialists and stakeholders in the political and institutional domain (Hoefnagel 2005: 32).

One important and central value of public service broadcasting is independence. Here, the arm's length principle, which is also dominant in the cultural policy domain, is an important guiding principle in the organisation of public broadcasting. The regulation of public as well as commercial broadcasting is in the hands of a Media Authority (*Commissariaat voor de Media*). The authority regulates frequencies for local, public and commercial broadcasters and systematically monitors compliance with the rules on quotas, advertising and the protection of minors. Programming on the three national television channels and public radio channels is delivered by private non-profit broadcasting associations and member organisations representing different groups in society according to a corporatist model (Hallin & Mancini 2004). News and information are delivered by an independent foundation called the NOS (Dutch Broadcasting Foundation – *Nederlandse Omroep Stichting*). The governing body, NPO (Dutch Public Broadcasting – *Nederlandse Publieke Omroep*), is the main responsible entity, whose supervisory board is nominated by the Minister of Education, Culture and Science and appointed by the king's assent.

Another central value underlying the organisation of public service broadcasting is the principle of universality of content and access. Universality is historically tied to the scarcity of access in broadcasting, where a public service provision was needed to ensure the freedom of opinions and the democratic core values of society. Universality of content was needed to attract an audience that was as comprehensive as possible, and this was largely operationalised as broad and generalist programming on one or more broadcast channels, including mass-appeal entertainment programming. In many European public broadcasting policies, universality is safeguarded through legislation promoting media diversity. Diversity is reflective in that the media reflect audience preferences and address the media consumers' expectations (Van Cuilenburg 2007, Van der Wurff 2004). The values of universality, both in content and in access, are under increased pressure by technological developments as well as individualisation trends. Audiences are demanding more distinctive and more thematic and personalised/individualised content as well as presence and ease of access on all relevant media and on-demand platforms.

Both issues of universality and independence remain relevant as well as contested in recent debates. In the run-up to the new Media Act of 2016, heated debates followed plans to constrain entertainment programming as well as to curtail the independence of the NPO by allowing partisan appointments in management and the supervisory board (D'Haenens 2018). In the end, the issues about independence were resolved by precluding direct appointments of the management and the boards. Entertainment programming has been removed as one of the central tasks of public broadcasting. However, it has not been prohibited and subsequently there have not been many changes in the NPO's programming. Interestingly, the issue about entertainment has not been resolved, but the new Media Act does open up the possibility of further restrictions on entertainment programming in the future.

6.3   Media Policy as Cultural Policy

Media policy in the Netherlands is still affected by the remainders of the traditional pillarisation of Dutch society along religious and political lines. Public broadcasting had a monopoly until the late 1980s and was operated by not-for-profit, publicly funded private associations that represented the various social-religious groups—or 'pillars'—in Dutch society. The reflective diversity of media content was thereby safeguarded, as each group was entitled to its own broadcasting organisation, with the amount of its broadcast time depending on its size (Van Cuilenburg 2007). The Dutch media system is fairly unique in that respect, although the system is not unlike others in democratic corporatist European countries (Hallin & Mancini 2004). Over the past 25 years, the Ministry of Education, Culture and Science has tried to break down these old structures and to work towards a system inspired by models such as the British BBC. In the process, the ministry has increasingly emphasised the distinction between commercial and public media. The idea is that the former is aimed at large groups and is largely focused on entertainment, while the latter should target specific audiences—e.g., religious or ethnic minorities—and offer programmes at a 'higher' cultural level.

The strong and deliberate connection between media and cultural policy has its roots in the intense cultural political debates that took place in the 1980s. Here we can observe the typical—and classical—themes underlying the increased intertwining of media and cultural policy: the importance of non-profit cultural provisions, issues of low and high-quality culture, the cultural education of the masses, and resistance to commercial exploitation. Public media could be the ideal instruments to realise broad cultural policy objectives, and the system—as national cultural heritage—needed to be protected from external forces (Hoefnagel 2005).

There are two ways in which the cultural prerogative becomes especially apparent in media policy. The first is the quality issue of programming of public broadcasting. Not only was the broadcasting system meant to reflect the cultural identity of societal groups (the 'pillars'), it also needed to represent national culture and the arts as a cohesive frame of reference for the development of individuals and groups. Media was to retain and enhance cultural values. According to the Scientific Council for Government Policy (WRR 1982), media policy was legitimised not by the individual preferences of audiences but by the high cultural standards of its content. In order to achieve this, broadcasting needed to adopt a similar system of quality control as the arts, whereby professional quality standards were independently assessed. This resulted in a system of quota for public broadcasting, which persists to this day. The minimum amount of programming cultural and artistic content was set at 25%, for news and information this was set at 35%, while entertainment programming was maximised at 25% (Den Hoed & Hoefnagel 2005: 20).

The latter already hints at another phenomenon in which we can clearly see the link between cultural and media policy. The issue of commercial broadcasting and the wider influence of commerce on the field of broadcasting echoes the debates in the 1980s about commercial versus subsidised culture. In broadcasting, this led to a watershed, resulting in a dual system with clearly separated commercial and public broadcasting. The latter became subject to a media policy that more strictly enforced the cultural responsibilities of the public channels. In addition, a dedicated funding body (the Fund for Dutch Cultural Broadcasting Production – *Stimuleringsfonds Nederlandse Culturele Omroepproducties*) was established to promote the development and production of high-quality artistic programmes by the national and regional public broadcasting corporations. It provided subsidies for radio and television programmes in the fields of drama, documentary, feature film, youth, new media and performing arts. Consequently, the deliberate programming of arts and cultural content became a way to counter the dumbing down of audiences by entertainment and commerce.

1989 to 2008: The Commercial Deluge
From 1989 onwards, the Dutch public broadcasting system was forced by European legislation to allow commercial broadcasting on its networks.

The choice for a clear divide between public and commercial broadcasting was explicitly made. The government could, by way of preferential treatment, allocate money and frequencies to public service broadcasting, provided there were special programmatic obligations, given the essential democratic and cultural features of this system. Commercial broadcasters would only be subject to very limited government requirements. This idea of a sharp profiling of the distinctive character of public and commercial broadcasting has always been the spearhead in successive cabinets' policies. For commercial broadcasters, the Dutch government never set more rules than was strictly required by European law, while extensive demands were increasingly placed on the public service broadcasters, given the specific national public interests they were meant to serve (Hoefnagel 2005).

In the two decades that followed, the increasing success of commercial broadcasting forced the public broadcaster to implement strategic responses that were by and large reactive and for the most part ineffective. By sharply profiling channels to cater to specific audiences and by increasing cultural and informational content, the government tried to counter the trend of decreasing market share for the public broadcaster. Nonetheless, by the mid-2000s, the market share of the one-time monopolistic public channels had tumbled to a mere 33% (Mediamonitor n.d.).

Interestingly, given this major watershed, public and commercial media still operate within one market for audiences, advertisers, and rights and distribution infrastructure. The legislator deliberately chose a policy for the public media that combined high-quality standards and regulations with a strategy of mass appeal. The alternative—that is, complementarity of content over the whole spectrum of commercial and public media—was deliberately not adopted. The argument was that willingly marginalising the public broadcaster by focusing solely on information and culture would drive the audiences into the arms of the commercial channels, thereby reducing the diversity of the total offer. The public broadcaster was to serve the nation and reflect national culture as a whole, in all its diversity.

A number of instruments were introduced in order for the public broadcaster to be able to compete with its commercial counterparts. While the strict regulations on advertising and sponsorship were eased, broadcasting organisations were forced to cooperate in a new, leaner organisational structure. In addition, the tasks of the public broadcaster were more specifically articulated, which ensured the pluriform nature of programming, high quality, representation and access. Also, the quota were specified: 35% information and education, 25% culture (half of which was dedicated to art), 50% Dutch-speaking, and 25% outsourced from independent producers.

A triad of very critical reports between 2003 and 2005 resulted in a period of fierce debate about the future of public broadcasting. The Dutch Council for Culture strongly criticised the cultural substance of public broadcasting (Raad voor Cultuur 2003). An external review committee was established to report on the way the public service broadcasting system could meet its social responsibilities. This committee's similarly critical report concluded that the system's joint responsibility was not working and that it was inefficient, indecisive, unprofessional and lacked leadership (Commissie Rinnooy-Kan 2004). And in 2005, the Scientific Council for Government Policy published its report *Focus on Functions (Focus op Functies)* on the future of media policy (WRR 2005). It advised the government to radically change its media policy from one in which each medium and infrastructure is subjected to separate policies to one that implements a vision on the functions of the media landscape as a whole. More specifically, the council suggested that public broadcasters should only focus on those functions that are not met by the system as a whole, including the commercial networks. This meant that entertainment as well as advertising should no longer be desirable or needed.

In reaction to these criticisms, a strong advocacy coalition of broadcast associations together with the left-wing opposition successfully defended the existing structure. Despite the opposition, the initial plans for a new Media Act, which was needed to align it with European media regulations, still included the proposal to no longer allow mass entertainment in the portfolio. Although the Labour Party joined the governing coalition in 2007 after years of having been in the opposition, the new Media Act was not radically transformed in this respect. Its major achievement was the inclusion of internet activities as central to the objectives of public service media, which reignited the debate about public broadcasting's role in society.

2008 to 2017: The Reculturalisation of Media Policy

Over the years, the neo-liberal agenda of government, backed by media entrepreneurs and commercial broadcasters, was successfully countered by a strong advocacy coalition of broadcast associations with changing political support from both the Labour Party as well as conservative religious parties (cf. Van den Bulck & Donders 2014). A major debate about the market activities and market appeal of public media raged throughout the ten years following the new Media Act of 2008. What this debate brought to the fore was the issue of the legitimation crisis of public media. Why would a government need to fund services that were already for a large part provided by market institutions? Should a public service be allowed to compete with market forces for the favour of mass audiences? What distinguishes (or ought to distinguish) public service media from its commercial counterparts?

A discussion from this period that exemplifies the strong paradoxical relation between public service media and the market involved the salaries of star news hosts, radio deejays and television personalities appearing on public media. It clearly shows that public and commercial media operate within the same market for audiences and advertisers but also that they compete for the same specialised labour. Some voiced their objection to the fact that the salaries of media stars were up to three times the salary of the prime minister. Opponents argued that it was ridiculous for taxpayer money to be spent on this and that if these personalities were so popular and valuable, commercial media should be the ones to capitalise on them. The public broadcasters countered by referring to the necessity of mass appeal as well as the distinctive qualities of the content that these personalities created. If they no longer had access to these kinds of stars, audiences would defer to commercial media and the media offer as a whole would deteriorate.

The latter also shows how important audience ratings remained. Even though the Media Act of 2008 allowed more online and non-linear activities for public service media, this did not counter the trend of an aging audience and public broadcasting's diminishing appeal to younger media users. This younger audience began consuming more and more international as well as commercial content, which is increasingly provided by internet-based platforms (e.g., YouTube, Facebook). The public service media were quickly losing their connection to these audiences. Even though the NPO's market share remained fairly stable over the years at around 30%, the reach of broadcast media was diminishing overall to the benefit of online content, user-generated content and non-linear international on-demand content.

This was underscored by matters of efficiency and organisation, which deepened the legitimacy crisis of public service media. A widely shared opinion among the public as well as in politics was that the organisation of the public media system, with its corporatist structure still well intact, was no longer fit for the twenty-first century. The Boston Consulting Group concluded that there were large efficiency gains to be achieved if this structure were replaced by an approach akin to the BBC (BCG 2011). The political coalition, which still favoured retaining the old structures, crumbled over the years, while at the same time public trust in the public media suffered. Following the Boston Consulting Group's advice, the government slashed the media budget in two waves of severe cost-cutting: under the successive cabinets of Prime Minister Mark Rutte (2010-2017), the publicly funded budget was cut by €175 million (from a total of €850 million). Savings were found in increased organisational, operational and programmatic efficiency (D'Haenens 2018).

Nevertheless, when compared to European counterparts, the Dutch public broadcasting system is not very expensive. A comparative study of 11 European public broadcasters by Raats et al. (2015) calculated that the NPO government grant amounted to €50 per capita, which was the lowest annual amount of all broadcasters. The much-praised BBC, for instance, receives €113 per capita. Another feature of the Dutch system is its income from advertising. Roughly 70% of its revenue is public money, but the remaining 30% is generated through commercial means, for the most part through advertising (23.2%). Again, this was the highest percentage among the 11 European public broadcasters studied by Raats et al. (D'Haenens 2018).

In 2016 a neo-liberal government coalition attempted to modernise the public media by introducing a new Media Act. The new Act made three radical changes deemed necessary for the public media to remain relevant. Media have become increasingly global, and viewers and listeners are turning away from traditional media in favour of YouTube, Netflix and other online digital content. The first major change was the reduction in the number of licensed public broadcast associations from 21 to eight, while smaller religious or politically ideological associations were discontinued altogether. A second related efficiency measure was to give more central power to the NPO in deciding content and strategy. Specifically, the government decided to strengthen the characteristic quality of public programming, setting criteria for distinctiveness, innovativeness and participatory content in addition to the already existing criteria of independence, pluriformity, cultural diversity and reliability. The third intervention was to restrict public broadcasting's programming to education, information and culture. In order to distinguish itself from commercial providers, it was decided that mass appeal entertainment should no longer be part of the remit of public broadcasting.

In conclusion, the Media Act of 2016 can be seen as a paradigmatic shift compared to the years preceding it. In order to enhance the legitimacy of public service media and to stifle the ongoing discussion about market competition, the government chose to re-culturalise media policy with a renewed focus on distinctive quality and innovative content (Raad voor Cultuur 2014). As mainstream programming can now be left to commercial networks, public media policy seems to have abandoned the underlying value of reflective diversity and moved towards a public service broadcaster that complements market failure (Van Cuilenburg 2007). In that respect, Dutch media policy has once again become increasingly similar to the broader cultural policy agenda. Nevertheless, entertainment content has not been prohibited, and to date, programming of the NPO has not significantly changed. Many programmes under the heading of 'culture' are still entertainment-based formats such as talent shows, quizzes, etc. Nevertheless, the new Media Act does open up the possibility of further limitations to entertainment programming in the future.

6.4   From Reflective Diversity to Complementary Diversity

Over the last 25 years, the public service media system in the Netherlands has undergone a number of major shifts, amounting to what may be labelled a paradigmatic change. The latest changes that have been made to the system have meant that the principle of reflective diversity has been abandoned. The public service broadcasters are no longer bound by universality in terms of content, as their remit now obliges them to explicitly differentiate themselves from commercial media. Distinctiveness and competitiveness should be achieved through high-quality innovative programming that is inspired by public values and in the public interest (Raad voor Cultuur 2014). Audience ratings should cease to be the predominant criterion for success; instead, public broadcasting should focus on audience reach. Who are their audiences and are they the ones that, in the light of their public responsibility, need to be reached? Reflective diversity has been replaced by what may be called 'complementary diversity'. Complementarity is the principle that public service media should supply content that is not provided by commercial broadcasters, or, to put it in more general terms, the main reason to subsidise public services is that their inherent objectives are not realised in the market (Donders 2012: 34). Public service broadcasting subsequently dedicates itself to redressing market failure.

Dutch media policy has abandoned the idea of full portfolio distinctiveness (Jakubowicz 2006), which ensures universality of content as a basic supply on generalist channels (including mass appeal, entertainment programming) and universality across the full portfolio of services, some of them specialised or tailored to specific audiences, adding up to a more extensive and comprehensive range of services (ibid. 13). While the full portfolio argument is still a guiding principle for many European public service media systems and might even have been operationalised in the

Dutch system, the Dutch government has chosen to fall back on a somewhat old-fashioned criterion of distinctive quality, failing to tie this in with the other aspect of universality: access. According to Jakobowicz, the discussion of quality, including all kinds of niche content, needs to be undertaken in the light of increasing personalisation options through digitalisation and multi-platform access. Here, the Dutch government has missed an opportunity. As far as access is concerned, this remains an issue of debate. Certainly, the public media are present in the online domain with their on-demand postponed viewing services. Nonetheless, they are bound to their own dedicated platforms, as they are legally prohibited to cooperate with commercial parties such as YouTube and Facebook. They thus have limited possibilities for personalising content per individual, and this kind of restriction of online content distribution may lead to innovation failure in the long run.

Media policy in the Netherlands has undergone paradigmatic changes. Severe financial cutbacks have resulted in weaker power arrangements, which in turn have opened up the possibility of a paradigmatic policy shift. This has resulted in a lean and relatively cost-efficient media system, allowing limited commercial cooperation and using technological opportunities and innovations. The latter shows that an economic paradigm has become more central over the years, as is apparent in the broader field of cultural policy. In the process, the system has lost its societal pluriformity in terms of reflectiveness and universality and has moved towards a more market-oriented reflection of identities and lifestyles. The paradigm of a media system representing traditional distinctions in society has lost its relevance and legitimacy. Over the years, the cultural paradigm has remained remarkably resilient in debates about the media. Media policy, even more than cultural policy, has embraced the discourse of efficiency, audience targeting, branding and innovation. The value of public media is again being legitimised through quality and distinctive content. While no longer being only instrumental, media policy is still sustaining its similarity to the broader objectives of cultural policy. Nevertheless, public media fulfil the essential public demands of safeguarding democracy and pluriformity and enhancing cultural values and participation. If such objectives are to be realised under restricted budgets and within the remainders of a market dominated by mainstream commercial programming, public media run the risk of marginalisation. Ultimately, media policy must address the issues of legitimacy, how public service media can adapt to changing circumstances, what we can expect from it, and how it should be organised and financed.

Bibliography

Bakker, Piet, and Peter Vasterman. n.d. *Media Landscapes: The Netherlands*. Accessed 20 November 2017. http://ejc.net/media_landscapes/the-netherlands.

BCG – Boston Consulting Group. 2011. *Efficiëntieonderzoek Landelijke Publieke Omroep*. In opdracht van het Ministerie van Onderwijs, Cultuur en Wetenschap. [Efficiency Assessment of National Public Broadcasting]. Amsterdam: BCG.

Commissie Rinnooy Kan. 2004. *'Omzien naar de omroep'. Rapport van de visitatiecommissie landelijke publieke omroep 2000-2004*, ['Looking after Broadcasting', Report by the Visitation Committee of National Public Broadcasting 2000-2004]. The Hague: SDU.

Donders, Karin. 2012. *Public Service Media and Policy in Europe*. London: Palgrave Macmillan UK.

D'Haenens, Leen. 2018. "The Netherlands: Organisational Transformation, a Means to Do More with Less?" In: Christian Herzog (ed.), *Transparency and Funding of Public Service Media–Die Deutsche Debatte im internationalen Kontext*, pp. 31-40. Wiesbaden: Springer Verlag.

Den Hoed, P., and F.J.P.M. Hoefnagel. 2005. *Beleid inzake media, cultuur en kwaliteit* [Policy Regarding Media, Culture and Quality]. Amsterdam: Amsterdam University Press.

Hallin, Daniel C., and Paolo Mancini. 2004. *Comparing Media Systems: Three Models of Media and Politics*. Cambridge: Cambridge University Press.

Hoefnagel, F.J.P.M. 2005. *Geschiedenis van het Nederlands inhoudelijk mediabeleid* [History of Dutch Media Content Policy]. Amsterdam: Amsterdam University Press.

Jakubowicz, Karol. 2006. "PSB: The Beginning of The End, or a New Beginning in the 21st Century?". Presentation at RIPE@ 2006 Conference: Public Service Broadcasting in the Multimedia Environment: Programmes and Platforms. Amsterdam.

Mediamonitor. n.d. [online]. *Televisie in 2007*. Accessed 25 October 2017. http://www.mediamonitor.nl/mediamarkten/televisie/televisie-in-2007.

Pots, Roel. 2000. *Cultuur, koningen en democraten. Overheid en cultuur in Nederland* [Culture, Kings and Democrats. Government and Culture in the Netherlands]. Nijmegen: Uitgeverij SUN.

Raad voor Cultuur. 2003. *Advies over het mediabeleid* [Advice on Media Policy]. The Hague: Raad voor Cultuur [Council for Culture].

—. 2014. *De tijd staat open. Advies voor een toekomstbestendige publieke omroep.* [De Tijd Staat Open: Advise on a future-proof Public Broadcasting System]. The Hague: Raad voor Cultuur [Council for Culture].

Raats, Tim, Hilde van den Bulck, Leen d'Haenens, Anne-Sofie Vanhaeght, Sanne Ruelens, Paulien Coppens, Nathalie Claessens, Miriam van der Burg and Elke Ichau. 2015. *Benchmark van de publieke omroep in Europa: een analyse van het aanbod, financiering en publieksbereik* [Benchmark of Public Broadcasters in Europe: Analysis of Supply, Financing and Audience Reach]. Brussels/Antwerp/Leuven: Vrije Universiteit Brussel, Antwerp University, KU Leuven.

Van Cuilenburg, Jan. 2007. "Media diversity, competition and concentration: Concepts and theories". In: Els de Bens (ed.), *Media between Culture and Commerce*, pp. 25-54. Bristol: Intellect Books.

Van den Bulck, Hilde. 2012. "Tracing media policy decisions: Of stakeholders, networks and advocacy coalitions". In: Monroe E. Price, Stefaan Verhulst, and Libby Morgan (eds.), *Routledge Handbook of Media Law*, pp. 17-34. London: Routledge.

Van den Bulck, Hilde, and Karen Donders. 2014. "Analyzing European Media Policy: Stakeholders and Advocacy Coalitions". In: Karen Donders, Caroline Pauwels and Jan Loisen (eds.), *The Palgrave Handbook of European Media Policy*, pp. 19-35. London: Palgrave Macmillan.

Van der Wurff, Richard. 2004. "Supplying and viewing diversity The role of competition and viewer choice in Dutch broadcasting", *European Journal of Communication* 19(2): 215-237.

WRR [Scientific Council for Government Policy]. 1982. *Samenhangend Mediabeleid,* Rapport aan de regering 24. [Coherent Media Policy. Report to the Government 24]. The Hague: Staatsuitgeverij.

—. 2005. *Focus op functies, uitdagingen voor een toekomstbestendig mediabeleid,* Rapport aan de regering 71. [Focus on Functions. Challenges for a Future-Proof Media Policy. Report to the Government 71]. Amsterdam: Amsterdam University Press.

'A More Holistic Approach to Problems'

An Interview with Hans Poll and Jacqueline Roelofs

Artist impression Groninger Forum
© NL Architects

'Embracing the future' is the main goal of the Groninger Forum, the new cultural centre in the heart of the city which will be completed by the middle of 2019. The impressive building will host a range of cultural institutions and functions, including the city library, a movie theatre, Storyworld (a museum of comic strips, animation and games) and debates. The marketing and programme director, Hans Poll: 'The Groninger Forum is to become an easily accessible meeting place for curious people of all ages and backgrounds. The programming will focus on three domains: current affairs & society, popular culture, and knowledge & technology. With our programming, we want to prepare people for the future by giving them an opportunity to get acquainted with the many new developments that are facing us. Themes that will be covered include nanotechnology, robotisation, artificial intelligence and popular image culture. Our principle is that it's better to have a future that you can see coming than a future that happens to you.'

The aim is to achieve integral programming whenever possible, combining the strengths of the individual functions in the shape of workshops, playgrounds, courses, exhibitions, lectures and master classes. Poll remarks that they are 'always playful and accessible, because fun is a condition for success.' There are literally no walls between the library, exhibition space, debate area and movie theatre. 'We are a single organisation and not a kind of multi-tenant office building. That makes it possible to highlight themes in a joined-up and multidisciplinary way,' he explains.

It is not only the Forum's programming that is geared towards meetings and interaction but also the striking new building. There will be activities aimed especially at audiences who are less likely to visit the city centre, such as families with children. 'It's no longer at the football club that we meet each other but at the library and soon also at the Groninger Forum,' says Poll. 'We have deliberately opted for an easily accessible building with a transparent column in the centre of an entrance hall which works its way up ten floors in the shape of an apple corer.' Attached to this column are multiple 'plazas' providing space for the library, interactive installations or workshops. 'And catering facilities, of course'.

The essence of the Groninger Forum fits perfectly into the legal function of the library as described in the Public Library Act (Wet Stelsel Opbenare Bibliotheekvoorzieningen, WSOB), which came into effect in 2015: helping people in their personal development and preparing them for their future. The public library is currently in transition from being a traditional lending library to a public and educational institution, Jacqueline Roelofs explains. She is the market and innovation manager at Biblionet Groningen, the network of public libraries in the province of Groningen. 'The new library act, which enshrines the five core functions—reading, education, information, debate, and arts and culture—provides helpful support. We have come to focus on a broad range of activities aimed at improving the literacy and digital skills—twenty-first-century skills—of vulnerable groups. Whereas we used to get our knowledge from books, we now have a variety of sources at our disposal. Think of films, websites, virtual reality and games. That is why the integration of the city library into the Groninger Forum is a logical step.' Poll: 'It's no longer just the librarian, curator or programmer who decides which sources matter; people do that themselves these days, with the help of social media.'

The new library act specifies the role of the three levels of government in the library system. The basic principle is that he who pays the piper calls the tune, explains Roelofs. 'While this layered system does offer support to local and provincial governments, it unfortunately also leaves them a lot of room for interpretation. Elected representatives are free to set policy priorities, and that doesn't always work out well for libraries. There is room for improvement in the current law to create more certainty for libraries.'

One of the problems, she explains, is that local governments are supposed to set the direction but do not always act accordingly. 'Local governments should take a more holistic approach to problems and ask themselves what institutions such as ours can contribute jointly. Which social objectives do you want to achieve as local government together with the library and other institutions? Greater participation, fewer people with low literacy, anything else?' Too often, local governments still regard libraries as purely cultural institutions and fail to recognise the broad range of social and educational activities they undertake. 'We are talking to the alderman for culture, but we would like him to be joined by his colleagues for social affairs and education.'

The main challenge according to Poll is for the local government to be aware of the hybrid organisation that Forum is. 'We have chosen to achieve various goals across a range of policy areas by means of crossovers and more diffuse forms of transferring information, but that requires flexibility from the donor organisation. The city of Groningen understands this, but now this needs to be turned into clear and comprehensive annual agreements. The challenge for us is to continue to inspire a wide audience with our programming, making every Groninger feel at home here and say: "It's always exiting to go to the Forum."'

Jack van der Leden

7.   Cultural Education Policy

Its Justification and Organisation

Teunis IJdens and Edwin van Meerkerk

Introduction

The inclusion of cultural education as a separate policy area in this book on *cultural* policy in the Netherlands is not self-evident. Cultural education is a hybrid field. It includes learning and teaching arts and cultural subjects at primary and secondary school (formal education) but also acquiring and transmitting arts and aesthetic/cultural competencies in other, non-formal and informal settings: e.g., art and music classes as a leisure activity, the educational activities of museums and other cultural organisations, and 'learning by doing' as an amateur. A chapter regarding cultural education at school might therefore just as well have been part of a book on Dutch *education* policy, while out-of-school cultural education might be part of a book on *leisure* policy.

The fact that cultural education policy is often considered a branch of *cultural* policy reflects a key problem in Dutch cultural education policy itself: its justification from the perspective of arts and culture and its virtual absence in mainstream education policy. Schools, especially primary schools, are often criticised by arts and cultural professionals (and by parents who value the arts and culture highly) for doing too little and not doing it properly. While this is not a crucial issue in official education policy—to put it mildly—several initiatives to promote cultural education at school have been taken from the perspective of arts advocacy and cultural policy. One can imagine that this may well reproduce the often-cited gap between 'school and culture' instead of narrowing it. There is an obvious paradox or vicious circle here: the deplored marginal position of the arts in school (Raad voor Cultuur & Onderwijsraad 2012) is supposed to be improved by measures that are marginal to schools.

This chapter explores cultural education's hybrid character as a policy domain as well as continuities and discontinuities in Dutch cultural education policy since the 1990s. Section 2 addresses the *justification* of public policy based on values attributed to cultural education. The desired and expected benefits of cultural education for individual learners and for society vary from arts-centred learning effects to various non-arts outcomes, and from broad values to more or less specific goals. Section 3 analyses the *delineations and jurisdictions* of cultural education: how cultural education is defined, in which settings it is practiced, and which government levels and agencies are responsible and accountable for developing and implementing cultural education policy. Sections 4 and 5 analyse *changes* in Dutch cultural education policy at the national level, especially regarding arts education at school, since the 1990s. These consist of some system-level updates as well as the launching of compensatory, additional and temporary programmes; and a shift in policy goals from promoting cultural participation *through* arts education to promoting quality *in* arts education. Section 6 focuses on the vicissitudes of non-formal arts education, partly at the national policy level but largely at the local level. The final section 7 summarises the main arguments, draws conclusions, and explores policy issues for the next decade.

The term cultural education policy deserves a final introductory note. In this chapter, we generally use the broad term 'cultural education'. In the Netherlands, this refers to learning and teaching competencies in doing, making, understanding, enjoying and appreciating art (in the broadest sense) and cultural heritage. Learners are persons of all ages in various settings, but the vocational education and training of artists and cultural professionals is not included. Our focus is on *arts* education at primary and secondary school, without omitting non-formal arts education. By 'cultural education policy', we mean any public policy—i.e., 'decisions (including both actions and non-actions) of a government or an equivalent authority' (Weible 2014: 4)—with regard to cultural education and its systemic conditions, especially regulation and funding. This includes policies at the national level, the level of the provinces, and the level of municipalities. It also includes policy networks of governmental and non-governmental actors (Rhodes 2008): the social structure of the 'cultural education polder' in the Netherlands at different levels and across levels of policy.

7.1   The Value of Cultural Education

Public policy regarding cultural education, like any other policy, needs to be justified. Cultural education policy ultimately rests on the belief that cultural education is somehow beneficial for individuals and society and that it deserves public support and care. However, what benefits is cultural education supposed to provide?

Arts and culture may be regarded as valuable in themselves, as a part of every person's life and as a unique quality of society. Learning arts and aesthetic competencies and learning to understand and appreciate the arts and cultural heritage is a primary and unique outcome of cultural education. Nevertheless, while this is also the most desirable outcome and sufficient justification for some, others may desire, expect or demand more far-reaching benefits for individuals and for society.

Experts around the world consider many different benefits to be relevant for assessing the impact or outcome of arts education (IJdens 2018a). An analysis of correlations between ratings of 50 different items indicated five distinct but not mutually exclusive types of expected benefits:

a. benefits for *creativity and innovation* in education and society;
b. benefits for *arts and aesthetic competencies*;
c. *intercultural* benefits (transcultural awareness, dialogue among cultures, appreciation of cultural diversity);
d. *political* benefits (e.g., democracy, citizenship);
e. various *other non-arts* benefits (reducing school dropout rates and absenteeism, mental and physical health and well-being, achievement in school, young people's employability, etc.).

Creativity and innovation benefits were rated highest, arts and aesthetics benefits came next, intercultural benefits in third place, political benefits fourth. Other non-arts benefits were rated last, on average, but still more positive than negative. Dutch experts rate arts and aesthetic benefits equally high as other European experts but place less value on creativity and innovation benefits and on political, social and other non-arts benefits.

The discourse on 'creativity and innovation' or 'twenty-first-century skills' has attracted much attention in the Netherlands and elsewhere. This discourse emerged in the United States as early as the 1980s; it was adopted by the European Union in its 2000 Lisbon Strategy and carried further by the OECD in its Innovation Strategy (OECD 2010). The OECD's Centre for Education and Innovation (CERI) included education and training in the arts in its research programme, as a field that is (supposedly) strongly associated with creativity and innovation. However, the publication by the OECD of a review study of research into the assumed impact of arts education on various non-arts skills (Winner, Goldstein & Vincent-Lancrin 2013) soon tempered exaggerated claims of so-called transfer effects, including its impact on thinking skills and creativity. The authors concluded that there is no conclusive evidence for transfer effects of arts learning to other domains, and that research into the impact of arts education needs first and foremost to establish a solid theoretical and methodological framework.

Although this OECD study seemed to bring the debate back to learning arts and aesthetic skills as a goal in itself, justifications of cultural education policy keep oscillating between 'intrinsic' and varying non-arts benefits. In

2015, in the wake of the OECD report but in spite of its main conclusions, a new funding scheme for music education at primary school in the Netherlands again stated that a solid cultural education is important for children's and young people's creativity, for the development of twenty-first-century skills, and for society's creative capacity (*Staatscourant* 13 October 2015). In a policy paper that was published as this chapter took its final shape, the new Minister of Education, Culture and Science firmly stated that culture primarily has its 'own, intrinsic value' and that culture is 'a counterforce of crucial importance' when 'rationalisation and return on investment are dominant issues in society' (Van Engelshoven 2018). In committing extra resources for music education at school, Van Engelshoven first stresses music's intrinsic value but then refers to neuroscientific research highlighting connections between musical skills and various cognitive, motor, emotional and social skills. The 'music is good for the brain' argument has replaced the discredited 'music makes you smart' argument as a key asset in music education advocacy in recent years (cf. Haanstra 2012, 2016).

These examples just go to show that policies and policy programmes are often justified by referring to supposed wider benefits of cultural education for individuals and society. Evidence for such outcomes may be lacking or poor, or not really refer to education and training but only to engaging in practicing an arts discipline itself—like listening to music or playing music. However, even generally acknowledged and proven benefits of cultural education should not be confused with benefits and goals of cultural education *policy*. A policy—choosing priorities for allocating public resources, setting goals, devising programmes and implementing them—that refers to cherished values of cultural education may be legitimate because it is thought to be 'for the good', but that does not necessarily mean that it is also effective and efficient (cf. Hoogerwerf & Herweijer 2008). In fact, statements regarding policy goals (not only for cultural education) vary greatly, from expressing values (what is good or bad about something) and indicating directions (where to go or not to go) to specifying targets: situations that must be achieved within a certain period of time. In section 4 we will show that cultural education policy in the Netherlands is diligent in allocating resources, hesitant in choosing directions, and reluctant in setting targets and measuring policy impact.

7.2   Delineations and Jurisdictions

This section describes the cultural education policy field in the Netherlands, starting with necessary *delineations* (definitions and distinctions), then the system of *jurisdictions* in this field (the division of authority, responsibility and accountability) and finally the *political context and status* of cultural education policy.

Delineations

Delineations of cultural education policy must start with a general definition of cultural education. In the Netherlands, the term cultural education (*cultuureducatie*) was introduced in the 1990s to incorporate arts education as well as cultural heritage education. The new name implied that in cultural education policy, a broad definition became dominant, shifting its focus from the 'high' arts to all cultural expressions. The glossary of the National Centre of Expertise for Cultural Education and Amateur Arts (LKCA) defines cultural education as 'deliberate learning about and with arts, cultural heritage and media through targeted instruction, at school as well as out of school' (https://www.lkca.nl/primair-onderwijs/begrippen#). So arts education is one of the three areas of cultural education, next to cultural heritage and media education.

In these definitions, 'school' means primary and secondary education, not vocational training. Out-of-school generally means in leisure time, as a voluntary activity. This refers to an important distinction in settings of learning that applies worldwide: formal education, non-formal education and informal learning. A glossary of the UNESCO Institute for Lifelong Learning (UIL 2012) states that *formal* learning 'takes place in education and training institutions, is recognised by relevant national authorities and leads to diplomas and qualifications. Formal learning is structured according to educational arrangements such as curricula, qualifications and teaching-learning requirements.' This applies fully to arts education at primary and secondary school. The UIL defines *non-formal* learning as 'learning that has been acquired in addition or alternatively to formal learning'; in general, it has a similar but more flexible structure as opposed to formal learning, and it 'usually takes place in community-based settings, the workplace and through the activities of civil society organisations'. Taking arts classes or cultural heritage courses as a voluntary leisure activity are typically non-formal cultural education. The UIL glossary finally defines *informal* learning as 'learning that occurs in daily life, in the workplace, in communities and through interests and activities of individuals' in any given place, form or context. Informal learning in arts and culture happens through attending cultural events and visiting cultural venues but also intentionally, e.g., by learning to play music or to make a video with friends, in the family or through the internet. However, these forms of informal learning are usually not included in cultural education as it is understood in the Netherlands but labelled as cultural participation or amateur practice.

In connection with different settings of learning, another delineation again refers to the hybrid character of the cultural education field. Cultural education practice is embedded in, dependent on and inspired by different 'parental' or related fields that each have their own structures, beliefs, logics and dynamics. In the Netherlands, these are the fields of education, the arts, cultural heritage and leisure.

These are analytical distinctions, based on the defining characteristics of the settings of arts and cultural learning and of related broader fields, but they have a strong *institutional* dimension. The different settings of arts and cultural learning and 'parental' fields have different organisational shapes and different values, and actors within these settings and fields have different ways of doing things. These are real differences, marked by boundaries and conventions that cannot be removed or changed easily. Yet these institutional domains are also *historical* phenomena, which means that they emerged, evolved and were constructed *and* that they are not static and resistant to change. We will consider the possibility of shifting boundaries at the end of this section.

Jurisdictions

Cultural education's multiple hybridity has two important consequences. First, it means that professional and organisational thinking and behaviour in this field can be seen from different perspectives, depending on different field regimes and cultural education settings. What to do and how to do it well: these are potentially controversial issues when professionals and organisations from different fields, settings and disciplinary backgrounds enter into common situations. In the Netherlands, as in other countries, projects and programmes for cooperation between schools and arts and cultural actors provide rich case histories of encounters between the major regimes of formal education and the arts (cf. Dieleman 2010, Hoogeveen & Beekhoven 2016). Subsequent government programmes aimed at improving the collaboration between schools and cultural institutions—each new programme implying that previous efforts did not succeed in bringing about lasting relationships—affirm the difficulty of bringing the two worlds together.

The second consequence of cultural education's hybridity is similar to the first, but it concerns the level of policy jurisdictions with regard to regulation and funding. It is remarkable that, in the Netherlands, legislation and other forms of ruling with regard to cultural education are considered to belong to cultural policy rather than to education policy. This is fully understandable as far as the national funding of arts and cultural organisations is concerned, in conjunction with (urgent) appeals to these organisations for educational activities. Nevertheless, since the 1990s, most national policy initiatives regarding arts education at school were also taken by the *cultural policy* departments of the Ministry of Welfare, Health, and Culture (WVC) and its successor, the Ministry of Education, Culture and Science (OCW) instead of the departments or directorates for primary and secondary education. As a result, cultural education remains an 'outside' phenomenon from the perspective of many schools and teachers (Van Meerkerk 2016).

Yet, even though Dutch cultural education policy is predominantly cultural policy, its scope is restricted by the implications of education policy. The most important aspect of this is the constitutional tenet of school autonomy. As the OECD has remarked, Dutch primary and secondary schools 'are highly autonomous on matters related to resource allocation, curriculum and assessment as compared to other OECD countries. School boards are responsible for governance of schools and implementation of national education policy.' (OECD 2014). In other words, attempts to change the school curriculum from a cultural policy perspective face a double challenge, as they require a change in education policy as well as school policy.

Public policy authority over (cultural) education in primary and secondary schools lies nearly completely with national government. The Ministry of Education, Culture and Science funds all levels of education, private as well as public schools, through a lump sum allocation. There is a legal framework for regular public funding. The regulation and funding of non-formal cultural education are responsibilities of local governments. However, this policy lacks a legal framework: municipalities are free to grant or withhold funding depending on their political and financial priorities. As a result, the goals and scope of local policies differ widely depending on the political landscape in each municipality, and may even be contrary to the goals of cultural policy as laid down in the national government's Cultural Policy Act (CPA).

Besides the distinction between 'territorial' levels of government (national and local, and in some cases provincial), there is also a 'functional' division of funding and regulatory jurisdictions between government and semi-public agencies. For cultural education at school and out-of-school, the Cultural Participation Fund and the LKCA (National Centre of Expertise for Cultural Education and Amateur Arts) are the most important national agencies. Some cities (e.g., Amsterdam, Rotterdam) and provinces (e.g., Noord Brabant, Gelderland) have similar agencies for carrying out part of their policies.

Cultural Education Policy and Politics

When studying cultural education policy, one should not neglect politics. Public regulation and funding, policy measures and programmes generally depend on political decisions and justifications and may therefore be subject to political debate and conflict. However, in the case of cultural education, there seems to be a broad but rather indifferent consensus among politicians on its value. As a result, cultural education is hardly a political issue, even though much effort is spent by civil servants and professional stakeholders on developing and implementing policy measures. In other words, there may well be a lack of cultural education *politics* and an excess of cultural education *policy*.

As the political status of cultural education is low, an elaborate system of funding and regulation may be restricted in its legitimacy. Usually, this is not an issue in national politics, though it sometimes is in local politics— but mainly because of budget cuts. In other words, the central aspects of what Mark Moore calls the 'strategic triangle' of public value, sources of legitimacy and support (i.e. politics), and an operational infrastructure (Benington & Moore 2010) are off balance. While cultural education's public value is hardly questioned and the supporting infrastructure is guaranteed by structural funding, both political and public support for cultural education are weak spots in cultural education policy. As a result, cultural education has been an easy target for budget cuts, both nationally (with the abolishment of a reduced-fare pass for high school students in 2010) and locally, where music schools were closed in several towns after the financial crisis of 2008.

Prospects

In 2001, the OECD published six scenarios for the future of schooling (OECD 2001). The fifth scenario—'Learner networks and the network society'—directly relates to the distinction between formal and non-formal arts education. The scenario predicts the rise of 'communities of interest'. The OECD fears that this development will cause 'potentially serious equity problems'. If, for instance, informal facilities for acquiring aesthetic and cultural skills (through media, the internet, private networks) become more attractive and effective than learning and teaching arts at school, formal arts education may become obsolete (IJdens 2018b).

In the Netherlands and elsewhere, informal learning is usually not included in arts education or cultural education policy. The extension of learning opportunities in arts and culture beyond traditional institutions of formal and non-formal education will be a challenging issue in education policy, including cultural education, in the coming decades (Heijnen 2015, OECD 2016). With many Dutch centres for non-formal cultural education in dire straits after the austerity measures between 2011 and 2015, the local infrastructure differs greatly from one place to the next. Cultural education policy measures thus far have aimed at strengthening the bonds between schools and cultural institutions. The most prominent of these measures will end in 2020. Whether a new perspective on cultural education will surface—one that includes informal and non-formal education—is hard to predict. The shift from primary schools to integrated 'child centres', where non-formal cultural education is included in daylong programmes, shows that this tendency is indeed gaining a foothold.

In addition, social welfare tends to become a new context of cultural education practice. In this, Dutch cultural education follows a pattern that has been set elsewhere. In Germany, for instance, legislation has been enacted regarding youth care and family services (KuBi Online). Some cultural education professionals also envision cultural education becoming part of creativity-driven technological and economic innovation. The latter perspective is also visible in Dutch cultural policy (in spite of the doubts on the beneficial effects mentioned above). In the field of cultural education, a tendency towards the integration of social and cultural goals is visible, especially in the connection of cultural activities and healthcare. Whether this will result in a substantial shift in the institutional structure of the cultural education field is hard to tell.

7.3   Systemic Updates

Values and desired and expected benefits typically prevail in political and public *discourse* on policy, including political communication via public speech or social media by the Minister of (or Secretary for) Education, Culture and Science. Official policy itself consists of politically authorised *decisions* regarding: (a) systemic regulation and funding (e.g., of primary education), and (b) additional and usually temporary funding programmes for specific issues or situations (IJdens & Van Hoorn 2014).

This section gives a concise review of systemic, usually legal updates of regulation and funding since the 1990s, focusing on cultural education at primary and secondary school. The next section 7.4 gives an overview of additional policies and programmes for cultural education.

Cultural Education in the National Cultural Policy System
Systemic regulation and funding within the context of national cultural policy—which is under the responsibility of the Secretary for Culture—directly relates to arts and cultural education through the basic cultural infrastructure. This system has three pillars. First, since 1997, the Ministry of Education, Culture and Science has communicated that cultural organisations receiving direct government subsidies within the framework of the four-year planning period should have an educational programme. This has not changed in principle, but the emphasis on education and additional measures to promote it have varied from one period to another. Second, the ministry subsidises (since 1983) a national institute or centre of expertise for arts and cultural education that was first called the LOKV, and then Cultuurnetwerk Nederland (from 2001), and in 2013 it was renamed the LKCA (National Centre of Expertise for Cultural Education and Amateur Arts). Third, the Cultural Participation Fund, one of the national public cultural funds, was established in 2009 to support cultural education and participation through various subsidy schemes.

Primary Education
Systemic goals for cultural education at primary school are laid down in the Primary Education Act. It states that primary schools must ensure continuity in pupils' development and facilitate their emotional, cognitive and creative development as well as their acquisition of necessary knowledge and social, cultural and physical skills (Art. 8). They must also acknowledge that pupils grow up in a pluralistic society, stimulate active citizenship and social integration, and ensure that pupils learn about the various backgrounds and cultures of their peers. The Act further defines seven statutory learning domains (Art. 9), including 'artistic orientation'. Each learning domain has official core objectives (attainment goals), specifying what pupils should have learnt by the time they leave primary school. 'Artistic orientation' currently has three such attainment goals: 1) children learn to use images, language, music, play and movement to express feelings and experiences and to communicate; 2) children learn to reflect on their own work as well as that of others; and 3) children acquire some knowledge of, and estimation for, aspects of cultural heritage.

Statutory changes affected the title of cultural education as a learning domain (from 'creative expression' to 'artistic orientation') as well as the number of core objectives and their description. The number of core objectives for art and culture in elementary schools was reduced from 19 in 1985 to three in 1998. Although the measure was presented as an efficiency and deregulation operation for all learning domains, it is striking to note that the net result of the operation was the reduction of the relative import of cultural education, as core objectives for this learning area dropped from 16% of the total number of core objectives in 1985 to 5% in 1998 (IJdens & Van Hoorn 2014).

Secondary Education

From 1993 to 2006, preparatory scientific and higher vocational secondary schools were obliged to teach fifteen subjects in the first two school years (lower secondary), including two arts subjects (e.g., music and visual arts, visual arts and drama, or dance and music). Since 2006, schools have been free to choose subjects as long as they meet 58 core attainment goals for seven learning domains, including five goals for the 'arts and culture' domain. While lower secondary education balances general education with teaching various subjects, including the arts, upper secondary education focuses strongly on exam programmes for four different 'profiles'. Arts subjects are part of the 'culture & society' profile (*Kerndoelenboekje* 2010), but pupils in other profiles focusing on natural sciences or economics can choose arts as an extra.

The most important systemic update since 1993 with regard to cultural education at secondary schools has been the introduction of the subject Cultural and Artistic Education (*Culturele en Kunstzinnige Vorming*, CKV) in 1999, in addition to existing arts subjects like music and visual arts. This new subject is explicitly intended to stimulate pupils' cultural participation during school and afterwards in adult life by getting them acquainted with the professional arts. Visiting arts and cultural events and reflecting upon these experiences in a portfolio was a key element in CKV. This made it very different from the existing arts subjects that focus on practical arts skills and knowledge of the arts. CKV was first introduced only in secondary education preparing for higher vocational training and university. It was not introduced as an exam subject at preparatory middle-level vocational schools until 2003. Yet considerably less instruction time is still spent on arts and culture in preparatory middle-level vocational education. This inequality is striking, given the often-voiced argument that there should be equal access for all students to the arts, culture and cultural education, and considering the fact that over 40% of all pupils in the third year of secondary education attend this type of schools, relatively many of whom come from lower-educated and lower-income families.

Despite severe criticism about the lack of visible effect and the quality of the lessons—voiced by pupils, in the media and in parliament—CKV is still part of the curriculum. In an attempt to strengthen its status, beginning in 2018 it will be assessed with formal grades instead of the current method of marking pupils' participation as sufficient or insufficient.

With regard to cultural education at secondary schools, the debate has further focused on the practical and theoretical competencies required in exam programmes, in relation to arts teachers' training and qualifications. These discussions take place in the context of education and teacher policies, not cultural policy. However, on one point, this debate crossed the blurred line between the two domains when an investigation committee on the arts subjects (*Verkenningscommissie Kunstvakken*) evaluated the arts curriculum in high schools. Its advice resulted in the cancelling of the obligation for pupils to visit cultural institutions as part of their CKV portfolio, thereby severing the ties—policy-wise at least—between secondary schools and the cultural sector. So, at the level of secondary schools, the only major change in cultural education policy after the introduction of the CKV course—with its emphasis on participation and the introduction of exam programmes in the regular arts subjects in lower and upper secondary—was the abolishment of the obligation to actually visit cultural institutions during CKV.

Here, as in primary education, the lack of consistent policy is likely to result in increasing differences between schools that offer a rich, high-quality arts curriculum and schools in which classes on arts and culture are restricted to the bare minimum.

Prospects

After government-sponsored local and regional initiatives to boost the arts and culture curriculum for primary schools were introduced since 2013, supported by the National Centre of Expertise for Curriculum Development (SLO), a recent report outlining the government's so-called 'vision trajectory' of education up to 2032 (*Onderwijs 2032*) has sparked debate on the future of Dutch education. The proposals, which were made public in early 2016, directly affect cultural education. Art and culture are presented as an essential element of the children's and young adults' personal development. The report proposes a minimum of three hours per week for art and culture, both in primary and in secondary education. In order to teach twenty-first-century skills, professional experts—which in the case of cultural education are artists, musicians and designers—need to be brought into the school to ensure the societal relevance of the curriculum.

These proposals are directly in line with the previously mentioned policy initiatives to promote connections between schools and cultural institutions. So far, however, none of the measures has had a lasting effect.

At the beginning of the second four-year period of the Quality Cultural Education programme (*Cultuureducatie met Kwaliteit*, CmK)—one of the additional, temporary programmes addressed below—the Secretary for Culture already hinted at the further continuation of the programme. This is enough to make one wonder whether the underlying problematic is not structural and whether the system is in need of more structural measures.

7.4   Additional Programmes

While various desired and expected benefits play an important role in discourses on the value of cultural education and hence in the justification of cultural education policy, operational cultural education policy in the Netherlands since the 1990s has boiled down to two main goals: to promote cultural *participation* and to promote *quality* cultural education. In this section, we will show the shifting weights of these two goals in four additional funding programmes for both formal and non-formal cultural education—one more case in point of the hybrid character of cultural education policy.

Two national policy programmes since the 1990s aimed explicitly to promote cultural education in school: Culture and School (1997-2012) and Quality Cultural Education (since 2013). Two other programmes focused on non-formal cultural education and amateur arts but also had links to formal cultural education: the Cultural Outreach Action Plan (2001-2008; *Actieplan Cultuurbereik*) and the Cultural Participation Scheme (2009-2012; *Regeling Cultuurparticipatie*). All these additional programmes explicitly refer to cooperation between central and local governments and some also to relations between formal (in-school) and non-formal (out-of-school) cultural education.

Culture and School
Stimulating cultural education at school as a form of stimulating cultural participation in later life is a policy goal directed especially at children and young people from disadvantaged families, and children with a migrant background. In the mid-1990s, there was a consensus that a more coherent policy regarding cultural education was necessary. Differences in cultural upbringing were deemed to be too significant, and the position of the arts in schools was perceived to depend too much on the enthusiasm of individual teachers and headmasters. By focusing cultural education policy on schools,

children from all classes and backgrounds could be reached. The underlying goal was to promote appreciation of the arts and as a result to stimulate participation in the arts in later life.

The Culture and School programme was a direct result of a rearrangement of ministerial departments, which led to the establishment (actually, reestablishment) of the Ministry of Education, Culture and Science (OCW). The policy brief *Culture and School* (1996) stated: 'Culture and education are not separate worlds. They are indissolubly connected, they stimulate and mutually influence each other.' (Netelenbos & Nuis 1996: 9). The programme continued earlier policy initiatives to foster collaboration between schools and cultural education professionals outside the school, in order to enhance the quality of the teaching of arts subjects (Hagenaars 2008: 12). This perceived lack of quality, which was nowhere defined or substantiated, would become a recurrent theme in cultural education policy over the following decades. Behind Culture and School lay the assumption that an early encounter with arts and culture would result in higher degrees of participation in later life. In line with this reasoning, the project gradually shifted its focus from secondary education (especially the introduction of CKV: see above) to primary education. Cultural education thus served as a means to promote cultural participation, and collaboration between schools and cultural institutions was a key element in this policy (Van Hoorn 2013). The latter goal was continued in the Quality Cultural Education programme (CmK) after 2013.

An additional policy measure provided further stimulus. Since 2004, elementary schools have been offered a subsidy of €10.90 per child for developing a vision on cultural education as well as for implementing and executing a cultural policy in school. Strengthening ties between schools and their cultural environment was again referred to as a key condition and objective. The measure was a huge success in terms of its scope: between 2004 and 2009, the number of participating school rose from 10% to 80%. It ran until 2012, when the funds were reallocated to the lump-sum budget for the schools. Schools are now required to justify their expenditures from this budget in their annual accounts, though no restrictions apply for the size of their spending on cultural education from this budget. In practice, however, additional budgets and temporary incentives may serve as an implicit argument for underspending on cultural education as a regular learning area (IJdens & Van Hoorn 2008, Van Meerkerk 2012, Sardes/Oberon 2016).

Parallel to this funding instrument, elementary schools were stimulated to appoint a coordinator for cultural education who was to be charged with the development of a school policy for arts and culture as well as maintaining contacts with their cultural environment. At the local and regional levels, intermediary agencies were funded to mediate between schools and cultural institutions. These agencies drew up annual 'cultural menus' for the schools, presenting the educational offerings from cultural institutions and other suppliers. The school coordinators could then use these menus to put together a programme for their school.

Cultural Outreach and Active Cultural Participation

The integration of cultural education policy with participation goals was confirmed in the Cultural Outreach Action Plan of 2001-2004 (*Actieplan Cultuurbereik*), a new programme co-funded by the national government, provinces and municipalities with more than 90,000 inhabitants. The programme aimed 'to involve more people in culture, especially newcomers such as immigrants and young people', and it defined culture in a broad sense: 'not just the performing arts or museums but also popular culture, e.g., pop music' (Cultural Policy in the Netherlands 2006).

In addition to the 'central' Culture and School programme with measures directly aimed at schools and under the direct responsibility of the Ministry, a 'decentral' programme with an earmarked budget was included in the first period (2001-2004) of the Plan. This programme aimed to make pupils in primary and secondary education familiar with culture through school, 'which is different from the aim to get young people in general involved with culture' (*Actieplan Cultuurbereik* 2001-2004; cf. IJdens & Hitters 2005). The second period of the Plan (2005-2008) aimed to promote 'cultural awareness' by way of participation and education but had no earmarked budget for cultural education.

After the Cultural Outreach Action Plan ended in 2008, its main elements were continued in a new subsidy scheme implemented by the Cultural Participation Fund (FCP). This including co-funding with provinces and cities for what was termed *active cultural participation*: amateur arts, cultural education, talent development and participatory culture.

Quality Cultural Education at Primary School

Dissatisfaction among arts teachers and cultural institutions with the artistic quality of arts programmes in elementary schools and the incidental nature of most cultural education policy measures led to a call for more focus on quality. An analysis of the aims of cultural education policy between 1995 and 2008 (Hagenaars 2008) showed an increase in emphasis on quality, from 34% of the goals that were referred to in official policy documents between 1995 and 2000 to 41% between 2000 and 2008.

The turn to quality was stimulated by two advisory reports: one by an ad hoc committee assessing the state of affairs in primary school arts education (Wagemakers 2003) and the other by the official Advisory Board for Education (Onderwijsraad 2006). The international context also helped. In 2006, the first World Conference on Arts Education under the auspices of UNESCO took place in Lisbon. For this occasion, UNESCO had a global survey conducted, which was led by Anne Bamford. Her report *The Wow Factor* (2006) is an analysis of policies in more than 60 UNESCO Member States. One of her conclusions was that it is better to have no arts education at all than to have bad arts education, as the latter would lead to a distaste for art. Though *The Wow Factor* provided no insight into the impact or efficiency of arts education policies, the publication led to an increased awareness of the importance of quality and accountability in arts education policy while simultaneously highlighting the importance of arts education as a goal in itself.

Although elements of quality were emphasised in the last years of the Culture and School programme, it was not until 2013 that a new programme was launched for primary school arts education that focused completely on quality. The ambition of the Quality Cultural Education programme (2013-2016) was to secure quality through four operational goals: improving the competencies of both generalist teachers and arts teachers; strengthening collaboration between schools and cultural institutions; developing a more coherent arts and culture curriculum for four to twelve-year olds; and developing better assessment tools for the arts and cultural curriculum. The latter two goals evidence a clear shift away from a policy aimed at cultural participation through cultural education at school towards one that focused on the way in which the arts and culture are being taught. The new programme focused on the conditions for quality, whereas before, policy measures were largely restricted to institutional incentives.

This shift, which confirms the findings by Hagenaars (2008) mentioned above, also has a great impact on cultural institutions, whose educational programmes were made subservient to the needs of schools (Van Hoorn 2013). The programme was continued for the years 2017-2020, despite the critical reception from policy researchers, who referred to the lack of a consistent plan for implementation and evaluation as well as the policy of addressing apparently structural issues through temporary, compensatory measures (IJdens & Van Hoorn 2014, Haanstra 2016). While such policy programmes usually draw quite a lot of policy and professional attention at different levels, the annual volume of public funding involved is only a fraction (6% on estimate for Quality Cultural Education) of the part of the regular national budget for teacher salaries that can be attributed to arts teaching at school (IJdens 2012).

The developments described above are not unique to the Netherlands. In other countries, similar policy initiatives have been deployed, focusing on temporary programmes to strengthen partnerships between schools, artists and/or cultural institutions. Under the umbrella of the Erasmus+ programme, the EU developed the CREARTE programme (Creative Primary School Partnerships with Visual Artists), which supported collaborations in Spain, Portugal, Cyprus, Great Britain, Sweden and the Netherlands (CREARTE website). CREARTE was based on the format of the earlier Creative Partnerships programme, an initiative of the British government. The Creative Partnerships started in 2002 and continues to date, despite its funding having ended in 2010. Another parallel initiative is the introduction of the Kulturagenten (cultural agents) in Germany. Although all these initiatives appear similar at first sight, there are important differences (Abs et al. 2016, Fink et al. 2017).

Music Education: A Case Apart

A final change in cultural education policy is the increased priority placed on music. In 2015, the Cultural Participation Fund introduced the subsidy programme known as Music Education Impulse (Muziekimpuls website). This new focus on music in cultural education policy merits description in more detail. The policy initiatives originated in discussions on the so-called 'Mozart effect', which holds that people who listened to classical music prior to performing an intelligence test increased their scores significantly. Despite this claim being doubted or even disproved (Hetland 2000, Thomson, Schellenberg & Husain 2001), the notion gained wide support and resulted in a vast array of music education programmes, both from within schools and cultural institutions and in cultural policy. Indications from brain research that there may yet be some truth in the claim (Scherder 2017) fuelled the continuing support for music education policies. The German programme 'Jedem Kind ein Instrument' (JeKI) served as a model for a similar programme in Rotterdam (Every Child an Instrument 2008). In 2009, the Cultural Participation Fund launched the programme 'Music in Every Child', which was followed by the 'More Music in the Classroom' programme in 2014. Backed by Queen Maxima and entertainment entrepreneur and now renowned patron of the arts Joop van den Ende, the latter programme gained nationwide media coverage, including a government-sponsored television programme promoting active musical performance among children. Most recently, Minister of Culture Ingrid van Engelshoven announced a doubling of the budget for the music impulse programme in her policy brief *Culture in an Open Society* (Van Engelshoven 2018).

Prospects

No substantial national evaluation of these additional, temporary programmes has been conducted, except the first Cultural Outreach Plan (IJdens & Hitters 2005). Evaluation has been restricted to national reports monitoring cultural education at primary and secondary school (Sardes & Oberon 2015), a process evaluation of selected local QCE programmes by LKCA (Kox, Meewis & Neele 2016) and several local or provincial evaluations and monitors of varying scope and quality. The school inspectorate, entrusted with the supervision of the additional means for cultural education, has so far only issued a report on drawing skills, leaving the efficacy of nationally funded measures unevaluated. The research that has been conducted has stressed the importance of teacher competencies and school leadership for the quality of cultural education (Van Meerkerk 2016).

There are no signs of policy initiatives to come to a structural, national system of evaluation and research on cultural education. Consequently, local governments and schools will most likely remain decisive in how cultural education is put into practice. This will presumably lead to a widening gap between the larger cities and smaller provincial communities, with increasing cooperation between cultural institutions and schools in urban regions but increasing marginalisation of cultural education in the less-populated localities.

This analysis of cultural education policy also brought to light the intricate policy network at several levels supported by the two pillars of education policy and cultural policy. At the level of primary schools, a shift from an emphasis on participation to quality in the policy goals could be discerned, while the underlying motives for this shift remained unclear, and hence the choices in cultural education policy were hard to assess. The only problem that everyone seems to agree on—the quality of teachers and hence their pre-service training and professional development—falls under the remit of education policy rather than cultural policy.

One could conclude that the developments in cultural education at school sketched above call for the incorporation of various additional programmes into the existing systemic funding and regulation—after a serious analysis and evaluation of the experiences and results of the programmes. But this is not likely to happen. Nor can we expect a new, more flexible system of funding and support combining market offers and not-for-profit community initiatives to be initiated. Rather, the developments of the past 25 years make it most likely that the system of additional programmes, with the same focus and the same beneficiaries, will continue under different names that reflect changing societal and cultural desiderata.

7.6 Vicissitudes of Non-Formal Arts Education

Engagement in amateur arts and taking classes in music, the visual arts, dance or drama in non-formal settings are generally seen as a 'good' leisure activity for citizens. National cultural policy since the 1990s has always paid some attention to amateur arts and out-of-school arts education as *active* cultural participation in relation to *receptive* participation (visiting performing arts, museums, etc.). But in 2007, the focus of national cultural policy shifted from cultural participation in general to active participation when Minister of Culture Ronald Plasterk published his policy paper *Art of Living* (Plasterk 2007). This also implied a further shift away from national campaigns to promote cultural participation to co-funding local participatory arts and cultural activities together with provinces and municipalities, a trend that had already started with the Cultural Outreach Plan of 2001-2004.

The national Cultural Participation Fund, founded in 2008 as an arm's-length government agency and operational since 2009, became the main instrument for this. The Fund subsidises amateur arts, participatory arts and cultural education projects and plays a crucial role in the implementation of additional national programmes for cultural education, while the Ministry of Education, Culture and Science remains fully responsible for policy directions, measures taken and available public funding (IJdens & Van Hoorn 2014, Van Rensen & IJdens 2010, Wils, Zweers & Berger 2012). In addition to the Cultural Participation Fund, the national infrastructure for non-formal arts education further consists of umbrella organisations in the voluntary arts field, employers' associations, labour unions and professional associations as well as the National Centre of Expertise for Cultural Education and Amateur Arts (LKCA). The latter and the CPF are state-funded institutions in accordance with the Cultural Policy Act of 1993, but apart from this, there is no legislative framework whatsoever for public funding and regulation in the field of non-formal arts education.

Opportunities for non-formal arts education are available all over the Netherlands, and 'market supply' prevails. Arts classes, workshops and courses are supplied by many private arts teachers and artists, by music schools and multi-disciplinary arts centres, by voluntary associations (e.g., amateur theatre groups, church choirs), by informal groups and clubs, and increasingly through the internet. Public funding is local and is subject to shifting political priorities, as there is no legal obligation for municipalities regarding culture.

Since 2009, financial pressure on various local services—including but not exclusively cultural—has increased due to the economic crisis and diminishing municipal revenues. Budgets for music schools and centres for the arts were cut, or they were restricted to offers for specific groups, mainly school-related programmes. In other cases, funding was terminated altogether. Subsidies were also relocated to schools in an effort to create local 'markets' for cultural education and to promote 'ownership' of cultural education in the schools. At the same time, national government support for cultural institutions was increasingly tied to the obligation to invest in educational programmes and collaboration with schools. Thus, the local infrastructure for non-formal arts education in many municipalities became increasingly dependent on temporary, project-based subventions instead of regular public funding (Van Hoorn & Hagenaars 2011). These subsidies generally demanded closer ties between arts education centres and other cultural institutions and schools. As a result, cultural education policy for out-of-school educational settings was redirected towards formal education.

Arts education centres and music schools in many cities and towns have certainly suffered severe budget cuts or were forced to close their doors altogether. The sum of all budget cuts was estimated at approximately 500 million euros, taking all levels of government together. Teachers were fired and in some cases rehired as freelancers by their former employers. In other cases, new local organisations emerged, initiated by self-employed arts teachers and artists or by other private or non-profit organisations and associations. If one considers public funding of local centres for non-formal arts learning as a typical feature of Dutch arts education policies from the 1980s until the first decade of this century, these changes can be called a systemic shift towards privatisation. As such, it is a clear example of neo-liberal public management: more market, less government. Its impact on the structure of provision (supply) and on employment in the non-formal arts education sector is undeniable. However, its impact on demand and participation is questionable. Percentages of the Dutch population engaging in arts and creative leisure activities (approximately 40%) have not dropped since 2013, and neither has the proportion of these practitioners (one-third) who take arts classes and workshops (Neele, Zernitz & IJdens 2017). In 2009, publicly funded supply was estimated to cover no more than 20% of private demand for arts classes (Van den Broek 2010). Since then, the market share of publicly funded local and regional music schools and arts education centres has likely decreased as a result of local austerity policies, but in 2015 its share was still estimated at between 15% and 20% (IJdens 2015).

7.7 Conclusions and Prospects

Cultural education is a hybrid policy field, not only because of the institutional distinction between formal cultural education (at primary and secondary school) and arts learning in non-formal and informal cultural and social settings but also because of dual funding schemes and policies for cultural education at school. Funding and other policy instruments often have as their main aim to bring the two domains—culture and education—together in order to resolve perceived lacunae in educational practice and/or the cultural field. Cooperation between schools and cultural actors emerged as a primary operational policy goal.

Cultural education policy at the national level is largely restricted to formal education. Policy measures are therefore limited because of the prevailing dogma of school autonomy in determining the curriculum. Policy regarding non-formal education is mainly the concern of local government in collaboration with cultural organisations. Today, the Cultural Participation Fund as well as semi-public funds, national, provincial and local agencies and various interest groups participating in policy networks deal with both formal and non-formal cultural education.

In this chapter, we first analysed the organisation of cultural education policy in terms of delineations and jurisdictions. From this perspective, the main trend since 2001 was the growing interdependence between the national government—directly and via the Cultural Participation Fund—and local governments in policies for cultural education at primary school. With regard to the justification of cultural education policy, we have shown that policy goals and presumed benefits of cultural education did change over time. While participation as a goal was dominant in the 1990s, the quality of cultural education became more of a priority from around 2010. However, the continuing lack of priority given to comprehensive policy evaluation prevents a valid and reliable assessment of the outcomes of cultural education policies.

In sum, it can be stated that underlying values and systemic policy goals have hardly changed and that corresponding policies and instruments have followed the same pattern of stability over the past quarter of a century. However, the discourse on (benefits of) cultural education and the focus of special policy programmes have changed, and schools instead of arts and cultural organisations have become the prime object of cultural education policy. In fact, the combination of systemic regulation and general funding of schools with recurring temporary programmes can be considered a hallmark of Dutch cultural education policy since the 1990s, along with continuous efforts to coordinate policies at the national and local levels.

Dutch cultural education policy faces a series of challenges in the coming years. One important decision that has to be made is whether cultural education at school will remain primarily the object of compensatory and additional cultural policy programmes or be integrated into education policy. Current initiatives for redesigning the curriculum may signify a shift in the latter direction—if resources that are now allocated via compensatory and additional programmes are fully incorporated into the design and implementation of a new curriculum. Alternatively, cultural education policy may remain separate from education policy to serve the socio-cultural goals of cultural policy.

A second challenge for cultural education policy pertains to the cultural and societal benefits it aims to achieve. Will cultural education be legitimised because of its impact on creativity and ultimately economic growth? Or will it be seen as a means for personal development, or perhaps 'merely' as a means for stimulating artistic development? Minister van Engelshoven (2018) ostensibly endorses the latter position, although it remains to be seen whether her ambitions will be translated into policy initiatives.

From an institutional perspective, the gradual shift at the local level from primary schools to integrated 'child centres' presents an interesting challenge for cultural policy. In the Netherlands and elsewhere, informal learning is usually not included in arts education or cultural education policy. However, the extension of learning opportunities in arts and culture beyond traditional institutions of formal and non-formal education is a challenging issue in education policy, including cultural education, for the next decades (Heijnen 2015, OECD 2016). Given that many centres for non-formal cultural education are in financial trouble after the local government's austerity measures between 2011 and 2015, the local infrastructure differs greatly from one place to the next. Cultural education policy measures thus far have aimed to strengthen the bonds between schools and cultural institutions. The most prominent of these—the Quality Cultural Education programme for primary schools—will end in 2020. Again, as in 2017, the desire on the part of all parties involved to see this programme continued appears to be stronger than their interest in solid evidence of its impact and cost effectiveness. The Dutch polder of cultural education policy appears to be a sustainable system, for better or for worse.

Bibliography

Bamford, Anne. 2006. *The Wow Factor. Global Research Compendium on the Impact of the Arts in Education*. Münster: Waxmann.

—. 2013. "The Wow and What Now?", E. Liebau, E. Wagner & M. Wyman (eds.) *International Yearbook for Research in Arts Education* 1: 175-186.

Barresi, Anthony L., and Gerald B. Olson. 1994. "Arts Education Policy in the School Culture", *Arts Education Policy Review* 95(6): 23-30.

Bennett, Tony, and Mike Savage. 2004. "Introduction: Cultural capital and cultural policy", *Cultural Trends* 13(2): 7-14.

Benington, John, and Mark H. Moore. 2011. *Public Value. Theory & Practice*. Houndmills, Basingstoke: Palgrave Macmillan.

CREARTE website. Accessed 3 March 2018. ec.europa.eu/programmes/erasmus-plus

Damen, Marie-Louise 2010. *Cultuurdeelname en CKV. Studies naar effecten van kunsteducatie op de cultuurdeelname van leerlingen tijdens en na het voortgezet onderwijs*. [Cultural Participation and CKV. Studies into the Effects of Arts Education on Cultural Participation of Pupils During and After Secondary School]. PhD thesis, Utrecht University.

Dekker. 2013. Accessed 3 March 2018. https://zoek.officielebekendmakingen.nl/dossier/32735/kst-31289-159.html

Dieleman, Cock. 2010. *Het nieuwe theaterleren: een veldonderzoek naar de rol van theater binnen Culturele en Kunstzinnige Vorming op havo en vwo* [New Theatre Learning: Field Research of the Role of Theatre in CKV in Middle and Higher Secondary Schools]. Amsterdam: Vossiuspers UvA.

European Union. 2000. Presidency Conclusions, Lisbon European Council. 23 and 24 March 2000. Accessed 30 June 2018. http://www.consilium.europa.eu/uedocs/cms_data/docs/pressdata/en/ec/00100-r1.eno.htm.

Fink, Tobias, Doreen Götzky and Thomas Renz. 2017. *Kulturagenten als Kooperationsstifter? Förderprogramme der Kulturellen Bildung zwischen Schule und Kultur*. [Cultural Agents as Founders of Co-operation? Fostering Programmes for Cultural Education between School and Culture]. Wiesbaden: Springer.

Gabrieli, Chris, Dana Ansel and Sara Bartolino Krachman. 2015. *Ready to be Counted*. http://www.transformingeducation.org/.

Haanstra, Folkert. 2016. "Wat neemt de leerling mee van kunsteducatie? [What does a Student Take From Art Education?]", *Cultuur+Educatie* 44: 8-28.

Heijnen, Emiel. 2015. *Remixing the Art Curriculum: How Contemporary Visual Practices Inspire Authentic Art Education*. PhD thesis, Radboud University Nijmegen.

Hetland, Lois. 2000. "Listening to Music Enhances Spatial-Temporal Reasoning: Evidence for the 'Mozart Effect'", *The Journal of Aesthetic Education* 34(3/4): 105-148.

Hoogeveen, Karin, and Sandra Beekhoven. 2016. "Samen werkt het beter? De samenwerking tussen scholen en de culturele omgeving" [Co-operation Does the Trick? Co-operation Between Schools and the Cultural Environment]. In: Lenie van den Bulk (ed.), *Een kleurrijke basis. Ontwikkelingen en trends in het cultuuronderwijs*. [A Colourful Basis. Trends and Developments in Cultural Education], pp. 139-148. Utrecht: LKCA.

Hoogerwerf, Andries, and Michiel Herweijer. 2008. *Overheidsbeleid*. [Public Policy]. Alphen aan den Rijn: Kluwer.

IJdens, Teunis. 2012. "Een kwestie van onderwijskwaliteit" [A Matter of Educational Quality], *Cultuur+Educatie* 33: 8-29.

—. 2015. "Comparative Policy Research in Arts Education: Prolegomena for a Review". In: S. Schonmann, E. Wagner & L. O'Farrell (eds.) *International Yearbook for Research in Arts Education* 3. Münster: Waxmann: 439-445.

—. 2018a. "Arts Education Benefits and Challenges". In: Ben Bolden, Teunis IJdens and Ernst Wagner (eds.), *International Yearbook for Research in Arts Education* 5. Münster: Waxmann:187-205.

—. 2018b. "Studying Arts Education Policy and Governance: Concepts and Perspectives". In: Benjamin Jörissen, Leopold Klepacki & Lisa Unterberg (eds.), *Spectra of Transformation. Erlanger Beiträge zur Pedagogik,* 17. Michael Gohlich and Eckart Liebau (eds.). Münster/ New York: Waxmann: 69-88.

IJdens, Teunis, and Erik Hitters. 2005. *Landelijke evaluatie van het Actieplan Cultuurbereik 2001-2004.* [National Evaluation of the Cultural Outreach Action Plan]. Tilburg: IVA.

IJdens, Teunis, and Marjo van Hoorn (eds.). 2008. "Pegasus' vlucht gevolgd. Cultuur en School 1997-2007: doelstellingen, onderzoek en resultaten [Tracing Pegasus's Flight. Culture and School 1997-2007: Goals, Research and Outcomes]", special issue of *Cultuur+Educatie* 21.

IJdens, Teunis, and Marjo van Hoorn. 2014. "The Art of Arts Education Policy. An Exploratory Analysis of Public Management in Arts Education Policy". In: Marjo van Hoorn (ed.), *Quality Now! Arts and Cultural Education to the Next Level,* pp. 50-66. Utrecht: LKCA.

IJdens, Teunis, and John Lievens. 2018. "Understandings of arts education". In: Ben Bolden, Teunis IJdens and Ernst Wagner (eds.), *International Yearbook for Research in Arts Education* 5. Münster: Waxmann: 71-100.

Kerndoelenboekje. 2010. Accessed 3 March 2018. https://www.rijksoverheid.nl/documenten/ besluiten/2010/09/17/kerndoelen-onderbouw-voortgezet-onderwijs.

Klaassen, Cornelis A.C. 1983. "De zorg voor de cultuuroverdracht [Caring for Cultural Transfer]". In: Philip. A. Idenburg (ed.), *De nadagen van de verzorgingsstaat. Kansen en perspectieven voor morgen.* [The Latter Days of the Welfare State. Opportunities and Perspectives for Tomorrow], pp. 102-132. Amsterdam: Meulenhoff.

Konings, Fianne, and Barend van Heusden. 2014. "Evaluating Partnership, or How to Evaluate the Contribution of Cultural Institutions to an Integrated Curriculum for Culture Education in Primary Schools". In: Larry O'Farrell, Shifra Schonmann and Ernst Wagner (eds.) *International Yearbook for Research in Arts Education* 2, pp. 66-78. Münster: Waxmann.

Kox, Ronald, Vera Meewis, and Arno Neele 2016. *Gevalsstudies Cultuureducatie met Kwaliteit. Eindrapport.* [Case studies Quality Cultural Education. Final Report]. Utrecht: LKCA.

KuBi Online. Accessed 3 March 2018. https://www.kubi-online.de/artikel/kulturelle-bildung-sozialen-arbeit.

Mercer, Colin. 2002. *Towards Cultural Citizenship: Tools for Cultural Policy and Development.* Stockholm: Bank of Sweden Tercentenary Foundation.

Muziekimpuls. Accessed 3 March 2018. http://www.cultuurparticipatie.nl/subsidies/impuls-muziekonderwijs.html.

Netelenbos, Tineke and Aad Nuis. 1996. *Cultuur en School* [Culture and School]. The Hague SDU.

OECD. 2001. *What Schools for the Future? Education and Skills.* Paris: OECD.

—. 2010. *The OECD Innovation Strategy: Getting a Head Start on Tomorrow.* Paris: OECD.

—. 2014. *Education Policy Outlook Highlights: Netherlands.* Accessed 3 March 2018. http://www. oecd.org/edu/highlightsnetherlands.htm.

—. 2016. *Innovating Education and Educating for Innovation: The Power of Digital Technologies and Skills.* Paris: OECD.

Onderwijsraad. 2006. *Onderwijs in cultuur* [Educating Culture]. The Hague: Onderwijsraad [Advisory Board for Education].

—. 2014. *Een onderwijsstelsel met veerkracht.* Accessed 3 March 2018. https://www.onderwijsraad. nl/publicaties/2014/een-onderwijsstelsel-met-veerkracht/volledig/item7193.

Plasterk, Ronald. 2007. *Kunst van leven. Hoofdlijnen cultuurbeleid* [Art of Living. Principles of Cultural Policy]. The Hague: OCW.

Raad voor Cultuur & Onderwijsraad. 2012. *Cultuureducatie. Leren, creëren, inspireren!* [Cultural Education. Learning, Creating, Inspiring!]. The Hague: Onderwijsraad.

Rhodes, Roderick A.W. 2008. "Policy Network Analysis". In: Michael Moran, Martin Rein and Robert E. Goodin (eds.), *The Oxford Handbook of Public Policy*, pp. 425-443. Oxford/New York: Oxford University Press.

Sardes and Oberon. 2015. *Monitor cultuuronderwijs voortgezet onderwijs 2015* [Monitor of Cultural Education Secondary Education 2015]. Utrecht: Oberon.

—. 2016. *Rapport Monitor Cultuuronderwijs in het primair onderwijs en programma Cultuureducatie met Kwaliteit Peiling 2015/16* [Report Monitor Cultural Education in Primary Education and Programme Quality Cultural Education Assessment 2015/16]. Utrecht: Sardes/Oberon.

Scherder, Erik. 2017. *Singing in the Brain: over de unieke samenwerking tussen muziek en de hersenen.* [Singing in the Brain: On the Unique Cooperation of Music and Brain]. Amsterdam: Atheneaeum – Polak & Van Gennep.

Staatscourant 13 October 2015. Accessed 3 March 2018. https://zoek.officielebekendmakingen. nl/stcrt-2015-34149.html.

Thompson, William F., E. Glenn Schellenberg and Gabriela Husain. 2001. "Arousal, Mood, and the Mozart Effect", *Psychological Science* 123: 248-251.

Van Engelshoven, Ingrid. 2018. *Cultuur in een open samenleving.* [Policy Brief: Culture in an Open Society]. The Hague: Ministerie OCW [Ministry of Education, Culture and Science].

Van Hoorn, Marjo (ed.). 2013. "Cultuureducatie met kwaliteit: de volgende stap" [Quality Cultural Education: The Next Step], special issue of *Cultuur+Educatie* 38.

— (ed.). 2014. *Quality Now! Arts and Cultural Education to the Next Level.* Utrecht: LKCA.

Van Hoorn, Marjo, and Piet Hagenaars. 2011. "Projectsubsidies en de marktstrategie van centra voor de kunsten" [Project Subsidies and Market Strategy of Creativity Centres]. In: Teunis IJdens et al. (eds.), *Participanten, projecten en beleid. Jaarboek actieve cultuurparticipatie.* [Participants, Projects and Policy. Yearbook Active Cultural Participation]. Utrecht: LKCA/ FCP: 129-145.

Van Meerkerk, Edwin. 2012. Verplicht en vastgelegd, maar ook verankerd? Cultuureducatiebeleid 2008-2012. [Obligatory and Documented, but Anchored as Well? Cultural Education Policy 2008-2012]. In: Teunis IJdens, Marjo van Hoorn, Andries van den Broek & Chrit van Rensen, eds. *Jaarboek actieve cultuurparticipatie 2012* [Yearbook Active Cultural Participation]. Utrecht: Fonds voor Cultuurparticipatie: 75-107.

—. 2016. *Cultuureducatie met leerkrachten. Het CMK-programma vanuit de klas gezien.* [Cultural Education and Teachers. The CmK Programme viewed from the Classroom]. Arnhem: Cultuurmij Oost.

Van Meerkerk, Edwin, and Eelco van Es. 2016. "Kwaliteit meten is positie kiezen. Een kritische beschouwing van cultuureducatie en kwaliteit" [Measuring Quality is Taking a Stance. A Critical Analysis of Quality Cultural Education], *Cultuur+Educatie* 46: 76-84

Weible, Christopher M. 2014. "Introducing the Scope and Focus of Policy Process Research and Theory". In: Paul A. Sabatier and Christopher M. Weible (eds.), *Theories of the policy process*, third edition. Boulder, CO: Westview Press.

WPO. 2005. Accessed 3 March 2018. http://wetten.overheid.nl/BWBR0018844/2012-12-01.

WPO. 2017. Accessed 3 March 2018. http://wetten.overheid.nl/BWBR0003420/2017-08-01.

WVO. 2017. Accessed 3 March 2018. http://wetten.overheid.nl/BWBR0002399/2017-08-01#TiteldeelI

8. Culture for Everyone

The Value and Feasibility of Stimulating Cultural Participation

Koen van Eijck

8.1 Introduction

This chapter will address the stimulation of cultural participation through policy in the Netherlands. After presenting the rationale of the Dutch government for encouraging cultural participation, two recent initiatives will be discussed and presented as emblematic of the indirect and decentralised fashion in which this policy was executed. Next, we will look at trends in cultural participation in the Netherlands and critically evaluate their usefulness for policy evaluation. Finally, alternative criteria for policymaking and policy evaluation are presented that might be more directly geared towards the underlying policy goal of helping people to enjoy and make sense of the arts and culture.

8.2 Cultural Policy on Participation

From its inception, Dutch cultural policy has been involved in attempts to enhance cultural participation. The Ministry of Education, Culture and Science lists the following core issues for cultural policy:
- cultural participation and cultural education
- innovation and talent development
- donating to culture and entrepreneurship
- internationalisation (Ministerie OCW 2013)

Although these themes have consistently received a fair amount of attention from policymakers, the rationale for focusing on these issues has shifted over time. In a sense, encouraging participation and promoting education both serve the same purpose, which is enabling people to appreciate cultural offerings that they might not familiarise themselves with if this was not actively encouraged. That is why, in addition to subsidising artistic production and the cultural infrastructure, the government invests in encouraging people to learn about the arts and to participate in them both as an audience member and as an amateur artist.

It is important to note that the Dutch government is conspicuously reserved when it comes to interfering directly with the arts on the basis of notions such as substance or aesthetic value. The way in which subsidising occurs reflects this reservation. Cultural institutions that are deemed to belong to the country's Basic Cultural Infrastructure (BIS) receive direct funding from the national government. The Council for Culture offers advice in this regard to the government, based on artistic criteria but also additional requirements such as the ability to generate revenues or educational activities. In addition, cultural supply can be subsidised indirectly through mediating cultural funds that are mandated by the government to make artistic selections on its behalf. Instead of discussing the artistic product itself, much policymaking is thus centred around policy procedures, the process of reaching consensus or the management of distributing financial resources. Due to its history of pillarisation, where different pillars of society held different social and aesthetic ideals, the Dutch government has traditionally been preoccupied with pacifying various groups within society and seeking consensus rather than formulating artistic guidelines or quality criteria. As a result, much of the artistic decision-making is left to the cultural field itself. However, the art world increasingly became the rather exclusive domain of an incrowd of experts whose primary concern was the appreciation of their professional peers rather than their appeal among the wider public (Hoefnagel 2009).

In presenting the government's cultural policy agenda, Ministers and Secretaries regularly explain why they think supporting the arts is important. Rick van der Ploeg (1999), who was Secretary for Culture between 1998 and 2002 on behalf of the Labour Party, felt it was time that cultural policy focussed on the audience. He argued that the cultural sector was dominated by specialists catering to society's (cultural) elites while caring too little about serving a wider audience. Van der Ploeg observed that the audiences for the arts were rather homogeneous in terms of education, income, age (high) and ethnicity (white). Van der Ploeg's predecessor, who confronted the same problem, put arts education high on the policy agenda as a possible remedy against the general public's lack of knowledge about the arts (Nuis 1996). But such attempts to socialise the audience were less than effective as long as experts remained the sole determinants of which art was to be financially supported by government subsidies. Blokland (1996) argued that such experts tend to identify 'high quality' with notions such as innovation, originality or freshness. The general audience, however, is less interested in these qualities and instead seeks craftsmanship, beauty, tradition and experiential qualities that they often find lacking in the art that is subsidised on the basis of expert recommendations. In contemporary Dutch society, which is too egalitarian and multicultural to hold the taste of the cultural elite in high esteem, this had led to an increasing gap between the taste of the general public and much of the art produced with the help of government subsidies. And the audience in turn became increasingly elitist, since the subsidised arts reflected the elitist, experimental preferences of experts rather than those of the general audience, which felt increasingly alienated from the cultural activities offered by museums, theatres and concert venues.

Van der Ploeg attributed this lopsided situation to three misunderstandings. First, under the assumption that supply precedes demand, cultural policy had been focused primarily on the supply of culture and not the demand. This had seriously limited the reach of the subsidised arts, which were often too hermetic and exotic to gain a wide following. The second misunderstanding, which followed from the first, was the belief that the main purpose of subsidies was to allow cultural producers to work without any commercial pressure or other obligations but to produce 'quality' art. This led to a further retreat of artists into their own bubble of like-minded experts who became a more relevant frame of reference than the audience 'out there'. Third, this situation led to the idea that Dutch cultural policy worked well and needed nothing more than routine maintenance every four years (which is the policy cycle in which new subsidies are granted). For these reasons, Van der Ploeg wished to encourage cultural diversity in the arts and allocated resources to specific programmes or initiatives aimed at education and outreach to a new or broader audiences. Rather than endorsing the notion of the *democratisation of culture*, whereby major cultural works are disseminated to audiences that do not have access to these yet, Van der Ploeg was inspired by the notion of *cultural democracy*, where government supports the free choices that individuals make (see, e.g., Evrard 1997).

Some of Van der Ploeg's predecessors from shortly after Second World War had advocated that art should be made available to members of all social classes (the democratisation of culture). However, at the time this goal was still firmly grounded in the belief in the edifying or purifying effects of art participation as a form of *Bildung*. The focus shifted around 1965, when citizens' well-being became more central and it was acknowledged that people should be allowed to be culturally active on their own, very diverse terms (Oosterbaan Martinius 1990)· It was from around this period that the social and demographic distribution of the arts acquired more prominence on the policy agenda and the social relevance of the arts became a central concern. However, since the 1980s, the focus had shifted back to artistic quality, which the government felt should play a larger role in granting subsidies to artists. This situation ultimately led to the chasm between the art world and the public that motivated Van der Ploeg to alter the central assumptions of Dutch cultural policy. With the exception of the 1970s, Dutch cultural policy had since the Second World War largely been assuming that it was the audience that needed to move to the arts. With Van der Ploeg, the government was now asking the arts to move to the general public. He therefore argued that cultural policymakers and institutions should incorporate audience development more explicitly into their policymaking and organisations. He argued that enjoying art is an acquired taste and that cultural policy should aim to enable everyone to sample art and then decide whether they are hungry for more.

The emphasis came to lie once again on the cultural sector's responsibility towards the general public when Halbe Zijlstra became Secretary for Culture in 2010. In his 2011 policy brief, significantly entitled *More than Quality*, he argued that culture is relevant for connecting people, developing an identity and keeping traditions alive as well as for enhancing dynamics, creativity and innovation. He believed that, besides striving for artistic quality, the cultural sector should be more entrepreneurial and innovative in finding new audiences. This idea was essentially in line with the change in policy introduced by Van der Ploeg, although the concomitant cutbacks in government subsidies that Zijlstra introduced was not. Zijlstra, representing the liberal-conservative party of Prime Minister Mark Rutte, wished to make the cultural sector more entrepreneurial by applying what many considered to be a ruthless kind of shock therapy, cutting 20% of the national budget for the arts.

Zijlstra's successor, Jet Bussemaker (Social-Democratic Party), made a distinction between art's artistic, social and economic functions in her 2013 letter outlining her policy vision. She, too, argued that art is relevant for identity, self-development and creativity. It connects people, brings joy and helps solve societal problems. Like Zijlstra, she believed that art's right to exist lies primarily in its ability to connect to other social domains. She emphasised creativity and innovation as skills that can be fostered by participation in the arts and are socially and economically relevant. For these valuable effects of participation to surface, policymakers must encourage participation to allow people to decide for themselves which forms of art appeal to them, in line with Isaiah Berlin's notion of positive freedom to which Van der Ploeg also alluded. In her letter outlining her cultural policy plans for the 2017-2020 period, she reiterated that the audience for culture should not just increase in numbers but rather that the goal should be to reach new audiences that are more diverse in terms of age, education level and ethnicity.

According to the Scientific Council for Government Policy (Schrijvers et al. 2015), the main points that policymakers should be concerned with are indeed no longer the guaranteeing of artistic quality and autonomy, which would prevail if only an artistic perspective was taken into account. Rather, the policy focus has been moving towards the reconciliation of supply and demand and the embeddedness of artists and cultural institutions in society, which should enhance public support for the arts. Encouraging artistic producers to take the audience more into account is also believed to diminish the financial dependence of the cultural sector on subsidies and to encourage cultural entrepreneurship and creativity in business management. The Scientific Council is, however, quite sceptical about policymakers' emphasis on the social and financial impact of the arts. They argue that the arts deserve to be supported mainly for their intrinsic aesthetic value, which cannot be reduced to their social or economic significance—something that recent policymakers such as Zijlstra and Bussemaker emphasised. The government's rather instrumental view of the arts, the Council argued, runs the risk of imposing ever-changing goals on cultural producers that may turn out to be hard to attain and difficult to measure adequately, if at all. This is not to say that the Council believes the arts should ignore the public and focus on artistic excellence only. It also suggests taking the audience more seriously in the granting of subsidies and to develop more professional ways of conducting audience research.

8.3   How Does Dutch Cultural Policy Try to Enhance Participation?

It is clear that the Dutch national government values a high level of cultural participation and that its focus is on making the arts—in the broad sense including community art, folk art, popular art and amateur art activities— available to a more diverse audience. As stated above, the goal of encouraging participation by reaching new audiences has gained in prominence especially since Van der Ploeg took office in 1998. As a result, policy has become more balanced in that both supply and demand are now considered in need of explicit support and should be more attuned to one another. Regarding the demand side, we need to distinguish between initiatives taken to encourage receptive cultural participation (i.e., being an audience member) and active cultural participation (making art yourself as an amateur musician, actor, or painter). Below, we shall take a closer look at two programmes that have been developed in order to achieve both: the Cultural Outreach Action Plan (*Actieplan Cultuurbereik*) and the Cultural Participation Scheme (*Regeling Cultuurparticipatie*). Apart from these programmes, it is obvious that generic cultural policy that keeps cultural participation affordable by subsidising supply also supports participation.

Cultural Outreach Action Plan
Striving to increase and diversify the cultural audience, Van der Ploeg introduced the Cultural Outreach Action Plan, whose main goal was to help cultural institutions reach a larger and more diverse audience (IJdens & Hitters 2005). This initiative encouraged a unique cooperation between governments at the national, provincial and local level. All 12 Dutch provinces plus 30 municipalities with at least 90,000 inhabitants were asked to formulate specific plans for a more diverse cultural offering, create links between cultural sectors or disciplines, and reach out more actively to (potential) audiences. The initial four-year programme period (2001-2004) was extended for another four-year term (2005-2008). With this extension, the initial five goals of the Action Plan—1) strengthen programming, 2) make way for cultural diversity, 3) invest in youths, 4) make cultural potential visible, and 5) put cultural town-planning on the agenda—were reduced to one: 'Strengthening people's cultural awareness by increasing both the audience reach and active participation in arts and culture.' (Commissie Cultuurbereik 2007). For this purpose, a yearly budget of €13.7 million was made available by the national government, to be matched by a similar amount by provinces and municipalities.

In its evaluation of the Action Plan, the Cultural Outreach Committee (*Commissie Cultuurbereik*) noted that many participants were very pleased that the Action Plan had led to an extension of the set of criteria for evaluating arts projects (see also IJdens & Hitters 2005 and Huysmans et al. 2005). Those directly involved stated that the Action Plan had successfully argued against the primacy of artistic quality as a criterion and made room for additional criteria such as diversity, regional dispersion, audience reach or innovative connections between the arts and other sectors. Not surprisingly, community arts and educational projects were often mentioned as initiatives meeting these new or additional goals. By thus re-allocating a small portion of the cultural policy budgets, new initiatives could blossom that would not have received government support if artistic quality had been the sole yardstick by which they were judged. This is not to say that the artistic quality was not up to standards but rather that it is difficult for newcomers to successfully claim a piece of the financial pie that the government (at the national, provincial and municipal levels) can offer. Using the criteria of the Action Plan, innovation was indeed encouraged and new networks were created. As it was left to the local and regional governments to formulate their own projects, many different initiatives emerged, but not all of them were easily monitored or evaluated. Notwithstanding this drawback, provinces and municipalities had been forced to think hard about what they wanted to initiate and also what (measurable) outcomes they wished to achieve, which was a positive outcome in itself.

The Cultural Outreach Committee also noted that the Action Plan mostly encouraged newcomers to the field to apply for financial support. This led to much temporary innovation but also to the creation of separate circuits or networks that did not always lead to the anticipated opening up of existing cultural institutions to new audiences or collaborations through innovative programming or marketing. Another 'missed opportunity' was that, once the Action Plan was extended in 2005 and its goal was formulated more broadly, the special focus on youngsters and ethnic minorities lost much of its urgency among applicants.

Cultural Participation Scheme
The Action Plan ended in 2009 when its successor was launched, the Cultural Participation Scheme.[1] Although this Scheme managed to better embed its activities in existing policy practices and diminished the administrative burden for participating initiatives, its goals were insufficiently specified, leaving much room yet little clarity to local policymakers. The organisation of the Scheme was rather complex as well (IJdens & Van Rensen 2010), with different roles and responsibilities for the Ministry of Education, Culture & Sciences, the municipalities, the provinces and the newly established Cultural Participation Fund (*Fonds Cultuurparticipatie*). With the introduction of this new Fund, the focus shifted from the enhancement of receptive cultural participation (as an audience member) to the promotion of active cultural participation (as an amateur artist) and arts education. This shift in focus was announced in the 2007 discussion paper entitled *Art of Living* (*Kunst van Leven*) by Minister of Culture Ronald Plasterk (2007-2010), in which he presented his so-called ten-point-plan that was partly a follow-up of the Action Plan but also explicitly addressed arts education and the strengthening of relations between schools and cultural institutions. Thus, the Fund has been active in supporting artistic talent development programmes, the professionalisation of arts education in schools (with a focus

on primary education since 2013: see chapter 7 by IJdens & Van Meerkerk), encouraging interaction between amateur and professional artists, and initiating international cooperation (Fonds Cultuurparticipatie 2016). In 2016, the Fund spent just over €8 million on subsidies for such projects, which each had to match this financial contribution with additional resources. It is, however, difficult to evaluate how successful these investments have been, primarily because the goals were formulated in rather general terms. While arts education has benefitted especially from support by the Fund, other effects are harder to assess. The following issues were addressed as points of concern in a policy evaluation report:

–   The cross-cutting themes of innovation, diversity and anchoring were formulated in such broad terms that the surplus value of introducing these themes is questionable, as many initiatives came up with their own definition of these themes.
–   While successful initiatives had been developed at the local level, much of the resulting know-how remained within a specific municipality or province and not shared more widely.
–   Is was uncertain to what extent the supported initiatives would be sustainable, as lower governments believed the financial embedding was questionable in the longer term.
–   Many problematic issues encountered in the Action Plan were still there: unspecific goals and concepts, limited attention for financial embedding, and the continuing need for the exchange of knowledge, experience and inspiring examples (Panteia Research voor Beleid 2012).

In conclusion, it is clear that enhancing participation and diversifying the cultural audience have been on the agenda of Dutch policymakers since the 1990s. However, with the advent of the Cultural Participation Scheme, the focus had shifted from passive to active participation and education. The impact of the measures taken with an eye on audience diversification has been hard to establish, since no clear criteria were set and it is hard to isolate the effects of single policy measures from other forces (political, economic, social) affecting cultural participation. This is, of course, an issue that is far from unique for these specific policy initiatives. An additional complicating factor for evaluation was that much of the initiatives were launched at the local level rather than orchestrated by the national government, making the resulting activities too diverse for a proper evaluation of the net effects of this policy. It is, however, positive that the responsibilities of local governments as the prime locus for the policy on participation were recognised and that the national government benefitted from their experience catering to 'their' local cultural audiences.

The involvement of local governments and the concern for equal opportunities for participation fit with the so-called Nordic cultural policy model as identified by Toepler and Zimmer (2002). This model, which is also largely applicable to Dutch cultural policy, is characterised by a high degree of decentralisation. While the national government formulates aims regarding egalitarian access to the arts, regional and local institutions have a high degree of control and responsibility in the initiation and implementation. This is what we have seen above, where central policy goals were preferably realised by supporting local initiatives. It is also typical of this Nordic approach to support not just the high arts, as is the case in a much more centralised cultural policy system such as France, but to include a wider range of popular or grassroots cultural activities. In fact, it has been the explicit goal since Van der Ploeg to provide the type of cultural activities that appeal to groups far beyond the cultural elite. Given this characterisation, with shared responsibilities between different levels of government and much room for bottom-up initiatives to connect with local populations, it makes sense that cultural policy measures are not directly reflected in participation rates, as we shall see in the next section.

8.4 Trends in Cultural Participation in the Netherlands

The Cultural Participation Fund does not directly support receptive cultural participation, as it primarily focuses on amateur arts and arts education or talent development. This means that policy aimed at enhancing participation is no longer central on the governmental agenda. It can be argued, however, that supporting active participation and education may also stimulate passive cultural participation, as amateur artists and those receiving an arts education are more likely to become audience members of the professional arts (Vanherwegen & Lievens 2014). Nevertheless, it is clear that we should not expect recent Dutch government policy to have a visible impact on cultural participation rates, both active and receptive.[2]

Table 8.1 shows the trends in receptive participation between 2006 and 2014 for nine important artistic disciplines. The numbers demonstrate that museums and films welcomed a growing proportion of the Dutch population among their audiences. Museum visits increased from 49% in 2006 to 52% in 2014, while film attendance rose from 56% to 64%. Interestingly, both museums and movie theatres have invested quite a bit in technology (3D vision, surround sound), comfort (better seating, quality food), and interactivity (touch-screens in museums) in order to draw larger audiences.

Also, both are able to attract mass attention by programming so-called blockbusters, a term previously reserved for movies but now also applied to very successful exhibitions, typically of iconic artists such as Van Gogh, Rembrandt, Gauguin, Jheronimus Bosch, etc.

Table 8.1: **Trends in *passive* cultural participation in the Netherlands, 2006-2014 (% of the population who attended at least once in the preceding 12 months)**

	2006	2008	2010	2012	2014
Museum	49	47	50	48	52
Opera	6	5	6	4	4
Classical music	19	17	20	18	17
Ballet	7	7	7	6	6
Theatre	28	28	29	27	26
Musical	27	26	26	24	21
Cabaret / Comedy	24	25	25	22	22
Film	56	54	61	61	64
Popular music	27	31	29	27	30

Source: SCP (2015: 254)

The other disciplines appear to have struggled to keep up their attendance rates. Opera, classical music, ballet, theatre, musical and cabaret suffered from declining audiences since 2010. Popular music did better: it showed no clear trend but constantly hovered around 29%. Overall, receptive cultural participation has been rather stable. The most recent Arts Index Netherlands (www.cultuurindex.nl), which takes 2005 as its starting point (value 100), shows that participation declined only slightly to 97.4 in 2015. However, as Table 8.1 demonstrates, this apparent continuity conceals somewhat diverging trends in arts participation for different disciplines.

If we look at trends in active cultural participation, the findings look more bleak, despite the focus of policymakers on supporting amateur arts participation since 2009. Active participation was at 72.8, indicating a drop of over 25% since 2005. Note, however, that this downward trend is to a large extent caused by the steep decline in the number of students at centres for the arts in 2013, which is a consequence of policy changes at the local level. Many of these students have found alternative places or ways to educate themselves (IJdens 2015). A more detailed view is given in Table 8.2 (note that not all indicators were available in 2005).

The number of students at centres for the arts (public institutions for learning music, theatre, or the visual arts) diminished at an alarming pace between 2005 and 2015, from 447,930 to 252,042. Part of this decline can be attributed to the cutbacks in local government support for these centres,[3] which forced many of them to terminate their activities. In fact, the number of centres for the arts declined by 35%, dropping from 237 in 2005 to 155 in 2013, at a pace very similar to the diminishing number of students. With the possibility to enrol in arts education through these institutions seriously diminished, many students were obliged to find alternative ways to develop their artistic skills.

Table 8.2:   Trends in *active* cultural participation in the Netherlands, 2005-2015

	2005	2007	2009	2011	2013	2015
Students at centres for the arts	447930	475300	426573	407984	271700	252042
Members of music, singing or theatre clubs (%)	8.7	10.3	10.3	9.8	9.5	8.1
Musical instrument players (%)		11.5	10.9	9.5	9.2	9.1
Members of choir or informal singing groups (%)		9.4	8.7	8.1	7.8	7.9
Performers of theatre, musical, ballet (%)		14.4	12.6	9.8	8.3	8.1
Students of handcraft, painting, drawing, molding (%)		21.2	17.8	15.6	16.2	14.9

Sources: Arts Index Netherlands, www.cultuurindex.nl.

All other indicators of active cultural participation show declining participation rates as well. The most dramatic decline was in the percentage of performers of theatre, musicals or ballet, which dropped from 14.4% of the Dutch population in 2007 to 8.1% in 2015. There are a number of reasons for this general decrease in active cultural participation. Apart from the decreased number of places where courses can be taken, people have become busier due to the increasing number of possible leisure activities; the economic crisis may have made it harder for people to financially sustain their hobbies or lessons; and some of the learning may have shifted to online environments, where many tutorials can be found on YouTube, for example (Van der Zant & Van Eijck 2015). Thus, we should consider this trend against the backdrop of a more general shift in the ways people spend their leisure time. Similar to active cultural participation, receptive participation, sports, hobbies and voluntary work have all suffered from downward trends as well, while media use, including the Internet, has increased (Vinken & IJdens 2015). This trend is not unique for the Netherlands either, as it has been observed in many countries.

8.5   When is Cultural Policy on Participation Successful?

Tables 8.1 and 8.2 present trends in receptive and active cultural participation, showing that both active and receptive participation rates are clearly
declining, although the decline in the latter has been less dramatic. The
only exceptions to the downward trend were in museums, film and popular
music. Although Dutch film and pop music receive some government support, their relative successes surely cannot be attributed to this support,
as they are far less dependent on subsidies than the four more traditional
art forms (opera, classical music, ballet and theatre) and, moreover, much
of the supply comes from abroad. This raises two questions. First, to what
extent can we actually expect these trends to tell us anything about the
success of cultural policy? Second, what would be more relevant or feasible
measures of policy success, given what policymakers hope to achieve by
supporting cultural participation? These questions will be addressed below.

Politics and Trends in Participation
If we consider Tables 8.1 and 8.2 to be indicators of the success or failure
of Dutch cultural policy, there would be little reason for optimism. As
we have seen, the Cultural Outreach Action Plan aimed to support local
initiatives that were innovative and that targeted new audiences. The
intention was to create new networks or a new set of cultural practices,
provisions and supporting infrastructure for people who were not in the
audiences of existing cultural institutions. Among these new initiatives
were community art projects, multi-functional cultural spaces and studios,
arts education projects for children with special needs, open-air theatre
productions, small-scale festivals, poetry workshops, the making of songs
in local dialects, sanctioned graffiti decoration of public places, and the
creation of a website as a cultural biography of a city (*Regiegroep Actieplan
Cultuurbereik* 2008). Such initiatives, which often evolve at the edges of the
existing cultural infrastructure, will obviously not be noticed in national
survey data that use more traditional categories to map cultural participation. If subsidies were spent on less innovative initiatives, they were often
used to co-finance plans that were already existent and would have been
carried out anyway.[4]

    The Cultural Outreach Committee, endowed with the task of evaluating
the Action Plan, concluded that it was virtually impossible to offer an objective evaluation, as any appraisal would be subjective since their evaluation
was largely based on surveys and interviews with participating institutions
and policymakers. In addition, the potential impact of the Action Plan

cannot be isolated from other developments in the cultural sector. For example, when first evaluated, it was only implemented in the 30 largest municipalities, which complicates an assessment of net effects due to difficulties in comparing participation rates between these municipalities and those that did not participate, which were typically smaller (Huysmans et al. 2005). These differences were controlled for, but unmeasured differences between larger and smaller municipalities could obviously not be taken into account. By talking to many key players involved, the Committee was able to get a reasonable impression of the strong and weak points of the Action Plan as perceived by those involved, but an evaluation in the strict sense could not be carried out. Initiatives that were developed with the aid of the Action Plan may have been successful, but they were very much dispersed and singular, often lacking the long-term financial commitment to bring significant or lasting change to the cultural infrastructure.

It must of course be taken into account that the money reserved for the Action Plan or the Cultural Participation Scheme was only a fraction of the total national budget spent on arts and culture.[5] Also, while the Action Plan or the Scheme were being carried out, other initiatives with sometimes overlapping goals were taking place as well. The national government invested in cultural education through schools, libraries have re-invented themselves and sought to connect more with partners in the cultural sector (see chapter 7), archives have received funding to enhance their accessibility online, and investments have been made in urban planning to create synergies between cultural policy and public space. In this multitude of initiatives and funding opportunities, the impact of any specific measure is virtually impossible to isolate and assess unequivocally. It is little wonder, then, that no clear link between cultural policy and cultural participation can be observed at the national level. But we may also ask ourselves if these participation rates are the most adequate criterion for policy success, apart from the practical and methodological drawbacks. According to IJdens (2012), in general it makes little sense to translate relatively open policy goals into measurable targets.

Assessing Policy Success Through Participation Measures
We listed a number of methodological reasons for the relative uselessness of general participation rates to assess government policy. These are rather technical reasons why such data typically do not provide much ground for firm evaluative statements. The results of policy measures that make up only some two percent of the already modest budget of a relatively marginal policy field are unlikely to show up in trends in population surveys. But does it make sense to expect them to?

The answer is no, and not just for these methodological reasons. Unless we wish to measure the direct change in the number of people participating in the newly developed initiatives, these numbers are not very meaningful. Although one may secretly hope for a successful initiative to turn people into returning audience members, this assumption would be overly optimistic. Typically, getting a person to participate in a more or less innovative cultural activity once does not change this person's attitude towards cultural participation in the long run. Cultural dispositions and resources do not change overnight.[6] Nevertheless, it is not uncommon for policy evaluations to resort to such 'hard' empirical data in an attempt to provide a solid 'evidence base' for policy success (Belfiore 2004). The requirement of evidence-based policy is related to the notion of instrumental cultural policy, which refers to the tendency 'to use cultural ventures and cultural investments as a means or instrument to attain goals in other than cultural areas' (Vestheim 1994). Examples of such goals—which may be labelled 'extrinsic' as they can in theory be achieved by other means than the arts (Van den Hoogen 2012)—are enhancing social inclusion and cohesion, boosting creativity or gentrifying neighbourhoods. As mentioned above, Minister of Culture Bussemaker also argued that much of the raison d'être of cultural policy resides in art's ability to connect to other social domains.

Such external effects are never achieved directly but through changes in the skills, knowledge or attitudes of those who are subject to meaningful aesthetic experiences, either receptively or actively. Therefore, the ultimate reasons governments believe they must support cultural participation lie more in the (intrinsic) cognitive and emotional effects of participation on individuals which may, in turn, have an impact on society at large and which the government itself cannot affect directly, as that is the task of the cultural institutions that are being supported to contribute to these goals. Nevertheless, let us look again at some of the rationalisations given for cultural policy in this area.

In the discussion paper outlining her cultural policy plans for 2013-2017, Bussemaker pays explicit attention to the legitimisation of cultural policy. She argues for a broad conception of culture that encompasses 'the sharing of (creative) forms of expression, knowledge, experiences and opinions. It is a dynamic system in which we create and confront values, symbols and identities.' (Bussemaker 2012: 1). Cultural participation is thought to improve so-called twenty-first-century skills—i.e., the ability to respond to change and to be creative and innovative. Here, the individual benefits of engaging with the arts are transported to the economic realm with the argument that these skills are much needed in today's information society.

Other policy documents list a number of additional legitimisations for supporting the arts: identity formation, enjoyment, enrichment, enhancing tolerance and social cohesion, etc. In all cases, the envisioned effects start with a change in individuals' skills, knowledge or attitudes. Assessing the extent to which cultural policy contributes to these goals is very difficult. It would require looking more specifically at what happens in the encounter between audience and art, which is—again—assessing the task of cultural institutions rather than the government itself. But to strengthen the rationale for government support for these institutions, we should look closer at the effects of participation on individual audience members and understand how these might translate into an impact on society as a whole in order to evaluate the impact that the arts have on people's lives.[7] We should also keep in mind that there are many other ways in which people can participate in the arts and benefit from its effects besides attending performances or exhibitions.

A clear focus on what participation—either active or receptive—does with people would be in line with the fruitful notion of theory-based evaluation as a tool for evaluating the social impact of the arts (Galloway 2009). We have already seen that large-scale studies on participation rates are unlikely to inform us about the meaning or impact of cultural policy. Rather, one should investigate *what* works for *whom* under *which* circumstances and *why*. This is no longer an assessment of cultural policy but rather of the social impact of participating. We do argue that such research could help policymakers in identifying what kinds of institutions or projects are most likely to help achieve the desired goals that underpin cultural policy. Just looking at the relation between input (subsidised activities) and output (participation rates) does not tell us much about *how* people are affected by their participation and why. Theory-based evaluation instead assumes that evaluation should focus on the process by which potential change is effected, taking into account the contextualised processes that lead to a certain outcome. Given the constant multitude of influences on people's lives, it is indeed advised to evaluate how people experience specific activities in order to learn if and why these activities have a certain impact on them.

Another interesting element of this approach is that it requires a theory of why certain policy measures are expected to have specific effects. Such a theory would explicate the mechanisms that should be set in motion by one's intervention. Only such a theory would allow evaluators to assess which mechanisms must be mapped and monitored by way of evaluation. While such a rationalist approach is unlikely to determine policy decision-making, it would be helpful for policymakers to develop a deeper understanding of the factors determining the success of specific initiatives (or types of initiatives) in order to assess their potential merits. Finally, theory-based evaluation and its generative model of change can be used to establish what kinds of activities other than the subsidised arts may lead to the desired outcomes at the individual level. Can certain forms of popular art contribute to a desired attitude change, too? And which values are most effectively communicated through which types of participation? In order to answer such questions, policymakers should look at the quality of aesthetic experiences as well as their relation to the desired effects and how these are best realised. Doing so would make cultural policy more focused in its support of participation. It would also make the results of evaluations more meaningful and hence useful for further improving the aesthetic experiences offered by cultural institutions and the policy instruments to support them, also by allowing sensible suggestions for adjustments to be made during the runtime of a policy programme. This requires qualitative research in order to map the contextualised experiences of participants and assess to what extent these are likely to further the underlying policy goals. Are the experiences that are offered relevant for people's identity? Do they gain a better understanding of other people's viewpoints? Is their creativity called upon? Understanding when and why goals such as these are achieved will help policymakers and cultural institutions in focussing on the most promising cultural initiatives for increasing participation and enhancing their impact.

A second reason not to rely on formal participation rates when evaluating the impact of cultural policy is that the Internet and other (social) media increasingly offer gateways to the arts that are easily accessible and inexpensive yet scarcely incorporated into official statistics. Even if people do not attend cultural events, it can be argued that their interest or informal participation in the arts should in itself matter to policymakers. Through YouTube, Spotify and numerous other channels and media, people can satisfy many of their cultural needs virtually anytime, anywhere and at little or no costs. Formal attendance of events is therefore an increasingly inadequate indicator for assessing people's cultural practices. The same goes for active participation, for which inspiration and instructions are increasingly found online, too (Van den Broek 2010). Those who listen to classical music at home, borrow a novel or DVD from a friend, or download sheet music from the Internet all benefit from the positive effects that engaging with the arts may have. These 'participants' do not surface in the statistics typically used for policy evaluation purposes, but they do rely on the existing cultural infrastructure that enables them to satisfy their needs and develop their cultural skills. It thus makes sense to monitor such online and informal manners of participating as well.

In 2009, already 41 percent of the Dutch population used digital media to look at art or to listen to music categorised under the heading of 'canonised' art (Sonck & De Haan 2012). For popular art, this percentage was 53. Purchasing tickets or seeking information (e.g., opening hours, exhibitions) was done online by over half of the population, both for canonised and popular culture. These proportions have been on the rise since and will most likely continue to do so, given the fact that younger audiences are much more proficient in the use of digital media than the elderly. People between the ages of 18 and 34 are almost four times more likely than those aged 65 or older to enjoy culture through new media (55% versus 15%). For popular culture, there is an even greater gap between these percentages (85% versus 9%). Thus, cultural participation is expanding to the online world. If the government wishes to have more people enjoy the arts, it should take this development seriously and encourage the availability of the arts through (online) media. As in the case of science, it could be argued that access to publicly funded art through media should be available to as many people as possible. In addition, the effects of mediated arts participation can be assessed using the theory-based evaluation approach mentioned above, which allows for a comparison of different modes of cultural engagement.

8.6   Conclusions

While post-1945 cultural policy in the Netherlands has always been keen on reaching a wider audience for the arts, this goal was long legitimised by the idea that art would turn people into better, more civilised human beings. Although these goals have fluctuated somewhat over time, near the end of the twentieth century, Dutch cultural policy has taken a clear turn towards enhancing participation by obliging the recipients of subsidies to try to reach out to new audiences and take the audience perspective more into account. Several programmes have been initiated to encourage participation by developing new cultural initiatives targeting in particular younger audiences and people with a minority background. Given the decentralised approach in this endeavour, which has been typical of Dutch cultural policy since 2001, these initiatives have lacked clear measurable goals, and their overall success is therefore hard to assess. Moreover, when the Action Plan was replaced by the Scheme that succeeded it, the focus shifted largely to arts education and active participation.

In its policy plans for 2017-2020, the Cultural Participation Fund will continue to support arts education, especially in primary education and lower secondary education, as part of the policy priorities as set by the national government. In addition, it plans to sponsor innovative 'makers' as well as to encourage the cultural participation of the elderly and vulnerable groups. Third, the Fund hopes to increase public support for cultural participation by sharing stories of people's personal experiences with culture taken from their previous programmes. Again, direct measures for enhancing receptive cultural participation will not be taken. But supporting innovative makers may be the best way to create a larger and new audience for the arts. It is, of course, important that these new initiatives, if successful, are able to count on a more sustained type of support so they may have a more structural impact on participation. For now, the sector seems to be dealing with the following dilemma: innovative makers that reach new audiences are temporarily supported, but after the subsidies stop they are unable to continue their activities as they are also not likely to be included among the more established institutions that can count on sustained financial government support. Finally, it has been argued that the choice of policy instruments would benefit significantly if evaluation practices focus on the theorised effects that participation in the arts has on people, as the social impact of the arts necessarily comes about through meaningful cultural encounters affecting the skills, knowledge and attitudes of the audience. While ensuring the type of cultural activities that will fulfil these ideals is the responsibility of cultural institutions and other professional initiatives, it is the government who needs to decide where the money goes. This requires that policymakers know what types of offerings are most likely to help them achieve their policy goals, which are ultimately about offering people access to enriching experiences.

Notes

1. The end of the Action Plan was imminent given that it was a specific support measure from the national government aimed at provinces and municipalities, which by definition was temporary.

2. This is why, since 2013, the Cultural Participation Fund no longer engages in a discourse on expanding the audience but instead focuses on the meaning and quality of (active) cultural participation projects.

3. Vinkenburg (2015) estimated a decline of 9% in municipal funding for arts and culture between 2011 and 2015. These cutbacks particularly affected libraries and creativity centres.

4. Commissie Cultuurbereik (2007). *Van Stolling naar Stroming* [From Solidification to Flow]. The Hague: Koninklijke De Swart.

5. The Action Plan budget only represented 2-4% of the cultural budget of municipalities and some 8% of the budgets of provinces.
6. See, for example, Pierre Bourdieu (1984) for a theoretical account and Van Eijck & Knulst (2005) for an empirical assessment.
7. For a good example of this, see Otte (2015).

Bibliography

Belfiore, Eleonore. 2004. "Auditing culture. The subsidised cultural sector in the New Public Management", *International Journal of Cultural Policy* 10(2): 183-202.

Blokland, Hans. 1996. "Het pantser van de culturele elite en de ruggengraat van Nuis" [The Cultural Elite's Armour and Nuis' Backbone], *Nederlandse Staatscourant*, Jg.127, Nr.206, October 24: 6. available from: http://www.hans-blokland.nl/artikelen/pantser_nuis_96.htm.

Bourdieu, Pierre. 1984. *Distinction: A social critique of the judgment of taste*. London: Routledge.

Bussemaker, Jet. 2012. *Cultuur beweegt: De betekenis van cultuur in een veranderende samenleving* [Culture Moves: The Meaning of Culture in a Changing Society]. The Hague: Ministerie OCW [Ministry of Education, Culture and Sciences].

Commissie Cultuurbereik [Cultural Outreach Committee]. 2007. *Van stolling naar stroming*. [From Solidification to Flow]. The Hague: Koninklijke De Swart.

Evrard, Yves. 1997. "Democratising Culture or Cultural Democracy?", *The Journal of Arts Management, Law, and Society* 27(3): 167-751.

Fonds Cultuurparticipatie. 2016. *Jaarverslag 2016* [Annual Report 2016]. Utrecht: FCP [Cultural Participation Fund].

Galloway, Susan. 2009. "Theory-based Evaluation and the Social Impact of the Arts", *Cultural Trends* 2: 125-148.

Hoefnagel, Frans. 2009. *Een nieuwe toekomst voor het cultuurbeleid* [A New Future for Cultural Policy]. The Hague: WRR [Scientific Council for Government Policy].

Huysmans, Frank, Olivier van der Vet, and Koen van Eijck. 2005. *Het Actieplan Cultuurbereik en cultuurdeelname 1999-2003*. [The Cultural Outreach Action Plan and Cultural Participation 1999-2003]. The Hague: SCP [Social and Cultural Planning Agency].

IJdens, Teunis. 2012. "Culturele volksgezondheid? Over het nut van bevolkingsonderzoek naar cultuurparticipatie". In: Quirijn van den Hoogen. *Effectief Cultuurbeleid: Leren van Evalueren* [Effective Cultural Policy. Learning through Assessing], pp. 110-127. Amsterdam: Boekmanstichting [Boekman Foundation].

—. 2015. *Kunstzinnig en creatief in de vrije tijd: Monitor Amateurkunst 2015*. [Artistic and Creative during Leisure Time: Monitor of Amateur Arts 2015]. Utrecht: LKCA [National Centre of Expertise for Cultural Education and Amateur Arts].

IJdens, Teunis, and Erik Hitters. 2005. *Landelijke evaluatie van het Actieplan Cultuurbereik 2001-2004*. [National Evaluation of Cultural Outreach Action Plan 2001-2004]. Tilburg: IVA.

IJdens, Teunis, and Chrit van Rensen. 2010. "Cultuurparticipatiebeleid: leren en verbeteren". In: Teunis IJdens, Marjo van Hoorn, Andries van den Broek, and Tienke Hiemstra (eds.), *Jaarboek Actieve Cultuurparticipatie 2010: Bijdragen over kennis en beleid*. [Yearbook of Active Cultural Participation, 2010: Contributions on Knowledge and Policy], pp. 19-45. Utrecht: FCP [Cultural Participation Fund].

Ministerie van OCW. 2013. *Het Nederlands Cultureel Bestel*. [The Dutch Cultural System]. The Hague: Ministerie OCW [Ministry of Education, Culture and Science].

Nuis, Aad. 1996. *Pantser of ruggengraat: Uitgangspunten voor cultuurbeleid.* [Armour or Backbone: Principles for Cultural Policy]. The Hague: Ministerie OCW [Ministry for Education, Culture and Science].

Oosterbaan Martinius, Warna. 1990. *Schoonheid, welzijn, kwaliteit: Kunstbeleid en verantwoording na 1945.* [Beauty, Welfare and Quality: Art Policy and Legitimisation]. The Hague: Gary Schwartz / SDU.

Otte, Hanka. 2015. *Binden of overbruggen? Over de relatie tussen kunst, cultuurbeleid en sociale cohesie.* [Binding or Bridging? On the Relation between Art, Cultural Policy and Social Cohesion]. PhD dissertation, Groningen University.

Panteia Research voor Beleid. 2012. *Evaluatie Regeling Cultuurparticipatie 2009-2012.* [Assessment of Cultural Participation Scheme]. Zoetermeer: Panteia.

Regiegroep Actieplan Cultuurbereik [Steering Committee of Cultural Outreach Action Plan]. 2008. *Het is om de hoek: Acht jaar Actieplan Cultuurbereik* [It's Around the Corner: Eight Years of the Cultural Outreach Action Plan]. The Hague: Koninklijke De Swart.

SCP. 2015. *De sociale staat van Nederland 2015.* [The Social State of the Netherlands 2015]. The Hague: SCP [Social and Cultural Planning Agency].

Toepler, Stefan, and Annette Zimmer. 2002. "Subsidising the Arts: Government and the Arts in Western Europe and the United States". In: Diana Crane, Nobuko Kawashima and Ken'ichi Kawasaki (eds.), *Global Culture: Media, Arts, Policy and Globalisation,* pp. 29-48. New York: Routledge.

Schrijvers, Erik, Anne-Greet Keiser, and Godfried Engbersen. 2015. *Cultuur Herwaarderen* [Reassessing Culture]. The Hague: WRR [Scientific Council for Government Policy].

Sonck, Nathalie, and Jos de Haan. 2012. *De virtuele kunstkar: Cultuurdeelname via oude en nieuwe media* [The Virtual Art Cart: Cultural Participation via Old and New Media]. The Hague: SCP.

Van den Broek, Andries. 2010. *Mogelijkheden tot kunstbeoefening in de vrije tijd.* [Possibilities for Art Participation during Leisure Time]. The Hague: SCP [Social and Cultural Planning Agency].

Van den Hoogen, Quirijn Lennert. (ed.). 2012. *Effectief cultuurbeleid: Leren van evalueren.* [Effective Cultural Policy. Learning Through Assessing]. Amsterdam: Boekmanstichting [Boekman Foundation].

Van der Ploeg, Rick. 1999. *Cultuur als Confrontatie: Uitgangspunten voor het cultuurbeleid 2001-2004* [Culture as Confrontation: Principles for Cultural Policy 2001-2004]. The Hague: Ministerie OCW [Ministry for Education, Culture and Science].

Van der Zant, Peter, and Koen van Eijck. 2015. "Talentontwikkeling in tijden van verschraling: Jonge kunstenaars zoeken hun eigen weg [Talent Development in Times of Austerity: Young Artists Find Their Own Way]", *Boekman* 105: 24-27.

Van Eijck, Koen, and Wim Knulst. 2005. "No more Need for Snobbism: Highbrow Cultural Participation in a Taste Democracy", *European Sociological Review* 21: 513-528.

Vanherwegen, Dries, and John Lievens. 2014. "The Mechanisms Influencing Active Arts Participation: An Analysis of the Visual Arts, Music and the Performing Arts", *Sociological Inquiry* 84(3): 435-471.

Vestheim, Geir. 1994. "Instrumental Cultural Policy in Scandinavian Countries: A Critical Historical Perspective", *International Journal of Cultural Policy* 1, 57-71.

Vinken, Henk, and Teunis IJdens. 2015. "De slag om de vrije tijd. [The Batte for Leisure Time]". In: Teunis IJdens and Jan-Jaap Knol (eds.), *Zicht op Actieve Cultuurparticipatie: Thema's en trends in praktijk en beleid* [Active Cultural Participation: Themes and Trends in Practice and Policy], pp. 44-48. Utrecht: LKCA & FCP [National Centre of Expertise for Cultural Education and Amateur Arts & Cultural Participation Fund].

Vinkenburg, Bastiaan. 2015. *Financiering van de cultuursector 2005 – 2015. Kaalslag of cultuuromslag?* [Funding the Cultural Sector 2005-2015. Clearcutting or Change in Culture?]. Amsterdam: Kunsten '92 / Boekmanstichting [Arts '92 / Boekman Foundation]. Available from: https://www.kunsten92.nl/wp-content/uploads/2015/06/Financiering-van-de-cultuursector-Vinkenburg-Berenschot-22-juni-2015.pdf .

'A Strong Field Needs Variation and Experimentation'

An Interview with Saskia Bak

° Eva Broekema

Ontwerp uitbreiding Museum Arnhem.
Beeld: Benthem Crouwel Architects

A striking change in how museums have come to organise their exhibitions is that their departments dealing directly with the public—through education, marketing and what have you—get involved in the process at an earlier stage. Saskia Bak, director of Museum Arnhem, a museum for modern and contemporary art, recognises this development as a clear example of the growing focus on the museum visitor. According to Bak, this is one of the main successes of cultural policy in recent decades.

The recognition of the need to guide visitors through an exhibition in a way that makes it accessible for a wider range of people is a theme that has gained momentum in both museums and museum policy. It is representative of the current situation that this issue is being tackled from both sides. For quite some time now, top-down policymaking has been replaced by a growing responsibility on the part of cultural institutions. Museum professionals increasingly have a say in the shaping of policy. Bak considers this a good thing, as the most radical changes in this field are being initiated by museums. She sees how museums are fuelling the debate on diversity and establishing a meaningful connection between their collection and its (potential) public, and looking for ways to better involve this audience. When Secretary for Culture Rick van der Ploeg changed the emphasis of cultural policy at the turn of the century to focus on public outreach, the sector was not quite ready for this change. Nowadays, however, almost everyone agrees that initiatives to improve audience reach are laudable—and still necessary. However, there is also critique. Take for instance a museum that wants to communicate by organising an exhibition. Getting the message across better to its audience, should be an issue but not the only issue. Some fear that too strong a focus on the government's reasons for public outreach might cause the message itself to wither away outside of the limelight.

For Bak, maintaining a strong connection between the cultural sector and a rapidly changing population remains one of the biggest challenges for both cultural institutions and cultural policy in the years to come. One issue that will definitely influence museum practice is the ageing of the population. At a certain point in the not-so-distant future, museums will mostly be visited by a generation that was brought up in a digital world. Linear story structures will not be something these visitors are familiar with, which means that museums need to become better equipped at using different forms to present their collections and stories.

Another challenge for the cultural sector is of a more structural nature, according to Bak. Visual arts, design and the creative industries as a whole are organised in separate subfields. This is true for exhibition venues as well as for art schools. At the same time, artists, designers and other cultural producers are collaborating more and more, and their work is becoming more interconnected. This is a development that needs to be embedded much more in the overall structure. Paradoxically, this trend of professions mingling coincides with a growing focus on specialisation and craft. Chances are that these developments will gain momentum and will benefit from a more heterogeneous museum landscape. Museums can be expected to broaden their scope, Bak contends. They will soon be not only collecting and showcasing existing art but also commissioning new works, addressing societal themes in exhibitions from a theoretical perspective as well as organising debates. Even a single museum could take on a variety of roles on different occasions. A strong cultural field needs variation and experimentation, argues Bak, and therefore more room for experimentation is needed. In recent years, however, the possibilities for experimentation have declined due to cuts in public funding for culture and an increase in pressure to attract not only a more varied audience but also simply more visitors. Bak maintains that this is not necessarily problematic if the situation lasts for only a few years, but without experimentation, progress cannot be expected.

This changing landscape of museum functionality implies that museums should not all be expected to meet the same requirements. It also means that the assessment of policy requirements ought to focus on the process rather than on the final results—something that is contrary to current practice. The outcome can be different from what was envisioned, but it is important to know why and how to build on this in the future. The government should take on a stronger role in facilitating this. Bak recognises that this has been happening to a certain extent.

The austerity policy of previous years has led to a considerable loss of trust in the national government among cultural institutions. Institutions share the fear that, after having gone to great lengths to build a strong profile as demanded by the Ministry of Culture, they risk seeing their efforts come to naught when a new government poses different demands. Bak believes that cultural policy should acknowledge previous policy requirements and judge museums accordingly. The government should aim for consistency for longer periods of time, giving museums a better chance to build up a distinct profile. Such profiles will then make it easier and more valuable for museums to cooperate among themselves and with other types of institutions. This could lead to new and better ways of organising the different specialisations each museum has as well as to more cooperation and co-creation. The Modemuze initiative is a good example of this: a platform for the different collections of fashion and costumes owned by around a dozen museums, it benefits from a collective form of showcasing. Bak is pleased to see that museums are increasingly taking on responsibility for subjects like cooperation and inclusivity, both as individual institutions and as a sector.

Rogier Brom

9. The People's Palaces

Public Libraries in the Information Society

Frank Huysmans and Marjolein Oomes

Public libraries, together with public broadcasting, are the only publicly funded cultural institutions with a broad social reach which includes groups of lower socioeconomic status and immigrants. Despite this crucial role they play, public libraries seem to have reached a turning point in the first decades of the twenty-first century. While they have a potential role as treasure troves of knowledge and guidance in a world of information overkill, 'alternative facts' and dwindling reading motivation among school-aged children, their societal relevance has been challenged, while cutbacks have affected the physical presence and professional staffing of public libraries over the last five years. However, a new public library law tightening the connections between the public library sector and the national library in the Netherlands may provide new impulses. This chapter tracks the developments in Dutch public library policy and the practices implemented by libraries to reposition themselves in the information age and 'data economy'. It concludes by exploring how the public role of libraries can be made visible by developing new ways to measure the societal value of these people's palaces.

9.1 The Dutch Public Library Network in 2018

The public library network in the Netherlands is well over a century old. In 1908, the Central Association of Public Reading Rooms and Libraries was founded by six members from the cities of Groningen, Leeuwarden, Utrecht, Dordrecht, The Hague and Rotterdam. It was not before the 1960s and 1970s that public library services reached all corners of the country. Economic crises, reluctance from religious groups (both Roman Catholics and Protestants) and the Second World War were important obstacles to the expansion that was so greatly desired by proponents of the Reading Room Movement, which was more successful in other Western European countries such as England, Wales and Scotland (Black, Pepper & Bagshaw 2009, Schneiders 1990).

The most recent statistics available at the moment of writing (reflecting the situation in late 2016 to mid-2017) list some 150 public library organisations in the Netherlands that operate at approximately 770 main locations and fully fledged library branches. An additional 200 staffed access points with limited collections and 180 book collection points are scattered across the country. In total, 2.3 million children (0-17 years) and 1.4 million adults are registered as members. Yearly, roughly 65 million visits are made. In addition, over 2,500 primary schools are connected to the Library at School programme with public library organisations involved in such activities as bringing books to—or very close to—schools to support and strengthen education systems. Over 560,000 children enrolled at these schools (0-12 years of age) have access to a Library at School. In addition, 55 lower secondary schools with almost 50,000 students (12-16 years of age) are connected to the same programme (Koninklijke Bibliotheek 2017).

The Public Library Act (*Wet stelsel openbare bibliotheekvoorzieningen*, WSOB), effective as of 1 January 2015, stipulates that each of the 150 public library organisations fulfill five core functions:
- provide knowledge and information
- offer opportunities for development and education
- promote reading and literature
- organise encounters and debate
- introduce to art and culture.

Since these functions were introduced in a report jointly written a decade earlier by the Dutch Public Library Association (*Vereniging van Openbare Bibliotheken*, VOB) and the Association of Dutch Municipalities (*Vereniging van Nederlandse Gemeenten*, VNG), they have been standard practice in the public library sector. The 2015 Act elevated them to legal status in conjunction with a set of public values to guide how these functions were to be executed: independence, reliability, accessibility, pluriformity and authenticity.

Observing the core functions and public values in the Act, the range of public library services has extended beyond simply lending books. The parliamentary deliberation on the bill in 2014 made it clear that all five functions were to be mandatory for every public library organisation (albeit not for every individual branch). Moreover, Article 5 of the Act states that these functions 'contribute to the personal development and societal opportunities of the general public'—a statement that can be seen as referring back to the traditional role of the public library as it was conceived in the second half of the nineteenth century—namely, as an institution for empowerment through self-education (Black, Pepper & Bagshaw 2009, Greve 1906, Schneiders 1990, Wiegand 2015).

Indeed, in recent years the tasks and activities of libraries have expanded into various domains. Increasingly, libraries organise activities such as lectures, expositions, workshops and debates in the fields of literature, the arts, culture, politics and social issues. Their role in reading promotion takes shape in educational programmes aimed at primary and secondary schools and organisations for early childhood education such as daycare centres and playgroups for babies and toddlers. In extensive cooperation with social organisations, they address social issues such as low literacy and low digital skills through programmes for basic skills education and lifelong learning (Koninklijke Bibliotheek 2017).

Meanwhile, both traditional and new tasks and services are being given a physical and digital appearance, and new forms of reaching out to user groups are being introduced:

- the national digital library: a portal (onlinebibliotheek.nl) offering e-books for e-lending as well as online courses (leisure, personal development and basic skills), together with a separate website for youth (jeugdbibliotheek.nl)
- experiments involving knowledge exchanges and development of online communities
- introduction of 'performative spaces' (fablab / maker space / media lab) to several libraries, including in mobile form
- digital information desks with reliable information in the fields of health and health care, labour markets and government (including e-government).

In overseeing the network's shape in 2018, it is fair to say that the public library network performs a range of activities that is much broader than the outdated public image of the institution—as a book lending warehouse—would have it. The *central question* of this chapter concerns how this state of affairs has developed over the past 25 years and the extent to which this has implications for public library policy and evaluation. Three dimensions or 'threads' will be central to our analysis:

1. the extent to which public library policy was *centralised versus decentralised*;
2. the *narrow versus broad* conceptualisation of the public library's societal role; and
3. the (development of) *indicators* that measure the extent to which the library network is effectively performing its desired functions.

First, we give a historical sketch of the development of public library policy over the past quarter century divided into several phases (sections 9.2 to 9.5). Then, we direct our attention to the current situation, discussing the broadening functions that the public library serves, the innovations in library services, the status of physical libraries and the monitoring of the public library's functions (sections 9.6 to 9.9), before finally summarising our findings (9.10).

9.2   Public Library Policy, Part 1: 1975-1998

Public library policy in the Netherlands is predominantly local (municipal) policy. From the start of the public financing of public libraries in the early 1900s, local governments have been in charge of public library policy with the short yet notable exception of the period between 1975 and 1987, when an attempt was made to centralise the public library system with the first Public Library Act. This Act succeeded in strengthening and expanding the provision of public library services, especially in rural areas (defined as municipalities with less than 30,000 inhabitants). In the 1980s, however, an economic recession, in combination with the trend in public administration science to place democratic control at the level where citizens can enjoy the benefits of public services, led to the reinstatement of local governments as the principal level of public library policy. In 1987, the public library system was incorporated into the Welfare Act and then decentralised, a process that was eventually completed in 1989. The first Public Library Act of 1975 was history.

Already in 1993, public library policy shifted from the Welfare Act to the newly established Cultural Policy Act. Two articles were dedicated to public library policy. Article 11a arranged that a financial contribution for library membership would only be asked of children and adolescents if provincial or municipal governments so decided, but the contribution could only be at most half of the adult contribution fee.

Article 11b stipulated that the three levels of government 'promote that the library facility they finance or maintain participate in the lending traffic together with other library facilities' and that they build regional and national networks. These networks were to be built from the bottom up, with provincial networks comprising all local networks (public library organisations) within their territory, and with the national network consisting of all provincial networks. The networks were made responsible for such things as collecting and distributing library materials and other information sources, centralising their collection management (including automation), and providing library services for special groups (particularly for the visually impaired).

The library system had seemingly arrived in calm waters, but the truth was that storm clouds were gathering on the horizon. In the second half of the 1990s, two developments started to preoccupy librarians and policymakers alike. First, a structural decline in reading began to emerge in library statistics. From the beginning of the 1980s, researchers identified a decline in the amount of leisure time the Dutch invested in reading print media from as early as the 1950s (Knulst & Kalmijn 1988, Knulst & Kraaykamp 1996). Remarkably, this trend failed to emerge in the library lending statistics until book lending finally stalled in the 1990s. Second, the rise of networked computers as household equipment and the advent of the internet and the World Wide Web as sources of information threatened the informational function of the public library.

9.3   Decline in Membership and Book Lending

The inclusion of the public libraries in the Cultural Policy Act in 1993 marks, in hindsight, the beginning of a period of decline in usage figures. After almost a century of first slow and then rapid expansion, Dutch public libraries reached a peak in membership, collection and lending in the beginning of the 1990s (Fig. 9.1).

Figure 9.1 shows the rapid expansion of the public library system in the period 1960-1985. During this quarter century, the rise in loans kept pace with a growing number of registered users. Over the decade that followed, users and loans more or less stabilised, despite some fluctuations. The number of registered users peaked in 1994 at almost 4.6 million. The number of loans reached a peak in 1990, already at over 185 million items. Starting in the mid-1990s, however, a gradual decline in users went hand in hand with a much sharper decline in loans. Logically, this was the result of users borrowing fewer books per capita. It is imaginable that the introduction of lending rights was a determining factor. Several libraries started to charge a small fee for each borrowed book or other item. This additional cost may have led to patrons becoming more critical in what and how much they borrowed. In that case, one would expect to see an initial drop after which stabilisation would set in at a lower level. Instead, there is a continuing, steep decline in loans. In other words, there must be additional and more powerful explanations, which we will now discuss.

Ten years ago, a study of developments in the public library landscape looked into several possible explanations for the marked decline in memberships and loans (Huysmans & Hillebrink 2008: Ch. 5). Starting already in the 1950s, a gradual and steady decline in the amount of leisure time spent reading was observed in time-use diary studies. From 1975 to 2005,

Figure 9.1:   Expansion of the Dutch public library system (in millions)

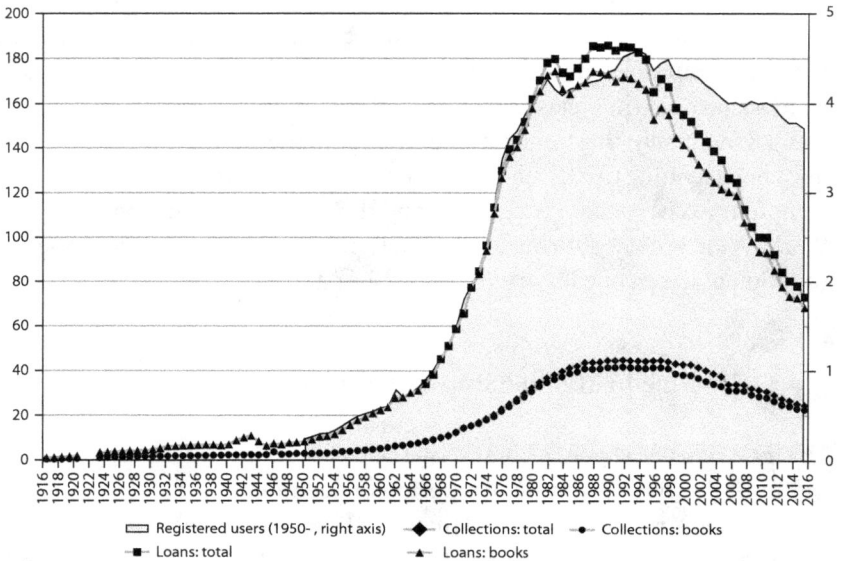

Source: Statistics Netherlands (https://opendata.cbs.nl/statline/#/CBS/nl/dataset/82469NED/
table?ts=1516800365480)

a series of studies every five years indicated a decline in the number of
Dutch citizens (12 years of age and over) reading at all, i.e., spending at
least one interval of 15 minutes reading a book, magazine, newspaper or
other reading material per week. For those who did read, the amount of
time spent reading declined only slightly. 'Fewer Dutch are reading' is a
more apt way of describing the trend than 'The Dutch are reading less'. A
recent study (Wennekers et al. 2018) using a time-budget survey allowing
for more fine-grained registrations of media use from digital devices has
demonstrated that this trend is continuing. The study also showed a very
pronounced decline for teenagers (12-19 years of age) and younger adults
(20-34 years) and much less so for the older population (seniors aged 65
years and older), for which the proportion of readers remained unchanged.

Looking at the data on a descriptive level, the simplest explanation would
be that age groups (or generations) have reacted differently to changes
in the media and reading environments, such as the rise of e-papers, e-
magazines and e-books as well as social media platforms such as Facebook
and on-demand video services such as Netflix. Younger people may be more
inclined than others to incorporate 'new media' into their media menus.
Older age groups may not change their patterns of media behaviour so

drastically, which would explain why 'traditional media' tend to exhibit considerable resilience when confronted with new competitors. Looking beyond the media environment, the number of options to fill one's leisure time shows no signs of decreasing. In other words, the number of options to choose from in spending one's leisure time both in and outside the media environment makes it less probable that reading books and other textual media will make the cut, although the probability may well vary with age.

9.4   Public Library Policy, Part 2: The Library Renewal Policy Programme (1998-2008)

In a 1998 memorandum to the ministry responsible for culture, the Council for Culture (*Raad voor Cultuur*) argued that the public library landscape— which typically had one library organisation in each municipality—would not be able to survive the dual challenges of the decline in reading and the trend towards digitisation. It advocated the scaling up of the library system by putting one organisation per region (each covering 400-500,000 inhabitants) with one governing board in charge of that region's library services. Each board was to be filled with representatives from the provinces and municipalities in the region, thereby forming political bodies: 'The local involvement of citizens could be organised through customer councils or panels, or other forms of public participation' (Raad voor Cultuur 1998: 8, translated by authors).

The Council's advice spurred a heated debate over the future of the public library system. Many deemed the proposed upscaling and particularly the phasing out of the local governmental level in library policy to be too abrupt a measure. As a way out of this debate, a committee was established, in good Dutch tradition, with the task of finding a way out of the deadlock. The Steering Committee on the Restructuring of Public Libraries, as it was called, was chaired by former Secretary for Culture Wim Meijer (who had successfully guided the 1975 Public Library Act through the chambers of parliament). After consulting stakeholders, the committee presented its final report, *Open Gate to Knowledge* (*Open poort tot kennis*), in 2000.

In its report, the Steering Committee upheld the Council for Culture's diagnosis that the public library system needed restructuring, but the nature of this restructuring deviated considerably from the Council's advice. In the view of the committee, small public library organisations should be merged into larger organisational units covering areas of at least 30-35,000 inhabitants but ideally (many) more. Local governments, however, were to

remain in charge of public library policy for its citizens. In the committee's
view, the regional level of government (i.e., the level of the provinces) should
act as the 'stage manager' of public library provisions within the province's
borders and should stimulate the following:
- cooperation between library organisations,
- cooperation between library organisations and other cultural, educational, knowledge, and other social organisations working at, and
  beyond, the local level,
- innovation and renewal as well as a change towards a more user-oriented
  organisational culture.

The responsibility for the functioning of the public library system *as a
whole* was to be positioned at the national level, 'enlarging its effectivity,
coherence, quality and pluriformity' (Stuurgroep Herstructurering Openbaar
Bibliotheekwerk 2000: 33). The national government could also formulate
'unsolicited' policy aims for library provisions, e.g., supplementary endeavours related to reading promotion, cultural education and international
cooperation.

The report concluded with a detailed implementation plan for the
restructuring process. It specified what was expected from the parties
involved: municipalities, provinces, the national government, local library
organisations, provincial support organisations and the Dutch Public Library
Association VOB (which was subsidised by the Ministry of Education, Culture
and Science as its de facto executive branch in developing programmes at
the national level). By and large, this plan was followed up in the subsequent
years, with the notable exception of its duration. Initially, a three-year period
was anticipated (2001-2003), but in practice, the implementation process
lasted more than seven years. In April 2008, the process was officially
concluded with a national conference in the new main building of the
Amsterdam public library.

During the 2001-2008 period, a steering group was formally in charge
of the restructuring process. It was supported by a 'process management
office' facilitated by the Ministry of Education, Culture and Science which
served as the force behind the restructuring endeavours. At the provincial
level, plans were developed for the merging of library organisations while
taking local/regional situations into account. In several cases, city libraries merged with the organisations of adjacent municipalities. Elsewhere,
libraries surrounding a city wished to remain independent from the city's
library and merged into a 'doughnut' structure. In regions without a city
functioning as a de facto regional centre, regional cooperation developed,

sometimes with multiple 'main libraries' forming in the most populous villages of an area.

One notable comment from the 2000 *Open Gate to Knowledge* report was that new legislation would take too much time and would only constitute a formal operation while the main task was to change public library *practices*. The Cultural Policy Act did not in any way preclude a restructuring of the sector, according to the steering committee. What *was* needed, however, was a set of agreements—in addition to the Act—between the three levels of government to be laid down in a covenant. In it, the three layers of government should outline their mutual responsibilities in the process of restructuring the library network. The first covenant covered the 2001-2004 period. When in the course of that period it became evident that more time was needed, a supplement to the covenant was devised and agreed upon to cover the years 2005 through 2007.

The main reason for the delay relative to the planning was the wide variation in the pace of the restructuring process between the provinces. In the northern province of Groningen, a cooperation agreement between all library organisations in the region was already in place at the beginning of the Library Renewal process, whereas in other provinces, it took several years for the merging to begin. However, at the conclusion of the process in 2008, the number of library organisations had been reduced from approximately 540 (ca. one per municipality) to just under 200 in 2008. By 2010, only 166 organisations remained. This also meant that the number of citizens served per organisation had risen to ca. 100,000, far exceeding the 30-35,000 that the Meijer committee had recommended as a minimum. However, the number of library branches and service points remained roughly stable in that period at approximately 1,080 (Bibliotheekmonitor 2018).

9.5   Public Library Policy, Part 3: A New Public Library Act (2008-2017)

It is fair to say that in 2008, when the Library Renewal Process was formally concluded, a new surge of energy emerged within the Dutch public library sector. The Steering Group's final report (Stuurgroep Bibliotheekvernieuwing 2008) and an in-depth analysis of societal factors expected to affect the public library sector in the decennium to come (Huysmans & Hillebrink 2008) provided directions for the sector that it was eager to take up. The Public Library Association even developed its own strategic vision, *Agenda for the*

Future (Vereniging van Openbare Bibliotheken 2008). In the meantime, the national government was not idle. A considerable budget (ca. 20 million euros annually) was reserved for library innovation in the years to come.

Putting this new energy into action was somewhat thwarted by a restructuring of the subsidised part of the cultural sector. At the national level, the Ministry of Education, Culture and Science intended to disentangle the implementation of its policy from the direct influence of the sector itself. The Public Library Association (VOB) was a hybrid organisation in that it was both a membership organisation governed by its members and an executor of policy programmes functioning on behalf of the national government (the Ministry of Education, Culture and Science). In theory, this could lead to situations in which public libraries could refuse to implement policy programmes and measures devised by the ministry and/or parliament.

The national government set up an advisory committee to devise an innovation strategy for the 2009-2012 period. In its report *Effective Innovation* (*Innovatie met Effect* 2008), the contours of the ministry's strategy to solve the VOB's 'possible conflict of interest' problem became visible: the VOB was no longer to be in charge of the national government's public library budgets. Instead, a so-called 'sector institute' was to be established from 2010, and the VOB itself was to be transformed into a trade association with a much smaller budget stemming primarily from its members' contributions.

In practice, the disentanglement of the national government's responsibilities from the sector's interests implied dividing the VOB into parts. This process was to take the better part of 2009, which begged the question of what would happen to the innovation budget in that same year. The advisory committee proposed that a small project office be established that would organise a call for innovation proposals and function as a jury for awarding the most promising proposals. The intention was to integrate this project office into the Netherlands Institute for Public Libraries, which was to become operational as of 2010 (*Sectorinstituut Openbare Bibliotheken*, SIOB). In the course of restructuring operations, it was decided that a separate entity, the Bibliotheek.nl foundation, was to be established as separate from the sector institute. Whereas the SIOB would primarily serve as a strategic entity, Bibliotheek.nl was designed to be an executive organisation, developing several digital services at a national scale for both back office (e.g., library data management) and front office (e.g., a national e-book lending platform) purposes. As of January 2010, three separate organisations were operational at the national level: the downsized 'new' Public Libraries Association (VOB), the Netherlands Institute for Public Libraries (SIOB) and Bibliotheek.nl (BNL). Although each organisation's responsibilities had been demarcated on paper, it took quite a long time for the organisations and the ministry to become used to both the new situation and to each organisation's ambitions.

When the dust had settled, another restructuring project was looming on the horizon: the development of a new Public Library Act. The legal basis for public library activities in the Cultural Policy Act (Articles 11a and 11b) dated from the pre-digital era. With the increasing prominence of digital libraries and of the distribution of e-content, there was a need to put local, regional and national governmental responsibilities on a new legal footing. It was felt, moreover, that incorporating the Royal Library (Koninklijke Bibliotheek, KB) would generate stronger coherence in the network. Additionally, the ministry claimed that incorporating the societal remit and function(s) of the public library system into the law would assist local policymakers in defining their libraries' budgets (Vereniging van Nederlandse Gemeenten 2015).

In January 2014, a bill was presented to the parliament. Over the course of the same year, the bill was passed by both the House of Representatives (*Tweede Kamer*) and the Senate (*Eerste Kamer*). It became effective on 1 January 2015. Both the sector institute (SIOB) and the national digital library organisation (BNL) were integrated into the existing Royal Library organisation. This meant that the public library sector was to be 'removed' from the Cultural Policy Act (Articles 11a and 11b).

9.6   From Act to Practice: Expanding Services

As part of discussions in both chambers of parliament, it was agreed that an evaluation of the Act would be conducted within five years. The senate also pressed for a mid-term review after two years. In December 2017, the Secretary for Culture sent a letter to both chambers accompanied by two research reports. Asserting that a two-year period is too short to observe any actual 'effects' of the act, the letter describes developments within the public library landscape in retrospect. Most notable is the appearance of several 'blind spots' in the landscape. In 2017, 16 of the 388 municipalities did not offer public library services in full concordance with the Public Library Act—i.e., operating on the basis of the five public values, offering all five core functions listed in the Act, and being a member of the national network (Van Mil et al. 2017). The Act does not require that municipalities maintain public library services within their territories. (The absence of such an obligation was a strong wish expressed by the Association of Dutch Municipalities in the run-up to the development of the bill.) In a small number of municipalities, a commercial supplier was asked to supply limited library services (mostly book lending only) for a reduced subsidy, whereas in others, local voluntary organisations started to run similar provisions. By and large, however, the 'official' public library network—consisting of locally and regionally subsidised, not-for-profit organisations that were members of the VOB—remained intact despite the budget cuts following the global economic crisis in the 2008-2015 period.

Once implemented, the new Public Library Act also brought a renewed awareness of the broad social role of libraries. The inclusion of the five core functions led to greater recognition that the library is more than just books; the functions also provided libraries and their subsidy providers with a framework for making arrangements for their tasks and purposes. The precise interpretation of the core functions within this framework is determined locally, but in general, tasks and activities of libraries are similar all over the country. In the field of 'reading and literature', collections for adults are supported by activities such as reading circles, literary courses, writer visits and campaigns. For children and adolescents, the library organises reading activities and participates in national reading promotion campaigns such as the Children's Book Week (*Kinderboekenweek*) and National Reading Days (*Nationale Voorleesdagen*). Through educational programmes such as Bookstart (*BoekStart*) and The Library at School (*de Bibliotheek op School*), they support institutions of pre-school, primary and secondary education in their reading promotion activities.

With a broad approach to art and culture, in many localities, the public library aspires to capture a central position in the local cultural life that is expressed in cultural activities and events and its collaboration with cultural institutions, with whom it shares space in many cases. Parts of the public library's collections—self-education books, music CDs, film DVDs and sheet music—are dedicated to this function, as are music study cells. Both the volume and the use of the collection of audio-visual materials, however, have experienced a sharp decline in recent years. Most probably this has to do with the rise of audio and video-on-demand services offered by TV channels, internet providers and companies like Netflix and Spotify (Koninklijke Bibliotheek 2017).

The 'encounters and debate' function is shaped by the simple observation that libraries are public buildings that are specifically designed for lounging (e.g., in reading rooms or reading cafés), meeting with friends, having a chat with other members of the community, or participating in activities such as lectures and debate evenings.

Although the far-reaching digitisation of recent years has put the public library's role of 'knowledge and information' under great pressure, its purpose of providing citizens with access to information and skills required to navigate the complex information landscape is still perceived to be valid, even more so in times of discussions and concerns about the detrimental effects of 'fake news' for democracy. This function takes shape with a curated collection of informational books, digital databases, information desks and (online) communities. In addition, people are supported in their digital skills, media literacy and searches for information with consultation hours and courses on various topics such as health and health care, labour markets, social media and e-government.

In contributing to a person's 'personal development and education', libraries provide access to information resources, computers, study rooms and materials. These facilities are often supplemented with events such as lectures, debates and training courses in which the learning and acquisition of knowledge and skills (e.g. in languages, information and media) are key. With the rapid emergence of new technologies in mind, libraries invite young people and adults to become acquainted with these new technologies in fabrication laboratories ('fablabs') and media labs.

Although many of the services mentioned were already part of the regular operation of libraries before the 2015 Act was adopted, some changes have become noticeable in recent years and seem to indicate a shift of focus in the fulfilment of tasks. Especially in the field of (adult) education, libraries are beginning to take up new activities and to expand old ones. The background of this shift is the rather radical system change at the national level that occurred in 2015, whereby the previous tasks of the central government in the domains of youth care, work and income, and health care were decentralised to the municipal level. The guiding principle behind this system change was the government's aspiration to develop 'from a welfare state to a participatory society' in which the strength, self-reliance and self-responsibility of citizens were paramount. Since this so-called 'decentralisation' of hitherto national government tasks came into effect, awareness has grown among both libraries and municipalities that local libraries had a role to play in implementing and realising local government policies designed to prevent and combat social disadvantages among vulnerable groups. The services provided by libraries—often in cooperation with other social organisations—concentrate on information provision and adult education and cover a wide range of domains: textual and digital literacy, health, child upbringing, personal finances, career development and the nature of labour markets, legal issues and e-government.

Overall, it seems justified to say that, over time, the activities of the library have covered a much wider field than just the cultural domain, a development that also becomes visible in the organisations with which libraries collaborate. In addition to cultural institutions and schools, libraries increasingly enter into partnerships with social service providers, health care institutions and financial and legal service providers (Koninklijke Bibliotheek 2017). The sources of financing for these new partnerships, projects and programmes also seem to be diversifying. Although the culture budget remains the main source of library funding, there has been a cautious shift towards financing from other policy areas. For social issues such as the prevention and combating of low literacy and basic skills education in particular supplementary subsidies at both the national and local level are added to regular budgets for starting up new projects, 'boosting' innovation through pilots and supporting the development of new programmes. Although such financing often still seems to be incidental, it appears to reflect and acknowledge the potential role of libraries in addressing broader social issues that transcend the cultural domain.

9.7   Innovation and the Rise of the Digital Library

The periods of library renewal and library policy review described in the sections above were driven by rapid developments in society, particularly in the technological field. Both the Council for Culture and the Meijer Committee (*Stuurgroep Herstructurering Openbaar Bibliotheekwerk*) argued, in 1998 and in 2000 respectively, that in addition to restructuring the library field, service innovation and renewal were pivotal to keeping up with the changing environment and surviving the challenges of digitisation. How this innovation was to be realised was determined by a committee chaired by the then deputy director of Leiden University's library, Josje Calff (*Adviescommissie Bibliotheekinnovatie 2008*). In its report, *Effective Innovation,* this Advisory Committee on Library Innovation recommended central control and implementation for innovation in the fields of digital infrastructure and digital content in particular. This belief was shared by the ministry, which reserved a substantial annual budget for library innovation to be spent under national control. The guiding principle was that the innovative capacities of the sector as a whole should be elevated, and for this, centralised coordination was deemed indispensable to ensuring the effective deployment of resources and energetic action.

The innovation strategy of 2009 and the subsequent foundation of the executive organisation *Bibliotheek.nl* in 2010 heralded a period of innovation with the purpose of constructing and managing a digital public library under national control. Activities were initiated to develop a common digital infrastructure to which all libraries are connected, providing library users with a low threshold and recognisable entry to an integrated library collection and innovative digital services. The most salient features of the digital infrastructure are the National Library Catalog Plus (NBC+), which provides information on all available titles held in Dutch public libraries and at the Royal Library; a joint website infrastructure (Website as a Service, WaaS) with a centrally arranged design and functionalities that local libraries can build upon to create their own websites; and an e-book platform through which members of public libraries can borrow e-books.

The development of the digital library continued after 2015, when the responsibilities of the sector institute (SIOB) and Bibliotheek.nl were incorporated into the Royal Library. At the time of writing, the digital library delivers different products and services made available via onlinebibliotheek. nl and bibliotheek.nl.

Although most of the national resources are made available with the aim of (further) developing the national digital library, several measures and projects have been set up to also boost innovation at a local level. The development of an innovation agenda in 2013 and the appointment of an Innovation Council (*Innovatieraad*) in 2014 by the sector institute (SIOB) formed the start of a centralised initiative to stimulate creativity and innovation at the local level and to scale up promising and innovative local projects and pilots. Examples include instruments and initiatives focused on online communities; programmes and facilities for the design of media labs and makerspaces; and innovative information services (both textual and digital) covering health care, the labour market and e-government.

This line of thought was continued in the subsequent innovation agenda (*Innovation Agenda 2016-2018*, Koninklijke Bibliotheek 2016), in which administrative partners (representatives of municipal, provincial and national library organisations) established a goal to—jointly—strengthen the innovative power of the sector in line with its five core functions. The agenda explicitly emphasises the broadening of library tasks and encourages the development of a digital platform on which the library innovations of the library sector are shared within the field.

9.8   Changes in Physical Accessibility

The drop in book lending and the rise of e-books and mobile devices have sparked a discussion about the future of the public library both in and outside of the library sector. The global financial recession following the US subprime mortgage crisis put more pressure on libraries. National and local policymakers were confronted with rapidly shrinking tax revenues. As public library subsidies formed a considerable part of the budget for culture, budget cuts were considered inevitable among local politicians. From 2010 to 2016, subsidies declined significantly, resulting in a decrease in library branches (by 9% from 2012 to 2016) and library staff (by 21% in fulltime equivalents and by 25% in persons from 2010 to 2016; Koninklijke Bibliotheek 2017, see Table 9.1). Locally, these figures varied widely, with some cities closing all but their central location. Moreover, in less densely populated areas, the number of bookmobile stops dwindled, offset in part by the opening of Library at School branches in primary schools. However, these locations mainly catered to the needs of school-aged children and did not provide a substitute for library services for adults.

Although the number of physical library branches has been declining, this does not mean that the value of a building housing a library is no longer recognised. In contrast, there seems to be renewed recognition of the importance of the library as a physical space among library professionals, politicians and researchers (Jochumsen et al. 2012, Skot-Hansen et al. 2013). Worldwide, new libraries are being built—often by star architects—and are expected to give an economic, cultural and social 'boost' to local environments. No longer are they quiet places filled with shelves of books; they are now designed to be vibrant meeting places, open learning and co-working spaces, innovation labs and 'community hubs'. In the Netherlands, not only are major cities such as Amsterdam, Utrecht, Arnhem, Tilburg, Groningen and Almere opening or building new libraries, but smaller towns such as Zoetermeer, Zwolle, Tiel and Leeuwarden are doing the same.

Table 9.1:   Income of Dutch public library organisations, 2005-2016 (in millions of Euros)

	2005	2006	2007	2008	2009	2010	2011	2012	2013	2014	2015	2016
subsidies												
from municipalities	380.1	388.5	401.9	422.9	445.7	457.8	456.8	452.1	438.4	420.9	415.3	406.8
from provinces	9.9	14.1	16.4	15.7	14.2	13.0	10.9	9.0	8.5	8.3	10.0	9.3
from other sources	5.7	6.4	6.5	7.2	3.7	2.7	3.6	3.5	2.6	2.4	3.6	2.4
own sources												
membership contributions	71.0	69.9	69.8	69.7	70.8	71.8	71.4	69.8	67.6	62.3	62.8	62.6
other	1.7	1.4	1.6	1.4	1.5	1.5	1.3	1.1	1.0	1.8	1.0	0.7
other sources	24.4	23.7	22.4	27.6	32.7	27.4	32.3	35.1	32.6	28.1	27.6	29.9
total	492.8	503.9	518.5	544.6	568.7	574.2	576.3	570.6	550.7	523.8	520.3	511.8
funding of municipalities as % of total subsidies	96	95	95	95	96	97	97	97	98	98	97	97
funding of municipalities as % of total income	77	77	78	78	78	80	79	79	80	80	80	79
membership contributions as % of total income	14	14	13	13	12	13	12	12	12	12	12	12

Note: All figures refer to the incomes of public library organisations only; subsidies of provincial support organisations (2016: € 32 million) and the national government (2016: € 44.9 million) are not considered unless passed on as subsidies to local public library organisations.

Source: Statistics Netherlands (https://opendata.cbs.nl/#/CBS/nl/dataset/70763ned/table?ts=1520466068473), last accessed 8 March 2018; own calculations.

Another trend in the physical appearance of the library is the increase in so-called 'multifunctional buildings'. Ideological motivations giving rise to multifunctional spaces in the 1970s and the *Kulturhus* in later years following Scandinavian examples were often the reason for building collective accommodations for libraries and for other community organisations and associations (Middelveld 2002). Currently, efficiency and effectivity are often cited as a cause of (sometimes forced) cohabitation. In 2016, 87% of all library organisations managed one or more branches housed in a joint building. The institutions with which they share the building are very diverse and range from schools to municipalities, from theatres to welfare institutions and from community centres to museums. The different institutions in such a building usually share space and functionality. To a lesser extent, they organise joint activities. Further integration, such as in the areas of shared personnel and subsidy management, is even more rare (Koninklijke Bibliotheek 2017).

9.9   A New Performance Story: Broader Functions Monitored

With the new Public Library Act (WSOB) coming into force in 2015, the five core functions of public libraries became legally fixed. In the perceptions of many, however, the library is still mostly a place with books and information. The relevance of such a place in our modern world is increasingly being called into question. As the pace of digitisation accelerates and as visitor preferences change over time, important questions are being raised regarding the role that libraries still play in a society overloaded with information. What will happen as the shift from print to digital continues? Will people still borrow books in a couple years? Is there still a role for public libraries in the Google era?

Motivated by the continuing pressure on government's budgets, both politicians and taxpayers want to know more strongly than before what value they are receiving for 'their' money. Libraries increasingly feel a need to make visible their contributions to community and policy issues such as combating low literacy and loneliness, bridging the digital divide, and stimulating social cohesion and community empowerment. This cannot be done solely in words and attractive policy statements but must be supported by a strong body of evidence based on facts and figures.

In taking up new tasks that were previously carried out by other institutions, libraries have been increasingly obliged to establish their accountability and legitimacy. For quite some time, evidence supporting their accountability and legitimacy consisted mainly of traditional statistics such as the number of registered users and visitors (and the percentage of the target population reached), the number of organised events, the number of books borrowed and the sizes of collections. Together with customer satisfaction surveys, these easy-to-count quantities gave a shallow impression of the quality of the services libraries provide to their users. In recent years, there is an increasing awareness that these traditional and easy-to-count statistics provide an incomplete picture of the broad role that libraries play in the community. At all governmental levels, the need for a better understanding of the roles of libraries—in line with their statutory tasks—has emerged. At the national level, instruments were developed to monitor the development and professionalisation of library services, particularly in the educational and social fields. These initiatives provide local libraries with better data for their evaluation and accountability. In conforming to the wishes of the national government, they also contribute to an all-encompassing overview of the state of affairs in the library system.

In this context, it is noteworthy that the Public Library Act includes an obligation (in Article 11) for all organisations within the national public library network to deliver data to the Ministry of Education, Culture and Science to support policy development. The nature of these data, their frequency and their time of delivery are elaborated in an additional ministerial ruling (Ministerie van OCW 2014). What stands out in this ruling is an emphasis placed on gathering data on the broad social functions of today's public libraries (see section 9.6).

Although the expansion of data collection on the wide variety of library services gives a more accurate impression of the broad functions that libraries fulfill, the data still provide scant information about the social impact that libraries actually have. When considering the value and contributions of libraries to society, if the focus is only on output and performance statistics, the most important question—what good does a library bring to its patrons and society as a whole?—remains unanswered. Thus, besides measures that better reflect the broad functions of libraries, new measures are also needed to provide better insight into the social value of libraries. The search for such measures has resulted in a growing body of studies on the social value, outcomes or impact of libraries that use various terms to describe the effects of library activities and services (see Huysmans & Oomes 2013, ISO 2014, Oomes 2015).

It goes without saying that measuring the effects of library services extends beyond what can easily be measured within library walls. Counting the numbers of participants in e-government courses does not reveal much about the benefits that these participants derive from their participation, the changes it has brought about in their daily lives, or about the extent to which the goals of the library programme have been achieved.

To determine the effects and value of public libraries, different approaches and methods come into play. Many international studies have used an economic approach, where valuation studies have attempted to assign a monetary value—known as 'return on investment'—to the benefits brought about by the library (Aabø 2005). Another economic approach is one offered by so-called impact studies that try to demonstrate how libraries contribute to the economic performance of a community by creating and stimulating employment or a creative knowledge environment while contributing to the quality of life and attractiveness of cities and villages as places of residence (Poll 2012, Urban Libraries Council 2007).

Most studies conducted in the Netherlands employ user surveys to measure outcomes and the perceived value at the level of individual library users. In these surveys, people are asked to give their estimations of the experienced benefits from the library (such as their improvement in digital skills or the reading skills of their children) or to provide their subjective opinion on the potential impact of libraries. Some studies examine the improvement of language skills or digital skills as the result of a library programme by using language tests or self-assessment questions. The scope of such studies ranges from evaluating the outcomes of individual library programmes or libraries to surveying public library outcomes at a national level (Hartkamp 2017, Kleijnen 2017, Nielen 2016, Oomes 2015, Van den Berg 2015).

The growing number of studies that try to quantify the inputs, outputs and/or outcomes of public libraries cannot be separated from the trends of 'new' public management putting emphasis on evaluating the effects of policies judged against their original intentions. A need to justify the invested taxpayer money has, as we have shown, affected the public library sector as much as it has other cultural sectors at the local, regional and national levels of government.

9.10   Conclusion

As primarily local institutions, public libraries are supposed to (or expected to) have a strong bond with their local communities and citizens. As this overview of policies and developments of the Dutch public library system from the mid-1970s has attempted to show, a curious fluctuation between centralisation and decentralisation of governance took place. The Public

Library Act of 1975 dictated by the central government was dropped after only a few years due to the economic recession of the early 1980s, which required substantial cuts in the state budget, and the new decentralisation trend in public administration studies. But towards the end of the 1990s, the pendulum swung once again as awareness grew that the challenges faced by the library sector would benefit from a more centralised approach. This notion led to the Library Renewal programme (2001-2008), which led to the mergers of library organisations. Soon thereafter, the national government took on a more dominant role by investing in and regulating a national digital content platform, well aware of how inefficient it would be if all library organisations had to connect separately to service providers.

Under the Cultural Policy Act that was the legal basis for public library policy from 1993 to 2015, public libraries were regulated only lightly. Library policy makers had to resort to covenants between the three levels of government to complement library legislation, especially during the phase of the Library Renewal programme. During these two decades, it was not always clear who was actually in charge. The Act itself did not fix the respective responsibilities of local, regional and national governments for the library system as a whole, and neither did the covenant between the three levels of government (2001-2004) and its supplement (2005-2007). Only in a new Library Charter (*Bibliotheekcharter*) for the 2010-2012 period were responsibilities clearly assigned (Vereniging van Nederlandse Gemeenten, Interprovinciaal Overleg & Ministerie OCW 2009). There is without doubt a great degree of truth in the assertion that the Dutch tradition of 'polderen' (negotiating at length until consensus is reached and a 'soft' regulation is attained) was in full swing in the public library sector in this period.

Public library policy is, both traditionally and internationally, primarily local policy. Municipal councils determine to a large extent what services local public libraries should provide to citizens through local subsidies. As in many other countries, the public library system in the Netherlands is organised and regulated from the bottom up, with regional and national governments supporting what occurs at the local level. Since the end of the Library Renewal Programme in 2008 and with the new Act of 2015, a tendency towards re-centralisation can be observed. To a large extent, technological developments have made this necessary, as efforts to establish digital portals and offer e-content are more efficiently undertaken at the national level for all libraries in the national public library network. The Royal Library currently plays a pivotal role in this network.

This central position extends to efforts to develop and implement national programmes to foster the broader—especially the more 'social'—functions that the public library network is to perform according to the 2015 Act. Not only are these functions *performed*, but indicators and measurement programmes are being developed and implemented to *assess* the extent to which libraries are succeeding at reaching the desired outcomes. Furthermore, library *innovation* is stimulated at the national level in agreement with the national network of regional library support organisations. Both from a practical and a policy perspective, therefore, the public library has been adapting to the changing environment. There is no evident reason why this will not be the case in the decades to come.

Bibliography

Aabø, Svanhild. 2009. "Libraries and return on investment (ROI): A meta-analysis", *New Library World*, 110 (7/8): 311-324. [https://doi.org/10.1108/03074800910975142, last accessed 14 March 2018].

Adviescommissie Bibliotheekinnovatie. 2008. *Innovatie met effect* [Effective Innovation]. [https://openaccess.leidenuniv.nl/bitstream/handle/1887/15086/Innovatie%20met%20 Effect.pdf?sequence=1, last accessed 8 March 2018].

Bibliotheekmonitor. 2018. Spreiding bibliotheken over het land [Distribution of libraries over the country]. [http://www.bibliotheekmonitor.nl/trends-bibliotheken/organisaties-en-vestigingen/spreiding-bibliotheken-over-het-land/item28, last accessed 3 March 2018].

Black, Alastair, Simon Pepper, and Kaye Bagshaw. 2009. *Books, Buildings and Social Engineering. Early Public Libraries in Britain from Past to Present.* Farnham: Ashgate.

Greve, Henri Ekhard. 1906. *Openbare leesmusea en volksbibliotheken.* [Public Reading Museums and Popular Libraries]. Amsterdam/Leipzig: Maas & Van Suchtelen. (PhD. dissertation, University of Amsterdam).

Hartkamp, Jannes. 2017. Monitor de Bibliotheek op School: Landelijke analyse basisonderwijs [Monitor Libraries at School: National Analysis Primary Education]. [http://pro.debibliotheekopschool.nl/dam/monitor/20171127-analyseresultatenmonitorpo2016-2017.pdf, last accessed 8 March 2018].

Huysmans, Frank, and Carlien Hillebrink. 2008. *The Future of the Dutch Public Library: Ten Years On.* The Hague: Sociaal en Cultureel Planbureau. [https://www.scp.nl/ dsresource?objectid=e226ca56-d730-4bd5-95b1-8bbfcf26bbcb&type=org, last accessed 8 March 2018].

Huysmans, Frank, and Marjolein Oomes. 2013. "Measuring the Public Library's Societal Value: A Methodological Research Program", *IFLA Journal*, 39 (2): 168-177. [https://doi.org/10.1177/0340035213486412, last accessed 14 March 2018].

ISO. 2014. *Information and Documentation: Methods and Procedures for Assessing the Impact of Libraries.* Geneva: International Organisation for Standardisation (ISO). [https://www.iso.org/standard/56756.html, last accessed 14 March 2018].

Jochumsen, Henrik, Casper Hvenegaard Rasmussen, and Dorte Skot-Hansen. 2012. "The Four Spaces – a New Model for the Public Library", *New Library World*, 113(11/12): 586-597. [https://doi.org/10.1108/03074801211282948, last accessed 14 March 2018].

Kleijnen, Ellen. 2017. *Route to Reading. Promoting Reading through a School Library: Effects for non-Western Migrant Students*. PhD. dissertation, University of Amsterdam. [http://hdl.handle.net/11245/1.547483, last accessed 8 March 2018].

Knulst, Wim P., and Matthijs Kalmijn. 1988. *Van woord naar beeld? Onderzoek naar de verschuivingen in de tijdsbesteding aan de media in de periode 1975-1985.* [From Word to Image: Enquiry into the Shifts in Leisure Activities Regarding Media between 1975 and 1985.]. Rijswijk: Sociaal en Cultureel Planbureau (SCP) [https://www.scp.nl/Publicaties/Alle_publicaties/Publicaties_1996_en_eerder/Van_woord_naar_beeld, last accessed 14 March 2018].

Knulst, Wim P., and Gerbert Kraaykamp. 1996. *Leesgewoonten. Een halve eeuw onderzoek naar het lezen en zijn belagers*. [Reading Habits. Half a Century of Research into Reading and its Stalkers]. Rijswijk: Sociaal en Cultureel Planbureau (SCP). [https://www.scp.nl/Publicaties/Alle_publicaties/Publicaties_1996_en_eerder/Leesgewoonten, last accessed 14 March 2018].

Koninklijke Bibliotheek. 2016. *Gezamenlijke innovatieagenda netwerk openbare bibliotheekvoorzieningen: Leidraad voor gezamenlijke innovatie in de periode 2016-2018*. [Joint Innovation Agenda for the Public Library System: Guidebook for Concerted Innovation 2016-2018]. The Hague: Koninklijke Bibliotheek. [https://www.kb.nl/sites/default/files/docs/gezamenlijke_innovatieagenda_2016-2018_def_0.pdf, last accessed 14 March 2018].

Koninklijke Bibliotheek. 2017. *Bibliotheekstatistiek 2016: Onderzoeksresultaten Gegevenslevering Wsob, 2016*. [Library Statistics 2016: Research Outcomes Data 2016]. The Hague: Koninklijke Bibliotheek. [https://bop.bibliotheek.nl/dam/bestanden/rapportage_bibliotheekstatistiek2016.pdf, last accessed 14 March 2018].

Middelveld, Henk (2002). *Kulturhus: Concept voor een lokaal netwerk*. [Kulturhus: Concept and a Local Network]. The Hague: NBLC/Biblion.

Ministerie van OCW. 2014. *Regeling gegevenslevering openbare bibliotheekvoorzieningen*. [Public Libraries' Data Delivery Scheme]. [http://wetten.overheid.nl/BWBR0035892/2016-01-01, last accessed 14 March 2018].

Nielen, Thijs M.J. 2016. *Aliteracy: Causes and Solutions*. PhD. dissertation, Leiden University. [https://openaccess.leidenuniv.nl/bitstream/handle/1887/37530/Nielen_Aliteracy_Causes_and_solutions_Dissertation.pdf?sequence=14, last accessed 8 March 2018].

Oomes, Marjolein. 2015. *De maatschappelijke waarde van openbare bibliotheken. Een enquête-onderzoek*. [The Societal Value of Public Libraries. A Questionnaire]. The Hague: Koninklijk Bibliotheek. [https://www.kb.nl/sites/default/files/publicatie_de_maatschappelijke_waarde_van_openbare_bibliotheken_in_nederland.pdf, last accessed 14 March 2018].

Poll, Roswitha. 2012. "Can We Quantify the Library's Influence? Creating an ISO Standard for Impact Assessment", *Performance Measurement and Metrics*, 13(2): 121-130. [https://doi.org/10.1108/14678041211241332, last accessed 14 March 2018].

Raad voor Cultuur. 1998. *Advies over de bestuurlijke organisatie van het openbare bibliotheekwerk*. [Advice on the Administration of Public Libraries]. The Hague: Raad voor Cultuur. [https://www.cultuur.nl/adviezen/media/advies-over-de-bestuurlijke-organisatie-van-het-openbare-bibliotheekwerk/item1538, last accessed 14 March 2018].

Schneiders, Paul. 1990. *Lezen voor iedereen. Geschiedenis van de openbare bibliotheek in Nederland*. [Reading for Everyone. A History of Public Libraries in the Netherlands]. The Hague: Nederlands Bibliotheek en Lektuur Centrum (NBLC).

Skot-Hansen, Dorte, Casper Hvenegaard Rasmussen, and Henrik Jochumsen. 2013. "The role of Public Libraries in Culture-led Urban Regeneration", *New Library World*, 114(1/2): 7-19. [https://doi.org/10.1108/03074801311291929, last accessed on 14 March 2018].

Stuurgroep Bibliotheken [Steering Committee on Libraries]. 2008. *Eindrapport Stuurgroep Bibliotheken 2002-2007*. [Final Report of Steering Committee on Libraries 2002-2007]. The

Hague: Stuurgroep Bibliotheken. [https://www.rijksoverheid.nl/binaries/rijksoverheid/docu-menten/kamerstukken/2008/04/11/eindrapport-stuurgroep-bibliotheken-2002-2007/6193c. pdf, last accessed 14 March 2018].

Stuurgroep Herstructurering Openbaar Bibliotheekwerk [Steering Committee on the Re-structuring of Public Libraries]. 2000. *Open poort tot kennis.* [Open Gate to Knowledge]. [https://www.rijksoverheid.nl/binaries/rijksoverheid/documenten/rapporten/2005/10/14/ open-poort-tot-kennis/bibliotheken-nota1.pdf, last accessed 14 March 2018].

Urban Libraries Council. 2007. *Making Cities Stronger: Public Library Contributions to Local Economic Development.* Chicago: The Urban Libraries Council. [http://www.urban.org/ publications/1001075.html, last accessed 14 March 2018].

Vakkari, Pertti, Svanhild Aabø, Ragnar Audunson, Frank Huysmans, Nahyun Kwon, Marjolein Oomes, and Sei-Chin Joanna Sin. 2016. "Patterns of Perceived Public Library Outcomes in five Countries", *Journal of Documentation,* 72(2): 342-361. [https://doi.org/10.1108/JD-08-2015-0103, last accessed 14 March 2018].

Van den Berg, Heleen. 2015. *From BookStart to BookSmart: About the Importance of an Early Start with Parent-Child Reading.* PhD. dissertation, Leiden University. [https://openaccess. leidenuniv.nl/bitstream/handle/1887/33033/Final_thesis.pdf?sequence=13, last accessed 8 March 2018].

Van Mil, Bill, Janine Mulder, Laura de Leeuw, and Paul Corten. 2017. *Midterm review Wet stelsel openbare bibliotheekvoorziening: Eindrapport.* [Midterm Review of Public Library Act: End Report]. The Hague: Kwink Groep. [https://www.rijksoverheid.nl/documenten/ rapporten/2017/11/22/midterm-review-wet-stelsel-openbare-bibliotheekvoorziening, last accessed 14 March 2018].

Vereniging van Nederlandse Gemeenten [Association of Dutch Municipalities]. 2015. *Lokaal bibliotheekwerk: Een handleiding voor gemeenten.* [Local Library Provision: A Guideline for Municipalities]. The Hague: VNG. [https://vng.nl/files/vng/publicaties/2015/20150521-lokaal-bibliotheekwerk.pdf, last accessed 14 March 2018].

Vereniging van Nederlandse Gemeenten, Interprovinciaal Overleg & Ministerie van Onderwijs, Cultuur en Wetenschap [Association of Dutch Municipalities, Association of Dutch Prov-inces and Ministry of Education, Culture and Science]. 2009. *Bibliotheekcharter 2010-2012.* [Library Charter 2010-2012]. [https://vng.nl/files/vng/vng/Documenten/Extranet/Cultuur/ Bibliohteekwerk/Bibliotheekcharter2010-2012.pdf, last accessed 8 March 2018].

Vereniging van Openbare Bibliotheken [Public Library Association]. 2008. *Agenda voor de toekomst. De strategie van de Vereniging van Openbare Bibliotheken voor de jaren 2009-2012.* [Agenda for the Future. The Strategy of the Public Library Association for 2009-2012]. The Hague: Vereniging van Openbare Bibliotheken. [https://vng.nl/files/vng/vng/Documenten/ Extranet/Cultuur/Bibliohteekwerk/dsc.pdf, last accessed 8 March 2018].

Vereniging van Openbare Bibliotheken & Vereniging van Nederlandse Gemeenten [Public Library Association & Association of Dutch Municipalities]. 2005. *Richtlijn voor basisbiblio-theken.* [Guidlines for Basic Libraries]. The Hague: VOB/VNG. [https://vng.nl/files/vng/vng/ Documenten/Extranet/Cultuur/Bibliohteekwerk/richtlijn.pdf, last accessed 14 March 2018].

Wennekers, Annemarie, Frank Huysmans, and Jos de Haan. 2018. *Lees:Tijd—Lezen in Nederland.* [Reading:Time—Reading in the Netherlands]. The Hague: Sociaal en Cultureel Planbureau. [https://www.scp.nl/dsresource?objectid=eb3ac332-95b5-4caa-baca-a1f5b3149059&type=org, last accessed 8 March 2018].

Wiegand, Wayne A. 2015. *Part of Our Lives. A People's History of the American Public Library.* Oxford: Oxford University Press.

10. Cultural Policy at a Crossroads?

How the Matthew Effect, New Sociocultural Oppositions and Digitalisation Challenge Dutch National Cultural Policy[1]

Erik Schrijvers

10.1   Looking Into the Future?

In *Fractured times: Culture and Society in the 20th Century*, a posthumously published collection of essays, the historian Eric Hobsbawm (1917-2012) argues that the high culture that was once the basic diet of the European elite is shrivelling fast—either unknown to new generations or else swamped by 'the present creative flood drowning the globe in image, sound and words, which is almost certain to become uncontrollable in both space and cyberspace' (Hobsbawn 2012: xv). *Fractured Times* has the rare quality of looking into the future of cultural life in Western society, discussing topics like ageing audiences and the prospects for artisan crafts in the wired twenty-first century. This final chapter of *Cultural Policy in the Polder* has a similar aim, though with a much more modest focus. It looks into developments that could influence the aims, the administrative level and the instruments of Dutch national cultural policy, in particular the Cultural Policy Act.

Can one describe developments that have not yet taken place? Hobsbawm felt he was looking 'guideless and mapless, to an unrecognisable future' (p. ix). On the one hand, he is right: even experts cannot make predictions, because data about the future can never be verified. On the other hand, the future is not fully undetermined either (Adam & Groves 2007). Therefore, instead of predicting the future, nowadays it is more common to use foresight to get some idea of what might happen. The aim of this is to try to identify possible consequences of policy for the longer term or developments policymakers should relate to (Van Asselt et al. 2010). Both of these aims will be pursued in this chapter.

But what developments or policy consequences should we look at? A lot has changed since the introduction of the CPA in 1993. The political consensus on cultural policy has crumbled under pressure from new political parties such as the Freedom Party (PVV) (Van der Meer 2016, Smithuijsen

2005). This has resulted in fluctuations in the level of culture budgets, which was the most drastic with the cuts implemented 2011. Economic globalisation and more open borders have put pressure on the facilities provided by the welfare state, including the facilities provided under the heading of cultural policy. There are also concerns about the changing composition of the population as migration and integration have become the subject of fierce political debate. For this reason, the binding function of cultural policy has once again come under the spotlight. Finally, there is digitalisation, which has left practically no area of civil society untouched.

In 1993, these and other developments were hardly on the radar of policymakers, if at all. In the previous chapters, various authors have analysed what has been happening since 1993 and what issues have arisen since then. Some of the above developments were also reviewed. In this concluding chapter, I attempt to extrapolate these developments to the future. Where possible, I will refer to the other chapters. As not all developments and the ways in which they may challenge cultural policy can be analysed in full, I have made a selection. In this chapter I will examine the transformation of the welfare state; new sociocultural oppositions that have emerged around the theme of migration; and the digitalisation of the cultural field. Each of the following three paragraphs will start with a short introduction to these developments, followed by an analysis of how they relate to cultural policy and the questions that may arise in the near future for policymakers as well as cultural institutions and academics.

10.2   Cultural Policy and the Transformation of the Welfare State

The history of cultural policy is closely related to the development of the post-war welfare state. After the Second World War, the broad consensus in Western Europe held that 'it was the responsibility of a well run public authority to deliver cultural nourishment no less than food, lodging, and employment' (Judt 2004: 377). Since the end of the Second World War, good housing, good nutrition, good healthcare, and good education have in theory been accessible to everyone. That also applies to an extensive and varied offering of high-quality culture, which eventually acquired a legal framework with the CPA in 1993. Long before that, in 1983, the right to 'cultural development' had been enshrined in the Dutch constitution.

However, the welfare state is now facing new challenges, including the internationalisation of the economy, the Europeanisation of government, an ageing population, low birth rates and an increased socio-cultural differentiation among citizens. The transformation of the welfare state is being accompanied by a redefinition of its principles, goals and instruments to adapt it to the new structure of risks and needs of contemporary societies (Van der Veen et al. 2010). Partly under pressure of impending cuts, the government is trying to unload its responsibilities in areas such as healthcare and social security and shift them elsewhere in society. Social protection entitlements have become more conditional, and the provision of services has become targeted at specific, vulnerable groups. Key to these efforts is a shift towards 'social development' or an 'enabling state' that prepares people to participate in society instead of simply compensating for their losses caused by societal risks (Morel et al. 2012). What do these challenges and trends mean for cultural policy? What changes have been made to policy and what effect can we expect from them?

A Greater Role for Market Mechanisms
The changes in cultural policy over the past few decades show a pattern that is quite similar to the changes in other policy domains of the welfare state. Since the mid-1990s, Dutch cultural policy has increasingly focused on encouraging artists and subsidised cultural institutions to be more entrepreneurial, the purpose being to strengthen the ties between the subsidised culture sector and society as well to wean institutions and artists away from their dependence on government funding. The underlying idea is that cultural institutions' licence to operate no longer lies exclusively in the public subsidy they receive but also in their capacity to raise funds. In other words: income has become a proxy for societal support.

The genealogy of cultural entrepreneurship presented by Kolsteeg in chapter 3 neatly illustrates the twofold character of cultural entrepreneurship. It shows that in political discourse, cultural entrepreneurship refers both to a new mentality in the culture sector and to a means of improving its financial stability. Thus, subsidised institutions must meet more and stricter requirements with respect to self-earned income; entrepreneurship has been added to the eligibility criteria for funding; and measures have been launched to encourage society to donate more money, such as the Gift and Inheritance Tax Act [*Geefwet*].[2]

Yet cultural policy differs in important aspects from welfare policies aimed at social protection. This type of welfare policy is characterised by a right to welfare provisions, such as unemployment benefits or social housing. In the domain of social protection, some of the responsibility has shifted away from the state to the citizen, who is expected to take care of himself more often. In the culture sector, there are no entitlements. Most change therefore takes place not between the state and the individual but between the state and cultural institutions. Although the individual responsibility of citizens was given an impetus through the Gift and Inheritance Act, its significance has remained fairly limited until now. The shifting of financial responsibility from government to cultural institutions and artists has in fact given the market a greater role in the culture sector. This move towards market mechanisms has major consequences in practice.

The Matthew Effect

The new funding regime in the area of cultural policy is causing growing differences in income between cultural institutions. The reason is that there are striking differences between cultural institutions' 'earning capacity' (Franssen & Beckers 2016; Schrijvers et al. 2015). The degree to which they succeed in finding alternative sources of funding, developing new revenue models, as well as exploring a broad range of different sources of income depends first of all on how 'entrepreneurial' the institutions' management is. But more trivial factors also play a role, for example the location, the type of activities offered, the scale at which the institution or organisation is active, and the type of visitor or audience that it attracts (Kloosterman 2014).

In particular, large cultural institutions in favourable locations that have a reputation in a specific area of specialisation can greatly improve their financial standing because they attract large numbers of visitors, are well-known and—since they tend to be situated in cities—have a huge network of wealthy friends and donors, often organised into 'circles of friends'. The others—in particular medium-sized cultural institutions with broader, more local collections or activities—often have trouble keeping their heads above water.[3]

This self-reinforcing process in which a good starting position leads to further advantages and a bad starting position produces further disadvantages is known as the 'Matthew effect' (Merton 1968; Rigney 2010).[4] This Matthew effect and the resulting lopsided growth of the cultural sector raises questions about how the government should treat high-earning subsidised institutions and institutions that are scarcely able to meet their financial commitments. One of the aims of cultural policy in recent years has been to make cultural institutions 'less dependent on government money and thus become more flexible and powerful' (Ministerie van OCW 2011). In this it has succeeded. The culture sector has indeed become somewhat less dependent on public investment. Yet its financial resilience is weak. Until now, a large part of the culture sector has in general not been able to improve its financial prospects (De Nooij et al. 2017).

Various reasons can be advanced as to why this situation will not change in the longer term either. A core argument here is that public support and private contributions are not communicating vessels. A decrease in public support does not automatically lead to an increase in private contributions from citizens, companies or private equity funds. New ways of financing the culture sector, for example crowdfunding, may be able to mobilise additional resources, but they can never replace public funding (Van den Hoogen 2018). At the same time, cultural institutions are becoming more vulnerable to external shocks—the economic crisis and the accompanying decline of tourism being a typical example.

Even the deployment of volunteers will ultimately not be sufficient to make cultural institutions more independent. The increased involvement and deployment of volunteers is desirable from the perspective of societal support for cultural activities. The number of volunteers has indeed risen sharply in the last few years, but there are also signs that they are displacing cultural professionals (Raad voor Cultuur & SER 2016). Since the culture sector features specialised tasks such as conservation, restoration and research, there is a clear limit to the replacement of cultural professionals. Crossing the line would inevitably lead to an impoverishment of the culture sector. Moreover, the expectations are too optimistic because the increase in volunteers seems in large part an effect of ageing and the improved health of elderly people. Future cohorts of senior citizens will definitely be smaller. Besides, the life of the average Dutch working person is getting busier. People have to work longer and are expected to perform caring duties as a result of the rolling back of the welfare state (Van den Brink 2017, Kremer et al. 2017), resulting in less time to contribute to cultural activities and institutions.

Last but not least, it is important to note that there is a serious chance that the Matthew effect will lead to the impoverishment of the cultural sector (De Nooij et al. 2017: 74). John Holden argues that publicly funded culture, homemade culture and commercial culture operate as a whole and in practice are interlinked (Holden 2015). Careers, ideas and money flow from one part to the other, often within one and the same institution, cultural activity or artist. Holden therefore proposes replacing the idea of separate spheres with an 'ecological' approach, concentrating on relationships and patterns within the overall cultural system. Following this approach, one should assume that changes within the publicly funded part of the culture sector will spill over into its other parts, disturbing and possibly even damaging the fabric of cultural life.

Conclusion

The Matthew effect challenges the aims of Dutch cultural policy, i.e. 'to create the conditions for maintaining and developing cultural expressions while spreading them socially and geographically or otherwise propagating them' (CPA: Art. 2). Officially, these principles are still in force today, but they have come under pressure as an effect of current policymaking. This will inevitably influence the level of amenities, their allocation and, eventually, also the type and quality of cultural offering and activities. For example, we can see the way museums are increasingly opting for blockbuster exhibitions to be sure of generating enough income (Van Aart & Brom 2017: 45). Cultural institutions are also using a shorter time horizon for their activities, as they are increasingly reliant on project subsidies. This tendency further strengthens the 'festivalisation' of culture. Yet another consequence is that the 'culture' part of cultural policy (Bell & Oakley 2014) implicitly moves to more economically viable disciplines like Dutch design, fashion and architecture, weakening art forms that are more dependent on subsidy.

10.3   Cultural Policy and New Sociocultural Oppositions

Demographic change is another development that influences cultural policy. The demographic composition of the Netherlands has changed dramatically as a result of mass migration. The arrival of citizens from the former colonies and increased labour migration have transformed the Netherlands into a multi-ethnic and multicultural society. The Netherlands is home to 1.6 million migrants with a Western background, 1.25 million migrants who belong to one of the four 'traditional' non-Western ethnic groups (Turks, Moroccans, Surinamese, and Antilleans), and more than 730,000 migrants from other non-Western countries (Jennissen et al. 2015: 11).[5] Already, in cities such as The Hague and Amsterdam, half of all young people are of foreign descent. Moreover, migration nowadays is becoming much more diverse in terms of countries of origin, educational levels, and length of stay. This development towards greater diversity within the flows of migration is often referred to as 'superdiversity' (Vertovec 2007).

Multicultural societies challenge cultural policy on at least two levels. A formal principle of cultural policy is to make art and culture accessible to society (see also Van Eijck in chapter 8 of this volume). However, an important underlying objective is to reduce the social distance between different groups of citizens. The Explanatory Memorandum to the CPA therefore refers not only to 'making cultural objects and events accessible' but also to 'promoting the opportunities for the public to participate in cultural values' and 'developing and maintaining cultural values'. This collective dimension of cultural policy is often overlooked, according to Lijster, Otte and Gielen in chapter 5. Apart from accessibility and participation, cultural policy involves the conservation, dissemination, and development of cultural values (Gielen et al. 2014). Multicultural societies thus face two interrelated questions (Delhaye & Van de Ven 2014). First, if the aim of cultural policy is to bridge the cultural divide between different groups of the population, it is necessary for them to have equal access to Dutch cultural institutions. Second, it is important to rethink established ideas on the cultural values that cultural policy aims to propagate.

Access to Cultural Institutions

Migrants were never encouraged to hold on to their 'own' cultural expressions, except for the period up to the end of the 1970s when public opinion held that they would return to their country of origin (Penninx 2016). From then on, adjustment to Dutch societal norms and individual emancipation were central policy objectives, while cultural values and preferences were considered to be a private matter. At the turn of the century, these policy assumptions came under fire from different directions, fuelled by conflicts in the Middle East and terrorist attacks by Islamist groups. Although the dominant frame since then is that migration policy has failed, it has now also been found that migrants have trouble accessing, for example, the labour market or (higher) education. Young people and members of the second generation in particular are much more focused on Dutch culture and society. However, they appear to have less trust in the institutions of Dutch society than people of Dutch origin (Huijnk & Andriesen 2016). They experience deliberate social and cultural barriers and feel that they are treated as outsiders. The mere fact that the majority of young people of Turkish and Moroccan descent were born in the Netherlands gives this sense of being unwelcome added impact (Huijnk et al. 2015).

No systematic research has been done on migrants' access to the culture sector. Nevertheless, policymakers have made attempts to improve the accessibility of cultural institutions for all. In 1999, for example, Secretary for Culture Rick van der Ploeg called for greater diversity in the culture sector (Ministerie OCW 1998 and 1999). He also presented plans that would allow the enforcement of an increase in diversity. However, the proposal to force cultural institutions to spend 3% of their budget on reaching new audiences encountered fierce opposition. The cultural sector stated that the measure would adversely affect artistic autonomy. Eventually, the proposal gave way to a few earmarked subsidies and dedicated projects.

Another important turning point was a 2009 study that looked at the state of cultural diversity in the Basic Infrastructure for Culture. The final report had the telling title *The Elephant in the Room*. It concluded that many cultural institutions were white bastions and that this was reflected in their programming, funding arrangements, staff policy and the membership of their supervisory boards. The Ministry of Education, Culture and Science responded by issuing the Cultural Diversity Code in 2010. Because the code was based on self-regulation, cultural diversity remained the responsibility of cultural institutions.

The first Rutte government continued this line of thought. The policy brief for 2013-2017 devoted only two sentences to the subject of cultural diversity: 'The new basic infrastructure will no longer provide scope for developments in the area of cultural diversity. The government [...] does not have a specific policy in this regard' (Ministerie van OCW, 2011). But in 2016, Minister of Culture Jet Bussemaker expressed her concerns with regard to the low level of cultural diversity in the subsidised culture sector. She felt that the audiences in the culture sector as well as the staff of cultural institutions did not constitute 'a reflection of the changing composition of the population'.[6] However, she did not propose a new policy.

Nativism and Its Critics
At the same time, another development has been taking place aimed at the assimilation of people with a migrant background instead of improving their access to cultural institutions. Duelund (2016) points to a resurgence of nationalism and collective identity politics in Europe, a trend that is increasingly reflected in national and regional cultural policymaking. This trend towards a more 'essentialist' approach to national identity making is manifesting itself in various ways such as the 'improvement of heritage at the expense of contemporary culture and art forms open to the world' and the 'primordial transformation of culture and identity and of the narratives of cultural institutions at the expense of the cosmopolitan view of identity formation' (Duelund 2016: 217). In the case of the Netherlands, Duelund points to the Canon of the Netherlands (2006) and the plans for a National History Museum (which were eventually abandoned).[7] He interprets both initiatives as a move away from the older multiculturalist approach, although he acknowledges the social constructionist approach used to present the Dutch Canon.

The budget cuts of 2011 clearly show the pattern described by Duelund, marking a shift in the content of cultural policy. Cuts to the arts (33%) far exceeded cuts to heritage (5%) and libraries (next to nothing). Moreover, 2012 saw the end of the subsidy to NiNsee, the National Institute for the Study of Slavery and its Legacy. The Ministry of Foreign Affairs also discontinued its subsidy to the Tropenmuseum, which was rescued by the subsequent government on condition that it merged with two other institutions. This resulted in two institutions specialising in the colonial past and non-Western culture being swept off the stage. This attitude is typical of many populist and 'nativist' political parties who, according to critics, have trouble assimilating 'foreign' cultural elements and 'embarrassing' periods and events from their own past—such as slavery, the colonial past and the history of migration—into the national paradigm (Duyvendak 2017).

The current government, which consists of the Liberal Party (VVD), the Social-Liberal Democratic Party (D66) and two Christian-Democratic parties (CDA and CU), also places a strong emphasis on national culture, national identity and national heritage as a means of binding different population groups together. For example, the coalition agreement states that cultural policy should increase knowledge of 'shared history, values and freedoms' because they are 'the anchors of Dutch identity in times of globalisation and uncertainty'.[8] And, according to the government, this requires more support for 'folk culture'.

This resurgence of nationalism and collective identity politics builds on a new sociocultural opposition that has emerged in response to more open borders, growing cultural diversity and immigration in European countries (see also Minnaert in chapter 2). This opposition is characterised by two extremes with on the one hand a group of people who are described as having open and confident attitudes, and, on the other, a group with closed and very distrustful attitudes. In between, there is a large majority with more neutral views and a moderate attitude. The terms used to denote the groups at the two extremes are 'cosmopolitan' versus 'nationalistic'-oriented citizens (Kriesi 2014) or, to put it more bluntly, the 'winners' and 'losers' of globalisation.

In the Netherlands, there is as yet no polarised landscape—i.e., one with two separate blocks and without any overlap or intermediate positions (Bovens et al. 2014). Yet feelings of cultural insecurity are being articulated by a growing number of political parties. Initially, these feelings were monopolised by populist parties such as Lijst Pim Fortuyn (LPF), the Party for Freedom (PVV) and most recently also Forum for Democracy (FVD). But their views on national culture, national identity and national heritage are also being adopted by other political parties, as the current coalition agreement shows. With the advent of a new political party, Denk (Think), which entered parliament in 2017 with three seats, an opposing voice is now also being heard. The party has its origins in migrant communities of different, although predominantly Turkish, backgrounds. The title of Denk's party programme is 'Thinking of the Netherlands', inspired by a canonical poem by the expressionist Hendrik Marsman in which he describes the Dutch landscape and mentality. Denk is opposed to parties that regard the Netherlands as 'unchanging, with a static culture and a uniform identity'.[9] Unsurprisingly, the party is also opposed to the culturalisation of citizenship. The party has not yet formulated a coherent cultural policy and is mainly focused on removing racist elements such as the tradition of Black Pete; decolonising the names of streets, bridges, tunnels and museums; and encouraging a colourful and more truthful perspective in the writing of history.

Conclusion

The Netherlands has an increasingly diverse population from a growing number of countries of origin and different cultural backgrounds but is also increasingly educated and therefore wants to participate in culture in the Netherlands. However, the principle of cultural diversity has disappeared from the agenda of cultural policy. Cultural diversity has become a responsibility of the publicly subsidised cultural institutions, which have repeatedly been found to be difficult to access for people with a migration background. At the same time, these institutions are confronted with a political discourse and policy proposals in which adaptation to Dutch culture is a key element, without a clear indication of what this culture consists of. The question is therefore not only what policy should the government pursue to reduce social differences among the population but also who should be responsible for it and at what level? Should the ministry do this? Or is it a task for the sector or even the shared responsibility of citizens, who will have to develop their own (political) initiatives?

10.4   Cultural Policy and Digitalisation

Cultural policy is also being influenced by digitalisation. Digitalisation should be distinguished from digitisation, which refers to the action or process of digitising, that is, the conversion of analogue data into digital form. Digitalisation, by contrast, refers to the adoption or increase in use of digital or computer technology by an organisation, an industry or a country. It refers to a host of powerful, accessible and potentially game-changing technologies like social media, mobile, cloud, analytics, the internet of things, cognitive computing and biometrics. Thus, digitalisation is about far more than simple technical innovation. It requires a wholesale remaking of infrastructures, legal environments, of business models and of cultural norms.

In his groundbreaking study *Art Worlds*, Howard Becker proposes to examine art as the product of 'an established network of cooperative links among participants' (Becker 2008: 34-35 [1982]). Yet Becker's cultural network has literally become a digital one, transforming everything connected to it and fundamentally altering the way cultural objects like music, film, books and even individual artworks are being produced, shared, distributed and consumed. In relation to digitalisation, much attention is typically paid to cultural institutions that are subject to market forces, such as cinemas, broadcasting companies and printing and record companies. Meanwhile, museums, concert halls, libraries and theatres are facing similar challenges, thereby blurring the line between the problematics of the so-called cultural industries and the publicly funded cultural sector and between cultural policy and media policy. Policymakers have anticipated some of the issues related to digitalisation, but other issues seem to have escaped their attention or simply seem too big to handle.

The Digitisation of Cultural Objects and e-Culture

In 2002, the Ministry of Culture issued its first policy document dealing with digitalisation. In its *Policy letter on e-Culture*, the ministry referred both to 'the artistic use of new media and the creative input of artists and designers to the development of digital applications and to the provision of digital access to heritage, the role of libraries in providing digital access to information and the Internet activities of public broadcasters' (Ministerie OCW 2002: 2). A lot of effort was put into trying to define 'e-culture'. According to the Council for Culture, e-culture was mainly about 'a new, digital dimension, a medium until recently unimaginable, to which the existing culture must relate and in which new culture is generated' (Raad voor Cultuur 2003: 5).

In the first decade of the twenty-first century, these and other policy documents set in motion different policies aimed at incorporating digital culture and digital technologies into cultural policy. The Dutch government started to subsidise digital art forms and stimulated the development of expertise on digital arts and culture by creating institutes like the Centre of Expertise for eCulture (*Expertisecentrum voor e-cultuur*), which later was succeeded by the the Virtual Platform (*Virtueel Platform*) and Platform 31. Nowadays, digital culture is considered to be part of the so-called creative industries and is being funded by the Creative Industries Fund NL (*Stimuleringsfonds creatieve industrie*).

Another important policy goal aimed to digitise the collections of cultural institutions. This often started with the digitisation of cultural heritage. Modern art is a bit less prone to digitisation, because modern and contemporary artworks are often protected by copyright law. The digitisation of material collections hosted by museums, archives and libraries is taking place at a very fast pace, with an interesting combination of public and private partners. These new partners—which include software developers, private companies and global media conglomerates—complicate the established relationship between government, cultural institutions and the public.

The Commodification of Access
The technological convergence caused by digitisation enables cultural institutions to develop and implement generic solutions. Yet, up until now, most parts of the culture sector have featured standalone digitisation projects (Papakonstantinou & De Hert 2012). Public libraries are an exception, but as Huysmans and Oomes point out in their chapter, the creation of a common digital infrastructure to which all libraries are connected demands a more centralised approach to public library policy. Without a national digital content platform, library organisations would have to connect separately to service providers, leading to all kinds of inefficiencies.

The development of a digital infrastructure also raises a number of questions. Public access and openness are best served through single, all-encompassing websites. These websites or 'platforms' enable new kinds of (interactive) participation and research, like crowdsourcing and the digital humanities. Yet the creation of single, all-encompassing platforms affects the current public access model and the legal systems supporting it, such as the copyright system, database law and the re-use of public information (Papakonstantinou & De Hert 2012). Once aggregated online, cultural content develops an independent existence, potentially exceeding the limitations and purposes of the cultural institutions that released it.

Moreover, major institutions in pre-digital sectors such as libraries, museums and cinemas partly lose control of access to their collections and the services attached to them, because private parties develop and own the software used to read, analyse and store digital sources (Gervais 2012).

Access to culture thus becomes a core value and a central commodity: it is 'to be given, had, shared, bought or rented' (Hylland 2017: 80). Access can take very different shapes, as can be illustrated by a comparison made by Papakonstantinau and De Hert of two platforms for digital reproduction: the private Google Art Project (now: Google Cultural Institute) and the public European culture website Europeana.eu. Whereas Europeana merely functions as a search engine and does not host any content itself, the Google Cultural Institute hosts a virtual collection of cultural objects and museum tours. Europeana refers visitors to the websites of museums, while Google Cultural Institute is a closed system. For example, it does not link to the twenty-plus Dutch museums whose collections it features. Moreover, 'Google art uses Google Maps and Street View technology, the search engine directs queries to the digitised images and the images are linked to educational content on YouTube (owned by Google) and to scholarly work registered in Google Scholar' (Hylland 2017: 72).

Frequently, a different logic comes into play, favouring 'views' and 'likes' as a means of ranking digital content, using sophisticated profiling techniques to tailor information to individual users (Van Dijck et al. 2016). Thus, the emergence of new, internet-based, digital infrastructures affects a wide range of decisions that used to be the prerogative of the management of cultural institutions and are now made by the parties that aggregate content and are often newcomers to the field. Cultural institutions will have to ask themselves whether and to what extent this helps to encourage interest in cultural activities. This requires openness about how these parties operate and what their added value is. Google is probably not primarily interested in helping cultural institutions to get more views but wants to collect even more data about people's preferences, including their cultural preferences. Yet parties like Google still refuse to disclose their contracts with cultural institutions and the way their algorithms work (Hylland 2017, cf. Pasquale 2015).

Regulating Digital Culture

Yet in the digital era, even more fundamental issues are at stake, because people increasingly make use of digital platforms such as YouTube, Netflix, iTunes or Spotify to access and consume cultural content and thus culturally develop themselves. This shift is signalled in the chapters by both Van Eijck and Hitters in this volume. Van Eijck observes that the internet and social media increasingly offer pathways to the arts. This is especially true for the younger generations: the younger people are, the more they tend to enjoy culture through new media. Hitters comes to similar conclusions when discussing public broadcasting and observes that younger audiences increasingly consume both international and commercial content provided by platforms such as Facebook and YouTube. As a result, the reach of the public media is diminishing overall—to the benefit of online content, user-generated content and non-linear international on-demand content.

Platforms like Facebook and YouTube are not regulated by the CPA or any other national regulations. Although the idea of stricter regulation of these tech companies is beginning to gain credence in Europe and beyond, a number of questions beg to be answered. These questions do not just concern the enormous size of these companies but also the regulatory regimes that should apply and the question of how these new digital infrastructures are to be regulated. This concerns platforms, search engines and algorithms (Van Dijck et al. 2016) and by extension even the internet itself (Mueller 2010, DeNardis 2014). Considering that the vast majority of cultural expressions is being produced, distributed and consumed digitally, policymakers ought to investigate and inform themselves about what digitalisation does to the public values that underpin cultural policy, such as cultural diversity, equality, artistic freedom and so on (Hoefnagels 2002). Meanwhile, regulatory actions may be needed to fix the current problems with the digitalisation of cultural content. Moreover, such regulation should facilitate the development of a worthy and potentially added-value initiative to unlock the full, public-good potential of digital technologies (Papakonstantinau & De Hert 2012).

A case in point is the growing personalisation of content, which leads to so-called 'filter bubbles' (Pariser 2011). These bubbles isolate users from diverging views, opinions or cultural preferences. Before the advent of digital media, news outlets generally featured the same content for all users. Nowadays, the same news websites are able to show each visitor personalised content. Personalisation is not a bad thing in itself. What matters is whether or not personalisation is self-selected (Zuiderveen Borgesius et al. 2016). Self-selected personalisation concerns situations in which people choose to encounter like-minded opinions exclusively. Pre-selected personalisation, on the contrary, is personalisation driven by websites, advertisers or other actors, often without the user's deliberate choice, input, knowledge or consent. In both cases, people may encounter only a limited range of cultural content, but with pre-selected personalisation the situation is quite different because people are unaware of it.

Personalisation can help people find what cultural content they like in a very effective way, based on their preferences. But it can also have an adverse effect on open-mindedness and the quality of the public sphere in which people develop themselves culturally. What is the right balance between these two qualities? Can we have both at the same time? Or should we try to safeguard the cultural domain from personalisation? Encouraging a greater digital presence of Dutch cultural institutions on the internet and social media is part of the answer and could provide a counterweight to excessive commercial tendencies (Hoefnagel 2002). But it might be wise to consider other interventions also, filling the regulatory vacuum in which online companies operate. When people move on to other cultural venues, cultural policy should probably follow suit.

Conclusion

Digitalisation propels the publicly financed cultural sector into a new constellation of stakeholders and into a new policy environment in which the distinction between different cultural sectors is blurred by technological convergence. It changes the authority of cultural institutions, creates liquid forms of ownership, adds new actors to the field and also challenges the concept of authenticity, which is central to large parts of the culture sector (Throsby 2001). Policymakers have reacted by stimulating digital culture and the digitisation of cultural content. Public access and openness are best served through single, all-encompassing websites and ohter generic solutions. An unresolved issue in many domains is whether to create a common digital infrastructure or allow cultural institutions to connect to the digital world individually, making them dependent on tech companies and leading to inefficiencies, because they will all reinvent the wheel. Moreover, the role these companies have in producing, structuring and distributing cultural content raises questions about safeguarding the public values that underpin cultural policy in the digital domain, both nationally and internationally.

10.5 Challenges for Dutch Cultural Policy

In what way do the three developments outlined in this chapter challenge Dutch cultural policy? Are there reasons to recalibrate cultural policy? Should new policy aims be added? Is the national level still the right level from which to address the questions these developments raise? Are planning and subsidies still an adequate means of achieving the aims of cultural policy?

Let me start with two observations. First, the CPA accommodated several major policy changes. It enabled policymakers to delegate greater financial responsibility to cultural institutions and individual artists by adjusting the criteria for subsidy allocation. The CPA further facilitated large and unevenly distributed budget cuts, partly aimed at the improvement of heritage at the expense of contemporary culture and art forms open to the world, thereby strengthening the ties between the nation- state and cultural policy. Last but not least, the CPA functioned as a means of mobilising support for digital media as a new art form and for the digitisation of heritage, artworks and information by cultural institutions.

The second observation I would like to make is that these changes were not accompanied by a fundamental political debate. Remarkably, the CPA was only meant to enable and stimulate ongoing political deliberation on the fundamentals of cultural policy.[10] But critics state that it has resulted in a 'shift away from ambitions for cultural policy to procedural exercises' (Van den Broek 2012: 236, Smithuijsen 2009). Attempts to include a fundamental political debate in the 'soulless' procedure of determining subsidies and grants (Ministerie OCW 2005) had hardly any effect. Because of its strong focus on maintaining the cultural infrastructure, the CPA stands in the way of a fundamental dialogue on the direction of cultural policy. This conversation is needed for a variety of reasons, which will be discussed below.

Countering the Matthew Effect

It is evident that the market mechanism has played an increasingly greater role in cultural policy. This trend constitutes a break with post-war cultural policy. The main legitimation for cultural policy in the first post-war decades was precisely that the market failed in delivering certain cultural amenities. Just as in other domains of the welfare state, the introduction of market forces into the culture sector has meant that organisations have started to focus more on society. They have also become more effective and efficient. At the same time, this trend is at odds with the principles of cultural policy which, after all, is intended to create the conditions for 'maintaining and developing cultural expressions and spreading them socially and geographically or otherwise propagating them' (CPA: Art. 2).

It is important to ask ourselves whether the market is the appropriate entity to encourage the provision of cultural expressions. Cultural policy is not just about allowing people to make choices, it is also about what they have to choose from. Apart from negative liberty (different options), positive liberty (personal development) is also important (Nussbaum 2011). However, promoting positive liberty requires that one has a view on the personal development of people based on normative principles concerning people, society and the world (Blokland 2013). A good starting point might be to discuss what cultural development should look like. What cultural needs do people have and what provision is needed as a result? What is the importance of cultural development for society at large? How can cultural policy help to better equip people for life in the twenty-first century?

Bridging the Divide

Dealing with cultural diversity also requires deliberation at a political level. It is striking to note how the principle of cultural diversity disappeared from the agenda of cultural policy as soon as political attention started to focus on migration and integration. Indeed, cultural policy itself has begun to place an increasing emphasis on national identity, history and 'Dutch' cultural values. The principal question seems to be how cultural policy should bridge the divide between migrants and people who feel culturally insecure. Should cultural policy tolerate and/or support the existing cultural differences as it has in the past? Or should it take a more active stance and endeavour to ensure that different perspectives are being acknowledged, without trying to make them fit into a single narrative, while at the same time doing justice to historical facts and the obligation to maintain high-quality cultural activities? Another pressing question is whether cultural policy should facilitate society's search for new ways of connecting and attempts to define a new 'we', or instead prescribe what is culturally valuable and how different groups should relate to that.

It will not be an easy choice. There are signs that the policy concerning cultural diversity is failing with regard to the participation of new population groups, some of whom have been in the Netherlands for generations, have Dutch nationality and feel a growing connectedness with the Netherlands and Dutch culture. At the same time, a part of the 'native' population feels alienated from the culture being offered within the framework of the CPA. Until recently, these were supported by a cosmopolitan elite but now a part of this elite is embracing a nativist perspective that takes feelings of cultural insecurity as a starting point and, by doing so, introduces a new agenda for cultural policy. But the question is whether that is an effective remedy. The 'culturalisation' of citizenship actually appears to widen the gap between different population groups (Duyvendak 2017). Moreover, it is still not known whether the proposed policy measures will actually reduce cultural insecurity. What is clear in any case is that cultural insecurity, as well as cultural diversity, is a subject that must be taken into serious account in cultural policy.

Digital Cultural Policy

However, the CPA is most problematic when it comes to dealing with digitalisation. To start with, the current sectoral approach is increasingly inappropriate as a means of addressing current issues. Many economies of scale are not exploited because of the sector-by-sector or even institution-by-institution approach. Especially smaller institutions experience the disadvantages of this. Moreover, due to the lack of shared digital facilities, the cultural sector is increasingly becoming reliant on the services of large digital platform organisations. The fact that these companies provide a limited amount of information on the way they organise their services cannot but weaken the bond between institutions and the public.

A second problem is the extent to which government can direct the digitalisation of culture. As long ago as 2002, Hoefnagel noted that the confrontation between culture, technology and government policy raised fundamental policy issues. He pointed out that, at the same time, the national government's ability to act in this area was diminishing. The ability of the national government to organise the market for digital applications and content is limited. Thus, it may be necessary to strengthen cultural policy at an international level. But at the moment, even international solutions seem to fall short. Although choices in the domain of internet governance do affect the culture sector, there is no appropriate cultural policy toolkit for adapting law in the face of technological change; it's still 'a tale of parallel worlds' (Burri 2016). Despite the disconnect of culture, technology and government policy, there is every likelihood that a genuine 'digital cultural policy' will go beyond the framework of the CPA.

Notes

1. Many thanks to Quirijn van den Hoogen and Edwin Meerkerk for their critical and helpful suggestions on earliers version of this chapter. I am also indebted to my two co-authors, Anne-Greet Keizer and Godfried Engbersen, of the edited volume *Cultuur herwaarderen*, on which a part of the paragraph on the Matthew effect is based.

2. The Gift and Inheritance Tax Act became effective on 1 January 2012 and contains a number of tax measures intended to encourage donations, allowing institutions with a 'Public Benefit Organisation' status ('Anbi') to develop more commercial activities. For an institution to qualify for this 'Anbi' status, 90% of its activities must be within the domain of the arts and culture.

3. See for example: https://www.cbs.nl/nl-nl/nieuws/2015/16/grote-musea-winnen-slag-om-bezoekers.

4. The Matthew effect refers to the Gospel according to St Matthew: '...for whosoever hath, to him shall be given, and he shall have more abundance:

but whosoever hath not, from him shall be taken away even that he hath'
(Matthew 13:12).

5. Dutch statistics distinguish between 'native' (*autochtoon*) and 'foreign'
(*allochtoon*) inhabitants, based on the country of birth of individuals and
of their parents. The numbers mentioned therefore include both migrants
(first generation) and their children (second generation).

6. This was written in a letter accompanying the publication 'Cultuur in Beeld',
a yearly overview of statistical material collected and published by the
Ministry of Culture.

7. In 2006, the cabinet launched its plan for a Museum of National History. In
2007, it chose the city of Arnhem to host the new museum, but during the
years that followed there was a continuing dispute on the exact location,
costs and course of the new museum. In 2011, the plan for the Museum of
National History was dropped by the Secretary for Culture. By then, the
plans had already cost €15 million. The National Open Air Museum in
Arnhem now hosts a digital presentation of Dutch national history, based
on the Canon of the Netherlands that was developed alongside the plan for
a Museum for National History.

8. See the government coalition agreement *Vertrouwen in de toekomst*, p. 19.
Available at: https://www.kabinetsformatie2017.nl/documenten/publica-
ties/2017/10/10/regeerakkoord-vertrouwen-in-de-toekomst.

9. See its programme *Denkend aan Nederland*, p. 7.

10. See, for example, the Explanatory Memorandum, which states that 'it is implicit in the system that an ongoing discussion of cultural policy is desirable
and necessary with regard to the precise content and scope of the culture
minister's responsibility', TK 1988-1989, 20 987, 3, p. 4.

Bibliography

Aart, Kimberly van, and Rogier Brom. 2017. "Wat zijn cultuurcijfers waard? Een blik op de
Cultuurindex Nederland" [The value of Cultural Statistics. Looking at the Dutch Arts Index],
Boekman, 113: 42-46.
Adam, Barbara, and Chris Groves. 2007 *Future Matters: Action, Knowledge, Ethics*. Leiden: Brill.
Asselt, Marjolein van, Franke van der Molen, Nina Faas and Sietske Veenman. 2010. *Uit zicht.
Toekomst verkennen met beleid* [Out of Sight. Exploring the Future with Policy]. Amsterdam:
Amsterdam University Press.
Becker, Howard S. 2008 [1982]. *Art Worlds*. Berkeley: University of California Press.
Bell, David, and Kate Oakley. 2015. *Cultural Policy. Key Ideas in Media and Cultural Studies*.
Routledge: London.
Bovens, Mark, Paul Dekker and Will Tiemeijer. 2014. *Gescheiden werelden? Een verkenning van
sociaal-culturele tegenstellingen in Nederland* [Worlds Apart? An Exploration of Socio-Cultural
Oppositions in the Netherlands]. The Hague: SCP and WRR.
Blokland, Hans. 2013. "Laat cultuurbeleid over aan de politiek" [Hand over Cultural Policy to
Politics], *Beleid en Maatschappij* (40) 4: 427-430.

Brink, Gabriël van den. 2017. *Moderne liefdadigheid* [Modern Charity]. Working Paper 25. The Hague: Wetenschappelijke Raad voor het Regeringsbeleid.

Broek, Andries van den. 2012. "Cultuur tussen collectieve verantwoordelijkheid en consumentensoevereiniteit" [Culture Between Collective Responsibility and Consumer Souvereignty]. In V. Veldheer, J. Jonker, L. van Noije and C. Vrooman (eds.), *Een beroep op de burger. Minder verzorgingsstaat, meer eigen verantwoordelijkheid.* The Hague: SCP: 213-253.

Burri, Maria 2016. "Global Cultural Law and Policy and the Internet: A Tale of Parallel Worlds", *Arts and International Relations* vol. 1, issue 1 (2016), pp. 148-181. Available at SSRN: https://ssrn.com/abstract=2748050.

Delhaye, Christine, and Victor van de Ven. 2014. "'A Committment to Cultural pluralism'. Diversity Practices in Two Amsterdam Venues: Paradiso and De Meervaart", *Identities: Global Studies in Culture and Power* 21(1): 75-91.

DeNardis, Laura. 2014. *The Global War for Internet Governance.* New Haven: Yale University Press.

Denk. 2016. *Denkend aan Nederland. Verkiezingsprogramma Denk 2017-2121* [Thinking of Holland. Election Programme Think 2017-2121]. Available at: https://www.bewegingdenk.nl/wpcontent/uploads/2016/11/Verkiezingsprogramma_DENK_2017-2021.pdf

Van Dijck, José, Thomas Poell and Martijn de Waal. 2016. *De platformsamenleving. Strijd om publieke waarden in een online wereld* [The Platform Society. The Battle on Public Values in an Online World]. Amsterdam: Amsterdam University Press.

Duelund, Peter. 2016. "The Impact of the New Nationalism and Identity Politics on Cultural Policy-Making In Europe and Beyond". In P. Madsen (ed.), *Challenging Identities: European Horizons*, pp. 212-221. New York: Routledge.

Duyvendak, Jan Willem. 2017. *Thuis. Het drama van een sentimentele samenleving* [At Home. The Drama of a Sentimental Society]. Amsterdam: Amsterdam University Press.

Franssen, Saskia, and René Beckers. 2016. *Culturele instellingen in Nederland; veranderingen in geefgedrag, giften, fondsenwerving en inkomsten tussen 2011 en 2014* [Cultural Institutions in the Netherlands; Changes in Giving Behaviour, Gifts, Fundraising and Income between 2011 and 2014]. Amsterdam: VU.

Gervais, Daniel. 2012. "Copyright, Culture and the Cloud". In: Sean A. Pager and Adam Candeub (eds.), *Transnational Culture in the Internet age*, pp. 31-54. Cheltenham: Edward Elgar.

Gielen, Pascal, Sophie Elkhuizen, Quirijn van den Hoogen, Thijs Lijster and Hanka Otte. 2014. *De waarde van Cultuur* [The Value of Culture]. Groningen: Onderzoekscentrum Arts in society, Rijksuniversiteit Groningen.

Hobsbawm, Eric. 2013. *Fractured times. Culture and Society in the Twentieth Century.* New York: The New Press.

Hoefnagel, Frans. 2002. *Internet en cultuurbeleid. Over de gevolgen van ICT voor het cultuurbeleid van de Nederlandse overheid* [Internet and Cultural Policy. On the Consequences of ICT for Dutch Cultural Policy]. The Hague: SDU.

Hoogen, Quirijn Lennert van den. 2018. "Values in Crowdfunding in the Netherlands", *International Journal of Cultural Policy.* DOI: 10.1080/10286632.2018.1433666.

Holden, John. 2015. *The Ecology of Culture. A Report Commissioned by the Arts and Humanities Research Council's Cultural Value Project.* London: Arts and Humanities Research Council.

Huijnk, Willem, and Iris Andriesen. 2016. *Integratie in zicht? De integratie van migranten in Nederland op acht terreinen nader bekeken* [Integration within Reach? A Closer Inspection of the Integration of Migrants in the Netherlands on Eight Terrains]. The Hague: SCP.

Huijnk, Willem, Jacco Dagevos, Merove Gijsberts and Iris Andriessen. 2015. *Wereld van verschil. Over de sociaal-culturele afstand en positie van migrantengroepen in Nederland* [Different Worlds. On the Socio-Cultural Distance and Position of Migrant Groups in the Netherlands]. The Hague: SCP.

Hylland, Ole. 2017. "Even Better Than the Real Thing? Digital Copies and Digital Museums in a Digital Cultural Policy", *Culture Unbound* 9(1): 62-84.

Jennissen, Roel, Godfried Engbersen, Meike Bokhorst, Suzanne de Leeuw, Mark Bovens and Laura Mulder. 2015. *Migratiediversiteit beter in beeld* [A Close Up of Migrationdiversity]. The Hague: Wetenschappelijke Raad voor het Regeringsbeleid.

Judt, Tony. 2010. *Post-war. A history of Europe since 1945*. London: Random House.

Kloosterman, Robert C. 2014. "Cultural Amenities: Large and Small, Mainstream and Niche—A Conceptual Framework for Cultural Planning in an Age of Austerity", *European Planning Studies*, 22(12): 2510-2525.

Kremer, Monique, Djurre Das and Erik Schrijvers. 2017. "Onzeker in het midden. Over de verbroken beloften van de midenklasse" [Insecure in the Middle. On the Broken Promises of the Middle Class]. In: Godfried Engbersen, Eric Snel and Monique Kremer (eds.), *De val van de middenklasse? Het stabiele en kwetsbare midden*, pp. 233-252. The Hague: WRR.

Kriesi, Hanspeter. 2014. "West-Europa: het toenemende belang van de culturele dimensie" [Western Europe: the Growing Interest of the Cultural Dimension]. In: Mark Bovens, Paul Dekker and Will Tiemeijer (eds.), *Gescheiden werelden? Een verkenning van sociaal-culturele tegenstellingen in Nederland*, pp. 59-78. The Hague: SCP and WRR.

Lagroup. 2009. *De olifant in de kamer; Staalkaart culturele diversiteit in de basisinfrastructuur* [The Elephant in the Room; Cultural Diversity in the Basic Infrastructure]. Amsterdam: LAgroup. Available at: http://files.goc.nl/files/pdf/Podiumkunsten/09%20Podium%20Olifant%20in%20de%20kamer.pdf

Meer, Tom van der. 2016. *Niet de kiezer is gek* [It is not the Voter Who is Insane]. Houten: Spectrum.

Merton, Robert. 1968. "The Matthew Effect in Science", *Science* 159(3810): 56-63.

Ministerie van Onderwijs, Cultuur en Wetenschap. 2011. *Meer dan kwaliteit: een nieuwe visie op cultuurbeleid* [More than Quality: a New Vision on Cultural Policy]. The Hague: Ministerie van Onderwijs, Cultuur en Wetenschap.

—. 2002. *Beleidsbrief eCultuur* [Policybrief eCulture]. The Hague: Ministerie van Onderwijs, Cultuur en Wetenschap.

—. 2005. *Verschil maken. Herijking cultuurnotasystematiek* [Making a Difference. Recalibrating the Cultural Planningsystem]. The Hague: Ministerie van Onderwijs, Cultuur en Wetenschap.

—. 1999. *Ruim baan voor culturele diversiteit* [Make Way for Cultural Diversity]. Zoetermeer: Ministerie van Onderwijs, Cultuur en Wetenschap.

—. 1998. *Cultuur als confrontatie: uitgangspunten voor het cultuurbeleid 2001 2004* [Culture as Confrontation: Principles for Cultural Policy 2011-2004]. Zoetermeer: Ministerie van Onderwijs, Cultuur en Wetenschap.

Morel, Nathalie, Bruno Palier and Joakim Palme. 2012. *Towards a Social Investment Welfare State? Ideas, Policies and Challenges*. Bristol: Policy Press.

Mueller, Milton. 2010. *Networks and States: The Global Politics of Internet Governance*. Cambridge, MA: MIT Press.

Nooij, Floor de, René Bekkers and Suzanne Felix. 2017. *Ontwikkelingen in giften, sponsoring en andere inkomsten van culturele instellingen in Nederland* [Developments in Gifts, Sponsoring and Other Sources of Income of Cultural Institutions in the Netherlands]. Amsterdam: VU. Available at: https://fci14.files.wordpress.com/2017/07/ontwikkelingen-in-giften-sponsoring-en-andere-inkomsten.pdf

Nussbaum, Martha. 2011. *Creating Capabilities*. Cambridge, MA: Harvard University Press.

Papakonstantinou, Vagelis, and Paul de Hert. 2012. "Legal Challenges Posed by Online Aggregation of Museum Content: The Cases Of Europeana and the Google Art Project", *9:3 SCRIPTed 314* http://script-ed.org/?p=713.

Pariser, Eli. 2011. *The Filter Bubble: What the Internet is Hiding From you*. New York: Penguin.

Pasquale, Frank. 2015. *The Black Box Society: The Secret Algorithms that Control Money and Information*. Cambridge, MA: Harvard University Press.

Penninx, Rinus. 2016. "'Integratie met behoud van eigen cultuur'? Terugkijken naar beleidsleuzen, beleidskeuzes en misvattingen daarover" [Integration While Maintaining One's Own Cultural Identity. Looking Back at Policy Rethoric, Policy Choices and Misunderstandings], *Groniek Historisch tijdschrift* 208/209: 203-217. Available at: http://rjh.ub.rug.nl/groniek/article/view/30224/27524.

Raad voor Cultuur. 2003. *eCultuur: van i naar e* [eCulture: from i to e]. The Hague: Raad voor Cultuur.

Rigney, Daniel. 2010. *The Matthew effect: How advantage begets further advantage*. New York: Columbia University Press.

Schrijvers, Erik, Anne Greet Keizer and Godfried Engbersen. 2015. "Cultuur herwaarderen" [Revaluing Culture]. In: Erik Schrijvers, Anne Greet Keizer and Godfried Engbersen (eds.), *Cultuur herwaarderen*, 17-59. Amsterdam: Amsterdam University Press.

Smithuijsen, Cas. 2005. "Tijd voor een radicale cultuurpolitiek? Over de wankele positie van kunst op de agenda van het openbaar bestuur" [Time for a Radical Politics of Culture? On the Feable Position of the Arts on the Agenda of Public Administration]. In: Frans Becker and Wim van Hennekeler (eds.), *Cultuurpolitiek*, pp. 17-36. Amsterdam: Wiardi Beckman Stichting.

—. 2009. "Langs de breuklijn tussen kunst en bestuur" [Along the Fault-Line Between the Arts and Public Administration], *Boekman* 81: 6-13.

Veen, Romke van der, Mara Yerkes and Peter Achterberg (eds.). 2012. *The Transformation of Solidarity. Changing Risks and the Future of the Welfare State*. Amsterdam: Amsterdam University Press.

Vertovec, Steven. 2007. "Super-Diversity and its Implications", *Ethnic and Racial Studies* 30(6): 1024-1054.

VVD, CDA, D66 and ChristenUnie. 2017. *Vertrouwen in de toekomst. Regeerakkoord 2017-2021* [Trusting the Future. Government Coalition Agreement 2017-2121]. Available at: https://www.kabinetsformatie2017.nl/documenten/publicaties/2017/10/10/regeerakkoord-vertrouwen-in-de-toekomst.

Zuiderveen Borgesius, Frederik, Damien Trilling, Judith Möller, Balázs Bodó, Claes de Vreese and Nathalie Helberger. 2016. "Should We Worry about Filter Bubbles?", *Internet Policy Review* 5(1).

'Production is Preceded by Talent Development'

An Interview with Sandra den Hamer

© Joost Bataille

When asked to review the past decades of film policy in the Netherlands, Sandra den Hamer mentions professionalisation and internationalisation as most notable 'successes'. Den Hamer is director of the EYE Film Institute in the Netherlands, and is the former director of the International Film Festival Rotterdam (IFFR) and winner of a Golden Calf (*Gouden Kalf*) for contributions to Dutch film culture. She emphasises how these major trends are interrelated. In part, internationalisation was caused by the exorbitant costs involved in the production of a film. 'If you watch the credits of most European productions—including Dutch films—you will see a large set of partners and funds listed,' explains Den Hamer. They each bring in part of the overall budget. 'Because (…) making films is just costly, and the funds of most countries are too limited in themselves to cover that budget.'

The increasingly international cooperation results in, but also presupposes, professionalisation. Movies of the first graduates of the Dutch Film Academy (established in 1958) sold millions of tickets to cinemas. At the moment, the market share of Dutch productions in total cinema admissions is precarious, depending each year on the particular titles being released. Nonetheless, commercially successful blockbuster productions of the last few years include *Viper's Nest* (*Gooische Vrouwen*) 1 and 2. This is unsurprising, in light of the fact that 'film policy in the Netherlands has been very successful in creating a strong production climate.' A contrasting example is Portugal, 'where film policy has always been regarded as *arts* policy, and where a few Portuguese directors regularly deliver award-winning films,' says Den Hamer, 'yet in the Netherlands, film policy is inherently economic. In terms of volume, in terms of budget, we have grown significantly. However, that does not correspond with the development of artistic quality. It is still very difficult to get Dutch films nominated for awards.'

In order to make progress in this regard, all the different parts of the chain should be taken into account: 'the production and screening of films, education and film critique, and platforms: they are all vital to the sector.' Fortunately, the Dutch government acknowledges the importance of festivals such as the IFFR and the International Documentary Festival Amsterdam (both are subsidised by the national as well as municipal governments). Like festivals, film theatres play an important role in the exhibition of films. In a guidebook for administrators of municipalities, policymakers and decision-makers, Den Hamer and Winnie Sorgdrager, the president of the board of Dutch association of cinemas and film theatres (NVBF), describe film theatres as 'a haven for relevant, yet commercially vulnerable films' with an 'essential role in the area of film education' (EYE, NVBF and Dutch film theatre consultation 2015: 9). These theatres are often subject to the policies of municipalities whose inhabitants are their primary audience. Nonetheless, 'there should be nation-wide agreements with municipalities on the public support for film theatres,' according to Den Hamer, precisely because of their local importance.

Meanwhile, other parts of the film chain—for example, the platforms that consumers use to view films at home, such as television and video-on-demand services—present even more urgent policy issues. 'Especially Netflix is increasingly important in the film industry,' confirms Den Hamer, 'A particular challenge in film policy for the upcoming decades is therefore dealing with these new mediums and their impacts.' Can we make the advent of Netflix and its competitors profitable for the Dutch film industry? At the moment, these revenues are cashed abroad. 'Ideally, part of the revenues of platforms in the Netherlands would be invested in new productions [...]. For film exhibition, a lower tax rate is in place; it may be possible for the government to add to this policy the condition that platforms invest part of their revenues in film production.'

At the same time, production should not become the sole focal point of film policy, argues Den Hamer. As mentioned before, current policy is mostly aimed at strengthening the production climate, 'yet production is preceded by talent development,' and for this, there is a need for 'free space wherein filmmakers can experiment and develop without necessarily generating "output"'. This idea is echoed in a profile of the audio-visual profession that EYE published in 2017, which states that professionals should make mistakes and learn from them in order to develop an authentic style and eventually deliver high quality. Thus, Den Hamer believes international residency programmes could play an invaluable role in artistic talent development in the Dutch film sector. It is precisely this part of the film climate in the Netherlands that could—and should—be significantly improved in the next 25 years of cultural policy.

Kimberly van Aart

Bibliography

Ylstra, Gamila and Rob Boonzajer Flaes (2017). *Beroepsprofiel audiovisueel* [Professional Profile: Audiovisual]. Amsterdam: EYE. Retrieved February 20, 2018, retrieved from: http://beroep-sprofielaudiovisueel.eyefilm.nl/index.html

EYE, NVBF and Dutch film theatre consultation (eds.) (2015). *Filmtheaters in beweging: handreiking voor bestuurders van gemeenten, beleidsmakers en -bepalers* [Film Theatres in Motion: Aid for Public Managers, Policy Makers, and Decision Makers]. Amsterdam: EYE, NVBF and Dutch film theatre consultation.

Epilogue: A Systemic View of Dutch Cultural Policy in the Next 25 Years

Quirijn Lennert van den Hoogen and Edwin van Meerkerk[1]

In this volume, a number of scholars from various Dutch universities and research institutions have shed their light on the past quarter century of the Dutch cultural policy system. This book as a whole, however, is not intended to be a historical overview. On the contrary, the book looks forwards with the aim of discovering the directions the Dutch cultural policy system might need to take in the coming decades. In this epilogue, we will take a step back and give ourselves free reign to use the insights brought to light in this book to dwell on Dutch cultural policy in the next 25 years. If anything, the analyses in the preceding chapters have revealed that Dutch cultural policy is very systematic: it developed into an intricate system with particular roles for policy agents and particular subsidy regimes for different types of cultural institutions. For example, there is the Basic Infrastructure for those institutions deemed indispensable to Dutch culture, the funds supporting the more experimental producers of culture, a different subsidy scheme for enhancing audience reach, and a specific budget for international cultural policy. Dutch cultural policy can truly be described as a *system*. Therefore, in this epilogue we will use a systems theory perspective as a guiding framework. Luhmann (1984) describes how social systems evolve as a consequence of the process of functional differentiation in society.[2] Each system that evolves deals with a particular issue, solving a particular societal problem. Luhmann refers to this as the *function* of social systems for society as a whole. In order to do so, each system develops its own internal logics and adjusts its internal operations to pressures from the environment as it sees fit.

We first revisit the question of why the cultural policy system developed. What was it designed for, and what are its benefits? These benefits tell us something about the societal function of the cultural policy *system*. Using the insights of the different chapters in this book, we will then describe in sections 2 and 3 of this epilogue some of the internal logics of the cultural policy system that became apparent as it developed over time, and how it reacted to pressures from the political and economic environment. Section 4 takes a more topical perspective, focusing on the most recent cultural policy document of the current Minister of Culture, Ingrid van Engelshoven

(Ministerie OCW 2018). As all the chapters in this volume have been written before this policy document was published, this epilogue is the only part of this book that devotes attention to it. Moreover, this policy document addresses two pressing issues introduced in the closing chapter by Erik Schrijvers: the impact of globalisation and digitalisation. We conclude by presenting three possible routes for the next 25 years of Dutch cultural policy. These routes are inferred from our systems theory perspective.

1.   Dutch Cultural Policy as a System

We cannot but start by recognising the achievements of the Dutch cultural policy system. In fact, the Netherlands has received international acclaim precisely for the systemic nature of its cultural policy (see Introduction). In chapter 1, Inge van der Vlies elegantly points out that the system balances two needs: the stability that cultural institutions need to be able to plan ahead and make autonomous choices about the content of their programmes and the political necessity to change policies when deemed fit. The Cultural Policy Act (CPA) provides the legal basis for a policy system in which the necessary, albeit bounded, freedom and stability for institutions and the possibilities for politics to change course are anchored. It does so by applying the rules of good governance: the CPA provides rules of conduct for politics, making the government a 'reliable' entity for the cultural sector.

The most notable rule in the CPA regards the position of expert advice in the system. While political influence is considerable at the level of the system as a whole, most notably in determining the overall budget and pointing towards social trends the cultural sector should address, its impact on individual subsidy allocations is limited. Here, the perspective of the cultural experts is leading: the cultural policy system firmly anchors the position of the Council for Culture and the national funds. Similar advisory bodies, although usually less permanent in nature, exist at the regional and local levels. The CPA even codifies this role of expert advice in line with the arm's length principle.[3] This allows the cultural policy system to function according to its particular logic, resisting pressures from politics as well as from the market. It is, in Luhmann's term, autonomous. Some of the chapters in this volume provide evidence of this autonomy, e.g. the chapter by Hitters on the media system, the chapter by IJdens and Van Meerkerk on cultural education, and the analysis of the role of the Council for Culture in the chapter by Van den Hoogen and Jonker. Providing this stability is exactly what the cultural policy system was designed for.

However, this stability also comes at a cost: it leads to an 'institutional turn' in Dutch cultural politics, which means that it is primarily geared towards the continued existence of cultural *institutions*. Despite efforts to correct this institutional orientation—e.g., the Basic Infrastructure (BIS) supports functions in the cultural sector rather than institutions—this focus has persisted. Various authors in this volume have pointed to the downsides of this institutional turn. Despite the central role of expert advice in the CPA, the system rewards organisational stability rather than artistic endeavour and values institutional achievements, such as covenants and collaboration, more than cultural outcomes. A final result of the focus on institutions is that the cultural policy system has been from its inception a closed field. Already in 1999, Secretary for Culture Rick van der Ploeg complained that 'Those who do not yet receive subsidy want subsidy. Those who already do, want more. [Cultural policy], then, is no longer an instrument for change, but a ticket to eternity.' (Van der Ploeg 1999: 18). Implicitly, the cultural policy system thus redefined the notions of art and culture as those expressions created within the system, excluding all others.

Schrijvers points towards a second objective of the CPA: to facilitate a fundamental political debate on the role of the arts, culture and heritage in society. In other words, the cultural policy system also allows another social system—politics—to function properly. However, this second objective has never been fully realised, as the political discourse on cultural policy has remained focussed on institutions rather than on questions regarding the role of the arts and culture in society. A clear example of this is the political reaction to the effects of the substantial budget cuts of 2013. In reporting on the effects of the cut, the continued survival of cultural institutions was presented as evidence of the resilience of the sector and its ability to function properly, even when downsized. Politicians remained oblivious to the question of what these institutions actually have been doing since 2013 and what cultural or societal effects their altered activities have yielded.[4] From a systems theory perspective, we can therefore argue that the political system is adapting itself to the logic of the cultural policy system, rather than the other way around.

The systems theory perspective, then, leads to the conclusion that the Dutch cultural policy system restricts its scope only to culture that is already subsidised, while excluding individual artists and (often temporary) grass-roots initiatives. Moreover, as Van der Vlies pointed out in her chapter, the broader context of administrative law as well as EU regulations inhibits the inclusion of commercial agents in the cultural policy system. In other words: even if there was a political will to include institutions from outside the subsidised circles, this would meet with legal barriers. Although politics still has considerable influence on the system, the central logic of the cultural policy system is not political. Nor is it cultural or artistic, for that matter—much to the chagrin of the cultural sector, we might add. Its key logic is *administrative* in nature, a fact that is frequently overlooked in cultural policy research.[5]

2.   The Inherent Logic of the Dutch Cultural Policy System

Although the CPA does not apply to regional and local authorities, they are mentioned as partners of the national government, which leads to inherent centre-periphery dynamics in the policy system. Moreover, various chapters in this volume testify to other logics inherent to the cultural policy system: it has a tendency towards compartmentalisation and towards rationalisation.

Centre-Periphery Dynamics
The centre-periphery tension is a key logic of the Dutch cultural policy system. While the CPA propagates a fair distribution over the country (Art. 2), the cultural sector naturally gravitates towards the most densely populated areas, the Rim City[6] and Amsterdam in particular. A logic consequence of the CPA's focus on institutions is that regions where most cultural institutions are located (i.e., Amsterdam) benefit most from national subsidies. Regional and local governments, particularly in the more rural parts of the country, have protested against the resulting lopsided distribution of national funds, arguing that artistic quality should be evaluated within its regional context.[7] The policy system first channelled the voice of local government by means of the so-called covenant negotiations (*covenantenoverleg*). These were instigated by Minister D'Ancona, the first Minister of Culture to work with the system. In keeping with the Dutch bottom-up tradition in government, cultural participation policies were based on local and regional plans (the Cultural Outreach Action Programme; see the chapter by IJdens and Van Meerkerk). And while digitalisation necessitated co-ordinated action on the part of public libraries, it turned out to be unfeasible to change the public library into a truly national one (see the chapter by Huysmans and Oomes). Moreover, local support for cultural facilities is important. Van Eijck points out that the bottom-up procedure of the Action Programme allowed policy efforts to be attuned to local circumstances. However, the downside is that the different operationalisations of the core issues addressed in the

programme (ethnic representation, access) lead to very different policy efforts.

This highlights a general weakness of the Dutch cultural policy system: compared to the education sector or the welfare system, the responsibilities of local authorities regarding cultural policy are, strictly speaking, non-existent. While local governments are expected to provide facilities for the dissemination of art and culture, such as libraries, art movie houses, theatres, and museums, they are not obliged to do so by law. Without such local institutions, a national system cannot properly attain its goals, nor can nationally funded institutions connect to their local environments in meaningful ways. The fact that the policy system does not provide more strict requirements for local authorities is a serious lacuna—and one that is hard to resolve, as national government cannot order municipalities to change their subsidy policies (see the chapter by Van der Vlies). Following its own logic, the cultural policy system resolved this problem by using the next-best thing: consultation rounds that aimed to align policy agents with particular courses of action.[8] In practice, this adds another bureaucratic step and extends the timeframe for producing cultural policy documents. Moreover, many feel that the interactions between national and local authorities are very ineffective (Council for Culture 2015).

Compartmentalisation of Cultural Policy
The examples of the Public Library Act (see chapter 9) and the Media Act (see chapter 7)—and also the Heritage Act (see Introduction)—indicate that the CPA does not cover all areas of cultural policy in the Netherlands. As the CPA typically underregulates the cultural sector, the legislature tends to opt for separate arrangements for those parts of the sector where more strict regulations are necessary. This is true for the conditions and regulations concerning the preservation of heritage objects and sites and issues of democratic representation and access in the media as well as the development of a national digital library infrastructure. This complicates the bureaucratic arrangements underpinning cultural policy, as cultural institutions may be forced to work under different policy regimes simultane-ously. National museums, for instance, are subject to the Heritage Act with regard to their collections, while as an institution they resort to the BIS for general subsidies, and for individual exhibitions, they apply for funding to the (public) Mondriaan Fund. As a result, cooperation between different types of institutions becomes more difficult. This tendency is in stark contrast to analyses that point to cross-sectoral developments (Council for Culture 2015), which blur the lines between art, heritage and media (see below).

Rationalisation and Economisation of Cultural Policy

Various chapters in this volume testify to the growing importance of extra-cultural reasoning in Dutch cultural policy, most notably the importance of the economic paradigm with its quantitative methods of evaluation. Lijster, Otte and Gielen highlight the fact that the Dutch cultural policy system is focused on the benefits of *individual* experiences rather than collective benefits. They see this as one of the major flaws of the system. Kolsteeg points out that the stress on entrepreneurialism has amounted to transplanting an economic rationale to the cultural sector to the point where self-generated income has become a yardstick for assessing societal support. Although Van den Hoogen and Jonker indicate that cultural and artistic values still provide the core of the reasoning behind actual decisions on subsidy allocations, their analysis, too, points to the increasing relevance of market and economic values. Ticket sales seem to have become the most important statistic used to assess the success of cultural policy. Hitters and Kolsteeg, however, argue that this economic turn in cultural and media policy actually prevents goal attainment, as the system does not stimulate cultural institutions to innovate or to address global issues such as migration, populism and the like. In short, the methods introduced for governance and accountability seem to be in opposition to the central goals of cultural policy. They do, however, fit the administrative logic of the CPA, and fit to the tendency towards bureaucratisation of the policy system.

This can also be seen in the evidence used to assess goal attainment. Huysmans and Oomes note that the statistics on lending do not shed light on public libraries' social values. New narratives of performance are necessary to provide data on their public role and the success of cultural policy. Van Eijck highlights the same problem, arguing that statistics on audience reach do not reflect new and informal forms of cultural engagement, which in many cases involve digital means. The current statistics, therefore, mainly attest to the failure of Dutch public cultural policy. What matters is *what* works *for whom*, under *which circumstances* and *why*. These questions necessitate qualitative rather than quantitative evaluations. In short, it is time to assign more political clout to different types of (narrative) evidence and hence to different values (Schrijvers et al. 2015, Van den Hoogen 2017). The alternative would be to work towards a system based on trust in the public role of culture, much like what is being advocated in education and healthcare—both public sectors suffering from (excessive) bureaucratisation. But currently, the cultural policy system does not allow for such a turn towards trust.[9]

Conclusion

Luhmann's prediction that systems inherently evolve towards more complexity holds true for the Dutch cultural policy system. As an inherent result of the system, bureaucratisation is seen as counterproductive to the achievement of policy goals and even an impediment to the autonomy of cultural institutions. The response to such criticism, however, is an impulse to refine the bureaucracy, making it ever more impenetrable for actors outside the system. This tendency towards ever-more complex bureaucratic arrangements is likely to increase in the coming years. The system will probably continue its present course of diversification in organisational structure and fine-tuning of administrative procedures, both in policy formulation and evaluation.

Regarding the latter point, we argue that the weak link that exists between policy goals and instruments and the evaluation of the effects of these instruments is an important challenge that the cultural policy system faces (Van Eijck in this volume, Van den Hoogen 2010 and 2012, Bunnik 2017). This gap between goals and evaluation is partly explained by the lack of an underlying vision on art and culture in society that would provide Dutch cultural policy legitimacy. This should be provided by a fundamental political debate on the issue. However, both in the CPA and in policy briefs issued by the ministry, cultural policy is legitimised from a pragmatic, systemic perspective. Even when subsequent Ministers of Culture make bold statements on the nature and necessity of art and culture, these statements are never connected to the policy itself but only result in more bureaucratic arrangements. The number of inter-government covenants and the increasingly specific definition of roles for non-government bodies is thus likely to grow. Only recently, a report on the structure of the policy system (Bureau Berenschot 2018) proposed that seven types of functions to be fulfilled (and thus subsidised) be identified, as opposed to the previously discerned two functions. As a result, an ever-more intricate web of functions, arrangements and institutions designed to cater to the needs and wishes of the public and the culture sector will become even more resistant to attempts to dismantle the bureaucracy of the cultural policy system.

3.   Is There a Future for an Inherently More Complex Policy System?

Current developments in the environment of the cultural policy system raise the question whether the system will be able to continue on this path towards more bureaucracy. Over the last 25 years, the Dutch cultural policy system may have been able to absorb pressures from its environment by expanding its administrative procedures. But that does not imply that this route will be effective in the coming decades. Currently we are experiencing a period of de-differentiation of functionally differentiated subsystems in society, rather than further specialisation. Technological developments, particularly the IT revolution, have allowed the blurring of boundaries between social spheres such as the arts, education, entertainment, news, leisure, sports and social action, to name but a few. The IT revolution also mutually enforces the process of globalisation: we are witnessing unprecedented speed and volume in the circulation of ideas, goods, services and people across the globe.[10] Furthermore, the move from a welfare state to a participatory society poses challenges to the cultural policy system. We now address this issue.

From Welfare State to Participatory Society
As indicated in the introduction to this book, the development of cultural policy in Western societies has been linked to the development of the welfare state. The provision of health care, welfare and education by the state has been as much a model for cultural provision as the cultural policy implemented during the Second World War was. However, the neoliberal climate that has been emerging since the 1970s has deeply undermined the welfare state logic. The alternative to the welfare state, embraced mainly in the Netherlands and the UK, has been dubbed the 'participatory society'.[11] A participatory society demands a more pro-active role of its citizens, presuming a more responsible attitude towards their community and their environment. As Schrijvers indicates, this provides a *moral* form of citizenship rather than a legal one: the citizen is expected—or obligated—to contribute to his or her society and is no longer 'entitled to' social benefits. We would note that this goes well beyond the mere financial relationship between government and cultural institutions: societal issues such as cultural diversity and proper payment for cultural work have increasingly been framed as responsibilities of the cultural sector itself without proper compensation for rising costs.[12] In other words, to be eligible for government support, artists and cultural institutions must take on additional responsibilities. Moreover, due to the growing importance of self-generated income, cultural institutions have increasingly relied on volunteer work (see Appendix). Currently, they rely on a generation of healthy but ageing citizens. Demographic developments, however, will frustrate this development. Moreover, increasing numbers of young adults find it difficult to balance private and work obligations, which bodes ill for future rates of volunteering but also for participation levels.

The shift towards catering to the needs of specific groups under specific conditions is also very problematic for the political support for the system. Fewer parties will be willing to support a full cultural system in society, in which generic cultural institutions cater to the needs of the whole population (at least on a rhetorical level). This is a marked difference between welfare and social policies on the one hand and cultural policies on the other. The chapter by Lijster, Otte and Gielen identifies the problems that cultural institutions encounter in truly engaging with grassroots initiatives and therefore becoming engaged in civil action. Artists with an ambition to confront the issues of their communities in their work do not see the institutions as proper platforms suited for their activities. The institutional focus of the cultural policy system does not stimulate the type of social engagement that is necessary to be successful in a participatory society. In spite of continuing efforts from within the cultural policy system, this increases the tension between the systemisation of cultural policy and the need to articulate other, more culture-related policy goals. In this respect, it is significant to note how Minister Van Engelshoven endorsed the Council's plea for a focus on the value, rather than the impact, of culture, while at the same time committing the government to the continued support of the existing institutional infrastructure. In her policy brief *Culture in an Open Society* (Ministerie van OCW 2018), Van Engelshoven follows the Council's latest advice, *Culture for City, Country and Region* (Raad voor Cultuur 2017), in which the value of culture is defined from the perspective of artists and consumers as well as from a historical and societal perspective. This line of reasoning does away with more fundamental considerations regarding the values underlying cultural policy in general (see also Drion, forthcoming)—i.e., art and culture as *dynamic* systems of social signification and identification.

Digitalisation and Globalisation

Schrijvers' chapter addresses digitalisation and globalisation quite adequately. Therefore, in this epilogue we will restrict ourselves to some general remarks pertaining to our systems theory perspective. Three issues should be addressed.

First, there is an obvious link between digitalisation, globalisation and the aforementioned tendency towards rationalisation of the cultural policy system. Digitalisation has allowed for expanding amounts of data to be produced and processed, feeding into the quantitative economic rationale that has become part of evidence-based policies. The global integration of economic systems also calls for more rational logics, particularly in smaller countries such as the Netherlands. However, we do not want to argue that such consequences of integration into the global economy are unintentional. Quite the opposite, rationalisation fits in very well with the Dutch mercantile attitude. But, as already indicated above, the civic value of general access that underlies cultural policies—or any other form of public service provision—may be seriously damaged as a consequence.

The second point also relates to those civic values: while digital technologies might seem to allow for unprecedented levels of access, the Matthew effect described in Schrijvers' chapter impedes greater access considerably. In a more market-oriented system, the larger institutions may fare well, but the diversity of provision and access are expected to become more limited. Moreover, the algorithms behind Google's search engines and commercial platforms such as YouTube and Facebook are not transparent. They are based on commercial rather than civic logics. Given the central role of the consumer's perspective in cultural policy, as advocated by the Council for Culture, this trend of decreasing diversity in the cultural offerings is likely to have a significant impact. Cultural institutions will increasingly feel the need to cooperate with these commercial partners, as will the public broadcasters (see chapter 6). However, the institution-centred logics of the cultural policy system seems ill-suited to counter the detrimental effects on the accessibility of public cultural and media provision.[13]

Third, the integration of the Netherlands into a global technological-economic system has made nationality a pressing issue. To what extent can Dutch culture remain Dutch? To what extent can a *national* cultural policy system be sustained in a globalising context? As long as there is a national authority that is willing to sustain a national system of cultural subsidies, this might seem a mute question. However, Minnaert and Schrijvers identify a new social cleavage between the so-called winners and the losers of a global economy. Up until now, the cultural policy system itself has been firmly supported by those with a cosmopolitan rather than an inward-looking perspective. Nonetheless, nativist tendencies have emerged, for example in the discussion surrounding plans for a National History Museum (between 2006 and 2011), in the increasingly national focus of international cultural policy as described by Minnaert in this volume and, more recently, in the focus on heritage as one of the four pillars of cultural policy (Raad voor Cultuur 2017). The latter has given rise to the view that visiting Rembrandt's *Night Watch* and singing the national anthem should be part of the school curriculum (see below). Clearly, cultural institutions are being called upon to cater to people experiencing 'cultural insecurity'. How the sector deals with these issues will undoubtedly impact political and public support for a publicly funded cultural system.

4.   The Current Regional Turn in Dutch Cultural Politics

As the chapters in this book were written before the publication of the current government's most recent policy document, Culture in an Open Society (*Cultuur in een Open Samenleving*), we will briefly reflect on this document here. We start with a rather elaborate quote from its introduction, in which Culture Minister Ingrid van Engelshoven places her cultural policy firmly in the liberal tradition dating back to Karl Popper, from whom she borrowed the title of her policy brief:

The Netherlands is an open society; a country in a delta area, where ideas flow in and out naturally. Just as the river Rhine cannot be stopped at Lobith [near the German border], neither can art or heritage be held back by national borders. The separation between inside and outside—the straight line between what happens here in the Netherlands and what happens in the rest of the world—is fictitious, and we have known that for a long time. [...]
Culture has, first of all, its own intrinsic value. It expresses one's deepest thoughts or feelings; it can convey beauty and refinement or conflict and coarseness. Furthermore, culture has an important societal function; it is a measure of *zeitgeist*. Culture can be ahead of its time, and thus determine the spirit of the age. [...] in our times, these societal functions are indispensable. When rationalisation and efficacy are the dominant themes in society, culture as a counterforce is of crucial importance.
At a time when many people have a hard time keeping pace with the rapid succession of developments, large groups of people have feelings of insecurity. Fear of the unknown spurs a longing for one's own. This is quite understandable in itself. However, it must not lead to fear and cultural conservatism becoming the dominant principles for society as a whole. An open society like the Netherlands cannot afford to stand still. Art resists stagnation. When the nation threatens to doze off, artists will arouse it. Meanwhile, it is important to preserve a mainstay. A society that knows only renewal and confrontation is uninhabitable. A healthy society balances the new with the familiar. (Ministerie OCW 2018: 3-4)

Minister Van Engelshoven strikes an eloquent balance in this text between the cosmopolitan and nativist perspectives on arts and culture while also addressing the most pressing issues discussed above. The text reflects the composition of the current coalition government of social-liberal democrats (D66), liberals (VVD) and Christian-Democrats (CDA). Whereas D66 has a strong cosmopolitan orientation, the latter two parties have in recent years adopted an inward-looking, conservative perspective in response to the rise of right-wing populism. On the one hand, the document stresses the importance of national culture and heritage. Van Engelshoven announces that she will support heritage as well as cultural and democratic education. Two concrete proposals that were already made during the elections are the inclusion in the national curriculum of school visits to the *Night Watch* in the Rijksmuseum as well as the national anthem and its importance in the Dutch rebellion against Spanish rule in the sixteenth century (which goes against the constitutional freedom of education, as described in the chapter by IJdens and Van Meerkerk).[14] On the other hand, the document stresses the importance of the arts in providing a dynamic and open society. The document is the first of its kind to devote an entire section to the *intrinsic* value of the arts and culture. In other words, the new Minister seems to be setting a course between Scylla and Charybdis.

The document also addresses the future of the current policy system. Just as at the start of the CPA 25 years ago, the proposals are very pragmatic. The government takes up the Council for Culture's suggestion for a regionally based national system. It repeats the new formulation of policy aims to be included in the CPA from the latest advisory document (Council for Culture 2017). The Council suggested four perspectives for defining the values underlying cultural policy. The first is the creative or professional perspective, which focuses on artistic quality. The second is the receptive perspective, in other words the perspective of the audience. The other two approach the value of culture from the perspective of history, where cultural value is related to the current notion of diversity as well as national identity, and from the societal perspective, which incorporates both the cosmopolitan and nationalistic outlooks on culture. These perspectives are broader and more encompassing than the current central values of the CPA—quality and diversity—while making the definition of cultural value dependent on what people (artists, audiences, politicians) experience as valuable.

By including these four perspectives in the Cultural Policy Act, cultural policy might be able to address the issues raised above. However, by defining value in terms of perspective, cultural policy would be letting go of control over its own legitimacy. In addition, Van Engelshoven refrains from commenting on the Council's quite detailed suggestions for restructuring the system. The system once again seems to be only *added to*: local authorities are called upon to produce a vision on the cultural infrastructure in their region (called a 'profile'), which will form the basis for conversations between regional and national authorities. The outcomes of these conversations will be laid down in a discussion paper written by the Minister of Culture, the document that starts each four-year policy cycle. Other than that, everything seems to be proceeding as usual: discussion paper, subsidy applications by institutions, independent advice by the Council for Culture, followed by the decisions on subsidy allocations by the Minister and the final approval of cultural policy by Parliament. This procedure is scheduled to last from May 2018 to 1 January 2021—nearly two and a half years. Hence, we are inclined to read the current debate as yet another example of the internal tendency of the policy system to react to pressures from the outside by making the dynamics of the system more complex and complicated rather than providing a more fundamental reorientation of cultural politics for the coming decades. Though this may suffice for the policy period of 2021-2024, it is questionable whether such a system will make it beyond that time frame.

5.   Three Scenarios for the Coming Decades

Looking at the future of the cultural policy of the Dutch nation-state, we can ask ourselves whether there will be a *cultural* policy or a *Dutch* cultural policy in 25 years. Three possible scenarios can be inferred from our systems theory perspective.

In the first scenario, the cultural policy system's strategy of adding new arrangements and requirements is successful in the sense that the system survives. It is able to absorb pressures from the political and social environment through further waves of bureaucratisation, securing cultural institutions' existence and freedom to manoeuvre at a national scale. In this scenario we must, however, seriously question whether the cultural policy system will be able to connect to new generations of artists and audiences, both of migrant and native descent, because what the cultural institutions have on offer is hardly relevant to them. Furthermore, cultural institutions may have a hard time connecting to what Holden (2015) has called the 'home-grown' and the 'commercial' spheres of culture, two vital elements in cultural ecosystems. As Van der Vlies pointed out in this volume, EU legislation regarding the public support of enterprises render it impossible to join forces with commercially oriented culture. Thus, the cultural policy system will remain a closed system. In this case, cultural policy does run the risk of losing touch with society. It is doubtful whether the cultural policy system will be able to promote the societal relevance of arts and culture, precisely because of its bureaucratic measures. In short, this might be a scenario of isolation, though the BIS may continue in its current form, providing a backbone for the cultural sector as a whole.

The second scenario is a breakdown of the national system. Instead, the cultural sector will rely on local and regional support for vital public cultural facilities. Such a scenario may be fully in line with the trend towards decentralisation we have seen in other policy areas such as health care and welfare. In this scenario, national quality standards may be difficult to sustain, but local support and embedding of cultural institutions may be promoted more easily. The cultural sector's distrust of national government, sparked by the wave of budget cuts around 2013, has propelled artists and institutions to look towards local governments. The latter are already eager to take over the lead in cultural policy. Major cities like Rotterdam and Amsterdam already have the appropriate infrastructure—a Council for Culture, a culture fund, institutions with international appeal—in place. Other cities are creating alliances to achieve sufficient mass, such as the coalition 'We the North', the Eindhoven *brainport* region, Brabantstad, and the alliance between Arnhem and Nijmegen. With the European Union increasingly taking on its role in cultural policy and focussing on regional rather than national cooperation, the national level will soon become redundant. From Van der Vlies' chapter on legal aspects of cultural policy, we deduce an important corollary to this development. The kind of intergovernmental collaboration that is necessary for this regional turn has no basis in the law. For such a turn to become a permanent, even fundamental part of cultural policy, this has to be repaired, in which case a successor to the CPA must provide an enabling framework to guarantee a reliable and productive cultural policy system. Moreover, if a new CPA does not contain the necessary regulations for local authorities, the risk of creating 'blind spots' is significant.

A scenario in which there is no culture may seem hard to imagine. As humans are cultural beings, cultural provision will always somehow be organised. However, it may not be a *public* form of cultural provision. This is the third scenario: no pubic cultural policy will survive in the Netherlands. The cultural needs of the population will be catered to by commercial parties and private initiative only. Already, private funding is taking on an increasingly important role in the cultural sector, from museum subsidies by the BankGiro lottery to the music education scheme initiated and co-funded by the VandenEnde Foundation. This seems to be a scenario in which the

Matthew effect will fully take root, as a diverse, professional provision of culture may be feasible only in densely populated areas (Schrijvers in this volume; Van Maanen 2009). Particularly costly forms of art, i.e., the live arts, will be difficult to sustain professionally. Only those performances that attract large audiences for longer periods of time will be commercially viable. Museum exhibitions, sponsored by private donors and commercial sponsors, will tour the nation. Popular musicals will dominate the stages. The longest performing theatre project in the Netherlands at this moment, *Soldier of Orange*, receives no government support and yet has attracted record numbers of spectators since 2010 and is still being staged in 2018. Outside the larger cities, amateur activities are the only viable option. In this scenario, national cultural heritage may suffer, though it cannot be ruled out that national politics will pick up the responsibility for heritage based on a nativist perspective. In that case, cultural policy will be transformed into heritage and identity policy.

Only in the first scenario can the cultural policy system's focus on the continued existence of cultural institutions survive, though this may come at the cost of audience reach and social efficacy. But that may be the price to pay for any public policy system, because it may be the case that such a system inevitably focuses on administrative logics. Democratic control of expenditures necessitates democratic procedures. Demands for transparency in government—legitimate demands—unavoidably lead to calls for more data on the functioning of a sector. And that in turn leads to an administrative rather than societal logic that tries to balance the demand for continuity of the sector and the ability of politics to intervene, with which we started in chapter 1. The CPA does strike that necessary balance. The real question, therefore, is how to balance this administrative logic with the goals of cultural policy and the reality of cultural processes in society. Our answer would be that the current course of the Dutch CPA system towards more bureaucratic specialisation is not the answer, as it will only create further rifts between the policy system, the cultural sector *and* politics.

Notes

1. The authors are grateful for the useful comments by Erik Schrijvers and Sara Strandvad on earlier versions of this epilogue.
2. Interestingly, Luhmann has extended his analysis of society to the arts as well (Luhmann 1995, translated in 2000) but here we will restrict ourselves to his more general description of social systems theory. This is because his later book only focuses on art, ignoring heritage or culture in general.

3. In Dutch, this arm's length principle is referred to as the Adage of Thorbecke, named after Dutch statesman Johan Rudolph Thorbecke (1789-1872). He was responsible for drawing up the Dutch constitution. In 1862, when he was prime minister, he explained in parliament that the government should not be the judge of the arts and sciences (Pots 2010).

4. Indicative of the blind spot in politics is the discussion regarding so-called production houses in the Dutch theatre system, a category of institutions devoted to experimenting and developing new theatre talent. The entire category was removed from the BIS. Institutions such as Toneelschuur in Haarlem and Grand Theatre in Groningen managed to survive (on local subsidies). However, their role and function in the Dutch theatre landscape have changed considerably. Moreover, the Matthew effect, as discussed in the chapter by Schrijvers, results in cultural institutions reverting to 'blockbuster' strategies, catering to audience groups that are already culturally active.

5. This may be explained by the fact that the systems theory perspective is far more common in law and administrative sciences than in cultural policy research. The formal and abstract nature of systems theory fits in particularly well with systems that are supposed to continue their operations without the influence of individual persons and interest. For example, the personal opinions of a judge should not matter in court rulings. Law was one of the major inspirations for Luhmann, in addition to calculus (see Borch 2011).

6. The Rim City ('Randstad') is the name for the metropolitan area in the West of the Netherlands. It encompasses the cities of Rotterdam, The Hague, Leiden, Amsterdam, and Utrecht and all towns in between. The Rim City is home to 7.1 million people (41,7% of the total population) and has a gross domestic product 367 billion euros (2016), 52,2% of the Dutch GDP.

7. See, for example, the argument put forward by the northern provinces in *We the North*, available on: http://www.wethenorth.org/ [accessed 30 March 2018].

8. Article 6 of the CPA explicitly mentions the possibility to cooperate with municipalities and provinces, negotiating administrative covenants (*bestuursovereenkomsten*).

9. The problem is not restricted to the cultural policy field. Currently, discussions are taking place on redressing the administrative pressures in health care and education, which due to the focus on new public management (see Van den Hoogen 2010) have also experienced a decline in trust in the professional capabilities of doctors and teachers.

10. This has led to a situation of constant fluidity of organisations and institutions, characterised as 'liquid modernity' by Bauman (2000). The trend seems to refute the notion of differentiation in society that is so central to Luhmann's theory.

11. The concept has been coined in the King's speech (Troonrede) of 2017, the King's annual address to parliament at the start of the parliamentary season.

12.   Interestingly, until 2015, the social economic position of artists and cultural workers was the remit of the Ministry of Social Affairs rather than the Ministry of Education, Culture and Science. In the policy document by Jet Bussemaker (Ministerie OCW 2015) and by Van Engelshoven (Ministerie OCW 2018), the issue is fully relegated to the cultural institutions.

13.   This is one of the reasons why the Council for Culture (2015 and 2017) has argued for a more local perspective in the national cultural policy system, as in their view, cultural institutions should cooperate with small, locally based IT and creative firms. However, although this might be helpful, it does not solve the problem of the lure of 'infinite' access through global IT platforms such as Google, Facebook and YouTube.

14.   Interestingly, older generations used to know at least two of the fifteen verses of the Wilhelmus by heart, as these used to be taught in schools. Apparently, investing in math and language education over some decades has come at the expense of attention for cultural history.

Bibliography

Bauman, Zygmunt. 2000. *Liquid Modernity*. Cambridge: Policy Press.

Borch, Christian. 2011. *Niklas Luhmann*. London: Routledge.

Bunnik, Claartje. 2017. *Naar Waarde Gewogen. Een nieuw model voor kwaliteitsbeoordeling bij de toekenning van cultuursubsidies* [Weighted According to Value. A New Model for Quality Assessment in Cultural Subsidy Allocation]. Amsterdam: Boekman Foundation.

Drion, Geert. [forthcoming] *De waarde van cultuur* [The Value of Culture]. Amsterdam: Boekman Foundation.

Holden, John. 2014. *The Ecology of Culture A Report commissioned by the Arts and Humanities Research Council's Cultural Value Project*. London: AHRC. Available at http://www.ahrc.ac.uk/documents/project-reports-and-reviews/the-ecology-of-culture/ [Accessed 27 March 2018].

Luhmann, Niklas. 1984. *Soziale Systemen. Grundriss einer algemeinen Theorie*. [Social Systems. Foundation for a General Theory]. Frankfurt am Main: Suhrkamp.

Luhmann, Niklas. 2000 [1995]. *Art as a Social System*. Palo Alto: Stanford University Press. Translated from *Die Kunst der Gesellschaft*. Frankfurt am Main: Suhrkamp.

Ministerie OCW. 2015. *Ruimte voor cultuur: uitgangspunten cultuurbeleid 2017-2020*. [Space for Culture: Principles for Cultural Policy 2017-2020]. The Hague: Ministerie van OCW [Ministry of Education, Culture and Science].

Ministerie OCW. 2018. *Cultuur in een Open Samenleving*. The Hague: Ministerie van OCW. Available at https://www.rijksoverheid.nl/documenten/rapporten/2018/03/12/cultuur-in-een-open-samenleving [Accessed 27 March 2018].

Pots, Roel. 2010. *Cultuur, Koningen en Democraten. Overheid & Cultuur in Nederland*. [Culture, Kings and Democrats. Government and Culture in the Netherlands]. Amsterdam: Boom.

Raad voor Cultuur. 2015. *Agenda Cultuurbeleid 2017-2020 en verder*. [Agenda for Cultural Policy 2017-2020 and Beyond]. The Hague: Raad voor Cultuur [Council for Culture].

Raad voor Cultuur. 2017 [online]. *Cultuur voor stad, land en regio*. [Culture for City, Nation and Region]. The Hague: Raad voor Cultuur. [Council for Culture]. Available at http://

toekomst-cultuurbeleid.cultuur.nl/verkenning/cultuurbeleid-voor-stad-land-en-regio [Accessed 27 March 2018].

Schrijvers, Erik, Anne-Greet Keizer and Godfried Engbertsen (eds.). 2015. *Cultuur Herwaarderen* [Reassessing Culture]. The Hague: WRR [Scientific Council for Government Policy].

Van den Hoogen, Quirijn Lennert. 2010. *Performing Arts and the City. Municipal Cultural policy in the Brave New World of Evidence-Based Policy*. PhD. dissertation, Groningen University.

—. 2012. *Effectief Cultuurbeleid. Leren van Evalueren*. [Effective Cultural Policy. Learning from Assessing]. Amsterdam: Boekmanstichting.

—. 2017. "Over 'waarde' en 'waarderen' van de kunsten" [On 'Value' and 'Valuing' in the Arts], *Boekman* 29 (113): pp. 12-15.

Van der Ploeg, Rick. 1999. *Cultuur als confrontatie. Uitgangspunten voor het cultuurbeleid 2001-2004*. [Culture as Confrontation. Principles for Cultural Policy 2001-2004] The Hague: Ministerie OCW [Ministry of Education, Culture and Science].

Van Maanen, Hans. 2009. *How to Study Art Worlds? On the Societal Functioning of Aesthetic Values*. Amsterdam: Amsterdam University Press.

Overview of Dutch Ministers of / Secretaries for Culture and their most important cultural policy documents

In the Dutch political system, there is a difference between Ministers (*minister*) and Secretaries (*staatssecretaris*). Both are a member of the government.[1] Usually, a Ministry is led by one Minister and one or two Secretaries. They split the responsibility of the various policy areas of the Ministry among them. As a result, cultural policy can fall in the remit of the Minister or in the remit of a Secretary. Joint responsibility does not exist. While the Minister is ultimately responsible for the whole department, this only comes to the fore when discussing the Ministry's budget with Parliament. Moreover, a Minister is part of the Cabinet, attending its weekly meetings. A Secretary for Culture will only attend these meetings when cultural policy issues are discussed. The resignation of a Minister does not necessarily lead to the resignation of the Secretary, or vice-versa. To avoid confusion, Secretaries call themselves 'Minister' when operating on international level, e.g. in meetings of EU Ministers of Culture and Media.

Name	Years in office	Policy Documents
Elco Brinkman (CDA, Christian-Democrats) Minister of Welfare, Healthcare and Culture	1982 – 1989	Prepared the Cultural Policy Act and published several policy documents, always concerning parts of the cultural sector e.g. on arts and heritage policy.
Hedy D'Ancona (PvdA, Social-Democratic Party) Minister of Welfare, Healthcare and Culture	1989 – 1994	1992: *Investeren in Cultuur, Nota Cultuurbeleid 1993-1996* (Investing in Culture, Cultural Policy Plan for 1993-1996)
Aad Nuis (D66, Progressive -Liberal Party) Secretary for Culture and Media[*1]	1994 – 1998	1995: *Pantser of Ruggegraat, Uitgangspunten voor cultuurbeleid*[*2] (Armour or Backbone: Principles for Cultural Policy) 1996: *Pantser of Ruggengraat, Cultuurnota 1997-2000* (Armour or Backbone: Cultural Policy Plan 1997-2000)

Name	Years in office	Policy Documents
Rick van der Ploeg (PvdA, Social-Democratic Party) Secretary for Culture and Media	1998 – 2002[*3]	1999: *Cultuur als Confrontatie, Uitgangspunten voor het cultuurbeleid 2001-2004* (Culture as Confrontation, Principles for Cultural Policy 2001-2004) 1999: *Ruim Baan voor Culturele Diversiteit* (Make Way for Cultural Diversity – policy brief on diversity in the cultural sector) 1999: *Cultureel Ondernemerschap* (Cultural Entrepreneurship – policy brief on entrepreneurship in the cultural sector) 2000: *Cultuur als Confrontatie, cultuurnota 2001-2004* (Culture as Confrontation, Cultural Policy Plan 2001-2004)
Medy van der Laan (D66, Progressive-Liberal Party) Secretary for Culture and Media	2003 – 2006[*4]	2003: *Meer dan de Som, beleidsbrief cultuur 2004-2007*[*5] (More than the Sum, Cultural Policy Brief 2004-2007) 2004: *Meer dan de Som, Cultuurnota 2005-2008* (More than the Sum, Cultural Policy Plan 2005-2008) 2005: *Verschil maken. Herijking cultuurnotasystematiek* (Making a Difference: Recalibrating the Cultural Policy System – policy brief on the process of cultural policy, it led to the introduction of the Basic Infrastructure per 2009)
Ronald Plasterk (PvdA, Social-Democratic Party) Minister of Education, Culture and Science	2007 – 2010	2007: *Kunst van Leven. Hoofdlijnen Cultuurbeleid* (Art of Living. Principles of Cultural Policy) 2008: Subsidieplan Kunst van Leven 2009-2012 (Subsidy Allocations Art of Living 2009-2012)
Halbe Zijlstra (VVD, Liberal Party) Secretary for Culture and Media	2010 – 2012	2011: *Meer dan Kwaliteit: Een nieuwe visie op cultuurbeleid* (More than Quality: A New Vision on Cultural Policy – policy brief) 2012: Kamerbrief: Besluiten Culturele Basisinfrastructuur 2013 – 2016 (Policy Brief: Allocations Cultural Basic Infrastructure 2013-2016)

Name	Years in office	Policy Documents
Jet Bussemaker (PvdA, Social-Democratic Party) Minister of Education, Culture and Science	2012 – 2017	2013: *Cultuur Beweegt: De betekenis van cultuur in een veranderende samenleving* (Culture Moves: The Meaning of Culture in a Changing Society – policy brief) 2015: *Ruimte voor Cultuur: Uitgangspunten cultuurbeleid 2017-2020* (Space for Culture: Principles for Cultural Policy 2017-2020 – discussion paper) 2017: Kamerbrief: Besluiten Culturele Basisinfrastructuur 2017-2020 (Policy Brief: Allocations Basic Cultural Infrastructure 2017-2020)
Ingrid van Engelshoven (D66, Progressive-Liberal Party) Minister of Education, Culture and Science	2017 – present	2018: *Cultuur in een Open Samenleving* (Culture in an Open Society – policy brief)

*1 As of 1994 the responsible department is the Ministry for Education, Culture and Science.

*2 As of 1995 it became customary that a Minister/Secretary first publishes a policy brief detailing the principles for the new period. Institutions could tailor their applications for subsidy to the principles in the document.

*3 Van der Ploeg was succeeded by Cees van Leeuwen (LPF, List Pim Fortuyn) in the Cabinet Balkenende I (July 2002-May 2003). This short-lived government did not publish a cultural policy brief.

*4 Van der Laan left office when her party left the coalition government. The then current Minister of Education, Maria van der Hoeven (CDA), saw to cultural policy until a new government was formed after the 2007 general elections.

*5 The title of this policy brief refers to 2004-2007, it however discusses the period 2005-2008.

Note

1. In the Dutch political system members of government are linked to political parties but need not be a Member of Parliament before becoming a minister or secretary. In fact, when a member of parliament becomes minister or secretary, they vacate their seat in Parliament which is taken over by another member of their political party.

Appendix

Facts and Figures on Culture and Cultural Policy in the Netherlands

Kimberly van Aart, Rogier Brom, Bjorn Schrijen – Boekman Foundation
Thijs Hermsen – Humanities Lab, Faculty of Arts, Radboud University

The facts and figures in this appendix are meant to provide an overview of public cultural policy and the size of the cultural sector in the Netherlands. The appendix has several sections providing data on:

1. Population data and administrative organisation of the Netherlands
2. Public expenditures on culture and the arts
3. Distribution of cultural amenities over the country
4. The labour market for arts and culture in the Netherlands
5. Participation in amateur arts and media
6. Private donations to culture

While the data provide a backdrop for the information in this volume, the set-up of the appendix allows for it to be used independently to gain insight into Dutch cultural policy.

Boekman Foundation and the Arts Index Netherlands
The facts and figures in this appendix are compiled by researchers of the Boekman Foundation, who are also responsible for the Arts Index Netherlands. The Arts Index Netherlands is a comprehensive database of facts and figures on arts and culture in the Netherlands, ranging from the number of cinema tickets sold and the total income of public libraries to the percentage of people that practice amateur arts. Since its launch in 2013, the index presents reliable, relevant and longitudinal data on the Dutch cultural field every other year, in cooperation with over 30 organisations that have information available. For more information, please visit: https:// www.cultuurindex.nl

1. Population Data and Administrative Organisation of the Netherlands

Figure 1:   Population density in the Netherlands in 2017[1]

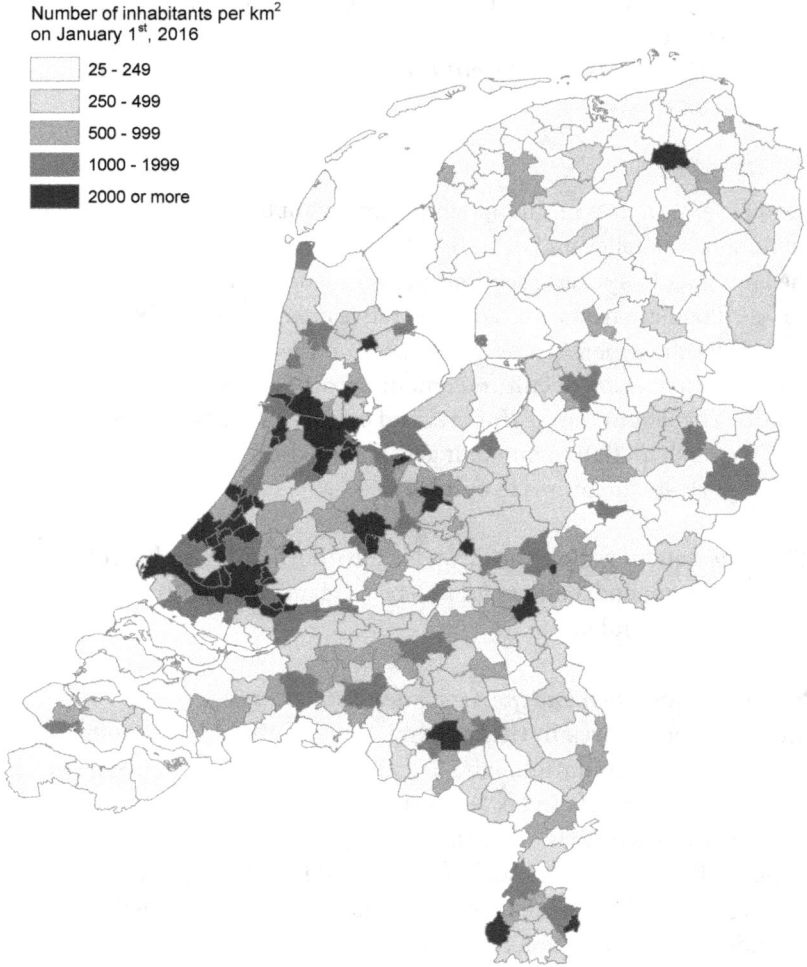

Number of inhabitants per km^2
on January 1st, 2016

- 25 - 249
- 250 - 499
- 500 - 999
- 1000 - 1999
- 2000 or more

Figure 2:   Share of inhabitants with a non-Western foreign background in total
population in 2017[2]

Share of inhabitants with non-Western foreign background
on January 1st, 2017 in %

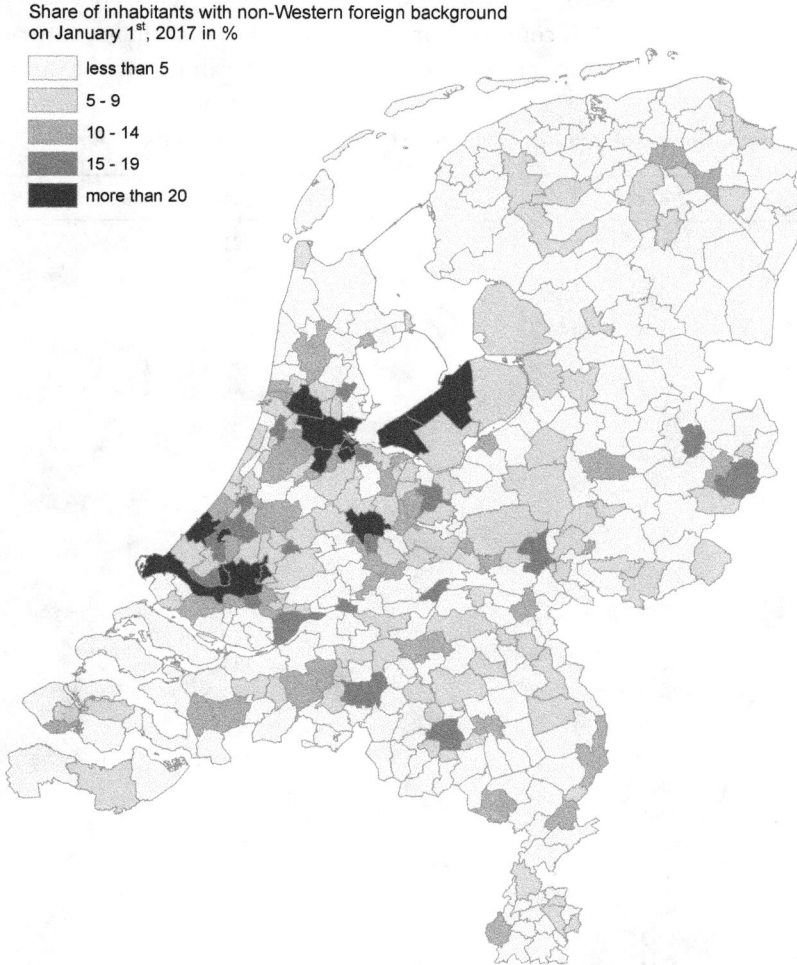

Data retrieved from Statistics Netherlands (CBS). Its population statistics
show 'with which country someone is closely related given their own country
of birth and that of their parents. For someone with a first-generation foreign
background, the origin is indicated as the country of birth of that person.
For someone with a second-generation foreign background, the origin
is indicated as the country of birth of the mother of that person. If the
mother's country of birth is the Netherlands, then the origin is indicated as

the father's country of birth' (translated from Statistics Netherlands, 2018, 'onderwerpen/classificaties' [subjects/classifications]). The figure shows the share of inhabitants of a municipality who were born in a non-Western country or who were born in the Netherlands who have at least one parent born in a non-Western country. Non-Western countries include countries in Africa, South America or Asia (excluding Indonesia and Japan) or Turkey.

Table 3:   Number of municipalities in the Netherlands, 1900-2016[3]

Year	Number of municipalities
1900	1,121
1910	1,121
1920	1,110
1930	1,078
1940	1,054
1950	1,015
1960	994
1970	913
1980	811
1990	672
2000	537
2001	504
2002	496
2003	489
2004	483
2005	467
2006	458
2007	443
2008	443
2009	441
2010	431
2011	418
2012	415
2013	408
2014	403
2015	393
2016	390
2017	388
2018	380

2.   Public Expenditures on Culture and the Arts

Table 4:   Government expenditures on cultural services in 1995-2016 (in million euros)[4]

	Government expenditures on cultural services (in million euros)		
Year	General government	National government	Local governments
1995	1,444	-	1,081
1996	1,457	-	1,113
1997	1,738	-	1,142
1998	1,853	-	1,266
1999	2,008	-	1,366
2000	2,177	-	1,493
2001	2,369	-	1,634
2002	2,533	-	1,811
2003	2,646	-	1,960
2004	2,700	-	2,002
2005	2,895	-	2,133
2006	3,007	-	2,197
2007	2,975	-	2,299
2008	3,333	-	2,574
2009	3,366	877	2,655
2010	3,386	948	2,646
2011	3,259	831	2,615
2012	3,194	850	2,568
2013	3,127	696	2,591
2014	3,033	720	2,476
2015	3,172	706	2,615
2016[5]	3,125	851	2,468

For 1995-2008, no data are available on the national government's expenditures on cultural services. When the figures on general government expenditures on cultural services in 1996-2016 are adjusted for inflation, based on the price level of 2015, the increase in expenditures in those years is 47%.

Historically, on average 87.8% of local governments' total expenditures on cultural services is covered by municipalities, and 12.2% by provinces.

Table 5:   **Number of institutions subsidised on a long-term basis by the Ministry of Education, Culture and Science (OCW) and national funds for culture in 2009-2020[6]**

	2009-2012		2013-2016		2017-2020	
	Number of subsidies	Million euros	Number of subsidies	Million euros	Number of subsidies	Million euros
Subtotal Basic Infrastructure for Culture (BIS)	172	411.1	82	329.8	91	345.2[7]
Subtotal national funds for culture	174	46.7	148	38	231	50.5
Cultural Participation Fund	26	5	18	3	29	3.8
Mondriaan Fund	27	2.3	26	2.6	28	2.8
Netherlands Film Fund	-	–	3	0.8	3	0.3
Dutch Foundation for Literature	3	0.2	8	1.2	13	1.4
Creative Industries Fund NL	-	–	11	3	15	3.4
Performing Arts Fund	118	39.2	82	27.4	143[8]	38.8[9]
Total BIS and national funds for culture	346	457.8	230	367.8	322[9]	395.7[8,9]

The Basic Infrastructure (BIS) consists of organisations that serve an indispensable function in the Dutch cultural sector at both a national and international scale. These are subsidised directly by the Ministry of Education, Culture and Science (for consecutive four-year periods). As dictated by the Cultural Policy Act (CPA), subsidy decisions are based on advice by the national Council for Culture. The Minister or Secretary of Culture, however, makes the final decisions. Deviations from the advice need to be substantiated as a consequence of the General Administrative Law Act (GALA, see chapter 1). As a rule, the Minister or Secretary follows the advice by the Council.

Apart from the BIS, (indirect) national funding is provided through six national funds for culture. Each fund caters to a particular discipline. These

funds in turn allocate both short-term and longer-term grants for organisations that are not part of the BIS. The funds have their own committees of
experts allocating subsidies. The funds' policies and criteria, however, are
subject to advice by the Council for Culture and are subsequently approved
by the Minister or Secretary of Culture.

When adjusted for inflation, based on the price level of 2015, the total
subsidies for the BIS and the national funds for culture decreased by 23.1%
in the 2009-2017 period.

Figure 6: **Overview of institutions in the Basic Infrastructure for Culture (BIS) in
2017[9]**

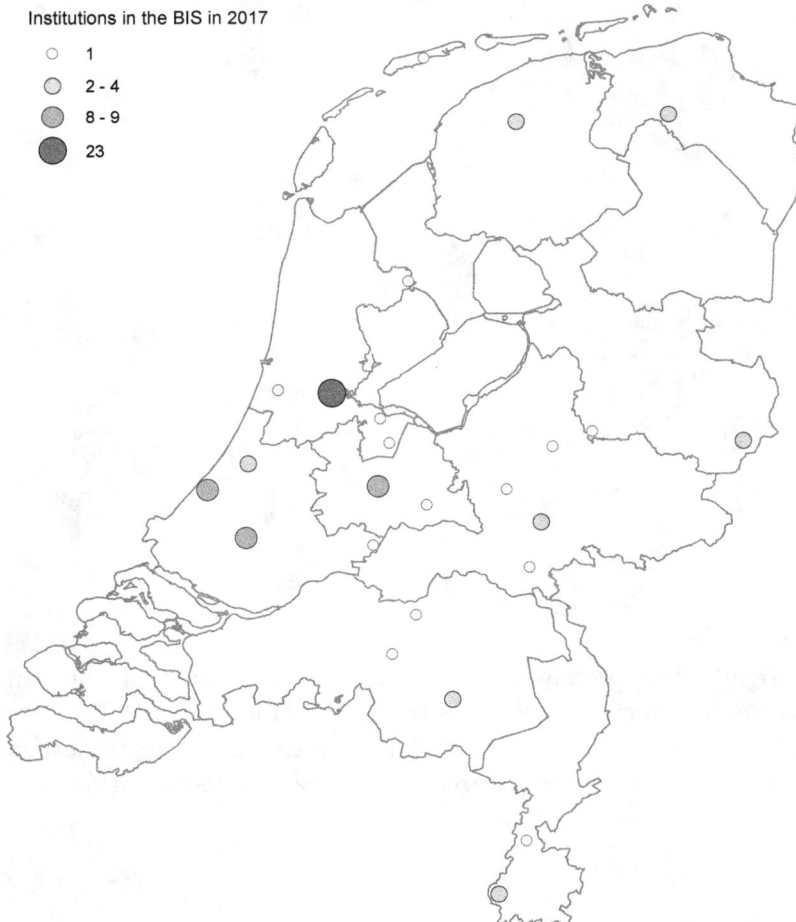

Institutions in the BIS in 2017
- 1
- 2 - 4
- 8 - 9
- 23

**Figure 7: Overview of institutions receiving long-term funding from national
            funds for culture in 2017[10]**

Institutions receiving long-term funding
from state funds for culture in 2017

○ 1 - 5
◔ 6 - 12
◍ 13 - 24
● 86

The figure above presents an overview of the distribution of long-term
subsidies by national funds for culture, based on the address of the receiving institutions. Nonetheless, it should be taken into account that these
addresses do not necessarily correspond with where these euros are really
spent.

Figure 8: Share of cultural sectors in BIS subsidies in 2017-2020 (in million euros)[11]

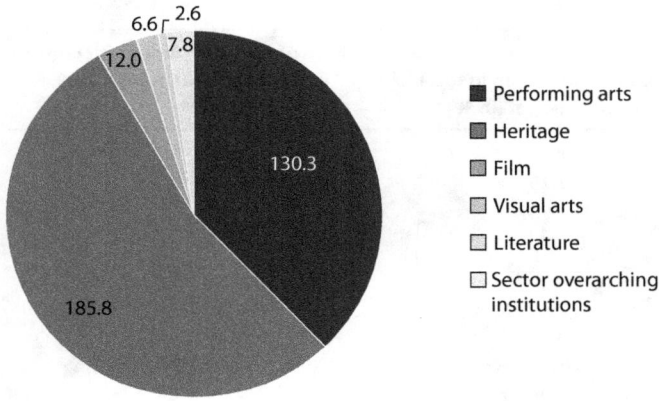

Legend:
- Performing arts
- Heritage
- Film
- Visual arts
- Literature
- Sector overarching institutions

Values: 2.6, 6.6, 7.8, 12.0, 130.3, 185.8

Figure 9: Share of performing arts subsectors in performing arts BIS subsidies in 2017-2020 (in million euros)[12]

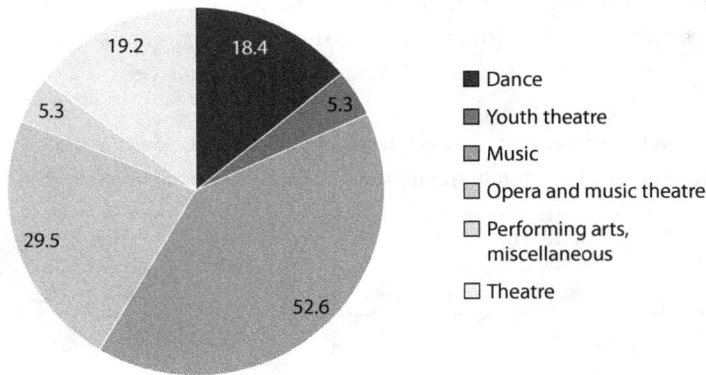

Legend:
- Dance
- Youth theatre
- Music
- Opera and music theatre
- Performing arts, miscellaneous
- Theatre

Values: 18.4, 5.3, 19.2, 5.3, 29.5, 52.6

Table 10: Share of national budget for culture in total national budget in 1993-2015 (in %)[13]

Year	Share of national budget for culture and media combined in total national budget (in %)	Share of national budget for culture in total national budget (in %)
1993	1.0645	-
1995	1.0179	-
1997	1.1150	-
1999	0.7924	-
2001	1.0846	-
2003	1.1338	0.4893
2005	1.2005	0.6151
2007	0.8510	0.4488
2009	0.7446	0.3789
2011	0.7789	0.3934
2013	0.7087	0.3126
2015	0.6630	0.2997

In the 1995-2001 period, government expenditures on culture are listed in chapter VIII27 of the Budget Memorandum (Miljoenennota) and include expenditures on media. Yet from 2002 onwards, new chapters list culture and media separately, in chapters VIII14 and VIII15 respectively.

Table 11: Expenditures on cultural services of general government levels in the Netherlands, in surrounding countries and in the European Union in 2016[14]

	Expenditures (in million euros)	Population	Expenditures per capita	Expenditures as % of GDP
Belgium	2,130.8	11,311,117	188.38	0.5
Denmark	1,867.1	5,707,251	327.15	0.7
Germany	11,741.0	82,175,684	142.88	0.4
The Netherlands	3,125.0[15]	16,979,120	184.05[15]	0.4[15]
United Kingdom	6,379.7	65,382,556[16]	97.57[16]	0.3
European Union (28 countries)	64,903.7[15.16]	510,277,177[15.16]	127.19[15.16]	0.4[15.16]

The data above are compiled by Eurostat and based on the Classification of the Functions of Government ('COFOG 99'). Within this classification, general government includes the national and local governments and social security funds. Function 8.2 'cultural services' is about the 'provision of cultural services; administration of cultural affairs; supervision and regulation of cultural facilities; operation or support of facilities for cultural pursuits (libraries, museums, art galleries, theatres, exhibition halls, monuments, historic houses and sites, zoological and botanical gardens, aquaria, arboreta, etc.); production, operation or support of cultural events (concerts, stage and film productions, art shows, etc.); grants, loans or subsidies to support individual artists, writers, designers, composers and others working in the arts or to organizations engaged in promoting cultural activities. Includes: national, regional or local celebrations provided they are not intended chiefly to attract tourists' (Eurostat 2011: 175).

Figure 12: **Share of self-generated income in cultural sectors in the Netherlands in 2015 (in %)[17]**

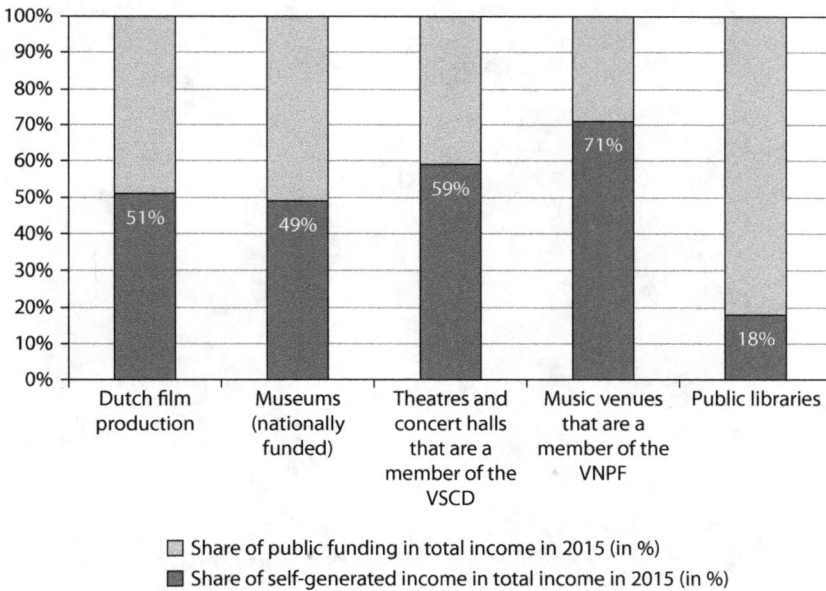

Share of public funding in total income in 2015 (in %)
Share of self-generated income in total income in 2015 (in %)

Note that the data above do not reflect music production and other fully privately funded cultural provision.

The VSCD is the Dutch Association of Theatre and Concert Hall Directors, and the VNPF is the Dutch Association of Pop Music Venues and Festivals. The figures for the VNPF above only account for music venues; festivals are excluded.

3.   Distribution of Cultural Amenities over the Country

Figure 13:   Overview of museums in 2016[18]

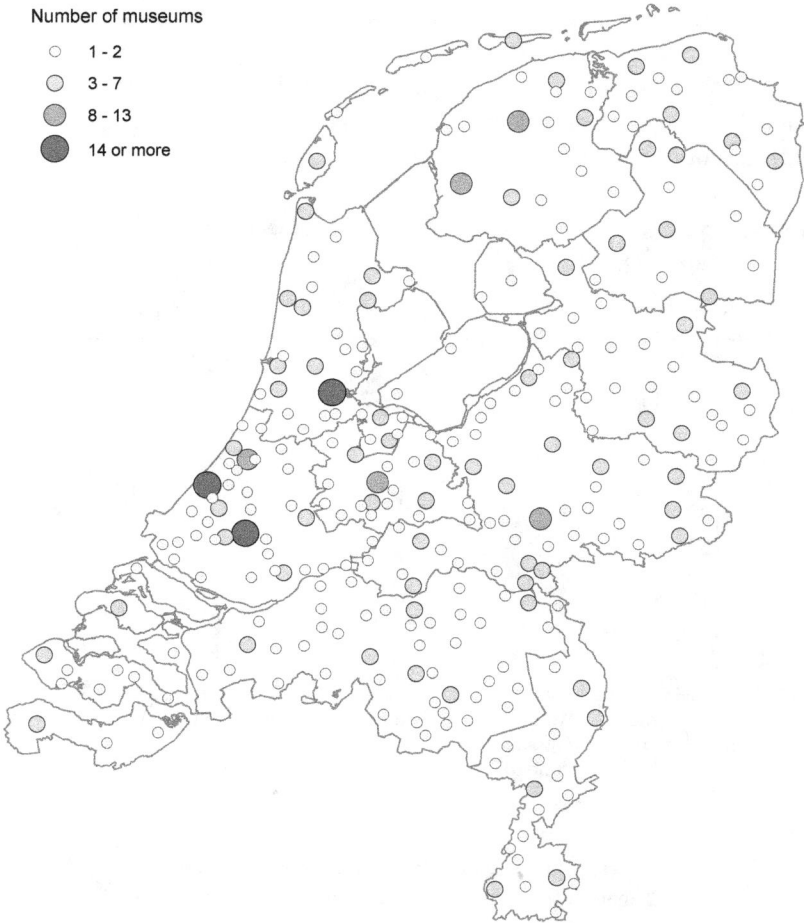

Number of museums
- ○ 1 - 2
- ○ 3 - 7
- ◉ 8 - 13
- ● 14 or more

The data are based on the museum population as defined by Statistics Netherlands (CBS), the Dutch Museums Association and the Cultural Heritage Agency (RCE). For this population, 'whether or not an institution is categorised as a museum is almost always based on the international definition of a museum of the International Council of Museums (ICOM)' (Statistics Netherlands 2017: 3).

Figure 14: **Overview of members of the Association for Theatre and Concert Hall Directors (VSCD) on 1 January 2018**[19]

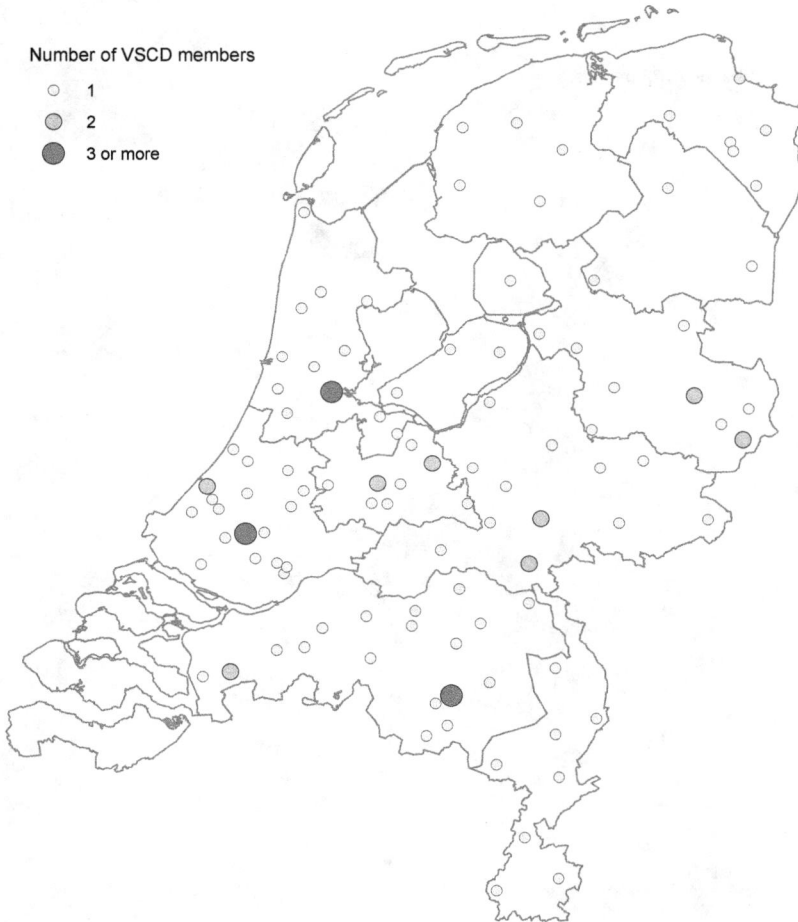

Note: This map does not reflect the number of halls available in a city, as in many cases one member of the association exploits several halls.

Figure 15:   Overview of members of the Association for Pop Music Venues and Festivals (VNPF) on 1 January 2018[20]

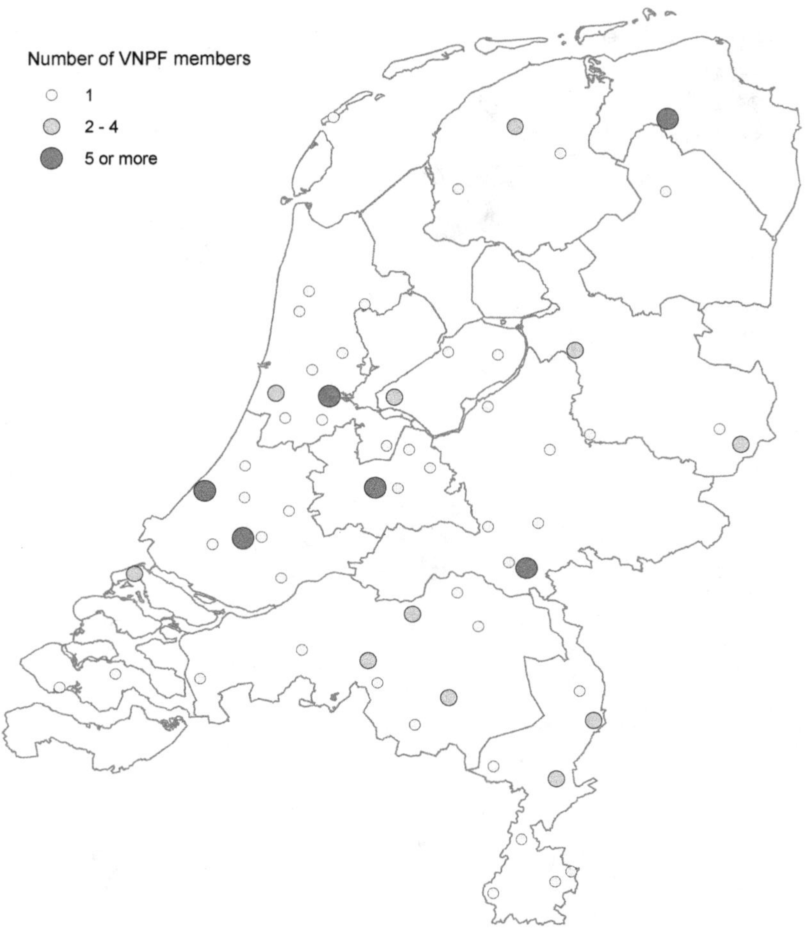

Number of VNPF members
- 1
- 2 - 4
- 5 or more

Figure 16:   Overview of built, non-archaeological national monuments on
31 December 2017[21]

Number of built, non-archeological
state monuments

○   less than 250

◐   250 - 750

◓   750 - 1750

●   7500

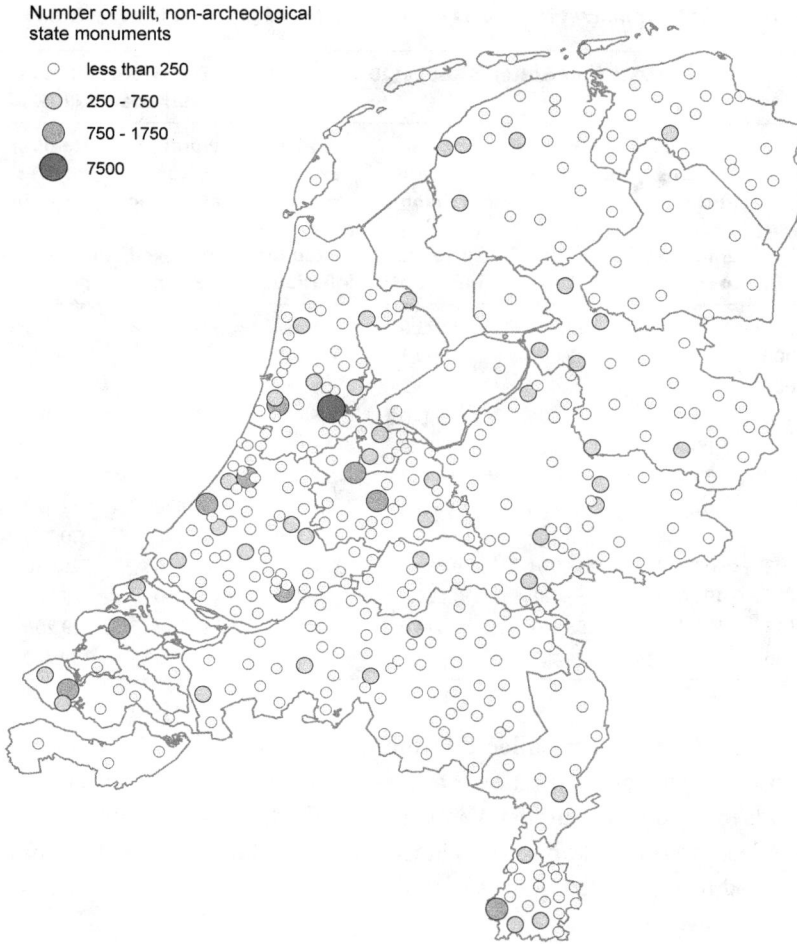

Note: The number of built, non-archaeological national monuments in
Amsterdam is 7,506.

4.   The Labour Market for Arts and Culture in the Netherlands

Table 17:   Labour market in the arts and cultural heritage sector in 2005-2016[22]

	Data from Rutten & Koops (2017)				Data from Statistics Netherlands (2017)	
	Number of jobs (including self-employed persons)	Number of companies	Production value in million euros, adjusted for inflation[23]	Added value in million euros, adjusted for inflation[23]	Number of jobs (excluding self-employed persons)	Number of FTEs (excluding self-employed persons)
2005	75,577	23,293	8,823.0	4,526.4	-	-
2006	77,207	25,049	9,099.3	4,664.0	-	-
2007	81,714	27,407	9,525.2	4,889.4	-	-
2008	85,202	30,204	9,501,0	4,880.9	-	-
2009	90,216	36,525	9,475.9	5,015.3	-	-
2010	98,001	44,090	9,841.7	5,226.4	47,550	32,470
2011	101,394	47,870	10,103.5	5,335.2	47,620	32,370
2012	101,738	50,322	10,036.4	5,348.1	45,440	30,770
2013	102,888	53,004	9,762.3	5,317.4	42,700	29,010
2014	105,033	55,888	10,399.4	5,727.4	43,250	29,560
2015	106,882	58,351	11,014.0	6,044.4	42,180	29,200
2016	-	-	-	-	43,110[24]	29,720[24]

The figures above are collected from different reports; while Rutten & Koops (2017) provide data over a longer period of time—thus showing trends in the overall number of jobs, including those hold by self-employed people, part-timers and so on—Statistics Netherlands (2017) offers more detailed insights with figures that also include FTEs, yet largely exclude self-employed people.

This sector is labelled slightly diffferently in diffferent sources. In the *Monitor Creatieve Industrie* of Rutten & Koops (2017), the sector is labelled Arts and cultural heritage (*Kunsten en cultureel erfgoed*). Statistics Netherlands (2017) labels the sector simply Arts (*Kunsten*). Both sectors include primarily performing arts, creative arts, supportive institutions, libraries, heritage institutions and museums, yet Koops & Rutten (2017) also include supporting funds, whereas Statistics Netherlands (2017) does not cover this subsector.

5.   Participation in Amateur Arts and Media

Table 18:   **Active and receptive cultural participation from April 2016-April 2017[25]**

	Active participation in artistic or creative leisure activities, share of the total Dutch population aged six or older, from April 2016-April 2017 (in %)
Visual arts	20
Music	19
Dance	9
Theatre	5
Creative writing	7
Media	12
Total	40
	Receptive participation in culture, share of the total Dutch population aged six or older, from April 2016-April 2017 (in %)
Exhibitions	40
Performances	44
Concerts	38
Film screenings	65
Reading	51
Total	84

Figure 19:   **Market shares of public and commercial television channels in total television ratings in 2017[26]**

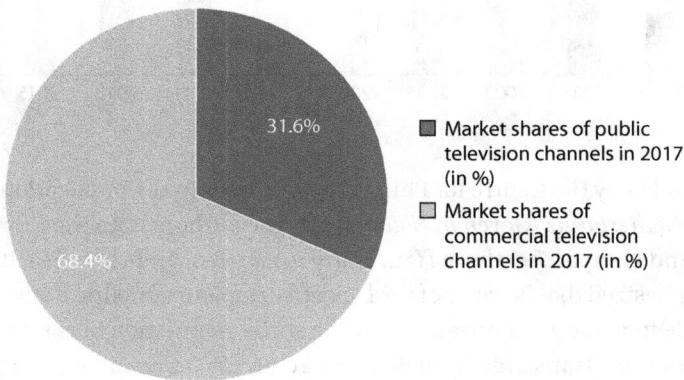

31.6%

68.4%

■ Market shares of public television channels in 2017 (in %)

☐ Market shares of commercial television channels in 2017 (in %)

The market shares of public and commercial television channels fluctuated slightly in the 2005-2017 period. It appears that in even years, public channels

had on average a higher market share (33.7%) compared with uneven years
(32.1%). This is probably the result of major, worldwide sports events (e.g.
Olympic Games, FIFA World Cup) being held in even years and broadcasted
by public television channels.

6.   Private Donations to Culture

**Figure 20:   Donations to culture from households, bequests, funds, companies
and charity lotteries in 1997-2015 (adjusted for inflation, based on the
price level of 2015, in million euros)[27]**

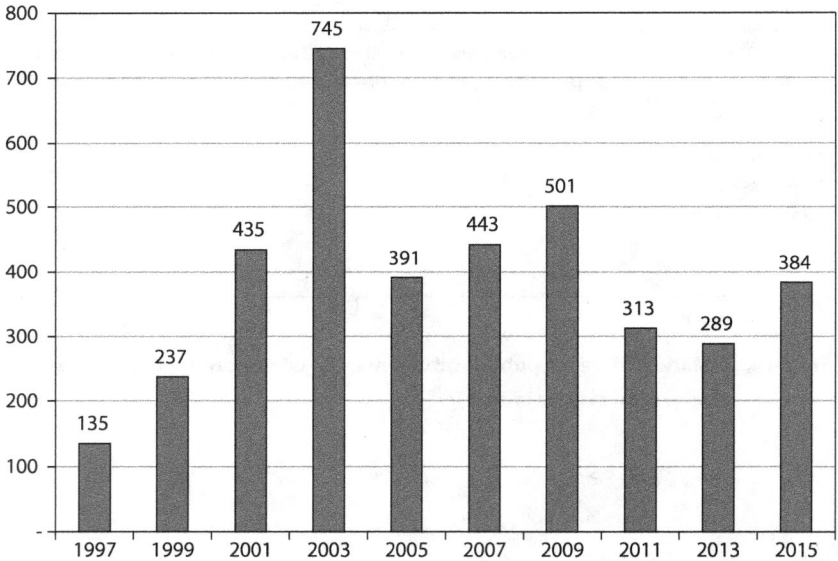

Data are compiled by the Centre for Philantropic Studies in the publication
Giving in the Netherlands (*Geven in Nederland*). The authors note that 'for
households and companies, these figures are estimates, and therefore it
should be emphasized that because of the lack of a complete sampling frame,
it is impossible to make generalisations for the entire population of capital
funds and bequests' (translated from Bekkers, Schuyt & Gouwenberg 2018:
241). Data have been adjusted for inflation, based on the price level of 2015.

Table 21:   Donations to culture via crowdfunding platform Voordekunst.nl in 2015-
2017, adjusted for inflation, based on the price level of 2015[28]

	2015	2016	2017
Total amount donated in euros	3,636,950	4,216,591	3,775,180
Total number of donations	46,142	54,191	56,820
Total number of donors	43,273	50,564	53,279
Total number of projects	690	777	749
Average amount per donation in euros	79	78	66
Average donation per project in euros	5,271	5,427	5,040
Average number of donors per project	63	65	71

Voordekunst is the main crowdfunding platform for artistic, creative and
cultural projects in the Netherlands, on which nearly 3,000 crowdfunding campaigns (i.e. projects) have been successfully completed since the
platform's inception in 2010.

For each project, a target amount is specified beforehand, as well as a
timeframe wherein that goal should be met. People may donate 10 euros
or more. When less than 80% of the target amount is raised, donations are
reimbursed. When 80-99% of the target amount has been raised, donors
have the option to request a reimbursement. The figures above include
such reimbursed donations.

Data have been adjusted for inflation, based on the price level of 2015.

Figure 22:   Share of cultural sectors in donations to culture via crowdfunding
platform Voordekunst.nl in 2017 (in euros)[29]

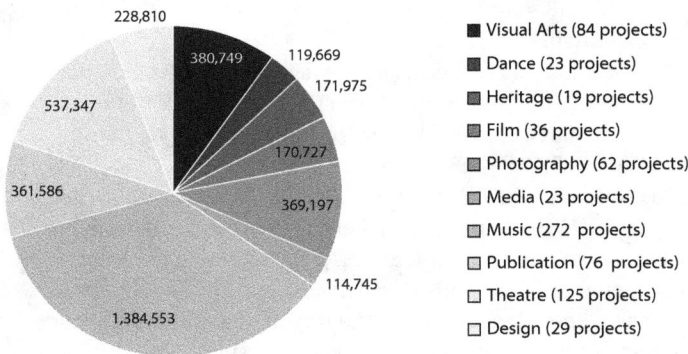

228,810
380,749   119,669
171,975
537,347
170,727
361,586
369,197
114,745
1,384,553

■ Visual Arts (84 projects)
■ Dance (23 projects)
■ Heritage (19 projects)
□ Film (36 projects)
▨ Photography (62 projects)
□ Media (23 projects)
□ Music (272 projects)
□ Publication (76 projects)
□ Theatre (125 projects)
□ Design (29 projects)

Table 23:   Volunteers in museums, libraries and performing arts venues in 2005-2016[30]

Museums	2005	2007	2009	2011	2013	2015[31]	2016[31]
Number of volunteers	19,667	21,329	23,720	29,205	31,019	33,867[31]	34,895[32]
Total staff (number of people)	8,143	8,598	9,146	11,580	12,010	14,253[32]	14,947[32]
Employees on payroll	6,563	6,760	6,938	8,060	8,333	9,606[32]	9,986[32]

Libraries	2005	2007	2009	2011	2013	2015	2016
Number of volunteers	-	-	-	6,825	7,516	10,828	13,489
Total staff (number of people)	-	9,080	9,060	8,340	6,695	6,813	6,639[32]

Performing arts venues	2005	2007	2009	2011	2013	2015	2016[32]
Number of volunteers/interns	5,100	5,700	6,400	8,600	8,100	10,400	10,200
Employees on payroll	9,600	9,900	10,400	10,000	8,800	7,700	7,700

For libraries and museums, the total staff includes all employed and non-employed, salaried staff. For performing arts venues, data only cover employees.

Notes

1.   Statistics Netherlands (CBS). 2018. *Regionale kerncijfers Nederland.* [Regional Key Figures of the Netherlands]. The Hague: Statistics Netherlands. Retrieved 11 April 2018 from https://opendata.cbs.nl/statline/#/CBS/nl/dataset/70072ned/table?dl=7F82.

2.   Statistics Netherlands (CBS). 2018. *Regionale kerncijfers Nederland.* [Regional Key Figures of the Netherlands]. The Hague: Statistics Netherlands. Retrieved 1 March 2018 from https://opendata.cbs.nl/#/CBS/nl/dataset/70072ned/table?dl=A288.

3.   Statistics Netherlands (CBS). 2018. *Regionale kerncijfers Nederland.* [Regional Key Figures of the Netherlands]. Retrieved 1 March 2018 from https://opendata.cbs.nl/statline/#/CBS/nl/dataset/70072ned/table?dl=A289. Statistics Netherlands (CBS). 2018. *Gemeentelijke indeling op 1 januari 2018.* [Municipal Layout per 1 January 2018]. The Hague: Statistics Netherlands. Retrieved from: https://www.cbs.nl/nl-nl/onze-diensten/methoden/classificaties/overig/gemeentelijke-indelingen-per-jaar/indeling%20per%20jaar/gemeentelijke-indeling-op-1-januari-2018.

Lisci-Wessels, Trudy. 2004. 'Ontwikkeling van het aantal gemeenten sinds 1900'. [Development of the Number of Municipalities since 1900]. In: *Bevolkingstrends*, 52 (4), 56-57. Retrieved 12 March 2018 from https://www.cbs.nl/-/media/imported/documents/2004/11/2004-k1-b-15-p056-art.pdf.

4.   Statistics Netherlands (CBS). 2015. *Overheid; uitgaven cultuur, sport en recreatie 1999 – 2012*. [Government; Spending Culture, Sports and Recreation 1999 – 2012]. The Hague: Statistics Netherlands. Retrieved 9 March 2018 from http://statline.cbs.nl/Statweb/publication/?DM=SLNL&PA=70130NED&D1=3,27,30,33,39&D2=a&D3=6,8,10,12-13&HDR=G2&STB=G1,T&VW=T.
      Statistics Netherlands (CBS). 2018. *Consumentenprijzen; prijsindex 2015=100*. [Consumer Prices; Price Index 2015=100]. The Hague: Statistics Netherlands. Retrieved 9 March 2018 from https://opendata.cbs.nl/statline/#/CBS/nl/dataset/83131NED/table?dl=87E6.
      Statistics Netherlands (CBS). 2018. *Overheid; uitgaven naar functies*. [Government; Expenditures per Function]. The Hague: Statistics Netherlands. Retrieved 6 March 2018 from https://opendata.cbs.nl/statline/#/CBS/nl/dataset/82902NED/table?dl=87ED.

5.   These are provisional data.

6.   Council for Culture. 2018. *Council for Culture*. Retrieved 14 March 2018 from https://www.cultuur.nl/english/item138.
      Database of the Ministry of Education, Culture and Science (OCW).
      Statistics Netherlands (CBS). 2018. *Consumentenprijzen; prijsindex 2015=100*. [Consumer Prices; Price Index 2015=100]. The Hague: Statistics Netherlands. Retrieved 9 March 2018 from https://opendata.cbs.nl/statline/#/CBS/nl/dataset/83131NED/table?dl=87E6.

7.   These expenditures include subsidies that museums receive via the Heritage Act (*Erfgoedwet*) for housing and collection management.

8.   Includes subsidies for 37 institutions for 2017-2020 whose subsidy applications were evaluated positively by the Performing Arts Fund in 2016, yet it became clear only in 2017 that budget was available to fund these institutions for the 2017-2020 period.

9.   Database of the Ministry of Education, Culture and Science (OCW).

10.   Database of the Ministry of Education, Culture and Science (OCW).

11.   Database of the Ministry of Education, Culture and Science (OCW).

12.   Database of the Ministry of Education, Culture and Science (OCW).

13.   Ministry of Education, Culture and Science (OCW). Miljoenennota's [Budget Memoranda] for 1995-2015 (including financial year report).
      Ministry of Education, Culture and Science (OCW). Year reports for 2007-2018.
      Statistics Netherlands (CBS). 2018. *Consumentenprijzen; prijsindex 2015=100*. [Consumer Prices; Price Index 2015=100]. The Hague: Statistics Netherlands. Retrieved 9 March 2018 from https://opendata.cbs.nl/statline/#/CBS/nl/dataset/83131NED/table?dl=87E6.

14.   Eurostat. 2011. *Manual on sources and methods for the compilation of COFOG Statistics. Classification of the Functions of Government (COFOG)*. Luxem-

bourg: Publications Office of the European Union. Retrieved 12 March 2018 from http://ec.europa.eu/eurostat/documents/3859598/5917333/KS-RA-11-013-EN.PDF.

Eurostat. 2018. *General government expenditure by function (COFOG)*. Luxembourg: Eurostat. Retrieved 2 March 2018 from http://ec.europa.eu/eurostat/web/government-finance-statistics/data/database.

15.   These are provisional data.

16.   These figures are estimates.

17.   Statistics Netherlands (CBS). 2017. *Openbare bibliotheken*. [Public Libraries]. The Hague: Statistics Netherlands. Retrieved 2 March 2018 from https://opendata.cbs.nl/statline/#/CBS/nl/dataset/70763ned/table?dl=80D1.
Bongers, Frank, Maartje Gielen, David van Kerkhof, Leonie Hermanussen, Maaike van Asselt, Dionne Faber, Nils Ellwanger, Stefan van der Veen and Leonie Gercama. 2017. *Economische ontwikkelingen in de cultuursector, 2009-2016*. [Economic Developments in the Cultural Sector]. Utrecht: APE, Dialogic.

18.   Statistics Netherlands (CBS). 2017. *Musea in Nederland*. [Museums in the Netherlands]. The Hague: Statistics Netherlands.
Statistics Netherlands (CBS). 2017. *Musea; collectie, bezoeken, tarieven, tentoonstellingen, werkgelegenheid*. [Museums; Collections, Visits, Tariffs, Exhibitions, Employment]. The Hague: Statistics Netherlands. Retrieved 2 March 2018 from https://opendata.cbs.nl/statline/#/CBS/nl/dataset/83533NED/table?dl=4717.

19.   Association of Theatre and Concert Hall Directors (VSCD), personal correspondence.

20.   Association for Pop Music Venues and Festivals (VNPF), personal correspondence.

21.   Cultural Heritage Agency (RCE). 2018. *Number of national monuments per end of the month*. Retrieved 12 March 2018 from https://erfgoedmonitor.nl/databank.

22.   Rutten, Paul and Olaf Koops. 2017. *Monitor Creatieve industrie 2016*. [Monitor Creative Industries 2016]. Hilversum: iMMovator.
Statistics Netherlands (CBS). 2017. *Cultuur in beeld 2017 (maatwerktabellen)*. [Culture in the Spotlight 2017]. The Hague: Statistics Netherlands. Retrieved from https://www.cbs.nl/nl-nl/maatwerk/2017/44/cultuur-in-beeld-2017.
Statistics Netherlands (CBS). 2018. *Consumentenprijzen; prijsindex 2015=100*. [Consumer Price Index, price index 2015=100]. The Hague: Statistics Netherlands. Retrieved 9 March 2018 from https://opendata.cbs.nl/statline/#/CBS/nl/dataset/83131NED/table?dl=87E6.

23.   Data have been adjusted for inflation based on the price level of 2015.

24.   These are provisional data.

25.   Neele, Arno, Zoë Zernitz and Teunis IJdens. 2017. *Kunstzinnig en creatief in de vrije tijd. Monitor Amateurkunst 2017 – Technisch rapport*. [Artistic and Creative during Leisure Time. Monitor Amateur Arts 2017 – Technical Annex]. Utrecht: National Centre of Expertise for Cultural Education and

Amateur Arts (LKCA). Retrieved 13 March 2018 from http://www.lkca.nl/over-het-lkca/publicaties-lkca/monitor-amateurkunst-2017.

Neele, Arno, Zoë Zernitz and Teunis IJdens. 2017. *Voluntary Arts in the Netherlands 2017: Practitioners and Facilities.* Utrecht: National Centre of Expertise for Cultural Education and Amateur Arts (LKCA). Retrieved 13 March 2018 from http://www.lkca.nl/~/media/downloads/publicaties/2017/en_nmak%202017.pdf.

26. Dutch viewer audience measurement service in the Netherlands (SKO). Year reports. Retrieved from https://kijkonderzoek.nl/jaarrapport-kijkcijfers.

27. Bekkers, René, Theo N.M. Schuyt and Barbara Gouwenberg (eds.). 2018. *Geven in Nederland 2017: huishoudens, nalatenschappen, fondsen, bedrijven, goede doelenloterijen en vrijwilligerswerk. Jubileum-uitgave.* [Giving in the Netherlands 2017: Households, Bequests, Funds, Companies, Charity Lotteries and Volunteering. Jubilee Edition]. Amsterdam: Lenthe.
Statistics Netherlands (CBS). 2018. *Consumentenprijzen; prijsindex 2015=100.* [Consumer Prices; Price Index 2015=100]. The Hague: Statistics Netherlands. Retrieved 9 March 2018 from https://opendata.cbs.nl/statline/#/CBS/nl/dataset/83131NED/table?dl=87E6.

28. Transactional data provided by Voordekunst.
Statistics Netherlands (CBS). 2018. *Consumentenprijzen; prijsindex 2015=100* [Consumer Prices; Price Index 2015=100]. The Hague: Statistics Netherlands. Retrieved 9 March 2018 from https://opendata.cbs.nl/statline/#/CBS/nl/dataset/83131NED/table?dl=87E6.

29. Transactional data provided by Voordekunst.

30. Statistics Netherlands (CBS). 2015. *Musea; bezoeken, tarieven en type collectie, 1993 – 2013.* [Museums; Visits, Tariffs and Type of Collection, 1993 – 2013]. The Hague: Statistics Netherlands. Retrieved 12 March 2018 from https://opendata.cbs.nl/statline/#/CBS/nl/dataset/82038NED/table?dl=8367.
Statistics Netherlands (CBS). 2017. *Musea; collectie, bezoeken, tarieven, tentoonstellingen, werkgelegenheid.* [Museums; Collection, Visits, Tariffs, Exhibitions, Employment]. The Hague: Statistics Netherlands. Retrieved 12 March 2018 from https://opendata.cbs.nl/statline/#/CBS/nl/dataset/83533NED/table?dl=8276.
Statistics Netherlands (CBS). 2017. *Openbare bibliotheken.* [Public Libraries]. The Hague: Statistics Netherlands (CBS). Retrieved 12 March 2018 from https://opendata.cbs.nl/#/CBS/nl/dataset/70763ned/table?dl=8278.
Statistics Netherlands (CBS). 2018. *Professionele podiumkunsten; werkgelegenheid, baten en lasten.* [Professional Performing Arts; Employment, Benefits and Costs]. The Hague: Statistics Netherlands. Retrieved 12 March 2018 from https://opendata.cbs.nl/statline/#/CBS/nl/dataset/70810NED/table?dl=8281.

31. Figures on museum staff are based on the museum population. This population was redefined by Statistics Netherlands (CBS) and the Dutch Museums Association in 2015, therefore one should analyse and interpret trends in 2005-2016 with caution.

32. These are provisional data.

Authors' Biographies

Koen van Eijck is professor of Cultural Lifestyles at the Department of Arts and Culture Studies at Erasmus University. His research and publications focus on social inequality and trends in cultural participation and taste patterns, arts education and talent development, the perception and appreciation of visual art and (classical) music, and cognitive sociology. He teaches courses on general sociology, philosophy of science, (cultural) consumption, and arts perception in the Bachelor's, Master's and Research Master's programmes of the Erasmus School of History, Culture and Communication.

Pascal Gielen is full professor of sociology of art and politics at the Antwerp Research Institute for the Arts (Antwerp University, Belgium), where he leads the Culture Commons Quest Office (CCQO). Gielen is editor-in-chief of the international book series *Arts in Society*. In 2016, he became laureate of the Odysseus grant for excellent international scientific research awarded by the Fund for Scientific Research Flanders in Belgium. His research focuses on creative labour, the institutional context of the arts, and cultural politics. Gielen has published many books that have been translated into English, Korean, Polish, Portuguese, Russian, Spanish and Turkish.

Erik Hitters is Associate Professor at the Erasmus School of History, Culture and Communication of Erasmus University Rotterdam. He has co-founded and is managing director of ERMeCC, the Erasmus Research Centre for Media, Communication and Culture. He holds a PhD in Social Sciences from Utrecht University. He lectures for the MA programme in Media Studies and IBCoM, the International Bachelor in Communication and Media. Erik's research interests and publications focus on transformations in the media and creative industries.

Quirijn Lennert van den Hoogen teaches art sociology and arts policy at the University of Groningen. His research interests include cultural policies, theatre systems and the cultural policy of cities and their societal impacts. He has worked as an official for cultural policy in the Netherlands at the provincial and municipal levels. From 2007 to 2017, he was editor-in-chief of the Dutch *Handbook for Cultural Policy* (Reed Business). From 2010 to 2017 he was chair of the advisory committee of the Groningen Art Council. He initiated the Dutch Network for Cultural Policy Researchers. He is a member of the European research group STEP (Project on European

Theatre Systems) and a member of the Research Centre for Arts in Society at Groningen University.

Frank Huysmans studied sociology and communication sciences at the Radboud University Nijmegen, where he obtained his PhD studying media use and time structures in families (2001). From 2001 to 2010, he worked at the Netherlands Institute for Social Research (SCP) as a senior researcher in media use and cultural participation, and from 2010-2012 as program manager of research and knowledge sharing at the Netherlands Institute for Public Libraries (SIOB). Since 2005, he has been extraordinary professor of library science at the faculty of Humanities of the University of Amsterdam, a position he combines with his own practice as independent researcher, consultant and speaker in the public information sector (WareKennis, The Hague).

Teunis IJdens studied graphic design at the Academies of Art in Arnhem and Enschede, and sociology at the University of Nijmegen. His research areas for many years have been cultural policy and the arts labour market. He has worked as a researcher at the universities of Rotterdam, where he received his PhD in 1999, and Tilburg. Since 2013 he has been a researcher, adviser and editor at the National Centre of Expertise for Cultural Education and Amateur Arts (LKCA). IJdens is co-founder of the European Network of Observatories in the Field of Arts and Cultural Education (ENO), linked to UNESCO.

Florine Jonker finished her Bachelor and Research Master's degree in Arts and Cultural Studies at the University of Groningen with a focus on the cognitive and intrinsic values of art experience. She wrote her Master's thesis on the synthesis of cognitive and philosophical approaches to the concept of aesthetics.

Johan Kolsteeg worked as a concert programmer and producer in the worlds of classical and contemporary music before moving to education and research at the Utrecht University of the Arts. He now works at the University of Groningen, specialising in his research interests of cultural entrepreneurship and cultural leadership.

Thijs Lijster is assistant professor in the philosophy of art and culture at the University of Groningen and postdoctoral researcher at the Culture Commons Quest Office of the University of Antwerp. He studied philosophy in Groningen and New York, and received his PhD at the University of Groningen in 2012. He was awarded the ABG/VN Essay prize in 2009, the Dutch/Flemish Prize for Young Art Critics in 2010, and the NWO/Boekman dissertation prize in 2015. His publications include *De grote vlucht inwaarts* [The great leap inwards, 2016] and *Benjamin and Adorno on Art and Art Criticism* (2017). He was also editor of the books *Spaces for Criticism. Shifts in Contemporary Art Discourses* (2015) and *The Future of the New. Artistic Innovation in Times of Social Acceleration* (2018).

Edwin van Meerkerk is associate professor in arts education and cultural policy at Radboud University Nijmegen and director of education at the Radboud University Faculty of Arts. His research focuses on arts education in elementary schools and high schools, teacher education as well as arts education policy. He is editor of *Cultuur+Educatie*, the national journal on arts education in the Netherlands. Previously, he was visiting scholar at the University of Duisburg-Essen.

Toine Minnaert is assistant professor at the Department of Media and Culture Studies at Utrecht University. In 2016, he obtained his doctorate with a dissertation on the role of national identity in Dutch international cultural policy. His teaching focusses on the Minor programme Arts, Culture and Society (*Kunst, Cultuur en Maatschappij*), and the English-language Master's programme Arts and Society. His current research focusses on international cultural policy, cultural policy as identity policy, and the role of culture in the ties between diasporic communities and their native countries.

Marjolein Oomes holds a M.Sc. in Sociology from Tilburg University (2007). She was researcher and advisor at the Provincial Service Organisation for Libraries Cubiss (2007-2010) and advisor Research and Knowledge Sharing at the Netherlands Institute for Public Libraries SIOB (2010-2014). She currently holds the same position at the Royal Library, The Hague, where she works on a PhD-project developing and evaluating tools for measuring the societal impact and value of libraries.

Hanka Otte is a cultural policy researcher and holds a postdoc position at the University of Antwerp, where she is involved in the Cultural Commons Quest Office. Her research focusses on the question of what conditions are needed for a balanced artistic biotope and what (policy) efforts can be made to generate creative commons. Her PhD research in 2015 was about the relationship between arts participation and social cohesion. For a period of ten years, she has been working as a policy advisor on arts and culture for regional and local governments.

Erik Schrijvers is senior researcher at the Scientific Council for Government Policy. He has collaborated on several reports among which *Identification with the Netherlands* (*Identificatie met Nederland* 2007); *How unequal is The Netherlands?* (*Hoe ongelijk is Nederland?* 2014); *Revaluing Culture* (*Cultuur herwaarderen* 2015) and *Big Data in a Free and Secure Society* (*Big Data in een vrije en veilige samenleving* 2016). Between 2016 and 2017, he was attached on an interim basis to the Dutch Ministry of the Interior and Kingdom Relations, as secretary to the Information Society and Government study group.

Inge van der Vlies is professor emeritus of constitutional law and art and law at the University of Amsterdam. Formerly a part-time judge, she still acts as chairperson of appeal committees. In the past, she has been a member of the Council for Culture and many other advisory bodies for the state, and she has published many books and articles on the legal aspects of cultural policy. She is currently a member of the supervisory boards of various cultural institutions, including the Kröller Müller Museum.

Index

Access/Accessibility 25, 31, 41, 46, 47, 49, 60, 70, 71, 78, 97, 117-120, 125, 137, 146, 152, 153, 156, 161, 165, 166, 179, 197, 203, 207, 210-212, 215, 220, 231, 234, 244, 248-252, 253-257, 273, 278, 285

Actieplan Cultuurbereik (see Cultural Outreach Action Plan)

Advertising 152, 153, 156-159, 256

Advice/Advisor (expert or independent) 12, 18, 19, 22, 30, 39, 47, 50, 51, 55-57, 70, 73, 91, 107-129, 131, 196, 225, 228, 232, 270, 271, 281, 296, 297

Advisory Board for Education (*Onderwijsraad*) 170, 184

Aesthetic experience 98, 109, 136, 143, 178, 179, 208-210, 212, 280

Amateur (Arts) 20, 32, 86, 126, 169, 174, 181, 183, 187, 188, 195, 199-204, 183, 307

Amsterdam 14, 24, 27, 28, 61, 62, 68, 131, 175, 234, 248, 272, 282, 284, 305

Arm's length principle 72, 153, 187, 270, 284

L'art pour l'art 118, 127

Arts'92 (*Kunsten '92*) 90, 133

Arts Council (*Raad voor de Kunst*) 14, 22

Arts education 25, 170-194, 201-203, 205, 206, 211

Association of Dutch Municipalities (*Vereniging Nederlandse Gemeenten*, VNG) 220, 230

Association of Dutch Pop Venues and Festivals (*Vereniging Nederlandse Poppodia en Festivals*, VNPF) 301, 304

Association of Theatre and Concert Hall Directors (*Vereniging van Schouwburg- en Concertzaaldirecties*, VSCD) 301, 303

Attainment goal 178, 179

Audience development 98, 116, 121, 123, 198

Audience rating 158, 160

Audience reach 55, 90, 91, 94, 97, 100, 101, 111, 113, 121, 122, 160, 196, 200, 269, 274, 283

Audience targeting 93, 132, 154, 161, 206

Authenticity 220, 257, 266

Autonomy, of art and/or culture 32, 98, 108, 109, 112, 116-120, 123-126, 153, 199, 250, 270, 275

AWB (*Algemene Wet Bestuursrecht*) see GALA

Bamford, Anne 184

Basic Infrastructure (BIS) 21, 24, 37, 51, 72, 81, 95, 99, 101, 102, 110, 112, 113, 115-119, 127, 133, 196, 250, 270, 271, 273, 282, 284, 288, 289, 296, 297, 299

BBC 154, 158, 159

Berlin, Isaiah 44, 198

Bildung 109, 135, 197

BKR (see Visual Artists Scheme)

Blokland, Hans 44, 196, 258

Boekman, Emanuel 135, 137, 138

Boekman Foundation (*Boekmanstichting*) 70, 72, 291

Boltanski, Luc and Laurent Thévenot 108-110

Boltanski, Luc and Eve Chiapello 92

Bottom-up 12, 15, 103, 137, 145-148, 222, 239, 272

Bourdieu, Pierre 108, 127, 213

Branding 161

Brinkman, Elco 89, 287

Budget cut(s) 26, 27, 33, 46, 70, 79, 93, 100, 112, 135, 159, 161, 176, 188, 198, 205, 212, 216, 220, 230, 234, 239, 244, 245, 251, 258, 271, 282

Bureaucracy (Bureaucratisation) 11, 12, 15, 22, 31, 63, 112, 136, 140, 144, 273-276, 281-283

Bussemaker, Jet 27, 29, 50, 68, 79, 92, 95, 98, 112, 116, 124, 134, 137, 144, 198, 199, 208, 250, 285, 289

Canon (Dutch Canon) 23, 75, 76, 81, 133, 250, 261

Canonised/canonical art 16, 133, 211

CDA (Christian Democrat Party) 26, 79, 80, 251, 280, 287, 289

Centre of Expertise for Cultural Education and Amateur Arts 173, 175, 178, 187

Christian-Democrats 14, 26, 32, 79, 89

Civil sequence 134, 138-142, 143-145

Civil society 133, 138, 139, 142, 144, 173, 244

Cohesion 111, 208, 209, 236

Commercial / Commercialisation 59, 60, 91, 100, 131, 146, 148, 151, 155, 157-159, 161, 197, 230, 247, 256, 257, 260, 265, 266, 271, 278, 281, 283, 307

Commercial broadcasting 151, 153, 155-157, 160

Commercial media 152, 154, 156, 158, 160, 307

Commissariaat voor de Media (see Media Authority)

Compendium of Cultural Policies and Trends in Europe 69, 71, 72

Competitor / Competition 56, 59-61, 93, 100, 101, 109, 117, 159, 160, 225, 266

Complementarity 77, 156, 160, 161

Concert hall 11, 49, 73, 197, 253, 301, 303

Conflict of interest 56, 74, 228

Constitution (*Grondwet*) 41, 42, 44-46, 54, 175, 244, 280, 284

Council for Culture (*Raad voor Cultuur*) 18-20, 22, 24-28, 32, 33, 38, 49-52, 56, 68, 70, 78, 82, 96, 98, 107-129, 131, 133, 134, 147, 157, 196, 225, 232, 270, 277, 278, 282, 296, 297

CREARTE 185

Creative Partnerships 185

Creativity 48, 86, 109, 171, 172, 177, 190, 198, 199, 208, 210, 233

Creativity centre (Art Centre/Arts Education Centre) 177, 187-190, 204, 205, 212
Cultural democracy 108, 197
Cultural and Artistic Education (*Culturele en Kunstzinnige Vorming*, CKV) 179, 180, 182
Culture and School (*Regeling Cultuur en School*) 25, 181-184
Cultural diversity / Cultural Diversity Code (*Code Culturele Diversiteit*) 26, 70, 78-81, 120, 122, 123, 171, 197, 200, 216, 248-252, 256, 259, 276, 288
Cultural education 20, 22, 25, 33, 112, 120, 155, 170-194, 195, 197, 200, 207, 226, 270
Cultural Outreach Action Plan (*Actieplan Cultuurbereik*) 181, 183, 187, 189, 200, 201, 206, 207, 211
Cultural participation 20, 25, 26, 51, 97, 98, 102, 137, 161, 166, 170, 174, 178-191, 196-212, 238, 249, 254, 259, 272, 276, 307
Cultural Participation Fund (*Fonds Cultuurparticipatie*) 25, 51, 175, 178, 185, 201, 203, 211, 212, 296
Cultural Participation Scheme (*Regeling Cultuurparticipatie*) 181, 200, 201-203, 207, 211
Cultuur+Ondernemen (Culture+Entrepreneurialism) 26
Cultuureducatie met Kwaliteit (see Quality Cultural Education Programme)
Cutbacks (see Budget Cuts)

D'Ancona, Hedy 20, 29, 32, 78, 90, 111, 272, 287
D66 (Social-Liberal Party) 25, 37, 79, 80, 251, 280, 287-289
Data economy 119
Decentralisation 32, 203, 231, 238, 239, 282
Democracy/Democratic (see also Cultural democracy) 12, 15, 16, 41-45, 47, 71, 73, 102, 133, 151, 153, 156, 161, 171, 222, 231, 273, 280, 283
Democratisation of culture 16, 197
DENK (Muslim Party) 252
Department for Education, Culture and Science (see Ministry for ...)
Digital media 211, 253, 256, 258
Digital Media Platform 221, 224
Digitalisation 31, 70, 161, 243, 244, 252-257, 259, 260, 270, 272, 277-279
Digitisation 138, 225, 231, 232, 236, 252-254, 257, 258
Distribution 14, 19, 21, 24, 30, 32, 55, 100, 117, 152, 156, 161, 197, 229, 272, 302-305
Diversity (as policy goal/criterion) 19, 20, 29, 47, 49, 59, 74, 100, 107, 117, 132, 151-156, 159-161, 200, 202, 278, 280
Djazzex 54
Documentary 155, 266
Drama 155, 179, 187

Dutch Music Centre (*Muziekcentrum Nederland*) 85

Economic impact 27-29, 108, 190, 199, 238
Education Policy 20, 25, 33, 169, 175, 177, 186, 190
Efficiency 117, 120, 121, 125, 158, 159, 161, 178, 184, 236
Elite 135, 136, 196, 197, 203, 243, 259
Employership 29, 97, 187, 188
Entertainment 60, 154, 155, 157, 159, 160, 276
Entrepreneur(ship) / Entrepreneurial 26, 27, 30, 33, 47, 49, 55, 59, 63, 87, 89-104, 116, 118, 123, 124, 126, 157, 185, 195, 198, 199, 245, 246, 274, 288
Ethnic minorities 25, 26, 68, 154, 201, 211
European Charter 45
European Charter of Minority Languages 33
European Court of Human Rights 44, 45
European Culture Foundation (ECF) 103, 134, 138, 144-146
European Institute for Comparative Cultural Research (ERICArts) 70
European legislation 155, 281
European media regulations 157
European Union 13, 58-61, 171, 282, 300
European Union Charter of Fundamental Rights 45
Evidence / Evidence-based policy 25, 124, 137, 171, 172, 190, 208, 236, 274, 277
Experience (of art and culture) 98, 109, 136, 143, 178, 179, 208-210, 274, 280
Expertise 22, 54, 109, 113, 117-121, 123, 125, 253

Film 15, 204, 299, 301, 307, 309
Film Institute EYE 24, 265, 266
Film Production Fund 15
Fonds Cultuurparticipatie (see Cultural Participation Fund)
Formal attendance 210
Formal learning / Formal education 169, 173, 174, 176, 177, 181, 188, 189, 190
Fortuyn, Pim 75, 115
Forum for Democracy (FvD) 108, 251
Forum on European Culture 103
Freedom of (artistic) expression 41-48, 63, 151, 256
Freedom Party (*Partij voor de Vrijheid*, PVV) 26, 80, 108, 112, 115, 243, 251
Fund for Dutch Cultural Broadcasting Production (*Stimuleringsfonds Nederlandse Culturele Omroepproducties*) 155

General Administrative Law Act (GALA) 17, 18, 42-44, 47, 48, 50-58, 61, 63, 296
Gielen, Pascal 29, 124, 249
Gift and Inheritance Tax Act (Geefwet) 27, 245, 246, 260

Globalisation 13, 67, 81, 100, 133, 244, 251, 270, 276-279
Glocalisation 102
Good Governance 21, 29, 42, 43, 52-57, 73, 270
Governance, (Code) Cultural 26, 27, 107, 121, 122, 147
Grassroots (organisation, initiative) 97, 133, 136, 141, 146, 147, 203, 271, 277
GroenLinks (Green-Left Party) 79
Grondwet (see Constitution)

Hagoort, Giep 93, 94
Healthcare 177, 244, 245, 274
Heritage 12, 19, 20, 22, 23, 26-28, 31, 39, 47, 59, 73, 77, 78, 90, 109, 110, 112, 124, 155, 170, 173, 174, 178, 250-254, 258, 271, 273, 278-280, 283, 287, 299, 306, 309
Heritage Act 20, 23, 64, 273
High culture (High arts) 15, 173, 203, 243
Holland Festival 61, 62

Immigration (see Migration)
Impact, the Art of 138
Inclusion (Social) 26, 108, 144, 208
Income (Artists') 16, 28, 29, 71, 86, 87
Identity (Cultural) 68, 74, 78, 102, 103, 155
Identity (National) 23, 39, 67, 68, 74-77, 78-81, 92, 198, 209, 210, 250-252, 259, 280, 283
Independence 11, 54, 91, 101, 152-154, 159, 220
Informal learning 173, 175-177, 188-190
Informal participation 205, 210, 274
Information society 208, 219
Innovation 90, 94, 98-101, 111, 131, 138, 147, 161, 171, 177, 195, 196, 198, 201, 202, 221, 226, 228, 232-234, 240, 253
Intangible heritage 77
Integration 80, 102, 178, 244, 259
International Convention / Treaty 42, 45, 46, 54, 64
International Cultural Policy (ICB) 29, 30, 68, 69, 74, 77-79, 80-82, 144, 145, 269, 278
iTunes 255

Justification 50, 92, 16-171, 176, 181, 182, 189, 238

Kulturagenten 185
Kunsten'92 (see Arts'92)

Labour market 29, 221, 231-233, 249, 306
Legitimacy crisis 157, 158
Legitimacy of media (Policy) 152, 159, 161
Legitimation/Legitimacy 55, 125, 172, 176, 236, 237, 258, 275, 280
Leisure (Activity) 16, 100, 137, 169, 173, 174, 187, 188, 205, 221, 276, 307
Leisure time 223, 225
Lending rights 223
LKCA (see National Centre of Expertise for Cultural Education and Amateur Arts)

Local authority (Government) 18-20, 24, 25, 27, 28, 32, 33, 38, 43, 49, 61, 73, 82, 124, 134, 147, 166, 167, 175, 181, 186, 188-190, 200-205, 222, 225, 229, 231, 238, 239, 272, 273, 281, 282, 295, 300
Local identity 117, 118, 120, 121, 125
LPF (List Pim Furtuyn) 251, 289

Marketing (or to market) 90, 93, 94, 98, 118, 121-123, 127, 165, 201, 215
Market failure 160, 258
Mass entertainment 153, 157, 159, 160
Matthew Effect (Mattheüseffect) 243, 246-248, 258, 260, 278, 283, 284
Media Act 20, 152, 154, 157-160, 273
Media Authority (Commissariaat voor de Media) 153
Media policy 151-161
  as cultural policy 151, 154-160
  reculturalization 157-160
  values of 161
Migration 67, 68, 80, 100, 102, 244, 248-252, 259, 274
Ministry of Education, Culture and Science (Ministerie van OCW) 16, 25, 27, 29, 32, 52, 63, 70, 72, 74, 75, 77, 100, 102, 111, 133, 137, 144, 145, 152, 154, 175, 178, 182, 183, 187, 195, 201, 217, 226, 228, 233, 237, 250, 252, 253, 261, 285, 289, 296
More Music in the Classroom (Meer Muziek in de Klas) 185
Mozart Effect 185
Museum 11, 16, 18, 20, 21, 23, 26, 60, 73, 133, 136, 165, 169, 183, 187, 197, 203, 204, 206, 215-217, 236, 248, 252-255, 273, 282, 283, 301, 302, 306, 310
Music 15-17, 25, 28, 32, 33, 85, 86, 131, 132, 169, 172, 173, 178, 179, 183, 185,187, 204-206, 210, 211, 230, 253, 299, 307, 309
Music education 185, 186, 282
Music Education Impulse (Muziekimpuls) 185, 186
Music in Every Child (Muziek in Ieder Kind) 185
Music school 176, 188, 189
Music venue 20, 136, 301, 304
Muziekcentrum Nederland (see Dutch Music Centre)

National Centre of Expertise for Cultural Education and Amateur Arts (LKCA) 173, 175, 178, 187
National Centre of Expertise for Curriculum Development (SLO) 180
National culture 67, 78, 79, 81, 155, 156, 251, 280
National History Museum 23, 81, 89, 111, 250, 261, 278
National identity 67, 74-77, 79-81, 250, 252, 259, 280
National museums (Rijksmusea) 11, 18, 21, 23, 60, 73, 89, 273

Negative right 41, 258
Neoliberal (Neoliberalism) 137, 138, 157, 159,
      188, 276, 278
Netflix 159, 224, 230, 255
Netherlands Film Fund (Nederlands Film
      Fonds) 51, 296
New media (Art) 51, 155, 224, 255, 258
New Public Management (NPM) 32, 73, 107, 110,
      122-124, 238, 284
Non-formal learning / education 181, 187-189,
      190
Non-linear 158, 256
NPO (Netherlands Public Broadcasting) 153,
      154, 158-160
NOS (Dutch Broadcasting Foundation) 153
Nuis, Aad 25, 78, 111, 112, 126, 182, 196, 287
Nussbaum, Martha 44, 258

Objectification 110
On-demand 153, 158, 161, 224, 230, 256, 266
Onderwijsraad (see Advisory Board for
      Education)
Open market 59- 61, 63

Participation (see Cultural Participation)
Participatory society 137, 193, 148
Performing arts 21, 22, 25, 32, 90, 91, 155, 183,
      187, 299, 306, 310
Performing Arts Fund 27, 50, 85, 113, 117, 128,
      296
Pillarisation (pillars) of society 154, 155, 196
Plasterk, Ronald 78, 91, 112, 187, 201, 288
Pluralism / Plurifomity 151, 159, 161, 220, 226
(Policy) Evaluation 21, 24, 27, 31, 33, 91, 113, 116,
      118-125, 127, 134, 184, 186, 189, 195, 200, 202,
      206-210, 212, 221, 229, 237, 274, 275
Popular art 15, 85, 86, 132, 165, 183, 199, 203,
      204, 206, 210, 211, 283
Populism 102, 115, 274, 280
Populist party 26, 38, 80, 81, 108, 112, 251
Positive freedom/right 41, 198, 258
Pots, Roel 9, 14, 83, 107, 111, 125
Private initiative 18, 83, 107, 135, 282
Privatisation 18, 73, 89, 188
Professional (quality) standards 156, 282
Profit for Culture-Committee (Commissie
      Cultuurprofijt) 91, 99, 102
Programme Cultural Entrepreneurship
      (Programma Cultureel Ondernemersc-
      hap) 95-97, 98, 101
Public Broadcasting Corporation 155, 253
Public library 22, 165, 166, 219-240, 254, 272
Public Library Act 20, 22, 166, 220, 222, 225,
      229, 230, 236, 237, 239, 273
Public Library Association (Vereniging
      Openbare Bibliotheken, VOB) 220, 226
Public Service Broadcasting 151, 153, 156, 157,
      160, 219, 256
Public sphere 31, 133, 141, 143, 256

Public value 160, 176, 220, 229, 256, 257
PvdA (Social-Democratic Party) 79, 80, 92, 135,
      198, 287-289
PVV (see Freedom Party)

Quality 11, 16, 18, 20, 21, 25, 27, 29, 32, 33, 49,
      50-52, 54, 55, 78, 91, 98, 101, 107, 109, 112, 113,
      117, 119, 120-126, 131-134, 136, 137, 142, 144,
      154-156, 159-161, 170, 179, 180-184, 186, 189,
      196-201, 203, 210, 212, 226, 237, 244, 248, 256,
      259, 266, 272, 280, 282
Quality control 155, 156
Quality Cultural Education Programme
      (Cultuureducatie met Kwaliteit) 181
Quantification 110, 124, 238
Quota 132, 153, 155, 156

Reflective diversity 153, 154, 160
Religion/Religious parties 11, 54, 154, 157, 159,
      219
Representation 29, 122, 142, 156, 273
Rijksmuseum 24, 37, 76, 280
Rights 15, 20, 41, 42, 44, 45-47, 53, 56, 87, 108,
      152, 156, 198, 223, 244, 245
Risk 27, 90-92, 94, 99, 121
Royal Library (Koninklijke Bibliotheek, KB) 229,
      233

Schrijvers, Erik 31, 98, 124, 199, 246, 270, 271,
      274, 276-278, 283
Scientific Council for Public Policy (Weten-
      schappelijke Raad voor het Regeringsbeleid,
      WRR) 17, 31, 76, 77, 80, 89, 98, 124, 151, 155,
      157, 199
Self-Generated Income (Eigen-Inkomste-
      neis) 91, 92, 97-99, 245, 274, 276, 301
Skills 94, 96, 98, 166, 171, 172, 176, 178-180, 186,
      198, 205, 208-212, 221, 231, 232, 238
Social-democrat(ic) (see PvdA)
Social exclusion 110, 144
Soci(et)al impact 98, 100, 199, 208, 209, 212, 237
Social media 85, 166, 177, 210, 224, 253, 257
Social security 20, 245, 300
Societal support 91, 92, 98-100, 245, 274
Societal value 27, 98, 101, 102, 116, 219, 237, 274
Solidarity 102, 111
Spotify 210, 230, 255
Stimuleringsfonds Nederlandse Cultrele
      Omroepproducties (see Fund for Dutch
      Cultural Broadcasting Production)

Television 12, 78, 151-161, 185, 266, 307, 308
Theater Utrecht 122
Theatre venue 11, 120, 301, 310
Theory-based evaluation 209-211
Thorbecke, Johan Rudolph 135, 138, 284
Top-down 61-63, 136, 137, 143-148, 215
Training (of artists) 20, 170-173, 179
Transfer effects 171

Trans Europe Halles 103
Treaty on the Functioning of the European
    Union (TFEU) 59, 64
Trots op Nederland 80

UNESCO 22, 77, 173, 184
Universality 153, 154, 160, 161
Universality of content 153, 160
    of access 153, 161

Van den Ende, Joop 185
VandenEnde Foundation 282
Van der Laan, Medy 28, 78, 112, 288
Van der Ploeg, Rick 25, 26, 78, 90-92, 102, 112,
    122, 126, 196-200, 203, 215, 249, 271, 288
Van Engelshoven, Ingrid 25, 33, 37-39, 172, 185,
    190, 269, 277, 279, 280, 285, 289
Van Leeuwen, Cees 83, 289
Visual Artists Scheme 16, 17, 28
VNPF (see Association of Dutch Pop Venues
    and Festivals)

Vocational education 170, 173, 179
Volunteering, Voluntary activity 173, 187, 205,
    230, 247, 276, 310
VSCD (see Association of Theatre and Concert
    Hall Directors)
VVD (Liberal Party) 26, 79, 80, 91, 251, 280, 288

Welfare Act 16, 222
Welfare state 47, 231, 244-247, 258, 276, 277
WIK (Artists Income Provision Act) 28, 87
Wilders, Geert 115
WRR (see Scientific Council ...)
WWIK (Labour and Income Provision for
    Artists Act) 28, 87

Youth 15, 38, 112, 142, 155, 177, 200, 221, 231, 299
YouTube 158, 159, 161, 205, 210, 255, 256, 278, 285

Zijlstra, Halbe 26, 27, 70, 79, 80, 91, 92, 97, 112,
    115, 198, 199, 288

For Product Safety Concerns and Information please contact our EU
representative GPSR@taylorandfrancis.com
Taylor & Francis Verlag GmbH, Kaufingerstraße 24, 80331 München, Germany